# THE ART OF SOUND

JACK SACHER

Montclair State College

# The Art

*an introduction*

PRENTICE-HALL, INC.

JAMES EVERSOLE

University of Connecticut

# of Sound

## to music

Englewood Cliffs, N.J.

THE ART OF SOUND
*An Introduction to Music*
BY JACK SACHER AND JAMES EVERSOLE

©*Copyright 1971*
*by Prentice-Hall, Inc., Englewood Cliffs, N.J.*

13-048686-8
Library of Congress Catalog Card Number: 72-127548
Printed in the United States of America

Current printing (last digit:)
10  9  8  7  6  5  4  3  2  1

PRENTICE-HALL INTERNATIONAL, INC., *London*
PRENTICE-HALL OF AUSTRALIA, PTY., LTD., *Sydney*
PRENTICE-HALL OF CANADA, LTD., *Toronto*
PRENTICE-HALL OF INDIA PRIVATE LIMITED, *New Delhi*
PRENTICE-HALL OF JAPAN, INC., *Tokyo*

# ACKNOWLEDGMENTS

Brief mention in prefatory pages is scarcely thanks enough to the many who have contributed to whatever excellence we have achieved in this book. It is, of course, the only formal way open to us, and, if it seems somewhat impersonally expressed, our gratitude is nonetheless heartfelt.

Professors Alvin K. Fossner of Jersey City State College, Paul McCarty of California State University at Fullerton, Scott Huston of the University of Cincinnati College-Conservatory of Music, John Hamell of the Bronx Community College, New York, and Robert Hill of the University of Connecticut read the entire manuscript with great attention to detail and with many helpful suggestions. Parts of our text were read by Professors Mario Oneglia, Emily Waters, and Robert Soffer of Montclair State College, Sharon Spencer Maijkovic of Jersey City State College, Edward J. P. O'Connor, Hale Smith, Bruno di Cecco, and Robert Coleman of the University of Connecticut, Roy Abrahamson of Southern Illinois University, Don Vollstedt of the University of Colorado, James Palmer of Essex Community College, and Mr. Richard Westenburg, organist and choir director of the Central Presbyterian Church of New York City. Professor Fossner and Mr. Westenburg also assisted with photographic materials, as did Mrs. Zdenka Winters and Professor Charles Martens of Montclair State College. Additional aid was lent by the British Overseas Airways Corporation, the Italian Government Travel Office, Cedok, the Czechoslovak Travel Bureau, and Olympia Publishers, Prague.

Some special contributions were offered by Mr. Robert Tuggle, Education Director of the Metropolitan Opera Guild, Miss Cynthia Carter of the Metropolitan Museum of Art, and Professor Paul Price of the Manhattan School of Music, all of whom assisted in the selection and acquisition of photographic materials. The staffs of Columbia Artists Management, the New York Philharmonic-Symphony Orchestra, the Bettmann Archive, and the Music Division of the New York Public Library were also helpful in this regard.

Mr. John Kling read portions of the text and assisted in producing our recordings. Mr. Harvey Sollberger was helpful with the sections dealing with electronic music.

Mr. Ray Carlucci encouraged us at the inception of the book; Mr. Alan Lesure, Mrs. Maurine Lewis, and Mr. Raymond Mullaney have been of great assistance throughout every stage. Mrs. Liselotte A. van Staveren, of the Prentice-Hall staff, offered invaluable help in the preparation of the manuscript, as did Miss Donna Schutz, who not only typed it more than once, but offered many valuable suggestions.

Filippo Bonanni's *The Showcase of Musical Instruments* with an introduction and captions by Frank Ll. Harrison and Joan Rimmer (New York: Dover Publications, Inc.) is the source of engravings reproduced on pages 8, 22, 38, 50, 169, 175–77, 203, and 253. The photo of a scene from *Hair* on p. 168 is by Martha Swope. The photo of André Watts on page 208 is by G. Macdominik and is reproduced with the permission of Judd Concert Artists Bureau. The background illustration on pages 256–57 is by Walter Behnke. The portions of Berg's *Lyric Suite* that appear on pages 240–41 are reprinted with permission (Copyright 1927, Universal Edition, Vienna). The photo of Charles Ives on page 282 is by Frank Gerratana, Connecticut Sunday Herald, Norwalk, Connecticut.

TO

Josephine

AND

Sylvia

# PRELUDE

Because this book concerns the art of music, we urge the reader to keep in mind this principle: familiarity with the sound of music is an absolute prerequisite to understanding it. Verbalizations about sound cannot reveal the sound itself, but can only hint at it: the content of this book, therefore, will be greatly enhanced if the reader listens to the music discussed.

The appreciation of music may be taught or stimulated in many ways. Some books are essentially histories, others isolate types or genres of musical composition, and still others focus on the men who compose music. We have attempted to synthesize all three approaches by emphasizing types of musical constructions, viewing them not only in the abstract but also as manifestations of changing times and as results of the efforts of the creative intellects of individuals.

The discussions have been confined to compositions produced within the so-called Western societies—Europe, Russia, and the Americas. This is intended neither as a slight to other societies and cultures nor as a suggestion that Western music is better than other music. The limitations of space in this book and of time in a one-semester course in music have forced this kind of focus. The student who wishes to explore the musical art of other societies is referred to Section 10 of the Bibliography, *Folk Music and the Music of Other Cultures.*

Feeling that one can learn more about the essentials of music by becoming thoroughly familiar with a few compositions rather than superficially aware of many, we discuss only twenty works, in whole or in part, and examine them in a variety of contexts throughout the book. These works are included in a set of recordings that is an integral part of the text.

It will be to the reader's advantage to listen carefully to the music each time it is mentioned, focusing on the characteristics under examination. The more frequently the music is listened to, the more deeply will one perceive its art, and the more direct will be the transfer of understanding from these few compositions to others like them. Many other compositions are mentioned within the body of the text. In all cases, their titles are in the form best known to English-speaking audiences; in some cases, therefore, the original language will be used, while in others the English title will be cited (thus, reference is made to Hindemith's *Mathis der Maler* rather than *Matthias the Painter,* but an oratorio by Haydn is referred to as *The Creation* rather than *Die Schöpfung*).

There are a number of musical examples within the chapters. Each is identified by the measure or bar numbers taken from the complete line score (that is, the printed music, reduced to a single line of notation wherever possible) provided with the recordings. Once they are located in the line score, the examples can be given attention as the listener follows visually what he hears. A special section on notation, which follows this Prelude, deals with using the musical examples and following printed music while listening. This section should be given careful study.

The four appendices that conclude *The Art of Sound* contain much data and information and are arranged in ways that will assist the reader in research and study.

*Appendix A* is a summary of music history in chart form. It has been designed more as a source of review and perspective than of explanation or introduction.

*Appendix B* is a suggested list of recordings that can make up a basic listening library. The choices made in it are arbitrary and personal and are offered only as suggestions rather than definitive judgments. It is expected and hoped that the reader will supplement and revise the list in accordance with his own needs and developing interests.

*Appendix C* is a set of biographical sketches of over 200 composers. Every composer mentioned in the text is included, with at least the dates and nationality for each; other important composers are also included. Information concerning style, place in history, and any noteworthy predilections as to medium or genre are given in more extensive entries for major figures.

*Appendix D* is an extensive glossary designed to be useful in answering questions that may arise during any personal involvement with music. It includes the technical terms used within the text, pronunciations for foreign words, and definitions of a number of terms that will possibly be encountered in reading about music.

The *Bibliography* is designed to serve as an introduction to some of the many books dealing with the art of music. For the reader's convenience, it has been divided into several categories (*History of Music, Reference Books, Aesthetics, Composers,* and others) and is restricted to books in English.

# NOTATION

The musical examples in this text and the abbreviated scores accompanying the recordings will be more useful if the fundamentals of notation are grasped by the reader early in his study of music. Not all the material presented here need be memorized, but all of it contributes to an understanding of printed music.

Notes are used to symbolize two qualities, pitch and duration. Each quality is essentially a simple one, but notes become somewhat more complex symbols when they are given several meanings at once, including not only those of pitch and duration, but also various expressive meanings. The shape of the note indicates duration; its placement on a line or in a space indicates its pitch.

## Time

The durational value of a note symbol has a time value in relation to all the others, as indicated by this chart:

| | | | |
|---|---|---|---|
| o | = whole note | ▬ | = whole note rest |
| 𝅗𝅥 | = half note | ▬ | = half note rest |
| ♩ | = quarter note | 𝄽 or 𝄽 | = quarter note rest |
| ♪ | = eighth note | 𝄾 | = eighth note rest |
| ♪ | = sixteenth note | 𝄿 | = sixteenth note rest |
| ♪ | = thirty-second note | 𝅀 | = thirty-second note rest |

A dot after any one of these symbols multiplies its value by one and a half. The mathematic relationship among the notes and rests is obvious. A half note lasts twice as long as a quarter note, but half as long as a whole note. Thus, the temporal value is established by the nature of the head and the flag of the symbol. There are equivalent rests for each note, since silence must be measured also.

Modern notation also provides a system for the orderly arrangement of the temporal patterns of notes and rests for convenience in reading. The grouping of patterns of beats and notational symbols is arranged in *measures* or *bars*, the beginnings and ends of which are indicated by vertical lines. The number of beats within the measure is indicated by the *time signature*, a mathematical fraction found at the beginning of a piece or a section of a composition. The bottom number of the fraction identifies the type of note that normally receives the beat; the upper number indicates the number of beats to be found in each measure. Thus, in 3/4 time, the quarter note will be the "beat note," and there will be three of them (or their equivalent) in each measure.

Some time signatures (12/8, for instance) are compounded. Instead of one eighth note being the beat note, a group of three eighth notes may be the beat unit, with the result that there will be four beats in the bar instead of twelve. Such time signatures as 6/8, 9/8, 12/8, 15/8, 6/16 are referred to as *compound* signatures.

### Pitch

The durational symbols just discussed indicate pitch when they are placed on the *staff*, a group of lines and spaces, each having a specific pitch name. The most frequently encountered staff used in Western music has five lines. The staff may be extended higher or lower by the addition of further lines (and spaces) as required for the notation of individual pitches. These lines are called *leger* (or *ledger*) lines.

A *clef* is a symbol placed at the left end of the staff to identify the name of one of the lines, and, by calculation, the names of the other lines and spaces. There are three clefs in common use.

 The loop around the second line from the bottom determines that all notes placed on that line will sound as G above middle C.

G clef

𝄢 The dots above and below the fourth line from the bottom determine that all notes placed on that line will sound as F below middle C.

F clef

𝄡 The point in the middle of the symbol determines that whichever line it points to will be the middle C line.

C clef

Because pitches are given letter names from A to G, the lines and spaces on staffs with the G and F clef will be as follows:

G clef                                                    F clef

The pitch names continue above or below the staff with the addition of leger lines.

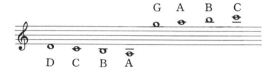

In the span of pitches from low to high, there will be several bearing the same letter name. There is a physical and mathematical relationship among the notes that accounts for this, as well as an aesthetic relationship. Notes that vibrate at frequencies of multiples of 2 with each other have a "oneness" that causes them to be named alike. Thus a pitch vibrating 440 times per second has an acoustical similarity to a pitch vibrating half as fast, 220 cycles per second, to a pitch vibrating twice as fast (880 *cps*), four times as fast (1760 *cps*), and so on.

The distance between a pitch and the next pitch of the same name is called an *octave*. While there are seven letter names for pitches, there are, in Western music at least, twelve different pitches within the octave; the distance between one of them and the pitch immediately above or below it is called a *half step*. In order to indicate all the pitches within the twelve-pitch octave on a seven-pitch staff, a set of symbols called *accidentals* must be used. There are three basic accidental signs: the flat (♭), the sharp (♯), and the natural (♮). The flat sign printed in front of a note indicates that the performer is to sound the pitch one half step lower than the natural note; if the note is preceded by a sharp sign, the note one half step higher than the natural note is to be sounded; the natural sign cancels all previous sharps and flats.

The reader will find that reference to a piano keyboard will be helpful in determining the natural, flatted, and sharped pitches. The following illustration shows part of the piano keyboard.

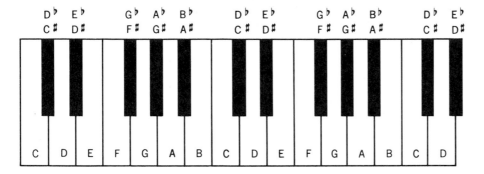

The white keys are given the letter names, the black keys are either sharps or flats. The note between C and D, for example, may be called either C-sharp or D-flat, its name depending on its relationship in musical theory to the other pitches of the music.

Often, particular sharps or flats are used throughout a composition or throughout a section of a composition. The indication of such a consistent use is indicated by a group of accidentals place at the left of the staff, between the clef sign and the time signature. This group of sharps or flats is called the *key signature*. When accidentals are needed within the piece of music and are not included in the key signature, the necessary sign will be placed immediately to the left of the note to be changed and will affect only that note and others of the same pitch name within that particular measure.

The following example, the first verse of *Greensleeves*, illustrates some of these essentials of notation. The numbers above some of the symbols are explained in the table below the music. Other notational symbols may be found in the *Glossary*, under *Symbols and Abbreviations*.

Green - sleeves is my on - ly light_____, Green - sleeves_____ my on - ly star.

Green - sleeves,_____ the sun of my heart _____,and who but my La - dy Green - sleeves?

1. G clef.
2. Key signature; in this case, the key is E minor, and all notes on lines or spaces named "F" are to be regarded as *F-sharp*.
3. Time signature; 6 beats per measure, the eighth note getting the beat. As usually sung, the speed is too fast for one to count six beats per measure, hence the listener may sense a pulse of two beats per measure, with a dotted quarter note ( ♩. ) getting the beat.
4. An incomplete measure; this note (an eighth note E) is used as a "pick-up," or rhythmic springboard into the first measure. To provide mathematical correctness, its time value is subtracted from the last measure of the composition.
5. Measure line, or bar line.
6. Accidental; here D-sharp is called for. Since D-sharp is not specified in the key signature, it must be indicated when desired.
7. D-sharp again specified, since it is required in a new measure.
8. Double bar; indicates end of a section.
9. D-natural; the singer is reminded that, in a new measure, any previous accidentals are automatically cancelled.
10. Double bar; the heavy second line indicates the end of the composition.

### Following a score or a musical example

A score reader must first be aware of the beat; once he senses the pattern of beats, he can move from measure to measure in time with the music, even if the individual notes are moving too quickly to be followed one by one.

The listener will also be aided in following printed music if he can detect rising and falling passages, and if he looks ahead to connect what is printed with what he is about to hear. The recognition of repetitions of rhythmic patterns and of melodic phrases is also a distinct aid to score reading and following. In *Greensleeves*, for example, the rhythmic group comprising the first measure is found in measures 2, 3, 5, 6, 10, and 11. Applying this sort of examination to musical examples without words will make score following much easier and listening more rewarding. The indications of instruments to be used should also be noted by the listener, since their unique sounds can give clues as to the place in a score.

# CONTENTS

# COMPANION RECORDINGS

Bach, J. S.: *Little Fugue in G minor*
Bartók: Piano Concerto No. 3, first movement
Beethoven: Symphony No. 5, in C minor, Op. 67, third movement (complete) and fourth movement (exposition only)
Berg: *Lyric Suite,* first movement
Berlioz: *Fantastic Symphony,* themes from the first and fifth movements
*Bicycle Built for Two, A* (in different settings)
Brahms: Trio in E-flat for Horn, Violin, and Piano, Op. 40, second movement
Debussy: *Voiles*
*Greensleeves* (Folksong)
Handel: "Every Valley" and Pastoral Scene, from *Messiah*
Mozart: Sextet, "Riconosci in questo amplesso," from *Le Nozze di Figaro,* Act III
_____: Symphony No. 40, in G minor, K. 550, first movement
Palestrina: *Agnus Dei II,* from *Missa Brevis*
Ravel: *Bolero,* thematic excerpt
*Requiem aeternam,* Mode VI (Plainsong)
Schubert: Quintet in A major (*Trout*), Op. 114, fourth movement
_____: *Erlkönig*
_____: *Im Frühling*
Smetana: *The Moldau*
Sollberger: *Music for Sophocles' "Antigone,"* second section
Verdi: Quartet, "Bella figlia dell' amore," from *Rigoletto,* final act
Wagner: Aria, "Du bist der Lenz," from *Die Walküre,* Act I
_____: Scene, "Siegmund heiss' ich," from *Die Walküre,* Act I
_____: Prelude to Act II of *Die Walküre*

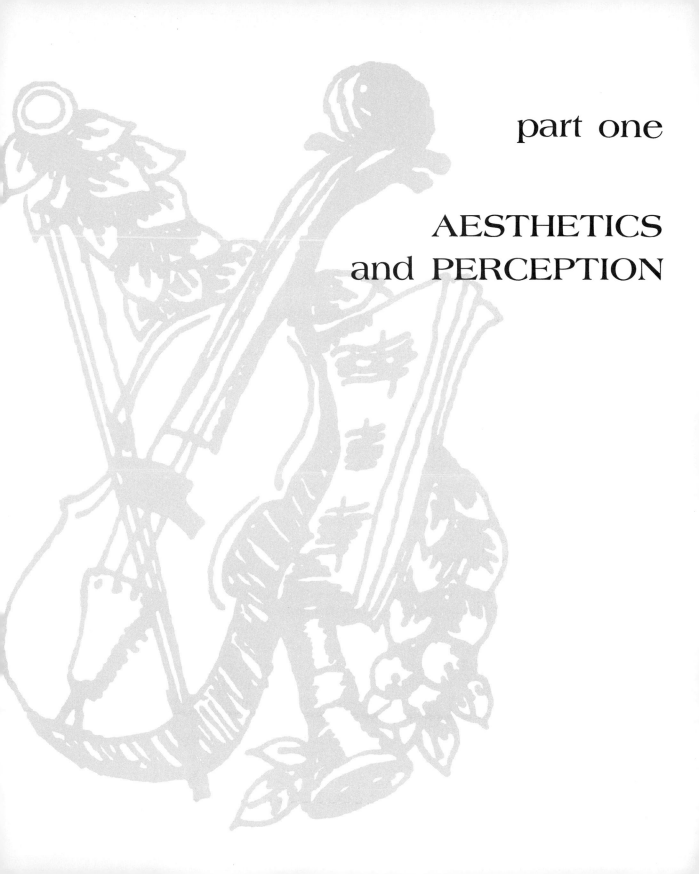

part one

# AESTHETICS and PERCEPTION

# 1 : AESTHETICS, ART, AND MUSIC

AS early man developed powers of reasoning and understanding, he realized that certain things he saw, heard, or did gave him a sense of pleasure. He may not have been certain why this happened or what caused it, but he knew it happened and recognized it as a factor in his life. Because of his ignorance and superstition, early man believed that he had to make token offerings to a variety of deities in order to insure his food supply and to guarantee abundant offspring and a happy life. He carved, he burned, he built, he danced, he chanted—all to appease the powers he thought divine. Believing that what pleased him would please the gods, he made his token objects and rites as beautiful as possible. At the same time, other human endeavors, such as signaling, body decoration, and the manufacture of weapons and utensils provided further opportunities for the creation of pleasing sounds, movements, and artifacts. Thus, out of a combination of activities deemed necessary for survival and a primitive sense of beauty, art was born.

Today, art is no longer just an outgrowth of activities necessary for survival. Many modern cultures are highly sophisticated and are able to take advantage of a great many mechanical and electronic devices that make life more comfortable. Such sophistication naturally breeds perceptivity—the ability to understand the reactions of our senses to various stimuli. Thus we are able to be more aware of life's pleasures, especially those that are derived from things beautiful.

It is only natural that today's man seeks to surround himself with pleas-

3

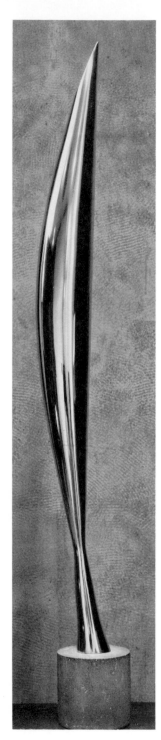

ure-giving sights and sounds. Some of these are provided by nature; others he creates himself. The world of art is in this latter category.

### *What is art?*

Art may be defined simply as the shaping of aural or visual media (words, sounds, paints, plastics, stones, and so forth) by a person in order to move or please himself or other men. Such a definition obviously needs some examination.

It is universally accepted that all art, in order for it to be art, must be man-made. This would immediately eliminate from the realm of art any natural objects or sounds—sunsets, flowers, views, people, calls of birds— even though they may be appreciated for their beautiful qualities. Art not only has to be made by man, but it also has to be recognized as art by man. In other words, it must evoke in someone some sort of response. This response is not always an emotional state of mind, such as joy or sadness, but may be an aesthetic reaction.

The nature of the aesthetic experience is purely an individual matter. No work of art is ever perceived by two people in precisely the same way. A painting or a symphony may cause one person to have a deeply involved aesthetic experience and another to have scarcely any reaction at all. This accounts somewhat for the wide range of art media (spatial, plastic, performing, aural, literary) and the ever-increasing number of works within each category.

Some people experience aesthetic gratification as a result of recognition and appreciation of the construction and form of the work of art. In others, this gratification may be caused by the subject matter of the work of art. In still others, the greatest response is the result of a combination of craft and subject matter. One person may view Delacroix's *Liberty Leading the People* (Colorplate 1) as a fine blend of light and color in a perfectly balanced form, while another may find the supercharged emotional content—a patriotic battle for freedom—a source of aesthetic reward. Does one respond to the finale of Beethoven's *Choral Symphony*

*Constantin Brancusi (1876–1957). Bird in Space (1927?). This bronze sculpture is a masterpiece of nonobjective art. The sculptor tries to capture the essence of flight itself, rather than describe beak, feathers, or wings. The simplicity of the design masks the craft and inspiration that must be fused in the achievement of an artistic experience. (Collection, The Museum of Modern Art, New York)*

because of its exultant setting of Schiller's poem *Ode to Joy*, or because of the superb manipulation of its thematic material, or because of a combination of the two? The reason for one's response does not matter, as long as aesthetic gratification is gained.

Art, then, is created by man for man's perception, and it arouses some sort of aesthetic response. The interaction between the artist and the perceiver is sometimes subtle, sometimes immediate. It changes as the history of man and his tastes change, and may even vary from day to day. The temperature in the concert hall as Stravinsky's music is being played, the food eaten by the viewer just before he confronts a Rembrandt painting, the emotional climate of a world in agony, and many other similar factors condition the creation or re-creation of art and our response to it.

Art is not only a result of many experiences, it is also a changing phenomenon, for it involves creation and response, both of which are conditioned by myriad factors of environment and personality. It is a process, a communication via words, shapes, motions, or sounds—an emotional contact between human beings.

Aesthetic gratification is a result of an experience with beauty. Because a painting or a song is "beautiful," it gives an aesthetic reward to the viewer or listener. In art, *prettiness* and *beauty* are different, the former implying an immediate yet somewhat trivial pleasing of the senses, the latter a quality of importance and deep aesthetic gratification. Thus, Picasso's painting *Guernica* or the prelude to the second act of Wagner's *Die Walküre* may be considered unpretty but beautiful. In *Guernica*, Picasso depicts horror and brutality in the starkest of ways. The agony of the people and animals injured and dying in an air raid is an obviously unbeautiful reality, but it is not the reality being viewed, it is an artist's concept of it. It is in the appropriateness and genius of expression of that conception that the beauty lies. *What* is said is ugly; *how* it is said is beautiful.

For someone who finds pretty melodies his main source of musical pleasure, Sollberger's *Music for Sophocles' "Antigone"* will probably be quite shocking, and the merging of a 2,400-year-old play with the newest of musical sounds may seem incongruous. Note, however, the ingenious fusing of sounds in order to mirror the meanings of specific words as well as the overall sense of the text in a work that is, *in its own stylistic terms*, beautiful.

This last point is significant, for it explains why artists are continually searching for new ways in which to express themselves. Concepts of beauty

**The nature of beauty**

*Pablo Picasso (1881–    ). Guernica (1937). The horrors of war have rarely been depicted so vividly as in this painting of the Basque town Guernica, bombed by German planes flying for General Franco. Picasso heightened the reality of pain, fear, anguish, and brutality by distorting houses, animals, and people. This distortion is intensified by the use of black, white, and grey, colors that give one a feeling of hopelessness and total calamity. (On extended loan from the artist to The Museum of Modern Art, New York)*

are continually changing simply because of change in the societies in which they are developed. The music of Bach or Beethoven is an expression of one aspect of their ages just as *Guernica* is an expression of an aspect of the twentieth century.

**The creator's role**     In addition to aesthetic communication, there may be other reasons for the production of an artistic work. The artist may wish to show something he has seen, or pass on his emotional reaction to an experience. He may wish to use his work to comment on a social or moral issue or to solve an emotional or aesthetic problem by exposing it and sharing it. He may desire to contribute to an environment within which some activity may take place (by designing an auditorium or decorating a conference room), or he may wish to create a tool that is both functional and interesting to look at. On the other hand, some artists will insist that they have no conscious goal at all, not even aesthetic communication. Aestheticians argue that this cannot be, for if the artist pleases himself, his self-gratification is, in a way, aesthetic communication.

A work of art is not necessarily directed by its creator to one person or perceiver, but to any beholder, and it thus becomes a universal utterance, an expression communicative to all men of all times or of an entire society and its age.

At the same time, the composer, painter, or any other artist of today has the responsibility for creating works that express today's societal and aesthetic values. Although the perceiver may not always wholly understand the artist's works, he must recognize the artist's responsibility for contemporary expression. Thus, when the creator asks the perceiver to "try to understand my work on its own terms," he is simply asking for recognition of contemporaneity. If the perceiver does not make the attempt, he is being completely unfair to the creator and, in a very real sense, unfair to himself.

### Music as an art form

Music is at the same time related to, and separated from, all of its sister arts. It is like them in that it is a vehicle for aesthetic expression and communication, but differs in that it is abstract and exists only in time, and not in space. This lack of specific verbal or visual imagery is such a hindrance to some that they try to ascribe additional, non-musical meanings to a musical composition to make it less abstract. On the contrary, music, to be valid, must be self-sufficient and free of dependence on stories or other extra-musical associations. Any art, of course, may arouse memories or suggest images to the individual perceiver; indeed, many composers have been inspired by pictures, legends, scenes in nature, and the like and have suffused their music with these associations. Almost invariably, however, the music is valid irrespective of the association. This has been borne out many times by teachers who have played such works as Smetana's *The Moldau* or Berlioz' *Fantastic Symphony* for students who had no knowledge of the "programs" or the music, yet who found the music artistically tenable and aesthetically satisfying. For many, the abstractness of music is its greatest quality, for they feel that through its abstractness the absolute in truth and beauty may be approached more closely. (See also Colorplate 2.)

In music, as in all of the arts, there are strong and important psychological forces. The arts stimulate the emotions, and psychology deals with emotions. Because of its psychological aspects, music is often used in religious services, mental therapy, and parades. In this functional realm, the emotional, aesthetic, religious, and other aspects of the human mind are so closely intertwined that it is impossible to separate them. For example, music in the church, religious paintings and statuary, the religious dances of many peoples, and even the architecture of the buildings that house the activities of religion give added emotional and aesthetic impact to man's worship.

There may, of course, be other functions for music. Music may provide background for conversation in a movie. It may be used to help create a placid environment for cows in order to encourage the production of milk, or it may be the medium for spontaneous expression as the spirit moves an improviser at a piano. Each is a valid function, but, when essentially musical values are subordinated to non-musical purposes, the result is most often a lessening of the aesthetic worth of the music.

It is as an art form that music serves man best. To understand the purpose of music is to understand the purpose of art. To appreciate music is to understand how and why it is created.

*Tromba Romana antica*

*Eugène Delacroix (1798?–1863).* Liberty Leading the People *(1830).
Stormy, colorful, allegorical, and overtly emotional, this
painting represents the epitome of nineteenth-century Romanticism.
Basing this work on an actual rebellion against Charles X,
Delacroix displays the typical Romantic conglomerate of
idealism and realism by juxtaposing the almost ethereal poise
of Liberty with the blood and dirt of rebellion. (The Louvre, Paris.
Photo: European Color Art, Peter Adelberg, Inc., New York)*

*Jackson Pollock (1912–1956). Autumn Rhythm (1950). One of the masterpieces of Abstract Expressionism, this painting not only illustrates the point that the subject matter of a work of art need not be a real object but also serves as an outstanding example of the artistic principles of rhythm and design as they may be found in the visual arts. The subtle placement of black, white, and brown masses results in an ebb and flow of line and shape perfectly suited to the size of the canvas and creates a strong feeling of graceful and rhythmic movement. (The Metropolitan Museum of Art, New York. George A. Hearn Fund, 1957)*

# 2 : THE PERFORMER AND THE PERCEIVER

MUSIC is unique among the arts because it exists only as sound. Few people can look at the printed score and mentally transform it into audible form, and few would care to experience music that way. The actual creation of the pitches called for by the composer is the most exciting aspect of the art of music; composers pine for live performances of their work, and people return again and again to hear compositions that are so familiar that many can hum every note.

It is the performer who mediates between the audience and the composer, bringing to life a series of dead symbols that provide guidelines for his playing or singing. In painting, the viewer can see precisely what the painter has wanted him to see; in literature, the reader can see the exact words and punctuation put on paper by the poet or novelist. The listener, however, cannot have such immediate contact with the composer, for the symbols of music have no reality of their own until they have been realized in sound. How they become sound is subject to so many varying factors that the re-creation of a single piece of music becomes a different experience each time it is undertaken, and performance becomes highly significant in its own right.

### What the performer does

The performer must make choices continuously, since such matters as tempo, dynamics, clarity of form, and the like create many problems of taste and temperament. Even more elusive are the choice of overall style and the degree to which the performer may alter tempo and other qualities. He must ask himself certain questions: Is the music basically a framework within which his own personality is given expression? Must he repress himself in order that the composer's wishes be the only focus of attention? May he add or blend his own musical tastes with those of the composer and, if so, to what extent?

This kind of choice is as perplexing and fascinating as any in music. It causes performers to study endlessly, to debate with critics and colleagues, to listen to other performers, and to examine themselves continually.

In approaching a musical composition, one of the first things a performer is aware of is its historical style, for his knowledge of the aesthetics of an age will determine the nature of his application of imagination to the printed note. He should know that he may not treat the rhythmic propulsion of a Bach composition with the rhythmic freedom appropriate to one by Chopin, nor may he invest a score by Mozart with the unbridled passion that would be suitable for a work by Puccini. He must balance this knowledge with an awareness of his audience's taste, for in some cases the ideal sound of a historical era may be too far removed from his own to be pleasing to his listeners.

Having ascertained the relationship of his performance to the historical demands of the music, the performer next examines more specific aspects of the score. He may be faced with a printed page that gives him only the pitches and rhythms to be sounded, with no performance directions at all. He may be directed to play certain passages with extreme rapidity, when he knows they will not be heard clearly in the hall in which he is to play. He will need to determine just how delicately a musical phrase should end, or how forcefully he may build to a rousing finale. In short, he examines all the elements of the music he is to perform with the ultimate goal of speaking for the composer and the composer's era by tastefully re-creating the essential meanings of the composition.

Every performer has his strengths and weaknesses; if he is astute, he will lean toward those musical styles he can do well, working with special care in those styles with which he may be less compatible. Invariably, these strong and weak points color his interpretation. Some pianists, for example, may move through the music of Mozart with a rather cold detachment, then catch fire in the passionate utterances of Scriabin. Many young players have difficulty coming to grips with both the grand gesture and extensive freedom of the romantic composers or the elegance of the classicists, and work best with the various genres of the twentieth century.

*Josef Danhauser (1805–1895). Liszt Playing before Kindred Romanticists (1840?).
His eyes fixed on a bust of Beethoven, Franz Liszt plays for Alexandre Dumas,
père, and George Sand (seated), the Countess d'Agoult (kneeling), and Victor Hugo,
Niccolo Paganini, and Gioacchino Rossini (standing). The scene is theoretically
in the Rome residence of Rossini, but it is unlikely that this gathering
really occurred. The painter's purpose was to bring together great artists whose
mutual understanding was a common bond against philistinism. (The Bettmann Archive)*

The consummate interpretation is met when technique is so firmly
under control that it seems not to be a factor at all. When one hears a
singer such as Leontyne Price, a violinist of the caliber of Isaac Stern,
or a pianist like Claudio Arrau, one really is less aware of technical skill
than of the ebb and flow of the composer's ideas as they are revealed in
exquisite tone, phrasing, and nuance. When the music itself is the focus
of all attention, rather than the skill or personality of the composer or
the performer, the art of musical performance has reached its apogee.

It is easy to say that a performer tries to bring to his audience the
original thoughts of the composer, but this is not enough. Not only may
the performer have his own ideas to bring to the music, including concepts of musical sound and style somewhat more relevant to his own age,

but also the intentions of the composer may have been veiled by inaccurate printing, changes in the meaning of notational symbols, and many other factors.

Because of this, the printed note is really a capricious thing. A blob of ink in the second space of the treble staff is called A, a pitch that is supposed to result from air waves vibrating 440 times every second.[1] In Europe, a pitch is considered to be A when it vibrates at a slightly different frequency (435 *cps* in some cases, higher than 440 *cps* in others). In Handel's time (first half of the eighteenth century), A was in some locales a whole step lower than our modern A, while in others it was about one half step lower. *A-440* is not necessarily sacrosanct within a country. When the late Charles Munch was the conductor of the Boston Symphony Orchestra, he had the orchestra tune to a higher pitch, and the "Boston A" of about 443 *cps* caused much unhappiness among the many wind players who had to have mechanical adjustments made on their instruments in order to play the higher pitches.

The question of pitch is not the only obstacle to exactness of performance, for there are other inadequacies of notation. For example, when a composer asks that a passage be played "moderately fast," he poses the musical equivalent of the conundrum, "How high is up?" How fast is "fast" and what does "moderately" mean? The interpretation of the rhythm of dotted quarters and eighths ( ♩. ♫♩. ♪ ) is another example of notational imprecision. According to the current rules of the rudiments of music, the dot adds the value of an eighth note to the quarter note, yet performers in the Baroque period often extended the length of the quarter note more than this and accordingly shortened the duration of the eighth note, thus resulting in a sound more accurately notated as follows: ♩.. ♫♩.. ♪ .

There are instances, too, in which the composer abdicates control so that the performer may give expression to his own creativity. The *cadenzas* in some concertos, for example, are free interpolations by the soloist at the end of a movement, without participation of the orchestra.

Improvisation, a free extemporization by a performer either on his own musical ideas or within limitations set by the composer, has been an

---

[1] The rate of vibrations per second is often indicated by a number plus the abbreviation *cps*, for *cycles per second*. Acousticians have recently standardized the abbreviation *Hz*, for *Hertz*, as the technical equivalent of *cps*.

aspect of musical performance throughout history. In *aleatory* music (Latin *alea*, "game with dice") the composer is content simply to provide an opportunity for improvisation by the performer, although the composer may offer limits as to the pitches, durations, or rhythms the improviser may use.

The foregoing discussion, it would seem, is concerned only with the solo interpreter. However, it applies equally to group performance, except that the interpretive decisions rest with a conductor. A further difference is that a musician who performs alone has no one to rely upon but himself, while the conductor must communicate his decisions to a host of

**Performance by groups**

*Sebastian Gutzwiller. Family Concert in Basel. Chamber music in the home was important in the "Biedermeier" ideal, a middle-class concept of warm family relationships and joy in simple comforts. In this painting, the performers are their own audience, and the lyricism of their music is suggested by the soft glow of the light flooding the room, the gentle contours of the many shapes in the picture, and the touches of family life. (The Bettmann Archive)*

performers, many of whom may have very strong opinions about the music themselves.

The conductor, therefore, is really much more than an interpreter. He is a leader, diplomat, autocrat, teacher, and, to no little extent, a disciplinarian. His job is complex, for he must be aware constantly of what is happening—and what should happen—in every one of the many instrumental or vocal parts sounding simultaneously. He must be able to hear all types of errors, ranging from an actual wrong note to a subtle miscalculation of interpretation. Moreover, he must know what changes the performers should make in order for them to conform to his interpretive decisions.

Although the conductor does most of his work in rehearsal, when he can verbalize his musical ideas and work them out carefully, the art of the baton is highly refined when the orchestra is playing before an audience, for the conductor must use his hands to set the speed, adjust the dynamics, signal players when to begin playing, communicate the style of the music, and modify its various components as the work progresses.

Most conductors use the right hand to inform the musicians of the nature of the pulse of the music and the left hand to communicate style and reinforce such things as changes in speed and dynamics. Usually, the first beat of each group of pulsations in the music is identified by a down-stroke of the baton; the directions of the other beats will vary with the number of beats in the rhythmic groups, or *measures*, of the composition. Some of the more usual baton patterns, as viewed by the audience, would look like this:

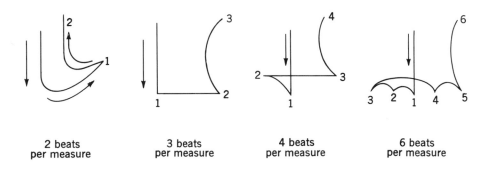

| 2 beats per measure | 3 beats per measure | 4 beats per measure | 6 beats per measure |

These beat patterns may be altered considerably to suit the demands of the music and the personal technique of the conductor, but, in general, they are universally employed.

Interpretation is sometimes more the result of a meeting of minds rather than the decision of one person. When a concerto is played, for example, the various aspects of interpretation are mutually agreed upon by conductor and soloist. When the soloist is a distinguished artist who appears only occasionally with the orchestra, differences of opinion are usually resolved in his favor, the conductor granting the soloist the courtesy of artistic hegemony. In one famous instance, the conductor of a concert in New York prefaced the performance of a concerto by Brahms with an announcement to the audience that the interpretation they were about to hear was solely that of the pianist, and that he, the conductor, disagreed so strongly with the pianist that he thought it important to disavow anything that was about to happen. Such moments are fortunately rare.

Conductors are assisted in the techniques of orchestral performance by the leader of the first violin section, the *concertmaster*, who sits in the outside seat of the front row of violins immediately to the conductor's left. The concertmaster's responsibility is twofold: he handles all incidental solos for the violin, and also advises the conductor in the all-important questions of the bowing of stringed instruments. Such problems as changing direction of the bow stroke, the type of bow stroke to be used to differentiate a loud (*forte*) from a soft (*piano*) sound, and other questions require a string specialist, and a successful orchestral performance leans heavily on the concertmaster's expertise.

In musical theater (musical comedy, opera, and other types), interpretation is a very complex matter. The conductor, singers, and stage director are all involved with what happens on the stage. The conductor is involved primarily with musical considerations, the director is responsible for physical action, and the singer must develop gestures, vocal inflections, and other musico-dramatic techniques to project a characterization. In highly integrated and well-rehearsed productions, the demands of both acting and music can be fulfilled, with the hand of the stage director as a shaping force. Where international stars are involved, or in situations where there are frequent changes in cast and conductor, performances often reflect uncoordinated concepts of characterization and music, primarily because of lack of rehearsal time. When it comes to actual performance before an audience, the dominant influence is that of the conductor; tempo, climax, and balance are the result of his leadership.

In chamber music, performers serve as co-equals in all aspects of performance. Occasionally, a member of a chamber group, such as the first

*Seventeenth-century opera in the French Embassy, Rome. Panoply may be observed on both sides of the footlights. (The Bettmann Archive)*

violinist in a string quartet, will act as leader, but only to get the group started and to indicate various points of interpretation along the way.

### The role of the perceiver

The evaluation of the performer's success is an extremely personal matter on the part of the listener. If that evaluation is to be positive, sensitive, and astute, the listener must consider carefully his responsibilities.

A work of art and what it communicates may be perceived on several levels of appreciation. Usually, the listener's response to music he is hearing for the first time is a personal, emotional one, and is stimulated by the overall impact of such qualities as loudness, tone color, speed, rhythm, accent, and other aspects of sound which may immediately impinge on his awareness.

Each subsequent hearing may result in a firmer grasp of more subtle factors, such as repeats of melodies, changes in texture, or variations of musical materials. In short, he becomes more aware of the craft of the composer. Emotional response will often become more pleasurable or significant as the listener combines his personal reaction with a conscious recognition of the craft of composition.

This ultimate combination of understanding and emotional receptivity, of "total appreciation," is the goal of the sophisticated listener. To attain it, he must commit himself to the idea that involved, active listening requires some sort of preparation. He may for example, acquire over a period of time a knowledge of the styles, traditions, and philosophies that have influenced composers to write in their various ways, and may deepen this knowledge through a familiarity with an ever-broadening repertoire of compositions of varying structure and style.

Awareness and depth of understanding of both live and recorded music can come only from repeated exposure, for musical and extra-musical meanings are not always easily detected and comprehended. In the case of many of the world's masterpieces, such meanings are like the petals of a flower, each one revealing deeper mysteries and feelings as it is unfolded.

After each listening experience, the listener ought to try to find answers to questions such as these:

Was there emotional, meaningful communication?

Was there more than one kind of emotion?

What devices created this sort of communication?

Were the melodies ingratiating? harsh? gentle? fragmented?

Does the music put greater emphasis on structure than on emotion?

What sort of structure did the composer employ?

The ordering of these questions is not casual. They proceed from the most personal observations to the more objective and sophisticated, since enjoyment of music may result not only from the power of music to move the soul, but also from its capacity to be an enchantress of the mind.

18

Thus, one might also ask himself, what happened to the musical ideas?

Is there one melody played over and over, each time with different instruments or voices?

Is there one melody alternated with other melodies?

How do contrasts (loud and soft, slow and fast, high and low) contribute to the nature of the musical ideas?

What gives the music cohesion? variety? climax? balance?

The records accompanying this book include a number of musical examples; some are complete, others are excerpts and fragments. The reader might practice his listening on them and become familiar with each one, noting that there are highly individual qualities in the music of each of the composers. One work or idea may appeal more than another, but decisions of preference should not be made until the compositions have been studied from several points of view. If possible, one should listen to recordings of the complete works from which the excerpts were taken, so that the excerpts may be heard in context.

One need not know a great deal of music literature to be a music lover. A person's treasury of art is essentially a treasury of the familiar, and it does not have to be huge to bring joy and enrichment. The greatest rewards come from reliving the emotional and intellectual experiences effected by a piece of music, and these rewards can be gained simply by listening to it again and again.

*William Hogarth (1697–1764). The Laughing Audience. One of the first artists to become a social critic, Hogarth satirized all elements of society in his engravings. The artist shows not only an audience enjoying what is apparently a very comic opera (note the three woodwind players in the foreground), but also the distracting influence of various dalliances in the first balcony. (The Metropolitan Museum of Art, New York. Harris Brisbane Dick Fund)*

*Basic principles underlying the study of art history*

BEFORE examining some of the interactions between art and life, it would be wise for the reader to become aware of some evaluative and analytical pitfalls encountered in any historical study of the arts.

One of the first principles of the study of art history is that each stylistic epoch has its own criteria for creating beauty; each period, therefore, must be evaluated on its own terms. Thus, one cannot use the same set of standards to compare William Shakespeare with Tennessee Williams to determine who is the better dramatist. To do so is to be unjust to both.

Further, there is a danger in the tendency to look upon each epoch as an improvement over a preceding one. Art is certainly in a constant ferment and evolution, but to suggest, for instance, that the music of Bach is better than that of Palestrina simply because it was composed two centuries later is to be blind to the beauties of two wholly different styles, each of which is aesthetically complete.

It must also be noted that each stylistic period is far more than a collection of art objects inspired by one basic impulse. On the contrary, every era presents the historian with a maze of contrasts and contradictions, a series of currents and counter-currents, each influencing the other. An example of this interaction is provided by a brief observation of the culture of Renaissance Europe, where such factors as affluence, climate, and religion helped create strikingly different styles of art.

In the north, a geographical area marked by harsh winters, political disunity, and general economic privation, there was a retention of a certain fundamentalism, a passionate seeking for truth, and an emotional religious faith that resulted in the Reformation. Paintings were often mystical and allegorical, and the sharp separation of one shape from another and the clear distinction between foreground and background, so often apparent in the work of such artists as Cranach and Dürer, seem to evoke the memory of medieval stained-glass windows, in which leaded frames set off one bold color from another.

In Italy, life was generally more affluent, and Italian art of the period reflects a more hedonistic and humanistic culture, a culture that sought pleasure for its own sake and was deeply concerned with the scientific, philosophical, and material aspects of man. Titian and other Italian painters produced sensuous studies of the human figure and bathed them in a glow of warm light and indefinite shadow.

Note the warm flesh tones and billowing draperies of Titian's *Venus and the Lute Player* and the stark contrasts and bold modeling of Cranach's *Venus* (Colorplate 3). The comparison reveals two different, yet contemporary, approaches to the same subject matter and illustrates the philosophical differences extant at the time.

Finally, it should be kept in mind that, although the interplay between historical events and artistic events is constant, the factor that most conditions the nature of an individual work of art is the shaping force *within* the artist, rather than specific, external events. A grasp of this principle will help one to understand how an artist can create even under the most adverse circumstances. For example, Mozart wrote some of his sunniest music when he was ill and despondent over finances and family tragedy. Milton suffered blindness, political persecution, and imprisonment during much of his artistic life, yet he produced many works of great merit; Cervantes survived the Inquisition and wrote *Don Quixote*.

### Forces influencing the arts

That there is a reflection in music, painting, poetry, and the other arts of the temper of an age is unquestioned. The maturation of a style or a specific work in the creator's mind is a long process, however, and the result will reflect more than a specific moment in time or a single state of mind. This should not reduce the importance of any interaction between art and life, for society is never free of the shaping forces of art, and no aspect of art can remain completely untouched by society. The unceasing flow of influences to and from the various forces of human life, including geography, war, economics, politics, and religion, has created a heritage of art and thought that has been in a state of change from the earliest times, and which has reflected the many aspects of man's society—the real, the ideal, and the unreal.

The interrelationships and cross-influences among the arts themselves are also important. Throughout history, stylistic currents in one or the other of the arts have conditioned the style of art in general. In France, the poetry of Verlaine, Baudelaire, Mallarmé, and others interacted with the painting of Monet, Manet, Pissarro, and other artists during the 1860's and 1870's, creating the stylistic force known as Impressionism. The climate was thus prepared for Debussy, whose music represents the same ideals translated into sound. The German Romantic art song could not have flowered without the flood of lyric poetry emanating from many literary figures, including Goethe and Heine; the grandiloquence of the Baroque is a stylistic element easily discerned in the music of Johann Sebastian Bach, the sculpture of Bernini, the poetry and periodic sentences of Milton, and the painting of Rubens.

The different strata of society interact, too, each influencing the other. The Negro spiritual, a religiously fundamentalist, passionate expression of faith and longing, has welled from an underprivileged group to exert a tremendous melodic, harmonic, and emotive pressure not only on a number of serious composers—working its way into their music via the idioms of jazz and the blues—but also on the dance and song of almost the entire Western world. The fact that gypsy qualities are often found in the music of Haydn and Brahms is another example of a musical influence exerted by a largely ignored, often mistreated segment of society.

Social dance and popular entertainment give other instances of social interaction; the former percolated through time and stylization into the highly refined Baroque *suite*, while the latter, through the medium of the socially not-so-acceptable *commedia dell' arte*, eventually influenced all forms of theater, including the opera.

### *Discipline and feeling—the romantic-classic struggle*

Change in the balance of emotion and reason has been a constant feature of the arts of Western civilization. Since both are always involved in the shaping of artistic communication, it is the relationship of one to the other, not the absence of one or the other, that identifies the temper of an age.

All artists are concerned with emotional communication. When they choose to express themselves in terms characterized by restraint, clarity of form, simplicity of diction, objectivity, and directness of expression, they are known as *classicists*. *Romanticists* are those artists whose works are identified by an outpouring of feeling, a tendency toward complexity, richness of color (or of sound or vocabulary, depending on the medium), a fascination with nature, a proclivity for the autobiographical, a quality of longing or aspiring to somewhat indefinable goals, and an approach to form that seeks to make every work quite personal and unique.

This polarity of attitude may be noted in two highly different manifestos. Consider first a part of the preface to Gluck's opera *Alceste*. Although the opera was first performed in 1767, the preface did not appear until two years later:

... my greatest labor should be devoted to seeking a beautiful simplicity, and I have avoided making displays of difficulty at the expense of clearness; nor did I judge it desirable to discover novelties if [they were] not naturally suggested by the situation and the expression.
.... the universal approbation of so enlightened a city [Vienna] has made it clearly evident that simplicity, truth and naturalness are the great principles of beauty in all artistic manifestations.[1]

Comparison of this eighteenth-century, eminently classical attitude with a letter written in 1856 by the nineteenth-century French composer Berlioz is informative:

I am for the music which you yourself call *free*. Yes, free and wild and sovereign; I want it to conquer everything, to assimilate everything to itself. ... The real problem lies in finding the means of being expressive and true without ceasing to be a musician, and to find new ways of making the music dramatic. ... There is still another stumbling block ahead of me in my attempt to write the music for this drama [*The Damnation of Faust*]. The emotions which I have to express affect me too much.[2]

One will notice Berlioz' interest in the unique ("new ways of making the music dramatic"), whereas Gluck downgrades novelty for its own sake. Berlioz admits to being personally involved with his music and its

---

[1]Cited by Alfred Einstein, *Gluck*, trans. Eric Blom (London: J. M. Dent & Sons, 1936, and New York: Farrar, Straus & Giroux, 1955), pp. 98f.
[2]In Ulrich Weisstein, *The Essence of Opera* (New York: Free Press, 1964), p. 213.

*The nave of Westminster Abbey, London (second half of the thirteenth century, partially rebuilt in the fifteenth century). The picture does not show the blaze of color created by stained-glass windows, but the slender piers of columns, pointed arches, and soaring roof epitomize the inventiveness and gracefulness of the arts in the Middle Ages and represent in stone the aspirant nature of the medieval outlook. (New York Graphic Society)*

subject matter, but Gluck's involvement is more impersonal. Berlioz wants his music to be all-consuming ("free and wild and sovereign"); Gluck stresses "simplicity, truth and naturalness."

## The periods of music history

The history of Western civilization can be discussed in terms of a perpetual swing between classic and romantic periods.[3] The Medieval era[4]

[3]A summary of traits, forms, men, and events of each historical era will be found in chart form in Appendix A.

[4]While many books will date the Medieval era from 1000, the time of the spread of staff notation, it is better to begin the study of Western music with the rise of polyphony, or many-voiced music (mid-ninth century).

(850–1450) was an overtly passionate age. The men of the time were consumed with a longing for a better world, attracted (in literature, at least) to the ethereal idealism of chivalry and monastic purity, and captivated by tales of great heroes and heroines battling insurmountable forces. The wearing of the heart on the sleeve is expressed in countless lyrics of sighing lovers, in the best tradition of romantic communication.

The ideals of the late fifteenth and most of the sixteenth centuries, on the other hand, included a greater emphasis on Greco-Roman aesthetics and reflected the calm, horizontal lines reminiscent of the classical concept. The arts of the Renaissance, especially in the south, reveal an interest in humanism, pride in man and his accomplishments, moderation, balance, and warmth of color. The north retained its medieval mysticism, combining it with the traits just listed for the south. For purposes of music history, the Renaissance may be dated from 1450 to 1600.

By the end of the sixteenth century, one can discern the beginning of a new era, signaled by a return to the patently emotional in all of the arts. Historians call this period the Baroque (1600–1750), a period of exuberance, splendor, excitement, drama, and romanticism. Although it was a time of such creative giants as Bach, Handel, Monteverdi, Milton, Rembrandt, Rubens, Bernini, and Molière, the origin of its name was less than complimentary. The extravagant expression of the period was

*Pieter Lastmann (1562–1649). David in the Temple (1613). The romantic impulse underlying Baroque art and music is revealed by contrasts of light and dark, rapt facial expressions, elaborate draperies and carvings, the crowd around the altar where David plays the harp, the complex interplay of diagonal and curving lines, and the suggestion of vibrant instrumental and vocal sounds (note the boy sopranos and altos). Above and behind the singers, from left to right, are violin, tambourine, trombone, tenor shawm (an ancestor of the oboe), bass viol, and, resting on a small table, a lute. (The Bettmann Archive)*

considered by its critics (among them Jean-Jacques Rousseau) to be a perversion of the absolute, the platonic, the disciplined, and the classic. And so "baroque," a word derived from either the Spanish *barrueco* ("misshapen pearl") or the Italian *baroco* ("illogical syllogism") and suggesting the extreme and the forced, was applied to a century and a half of artistic achievement.

The so-called Classical period, said to include the latter half of the eighteenth century and the first two decades of the nineteenth, began and ended in political turmoil. The era emerged from an artistically unsettled sub-period in the mid-eighteenth century, when some composers were relying on a combination of intimacy and ornamentation known as the Rococo, while others of a Preclassical persuasion were catalyzed into seeking a studied simplicity and discipline by the discoveries of Johann Joachim Winckelmann (1717–1768), an archaeologist whose *History of the Art of Antiquity* (1764) set down some of the major principles of Hellenic art.

The Classical period is familiar to most students, regardless of their major fields, because many of the personages of the era are encountered in the study of history at all educational levels. Washington, Jefferson, Franklin, Voltaire, and Goethe are characterized by the same elegance, poise, reason, dignity, and polish that are present in the music of Haydn, Mozart, Gluck, and the young Beethoven.

The graciousness of life discerned in the painting and poetry of the late eighteenth century (especially in the court of Louis XVI) masked an unrest and thirst for change that can be perceived even as the Classical period was evolving from the Baroque. The *Sturm und Drang* ("storm and stress"), a literary movement identified with Goethe, Herder, and Schiller, trumpeted a new concept of the individual in society and, venting a vigorous protest against inequality and injustice, presented an emotional appeal for social change.

The emotionalism of the late eighteenth century is often expressed with elegance and restraint, but by the early 1800's, unrestrained expressions of feeling and of individual attitudes were clearly in the ascendancy. In music, the pivotal figures in this change from classicism to romanticism were Beethoven and Schubert. Both expressed themselves in the concise language of classic thought, yet with a degree of personal involvement, surging lyricism, and dynamic communication that marked a distinct departure from the previous era.

The traits of any romantic era have already been discussed; it remains for the student to apply the general attributes of romantic expression

*Jacques Louis David (1748–1825).* Madame Desbassayne de Richemont and Her Daughter, Camille. *The simplicity of shape and line, combined with incomparable grace, dignity, elegance, and an indefinable blend of strength and softness, is strikingly evocative of the music of Mozart. (The Metropolitan Museum of Art, New York. Gift of Julia A. Berwind, 1953)*

Honoré Daumier (1808–1879).
Pyrotechnical Music (1853).
*The nineteenth century was
fascinated by unusual sound
effects and instrumental
combinations; the intense
controversy that frequently
surrounded their use is
indicated by Daumier's
satirical lithograph.
Substituting pots for
drums provides a
delightful pun for
English speaking readers
who often refer to
timpani as "kettle drums."*
(The Bettmann Archive)

Jensen. The Violinist. *Black chalk and
watercolor produce an interplay of line and
shape that suggests the quality of bowing and
fingering and the involvement of the performer,
who seems to have become a part of his instrument.*
(The Metropolitan Museum of Art, New York.
Bequest of Alexandrine Sinsheimer, 1958)

to the art of the nineteenth century and, to a great extent, that of the
twentieth century. Lurid subject matter; an ardent interest in the sights
and sounds of nature; expansion of the resources of tone color by expanding the number and variety of orchestral instruments; long-breathed
melodies glowing with passion; extended forms suitable to programmatic
subjects rather than to pre-established patterns of repetition and con-

trast; the emergence of virtuoso performers whose reputation was based largely on their ability to dazzle their listeners with technical effects; a host of strikingly individual composers who sought personal, novel, and trenchantly communicative forms of expression; a fascination with the exotic, the bizarre, the melancholic, and the historical, all tied up with a sort of philosophical escapism; a variety of dynamic effects involving tempo changes, gradual alterations of loud and soft, and subtlety of tone color; and an array of national and personal styles ranging from the grandiose and the vulgar to the intimate and the ultrasophisticated—these characteristics are all part of the recent past, the Romantic era.

Many writers date the Romantic era from the death of Beethoven (1827) to the death of Mahler (1911), or more generally, to the beginning of the twentieth century. It is misleading, however, to suggest that the era came to a halt with either date, in spite of the fact that the year 1900 is a convenient and logical date for the beginning of the Modern era. A study of the arts of the first half of the twentieth century reveals that romantic expression has been a major concern for many composers, artists, and writers.

Other creators did, however, begin to break with the romantic tradition, some as early as the first decade of the twentieth century. The Fauvists, Cubists, Dadaists, Impressionists, Expressionists, and Futurists

*John Constable (1776–1837). Salisbury Cathedral (1823). The Romantic poet, painter, composer, or novelist often found inspiration in the past or in nature, as Constable did when he painted the cathedral's slender spire, its Gothic character, and rural environment. The dramatic arch of the rainbow, stormy clouds, and writhing trees and greenery are part of the intensely emotional character of the Romantic gesture. (Victoria and Albert Museum, London)*

all presaged a movement toward a more objective art, although the movement did not become general until after World War II.

A number of factors have created a diversity of philosophy and life in the second half of the twentieth century that were not observable in previous epochs. Existing side by side are such disparate concepts as capitalism, socialism, and communism, religious fundamentalism, liberalism, and mysticism, experimentalism, reactionism, and staunch conservatism. The emergence of many newly independent states has stimulated strong national pride for some, while others, influenced by the rapidity of communication and ease of transportation, have espoused a more international and cosmopolitan mode of expression. The explosion of scientific knowledge has been recognized as only a partial boon to mankind, and many artists are evidencing serious concern for the role of man in a technological age. They are disturbed by man's apparent urge to destroy himself and pollute his world, by his frequent cruelty or apathy toward his fellows, and by the contradictions of an age of discovery and wealth that tolerates war, hatred, and poverty.

At this point in the mid-twentieth century, it is impossible to identify one basic musical style as typifying the Modern era. This is an eclectic age, an age of composers who borrow from the past and from one another, and, equally important, who experiment with resources of sound that have nothing in common with the practices of the past.

It would seem, however, that the musical world, having passed through a romantic period that lasted with influence and varying degrees of vigor until 1950 and having experienced some thirty or forty years of experimentation and artistic ferment, has entered a relatively objective era that reflects the search for clarity and logic that denotes a classical age.

The immediacy of communication may well have destroyed forever the possibility of separating the arts into specified periods. Through the miracles of electronics, the composer of today can hear, evaluate, and respond to music being performed halfway around the world, whereas the composer of a century ago had to wait months to learn of the musical creations of his contemporaries. This rapid interchange of style and experience is unprecedented in the history of music. Its impact on the definition of musical style is impossible to predict, but exciting to contemplate. (See Colorplates 4, 6, 7, and 8.)

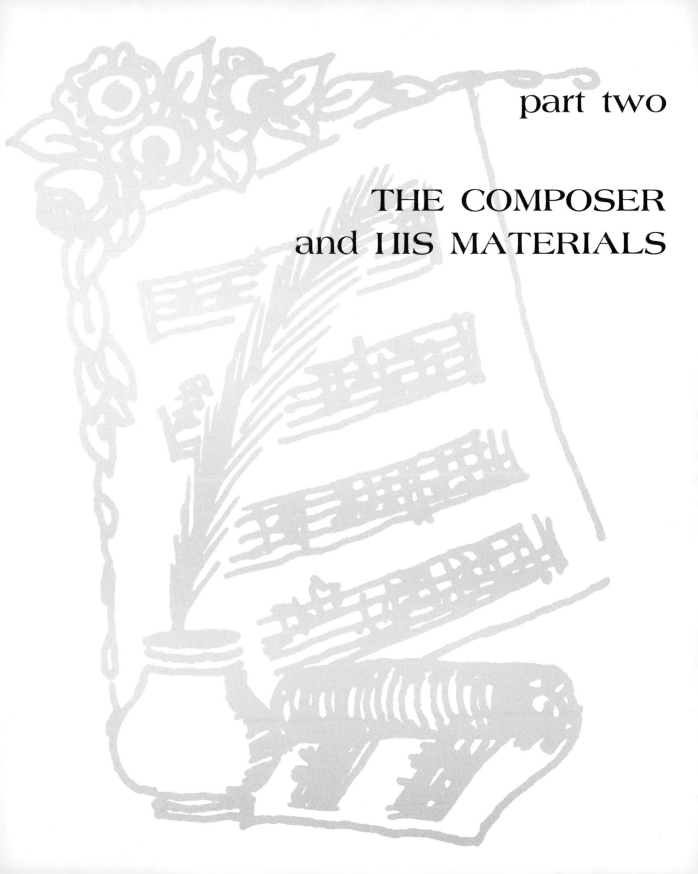

part two

THE COMPOSER
and HIS MATERIALS

# 4 : TOOLS OF PERFORMANCE

## *The nature of performing media*

THE sound quality of the voices or instruments involved in a performance plays a tremendous role in the kind of impact made by the music. Smetana's *The Moldau* is a case in point. Each of the scenes described in this composition depends for its effectiveness on the instruments used. At the very outset of the work, the music suggests the welling of the river's source; light, high, rapid movement is called for, hence flutes are used in fast, scale-like passages. The main theme of the river could have been assigned to any melodic orchestral instrument, but strings are specified, because Smetana felt that the depth and majesty of a great river could be expressed only by a massed group of instruments capable of a rich, soaring tone. (See also Chapter 12.)

Try to imagine Sousa's *Stars and Stripes Forever* played on recorders, or by a string orchestra. All the melodic and harmonic ideas would be there, but the inherent sound of the instruments would make the composition wholly different from what the composer had in mind. This inherent quality of specific instruments or voices is called *timbre*, or *tone color*. It is one of the major shaping forces in music and, in any live performance, is the very first sensation consciously or unconsciously perceived by the listener.

**Overtones**

All performing media utilize air set into motion by such vibrators as tendons (the voice), pieces of gut (stringed instruments), membranes (drums), reeds (most woodwind instruments), lips (brass instruments), or electronic devices, to mention but a few. Each vibration is a complex phenomenon, for the vibrating element quivers not only over its entire length, thus producing its lowest pitch, called the *fundamental*, but also in many shorter segments as well. Since the shorter segments vibrate faster, their pitches are higher. Each of these higher pitches resulting from a fundamental is called an *overtone*; with the exception of some sounds produced by electronic instruments, every musical sound is an agglomeration of a fundamental and its overtones.

The various overtones of any fundamental are unequal in strength, and vary from instrument to instrument or voice to voice as a result of differences in the shape of the instrument, the material of which it is constructed, the length and thickness of the instrument or the vibrating element, and the sensitivity or style with which it is played or with which the sound is produced. The relationships between the higher and the lower overtones result in the distinctive sound of an instrument or voice—its timbre.

**Vibrato**     The modern concept of beautiful sound often calls for a certain quality known as *vibrato,* a slight quivering or alternation between the written pitch and fractional pitches just above and below it. Singers and instrumentalists must be able to produce and control an expressive vibrato as an essential part of performance technique, although the degree of vibrato required is not the same for all historical epochs or for every composition. Voices of young children are weak in vibrato, hence the sound produced is rather "straight."

### Voices and how they are used

The singing voice is not only the most familiar medium of performance, but is also the most personal, flexible, and varied. No one voice is precisely like another; just as each speaking voice varies from person to person, a singing voice will vary, and for the same reasons.

**Voice types**     There are two basic types of voice, the lyric and the dramatic. Lyric voices are generally light, agile, and clear; dramatic voices have an exciting ring and a sense of weight and power. Although well-trained dramatic voices may be as flexible and agile as lyric ones, most dramatic roles in operas heard today call for less *fioritura* ("floweriness" or ornateness) than lyric roles. In oratorios, operas, and in some musicals, the roles of ingenues or young heroines are generally given to lyric voices;

dramatic voices are used for great queens, goddesses, or heroines whose singing is accompanied by fairly large orchestras. In operas composed in the nineteenth century, from which the bulk of the repertoire is taken, heroic roles are given most often to tenors; priests, fathers, and kings are sung by basses. If a role requires the performance of ornamental melodies, the part will be taken by a lyric voice; tragic or warrior-like roles will be sung by dramatic voices.

Voices are classified also by *range*, that is, how high or low the voice may comfortably go. A high woman's voice is called *soprano*, a low woman's voice *alto* (or, more formally, *contralto*). A high male voice is called a *tenor*, a low one *bass*.

In addition to range, the appellation "tenor," "soprano," and so on depends on timbre, for the soprano or tenor is immediately distinguishable from the alto or bass by virtue of the formers' greater brilliance and, in most cases, flexibility.

There are two important intermediate voice types. Midway between the alto and the soprano is the *mezzo-soprano* (literally, "middle-soprano"), a voice combining some of the weight and force of the dramatic soprano with the lower, richer qualities of the alto. Such a voice is often called upon to portray a temptress or villainess, and also an adolescent boy. Between the tenor and the bass is the *baritone*. One must distinguish between the operatic baritone and the baritone sound of the popular crooner. The latter is characterized by a charming and pleasing quality that rarely varies in color or dynamics, while the former, used in many types of roles, has a certain "ping" that is reinforced by a wide singing range, considerable dramatic power, and variety.

There are still other voice classifications. The *coloratura* is a voice with a truly unique flexibility and very wide range. The term is most often applied to a high, lyric soprano who can sing very ornate music, but it can be applied also to any voice with similar capabilities. The *spinto* is a particularly warm soprano or tenor voice that has both lyric and dramatic qualities. The *basso profondo* is a very deep voice with impressive sonority and weight, yet, understandably, relatively little agility, while the *basso buffo* has a less deep, rotund quality and a greater clarity, often combined with a certain dryness. The *basso cantante* ("singing bass") is a lyric, warm bass voice. The *Heldentenor* is an especially dramatic tenor, with great carrying power and weight. A very rare type is the *counter-tenor*, a high male voice capable of great feats of agility but without the projection or richness of sound of the more familiar lyric or dramatic tenor. It uses the *falsetto*, a technique by which a mature male singer can extend his range above its normal limits, although the resulting sound is somewhat weaker than the full voice.

A type of voice no longer encountered today is that of the *castrato*, a male singer emasculated just before the onset of puberty in order to combine the boy's larynx and voice production with the adult male's chest. Castrati, who dominated Italian opera during the Baroque era, were capable of performing extremely elaborate music of wide range with great power and trumpet-like timbre, but humanitarian considerations and a distaste for the bizarre resulted in a sharp decline in their popularity toward the end of the eighteenth century, although professional castrati were used in Italy even into the early decades of this century. Modern performances of Baroque vocal music usually use female rather than male voices for roles originally taken by castrati, because of considerations of range, timbre, and flexibility.

The table below identifies the voice types and ranges to be found in each of the vocal recordings accompanying this text:

| Verdi: | Quartet from *Rigoletto* | |
|---|---|---|
| | Duke | dramatic tenor |
| | Maddalena | mezzo-soprano |
| | Gilda | lyric soprano |
| | Rigoletto | baritone |
| Wagner: | Excerpts from *Die Walküre* | |
| | Sieglinde | dramatic soprano |
| | Siegmund | dramatic tenor (Heldentenor) |
| | Wotan | basso cantante |
| | Brünnhilde | dramatic soprano |
| Mozart: | Sextet from *Le Nozze di Figaro* | |
| | Don Curzio | lyric tenor |
| | Marcelline | mezzo-soprano |
| | Figaro | basso cantante |
| | Count Almaviva | basso cantante |
| | Bartolo | basso buffo |
| | Susanna | lyric soprano |
| Handel: | Excerpts from *Messiah* | |
| | *"Every valley shall be exalted"* | lyric tenor |
| | *"There were shepherds"* | lyric soprano |
| Schubert: | *Erlkönig* and *Im Frühling* | lyric baritone |

**Choral groups**  There are many names given to choral groups, none of which is used with consistent meaning. A *glee club*, for example, is theoretically devoted to short, sentimental or light-hearted songs for male voices, with one singer per part. In many schools, however, glee clubs sing all types of choral literature and may include both men's and women's voices, women alone, or men alone, and may range from relatively few singers to one hundred or more.

*Choir* is a term with religious overtones and suggests a group devoted to the performance of sacred choral music. However, choir refers also to any instrumental or vocal grouping in which the soprano, alto, tenor, and bass registers are represented. Furthermore, many school choirs, in spite of their frequent appearance in quasi-liturgical robes, perform choral pieces that are wholly secular in character, thus totally belying the original meaning of the word.

*Chorale* usually refers to a choral group that sings a wide variety of choral literature. The same term, however, describes such simple, rhythmically solid hymns as *Ein feste Burg* ("A Mighty Fortress") and *Nun danket alle Gott* ("Now Thank We All Our God"), works that were composed for the German Protestant Church.

A *chorus* usually has the largest membership of the several types of choral groups, and its literature will be taken from the entire spectrum of choral music. Many choruses, however, are quite small in number of singers, and, to confuse further the meaning of the word, *chorus* is also used to refer to a musical composition calling for many voices singing together (the "Hallelujah chorus," from Handel's *Messiah*, for example). A refrain is also colloquially called a chorus.

In addition to these four basic names, there are other combining forms, such as *a cappella choir* (devoted to unaccompanied sacred choral music, but misusing the term *a cappella*; see *Glossary*), *motet choir* (specializing in a particular genre of choral music), and *chamber chorus* (few singers per part). A *concert choir* is most often a select group of singers. A *madrigal group* is in theory devoted to the performance of the madrigal, but at times it performs works that are more appropriate to the chamber chorus. Such coined words as *Melodaires, Choralaires,* and the like usually refer to groups that are concerned with popular ballads, arrangements of show tunes, and various musical types chosen for values of entertainment.

### Instruments and how they are used

The variety of sound creators, or performing media, is almost infinite. The most familiar medium, of course, is the human voice, but man has

also supplied himself with a remarkable array of instruments, including everything from iron chains (as in Schoenberg's *Gurrelieder*) to wondrous machines that require years of practice and great skill if they are to be played well. The instruments used most frequently today represent but a fraction of those used throughout history.

Performing media are essentially melodic or nonmelodic, the latter producing sounds which either cannot be classified as to pitch or are limited to one pitch. The latter class includes the snare drum, cymbal, castanets, gourds, and tambourine.

Melodic instruments include not only such familiar media as piano, guitar, harmonica, and violin, but also timpani (or kettledrums, as they are also known) and the tape recorder (which may reproduce nonmusical sounds in a musical way). Instruments which are blown (brasses and woodwinds) or bowed and plucked (violin, viola, [violon]cello, double bass, harp, guitar, and banjo, to name just a few) are utilized by composers for carrying the melody. Besides the timpani, a number of other percussion instruments, including the xylophone and orchestra bells, can play melodies.

The strings, woodwinds, and brasses are considered to be orchestral "choirs," since each has soprano, alto, tenor, and bass "voices"; the range of each instrument is generally much wider than that of the corresponding human voice, however.

**Keyboard instruments**     A major feature of keyboard instruments is the efficiency with which they may be made to do many things at once. Many pitches can be sounded simultaneously and several melodies can be played at the same time. This group of instruments is popular for social purposes as well as for concert appearances, for these instruments are not only wholly self-sufficient, but are also very effective when used to accompany others.

The piano is perhaps the most familiar of all Western keyboard instruments. It employs strings stretched across a sounding board, and felt-lined hammers to strike them. Two particular attributes of the piano have made it a flexible and widely used instrument during the past two centuries. First, its key mechanism, or action, enables the player to vary his touch to alter dynamics and tone quality, hence the formal name of the instrument, the *pianoforte*—the "soft-loud." This action also allows for very rapid repetition of a single pitch without blurring or mechanical delay, and contributes to the intensity and drama of much piano music. The second major feature of the piano is its pedal mechanism. The three pedals found on large concert pianos allow the pianist to mute the sound or sustain some or all the notes played.

The organ is the most complicated of all musical instruments. The sound is the result of the blowing of air from a bellows through or across openings in pipes.[1] Since larger organs have several thousand pipes, considerable complications arise because their sounds must be controlled by the actions of one person. Before the invention of an electrically controlled air supply to the bellows getting a sound from some organs was more than a one-man job, for the air bellows had to be pumped by hand, a task usually relegated to young boys.

If an organ is used to play representative organ literature, it must have at least two keyboards. These keyboards are called "manuals." Most organs have three or four manuals, and there is one that has seven. Each manual controls a *division,* a group of pipes within which there are sets of like-sounding pipes—each producing a single pitch—called *ranks.* On a two-manual organ, the lower manual and its division will be called the *Great*[2] because it is the main division of the organ. The upper manual and its division is the *Swell.* The ranks of the Swell division are housed in a cabinet across the front of which is a set of slats resembling those of a venetian blind. The organist moves a pedal which opens and closes these slats, allowing the sound to swell, hence the name, or dwindle, thus contributing to the expressiveness of his playing. Organs also have a *pedalboard,* a keyboard and its division, that is activated by the feet.

There are Great and Swell manuals on all multi-manual organs. If there is a third manual, it will be the *Choir.* The Choir division's pipes are usually more delicate in sound, thus making for better choral accompaniments. The Choir manual may also be known as the *Positiv,* and some builders now label it the "Choir-positiv." Additional manuals may be known as *Solo* and *Echo,* either because of the nature of their sound or because of the placement of their pipes in relation to the rest of the divisions.

Each manual has a series of knobs, levers, or buttons called *stops.* Each stop controls a rank, and when the stop is pulled out, the organist may cause a pipe to sound by depressing a key on the particular manual to which the rank belongs. The sound an organist calls forth from his instrument is usually a composite of several ranks being played simultaneously. Richness and brilliance can be added to basic pitches by mixing them with higher sounds. *Couplers* can combine the stops found on one manual with those found on another.

[1]Electronic organs, which produce sounds by means of electrically driven generators, oscillators, or tapes, are also used extensively.

[2]European organs may have a different set of names for their various divisions.

The four manuals of the organ at Central Presbyterian Church, New York City. White tabs at top are couplers; knobs to the right are stops; buttons below each keyboard are pre-sets, which can engage many stops at the same time. (Photos by Alvin Fossner)

Organist Richard Westenburg at the console. His left hand plays the Choir manual, while his right hand activates a coupler. Above the Choir is the Great, then the Swell. The top manual is the Solo.

The console. The organ bench obscures the Swell pedals and pedal pre-sets.

Some of the pipes, grouped in five ranks. Different metals, sizes, and caps create distinctive timbres. These pipes are not visible to an audience.

The pedal-board, Swell pedals, and (left and right of the Swell pedals) pre-sets to be activated by the feet.

*Titian (ca. 1488–1576). Venus and the Lute Player. The subtle sweep of line from front to back and side to side, the gentle curves of draperies, human form, and other objects, the softness of the modeling, and the use of chiaroscuro identify the Southern Renaissance. (The Metropolitan Museum of Art, New York. Munsey Fund, 1936)*

*Lucas Cranach the Elder (1472–1553). Venus (1532). This famous painting of the Northern Renaissance is bold in color and form; the brilliant contrast of light and dark intensifies an already sensuous image. (Stadelisches Kunstinstitut, Frankfurt)*

*Colorplate* **3**

*Georges Seurat (1859–1891). Invitation to the Sideshow (1887–1888). Pointillism, a technique utilizing tiny dots of color, creates the purposeful vagueness of this evocative painting, in which the specific identity of an alto horn, trumpet, trombone, and, possibly, two clarinets is less important than the bittersweet image evoked. The hilarity and noise of the sideshow is muted here, for reality has been given a special twist by the artist. (The Metropolitan Museum of Art, New York. Bequest of Stephen C. Clark, 1960)*

*Colorplate* **4**

The tone quality and construction of the organ have been modified greatly over the centuries, as a result of both changing taste and mechanical improvements. The organ developed in the Romantic era included many expressive mechanisms (crescendo, tremolo, and couplers ad infinitum) and exotic and imitative tone colors. A Romantic organ almost invariably has such imitative stops as the clarinet, French horn, and English horn. The organ typifying the Baroque era is a much simpler instrument, with a generally brilliant and clear tone that stresses both the individuality of each stop and a consistency of timbre. In recent years, organ builders have re-created many old types, have constructed hybrids, and have produced electronic devices that are in some ways imitative of previous eras, and in others, unique to our own time.

The church organ is the only type of organ for which significant musical literature has been composed. Most organs heard today are in churches, although many concert halls also have them. The organs that are designed for theaters are sufficiently different to be considered as a separate category.

The theater organ is built with only one basic division, to which all the manuals may be connected. The lack of divisions creates a certain unity of color essentially foreign to the qualities sought by the great composers of organ music. The origins of this instrument are closely connected to the need for aural stimulation of the emotions during the era of silent movies; the advent of sound films with elaborate orchestral accompaniments signaled its demise for all but a devoted coterie of theater organ buffs.

Church organs usually have more pipes and varieties of sound than theater organs. The great theater organ in New York's Radio City Music Hall has actually far fewer ranks and pipes (and thus combinational possibilities of sound) than the rather modest-sized instrument in the Central Presbyterian Church on New York's Park Avenue. Interestingly enough, the world's largest organ is not in a church but in Convention Hall in Atlantic City, New Jersey. It has 33,112 pipes, 445 ranks, and 2 consoles (or sets of manuals), one with 5 manuals and one with 7.

A third major keyboard instrument is the harpsichord. Once the dominant keyboard device of Western music, the harpsichord yielded to the piano toward the end of the eighteenth century and remained in eclipse until the rebirth of interest in Renaissance and Baroque music in the mid-twentieth century. It blends easily with both strings and woodwinds, and is cherished for its clarity. Within the case there are strings that are plucked by *plectra* (singular: plectrum) made from crow quills or leather and held in place by wooden jacks that are activated by the keys. Larger models have two manuals (some even have a pedal manual), and both large and small models may have stops with which longer or shorter strings may be brought into play in order to achieve a variety of tone color.

The celesta is much less important in all respects than the piano, organ, or harpsichord, but its pleasantly muted, bell-like sound is encountered in a number of compositions of the nineteenth and twentieth centuries. The keys activate hammers that softly strike metal bars.

**Stringed instruments**     The largest number of members of the modern orchestra play the violins, violas, cellos, and double basses. To the strings are given the main burden of carrying melody and of providing buoyancy and orchestral sheen, and they have dominated the sound of the orchestra ever since the seventeenth century.

These instruments have four strings, made of gut or wire, which are caused to sound by the action of the bow or by being plucked with the finger (*pizzicato*). The bow may be drawn smoothly across a string, it may be bounced or hammered, and it may be played in such a way as to activate more than one string at a time.

The movement of the fingers of the left hand upon the strings is designed to make each string shorter in order to produce a higher pitch from it. This is called *stopping*; the stopping of more than one string at a time, combined with bowing more than one string at a time creates chords or simultaneous melodies and is called *double* or *triple stopping*, depending on the number of strings involved.

The modern string choir is but one group of instruments in the string family. A number of instruments, some of which have been quite important in the historical progress of music, are socially popular today. The guitar is especially significant in this regard; it and the lute, banjo, and mandolin differ from the violin group in that they are plucked only.

The guitar, lute, banjo, and mandolin are *fretted*; that is, they are equipped with thin strips of wood or metal across the neck of the instrument and under the strings to provide the player with a guide as to where to stop the strings. None has the singing resonance of the violin family. Although these instruments are used for the playing of chords as accompaniment, the lute and the guitar have an extensive body of melodic music written for them. Both were especially important during the sixteenth and seventeenth centuries and have consistently been popular.

A third group of strings, the viols, lay dormant from the end of the

The New York Pro Musica Consort of Viols playing at the Cloisters, medieval branch of the Metropolitan Museum of Art, New York. From left to right are Barbara Mueser, tenor viol, John Gibbons, harpsichord, Grace Feldman, treble viol, Judith Davidoff, tenor viol, and Alison Fowle, treble viol. (Courtesy of Columbia Artists Management)

Renaissance until the present. The recent revival of interest in older music has caused many players to take up instruments that were in vogue hundreds of years ago. Although less dramatic and vibrant than the tone of the modern string family, the viol sound is sweeter and seems especially appropriate to music of a somewhat intimate character.

The instruments played by the New York Pro Musica Consort of Viols reveal some of the basic structural differences between viols and the modern violin family. The frets can be clearly seen on the tenor viol in the right foreground; the modern violin family is not fretted. The C-shaped holes of the viols, their sloping shoulders, flat bodies, and high side walls are in sharp contrast with the violin, viola, and cello, which have "f" holes, squarish shoulders, swelling bodies, and narrow sidewalls. The double bass, however, retains characteristics of the viols. The viol bow, which is played with the palm facing up, uses wood that is either straight or slightly convex; the modern violin bow, played with the hand atop the wood, exerts greater tension on the hairs of the bow because of its concave-shaped wood. The violin, viola, and cello have four strings; the viol strings are thinner and more numerous, averaging six or seven in number.

The harp differs from the other strings in several respects. It has many strings, tuned to all the pitches of the major scale, but over several octaves; thus it can be played in all registers, from soprano to bass. The harp has an unusual mechanism that assigns a pedal to each string of a single pitch name; this pedal can raise or lower by a half step the pitch of all the strings of the same pitch name, regardless of the octave, and thus makes practicable the performance of the rapid runs and arpeggios so characteristic of the instrument. The harp's plucked sounds are striking and distinctive in slow passages as well as in fast ones.

**Woodwind instruments**

Except for the flute, all members of this choir are made of wood, although cheaper models of each instrument may be constructed of metal or plastic. In its earlier days, the flute, too, was made of wood; some players still prefer it that way, although metal instruments are the most widely used.

Modern woodwinds may be divided into three groups. The first has a single reed—a thin strip of cane—held in place against a mouthpiece. When the player blows against the thin gap between the reed and the mouthpiece, the air within the instrument is set into vibration and sound is produced. The acoustic length of the instrument (and therefore its pitch) is altered by opening and closing holes along the side of the tube by the fingers or by various levered mechanisms controlling pads which cover the holes. The important single reed instruments are the clarinets and saxophones.

The second group of woodwinds are the double-reeds, including the oboes, the English horn, the bassoon, and the contrabassoon. These instruments have two pieces of cane juxtaposed at one end; these are thinner and smaller than clarinet reeds in every way and produce a more nasal, biting sound.

A third type of woodwind, in which air is directed across an open hole, is the oldest of the three groups. The modern flute and piccolo are descendants of the ancient pan pipes and flutes and vary little from them in principle. The player blows against the edge of a hole in such a way that he causes the air stream to split and to vibrate within the body of the instrument. The piccolo, smaller than the flute, produces tones which are higher and more shrill. The family also includes alto and bass flutes.

The most significant ancestor of the modern flute is the recorder, undergoing a revival because of the broadening of the performing and listening repertoire. The recorder is held at an angle down from the mouth, in contrast to the flute, which is held at right angles to the mouth. Holding the recorder in this vertical position, the player directs his breath past a fipple, or wooden block, against a sharp edge, where it is split and directed down the length of the tube.

The recorder is built in various sizes and is essentially unkeyed, the holes on most models being covered directly by the fingers of the player.

*Hans Burgkmair (1473–1531).*
Emperor Maximilian Listening to a Concert. *Singers and a recorder player are at upper left; on the table at right are a viol, a spinett (a type of harpsichord), flutes, recorders, and with its characteristic curve, a crumhorn (a type of oboe). Atop drums in right foreground (and to the right of a harpist) are a trombone, lute, and a triangular, three-stringed monochord. In the left foreground is an organ. One man operates the bellows, another the keyboard.* (The Bettmann Archive)

It is less piercing and less dynamic in sound than the flute, and seems more appropriate for chamber music than for larger groups. As with the viols, recorders were parts of consorts during their heyday in the Middle Ages, the Renaissance, and much of the Baroque era.

Flutes, recorders, clarinets, saxophones, oboes, and bassoons exist in more than one size, all but the last including full choirs.

**Brass instruments**    Although the sound of the brass instrument is created by the same principle as the woodwind—by setting into motion a column of air within a tube of some sort—there are two distinctions to be made. First, brass players blow into a cupped mouthpiece rather than across a hole or against a reed. The player's lips vibrate, not a part of the instrument. Second, the brass player deals much more extensively with the overtones that result from the fundamental pitch of this instrument and he alters the fundamental by using different lengths of tubing and by dividing the column of air in the instrument through manipulation of air pressure and tension of the lip. Valves on most brass instruments are used to change the length of the instrument instantly by adding additional tubing so that a new fundamental is produced. A moveable slide, a U-shaped piece of tubing, fulfills the same function on the trombone. With the new fundamental, of course, a different set of pitches becomes available as overtones. This feature enables the modern brass player to play any pitch within the range of his instrument. The first overtone above the fundamental results from the division of the air column into halves and is the same note name as the fundamental but a higher pitch level (see *octave*, in the *Glossary*); the next overtone is five notes higher, the third is four notes higher and so on, with the higher overtones occurring very close together.

Prior to the development of valves early in the nineteenth century, players were restricted to the overtones resulting from a single fundamental and could not play others without changing instruments or inserting various lengths of tubing. Composers had to allow for this by giving brass players periods of silence within a composition before requiring them to play in a different key. Horn players of the Classical period overcame this limitation somewhat by inserting the hand in the bell of the horn, thus lowering or raising the fundamental by a half step. In the Baroque period, trumpet players used instruments designed so that they could play easily on the higher, closer overtones, thus making more notes available. The slide of the trombone has enabled the player to alter the fundamental pitch of the instrument ever since its origin (ca. 1400). The trombone is therefore the earliest of the modern brass instruments that could truly be described as flexible insofar as it can be used with ease in more than one key.

The four basic brass instruments employed consistently today are the trumpet, the French horn, the trombone, and the tuba. The trumpet is the brilliant soprano voice of the group; the trombone, the tenor, is the most powerful. The French horn is by far the most versatile, since its wide range and varieties of tone color allow it to blend well with many combinations of instruments and to meet many expressive demands, and one often finds it as part of the woodwind ensemble in chamber music. The tuba is the bass voice of the brass family, and, because of its bulk and awkward shape, is unsuited to a marching band. Its equivalent in that group is the sousaphone, a tuba reshaped into coils that rest on the shoulder of the player, thus facilitating carrying and playing when marching.

Other instruments in the brass family include the cornet (the mellow twin of the trumpet), alto horn, and the baritone horn; the names of the second two instruments indicate their roles in the brass choir. The Wagner tuba is a hybrid instrument having the flexibility of the cornet and the richness of the French horn. It is found in several sizes, and ranges from high tenor to low bass.

## Percussion instruments

The fact that many percussion instruments are nonmelodic should not lead the reader to consider them less important than those discussed above. Rhythm is the moving force in music, and most percussion instruments are basically rhythmic in character. Furthermore, the role of tone color is so vital to the way music is heard that the very variety of sounds derived from percussive effects makes this section of an orchestra fascinating and valuable. So many percussion instruments are used in the production of this variety that there is little point in attempting to list all that are used today.

There are many types of drums. Snare drums and bass drums are exclusively rhythmic and coloristic, and are especially prominent in much band music. Timpani, which are tunable and, therefore, melodic, are usually found in pairs or groups of three or four, and serve not only rhythmically and coloristically, but also harmonically, since they can reinforce bass notes with great strength or incisiveness. Tom-toms and tambourines are other rhythmic drums which serve to intensify sound by providing strongly individualistic colors.

The xylophone, vibraphone, marimba, orchestra bells (*Glockenspiel*),

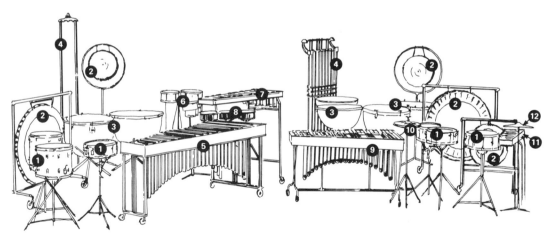

The Manhattan Percussion Ensemble, Paul Price, conductor. Note the variety of sticks and beaters used in performance (opposite page). Instruments are diagrammed and may be identified with this key:

| | | | |
|---|---|---|---|
| 1 | Snare drums | 7 | Xylophone |
| 2 | Tam-tams | 8 | Small drums |
| 3 | Timpani | 9 | Vibraphone |
| 4 | Chimes | 10 | "Sock" cymbals |
| 5 | Marimba | 11 | Orchestra bells |
| 6 | Bongo drums | 12 | Suspended cymbal |

| | |
|---|---|
| 13 | Tunable tom-toms |
| 14 | Brake drums |
| 15 | Tam-tam beater |
| 16 | Bass drum |
| 17 | Lg. suspended cymbal |
| 18 | Tom-tom |

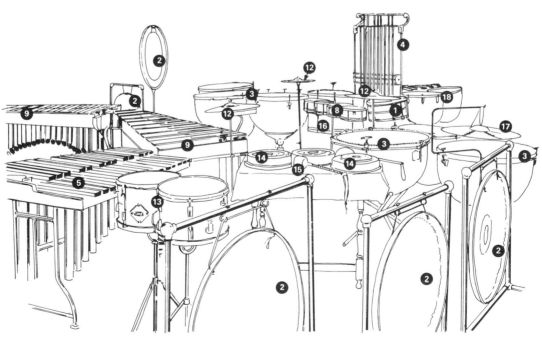

and chimes comprise a second group of percussion instruments in which the vibrating elements are arranged in a manner similar to the keys of the piano. The chimes are suspended metal pipes, open at the lower end; the others are sets of tuned blocks arranged on table-like frames. The xylophone uses wooden blocks struck with hard mallets of varying materials; the marimba, a lower pitched instrument, is played with soft mallets; the vibraphone has metal bars and an electric mechanism that gives an optional vibratory effect, while the orchestra bells are made of metal bars and are struck with brass, plastic, or rubber mallets. When the bells are used in a marching band, the bars are fixed in a lyre-shaped frame for ease in carrying; in this shape, the bells are known as the *bell-lyra*.

Except for the vibraphone, which produces a rather sweet, quiet sound, the tones of these instruments have a very distinctive quality that carries well over the rest of the orchestra. The xylophone has a clicking quality, the bells ring brightly, and the chimes ring with a deep sonority.

A host of miscellaneous instruments are found in the so-called "battery" of the percussion family. These include such metallic ones as the triangle, the cymbals, and the sleighbells; wooden ones such as castanets, woodblock, slapstick, and claves; and other exotic devices such as guiros (scraped jaw-bones), maracas (gourds filled with seeds or pebbles), and the Chinese gong (also called *tam-tam*).

**Electronic instruments**    The totally new medium of electronic music is fast gaining in importance and popularity. Of the several sound-generating devices available for electronic composition, the synthesizer is the most often used. Unlike earlier electronic media, which required the composer to record and re-record sounds in his studio in order to produce a finished composition that was played on a tape recorder in the concert hall, the synthesizer combines generators and modifiers into one unit in such a way that it may actually be "played," just as one plays a piano. Because it may be used in live performances, it extends the possibilities of electronic music from the studio to the concert stage, where it may serve as a solo instrument or be mixed with other instruments.

The synthesizer deals essentially with two types of sound, *sine tones* and *white noise*. Remembering that the timbre of any sound is caused by the presence and relative strengths of various overtones, the listener will be able to distinguish these two types, for a sine tone is a pitch with no overtones present at all, while white noise uses all possible overtones simultaneously with a resultant rushing windlike sound.

*A large electronic synthesizer. To the left are two tape decks and various generating units; in the center and also at extreme right are two speakers; a double keyboard identifies the main console, below which is the master mixer panel, through which various sounds, generating units, and so on, may be combined or isolated. (Photo by Laura Beauchamp, courtesy of Robert Moog, Inc.)*

ELECTRONIC WAVE PATTERNS

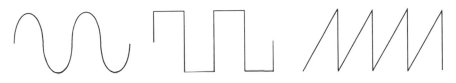

Sine          Square          Sawtooth

Many modifications of sine and white sounds may be made. Overtones may be added to sine tones or filtered out of white sounds, thus making great varieties of timbre possible. The two most common results of such modification are the somewhat bright *square wave* (fundamental plus odd-numbered overtones) and the more nasal *sawtooth wave* (fundamental plus all its overtones), so called because they show up on an oscilloscope in these patterns. All such sounds are available through the entire sound spectrum (20–20,000 cycles).

Electronic sounds may be changed and varied by other means. Two sounds may be fed simultaneously into an electronic switch that will cause them to alternate in predetermined time intervals. A "ring modulator" will multiply and divide two sounds, causing them and their multiples and divisions to be sounded simultaneously. A "reverberation unit" causes echo-like effects and may capitalize on the tendency of some sounds to decay, or fall off, after being created. There is, too, an infinity of dynamic variety possible, plus options for speeding up or slowing down the rate of musical motion.

Although the synthesizer is by far the most significant electronic instrument now in use, one might also cite as examples of electronic devices such instruments as the theremin, which uses an electronic force field interrupted by hand movements, and computers of various types, which can produce musical events when melodic, harmonic, and structural patterns are fed into their memory banks.

**Instrumental groups**    Instrumentalists may perform alone or in groups of various sizes. The orchestra is a large gathering of instrumentalists, with string players as its nucleus. The band is similar in size, but has few or no strings, its instrumentation being primarily winds and percussion. Those instrumental combinations not large enough to be considered bands or orchestras are categorized as chamber groups.

The orchestra is identified by a variety of names, including *symphony orchestra, philharmonic orchestra,* or *philharmonic-symphony orchestra*; all are synonymous.

Professional orchestras usually have enough players and a wide enough variety of instruments to perform the works of most composers of the Romantic period, whose works generally call for a string choir, woodwinds in threes, two or three trumpets, four horns, three trombones, and a percussion section of at least timpani, bass drum, snare drum, and cymbals. Such orchestras have about seventy-five members as a rule. More affluent orchestras in larger cities may have over a hundred members, but not all are required to play in every composition. Works of composers who lived earlier than the Romantic period generally call for smaller instrumentations and the size of an orchestra will be suitably reduced when such works are being performed. Orchestras may also be enlarged as necessary for works that call for unusually large instrumentations.

The major difference between a band and an orchestra is that the former is usually devoid of strings. The word "usually" is used, because, in concert, double basses are often a part of the band's bass voice for purposes of tonal richness.

Two schools of thought about the size of the concert-giving band currently exist. One school prefers a larger group, perhaps numbering between seventy-five and ninety players, in which emphasis is on richness and depth of sound. The other school suggests that a smaller group of about forty-five players is better, and that depth of sound should be sacrificed for the sake of versatility and clarity. The larger band bears the title of *symphonic, or concert band,* while the smaller one is referred to as a *chamber band* or *wind ensemble.*

The band in America is most prominent in colleges and universities; there are no full-time "city" bands of a caliber and stature equal to major professional orchestras. Its literature is largely contemporary, and today it is primarily an American institution, although some of the military-professional bands of Europe, England, and Canada are of exceptional quality. Many composers have been attracted by the band's brilliance and capacity for clear articulation of melody; hence, there are compositions exploiting its percussive sounds and clear instrumental colors.

Chamber music combinations number from two to sixteen players, each with a separate part to play (as opposed to a violin section in an orchestra, for instance, in which several players will be performing the same part). The combinations of instruments in chamber groups are almost limitless; some of the more popular ensembles are the *string quartet* (two violins, viola, cello), the *woodwind quintet* (flute, oboe, clarinet, bassoon, French horn), and the *brass quintet* (two trumpets, French horn, trombone, tuba). Piano trios (piano, violin, cello) and accompanied sonatas (piano and violin, piano and cello, and many other pairs) are also important.

PROMINENT PASSAGES FOR VARIOUS PERFORMING MEDIA
Works marked with an asterisk are found in whole or in part on the recordings accompanying this book. The instruments used in the recorded excerpts

from Ravel's *Bolero* are heard playing the melody in this order: sopranino clarinet, oboe d'amore, flute and muted trumpet, tenor saxophone, soprano saxophone. The final playing of the melody is a unison passage for flute, piccolo, French horn, and celesta.

*Choirs*

| | |
|---|---|
| Strings | Schoenberg: *Verklärte Nacht*; Schubert: Quintet in A (*Trout*);* Berg: *Lyric Suite** |
| Viols | Gibbons: *In nomine*; Byrd: various fantasies for strings |
| Woodwinds | Milhaud: *Le chemineé du Roi René* (woodwind quintet) |
| Recorders | Telemann: duo sonatas for recorders |
| Brasses | G. Gabrieli: *Canzona septimi toni* |
| Percussion | Varèse: *Ionisation* |
| Women's voices | Britten: *A Ceremony of Carols* |
| Men's voices | Schubert: *Gesang der Geister über den Wassern;* Brahms: *Alto Rhapsody* |

*Fully complemented groups*

| | |
|---|---|
| Band | Holst: Suites Nos. 1 and 2 for Military Band; many marches by Sousa |
| Baroque orchestra | Bach: *Brandenburg concertos* (there is no "standard" Baroque orchestra) |
| Classical orchestra | Haydn: Symphony No. 94 (*Surprise*) (without clarinets); Mozart: Symphony No. 39 (with clarinets; without oboes); Beethoven: Symphony No. 2 (full woodwind section) |
| Romantic orchestra | Wagner: Prelude to *Tristan and Isolde*; Tchaikovsky: Symphony No. 5 |
| Contemporary orchestra | There is no standard orchestration; compare Bartók's *Concerto for Orchestra*, Luening's *Concerted Piece for Electronic Sounds and Orchestra*, and Webern's *Symphony for Small Orchestra*, Op. 21. |
| Mixed voices | Mendelssohn: *Elijah* |
| Antiphonal voices | Verdi: *Sanctus* from "Manzoni" *Requiem* |

*Individual voices*

| | |
|---|---|
| Lyric soprano | Menotti: *The Telephone* (role of Lucy) |
| Dramatic soprano | R. Strauss: *Salome* (role of Salome) |
| Coloratura soprano | Handel: *Alcina* (role of Alcina); Donizetti: *Lucia di Lammermoor* (role of Lucia) |

| | |
|---|---|
| Mezzo-soprano | Bizet: *Carmen* (role of Carmen as performed on most discs); Verdi: *Il Trovatore* (role of Azucena) |
| Contralto | Verdi: *Un Ballo in Maschera* (role of Ulrica); Brahms: *Alto Rhapsody* (often recorded by mezzo-sopranos) |
| Lyric tenor | Mozart: *Don Giovanni* (role of Don Ottavio) |
| Dramatic tenor | Verdi: *Aïda* (role of Radames) |
| Heldentenor | Wagner: *Siegfried* (role of Siegfried) |
| Baritone | Menotti: *The Telephone* (role of Ben); Verdi: *Rigoletto* (role of Rigoletto) |
| Basso cantante | Mozart: *Don Giovanni* (role of Don Giovanni) |
| Basso profondo | Mozart: *Die Zauberflöte* (role of Sarastro) |
| Basso buffo | Rossini: *Il Barbiere di Siviglia* (roles of Bartolo and Basilio) |

### Individual instruments

| | |
|---|---|
| Violin | Many concertos (especially those by Brahms, Tchaikovsky, Mendelssohn) |
| Viola | Berlioz: *Harold in Italy*, second movement; Piston: *Concerto for Viola* |
| Violin and viola | Mozart: *Sinfonia concertante in E-flat*, K. 364 |
| Cello | Bruch: *Kol Nidre*; concertos by Dvořák, R. Schumann, Elgar |
| Double bass | Saint-Saëns: *Elephants*, from *Carnival of the Animals* |
| Harp | Donizetti: *Lucia di Lammermoor*, Prelude to Act I, scene 2; Tchaikovsky: *Waltz of the Flowers*, from *The Nutcracker* |
| Piccolo | Tchaikovsky: *Chinese Dance*, from *The Nutcracker*; Ravel: *Bolero** |
| Flute | J. S. Bach: Suite No. 2, for flute and strings |
| Recorder | Vivaldi: *Concerto for Sopranino Recorder and Strings* |
| Oboe | Berlioz: *Fantastic Symphony*, third movement (with English horn) |
| Oboe d'amore | Ravel: *Bolero** |
| English horn | Berlioz: *Fantastic Symphony*, third movement (with oboe) |
| Sopranino clarinet | Ravel: *Bolero** |
| Clarinet | Weber: Overture to *Oberon* (second theme) |
| Bass clarinet | W. Schuman: Symphony No. 3, fourth movement (*Toccata*) |
| Bassoon | Mozart: *Concerto for Bassoon*; Dukas: *The Sorcerer's Apprentice* |

| | |
|---|---|
| Contrabassoon | Ravel: *Conversations of Beauty and the Beast*, from *Ma Mère l'Oye* |
| Saxophone | Ibert: *Concertino da Camera*, for alto saxophone; Ravel: *Bolero**  |
| French horn | Mozart: *Concerto in E-flat for Horn*, K. 447 |
| Trumpet | Verdi: *Grand March*, from *Aïda*, Act II, scene 2; Ravel: *Bolero**  |
| Clarin trumpet | J. S. Bach: *Brandenburg Concerto No. 2* |
| Trombone | Wagner: *Lohengrin*, Prelude to Act III; Mozart: *Tuba mirum*, from *Requiem* |
| Bass trombone | Beethoven: Symphony No. 9, fourth movement (at "Seid umschlungen, Millionen") |
| Tuba | Mussorgsky-Ravel: *Bydlo*, from *Pictures at an Exhibition* |
| Timpani | Beethoven: Symphony No. 9, second movement; Shostakovitch: Symphony No. 5, last measures of *Finale* |
| Snare drum | Bartók: *Concerto for Orchestra*, beginning of second movement (without snares); Rossini: *La Gazza Ladra*, overture (with snares) |
| Bass drum | Berlioz: *Fantastic Symphony*, fifth movement |
| Chimes | Berlioz: *Fantastic Symphony*, fifth movement |
| Orchestra bells | Mozart: "Das klinget so herrlich" from *Die Zauberflöte*, Act I |
| Cymbals | Wagner: *Lohengrin*, Prelude to Act I (at climax, near middle) |
| Gong (tam-tam) | Mussorgsky-Ravel: *The Great Gate of Kiev*, from *Pictures at an Exhibition* |
| Castanets | Bizet: *Carmen* (Carmen's dance in Act II) |
| Celesta | Tchaikovsky: *Dance of the Sugar Plum Fairy*, from *The Nutcracker* |
| Wind machine | R. Strauss: *Don Quixote* |
| Piano | Concertos and sonatas |
| Harpsichord | J. S. Bach: preludes and fugues from *The Well-Tempered Clavier* |
| Baroque organ | Many preludes, toccatas, and the like by J. S. Bach; concertos by Handel |
| Romantic organ | Franck: *Grand Pièce Symphonique*, Op. 17 |

# 5 : TOOLS OF COMPOSITION

ALTHOUGH it is necessary to discuss melody, rhythm, harmony, timbre, and other musical factors as separate functions, music is a result of the interaction of all of them, and none can exist without being shaped by each of the others.

*Pitch* and *duration* are, perhaps, the two most vital of the materials with which a composer deals, for they combine to form the two basic elements of a musical composition, *rhythm* and *melody*. *Pitch* is the high or low quality of a sound, determined by the number of vibrations per second, or frequency, of air waves. The higher the frequency, the higher the pitch. *Duration* refers to the length of time that a pitch lasts, especially as it relates to the duration of other pitches.

Pitch and duration are indicated by notational symbols. Pitch is indicated by the placement of the note on the staff, and duration by mathematically related symbols. These symbols are whole notes ( 𝅝 ), half notes ( 𝅗𝅥 ), quarter notes ( 𝅘𝅥 ), eighth notes ( 𝅘𝅥𝅮 ), sixteenth notes ( 𝅘𝅥𝅯 ), and so on, each with an obvious *relative* time value. In electronic music, durations are thought of in terms of seconds and microseconds, and some composers have devised a different set of symbols to indicate time values.

### The interaction of melody and rhythm

A pattern of consecutive pitches recognizable as a logical or musically meaningful entity is called a *melody; rhythm* may be defined simply as patterns of long and short durations of sounds. Rhythm, whether it consists of repeated patterns or of irregular patterns, is as significant in establishing a recognizable melodic profile as is the sequence of pitches. There are two basic aspects to rhythm, *meter* and *tempo*.

### Aspects of rhythm

**Meter**    *Meter* refers to the organization of accent or beat in music. These accents are perceivable in duple (*binary*) or triple (*ternary*) patterns. In most music, the meter is regular; there is a feeling of groups of notes, the first note of each group being strongly accented. Other notes of each group are weaker in accent, although some of these weaker accents may be more stressed than others. Moreover, this strongly accented beat returns at equal intervals of time, unless the composer or performer gives specific directions to alter it. In *Greensleeves*, there are strong pulsations occurring predictably from the beginning of the song until the end of it. In the example below, the notes marked with *x* identify the places where the accents occur within each *measure* or *bar* (the groups of notes within the vertical lines).

**EX. 5.1**
*Greensleeves*, bars 1–4

Not all music is meant to be performed metrically. The flowing quality of the chant *Requiem aeternam* is an example of unmetrical rhythm. The rhythmic flow is established over a basic (but unaccented) beat represented in modern notation by the eighth note; the longer durations, represented by the quarter note, are not always double values of the basic beat. Often they are but slight prolongations, the extent of which is determined by various principles that take into account the endings of phrases, the rise and fall of pitch, word accents, groups of several notes per syllable of text, and the relationship of a single pitch to notes before it and/or after it.[1]

---

[1]The details of chant rhythm and expression have been carefully and clearly explained in publications by the Benedictines of Solesmes, a group of monks who have researched the performance practice of medieval chant. The reader is referred to Dom Joseph Gajard, *The Solesmes Method: Its Fundamental Principles and Practical Rules of Interpretation*, trans. R. Cecile Gabain (Collegeville, Minn.: The Liturgical Press, 1960) and *Chants of the Church*, edited and compiled by the monks of Solesmes (Toledo, Ohio: Gregorian Institute of America, 1953).

The rhythm of the first part (all before the first double bar) of this piece of Gregorian chant is made up of the free commingling of *ternary* and *binary* groups. The first syllables of *aeternam* and *dona* have ternary groups, in which the three eighth notes are joined by a common horizontal flag: ♪♪♪ . The binary groups (see *et*, [per] *petu* [a], *lu* [ceat]) are printed the same way: ♪♪ . Also contributing to the sense of pattern in this first part is the use of the same music for [do] *na eis Domine* and *luceat eis*, a repetition which provides a strong sense of melodic unity as well.

**EX. 5.2**
*Requiem aeternam, Mode VI, modern notation*

The term *Introit* identifies this selection as the introductory chant of a *Mass Proper* (see Chapter 9); *Mode VI* indicates which scale it is based on (*Hypolydian*) and which notes are the tonic and dominant (see discussion, p. 77). ⌐ is a clef identifying the note C; ♩ indicates the note to be encountered first on the next staff; vertical lines indicate phrases or pauses; double lines indicate the end of major sections, the end of a total composition, or a place at which a soloist or choir is to take over the melody. Graphs such as ◣ or ♩•• indicate two or more notes and are called *neumes*; the shape of individual notes is not necessarily an indication of duration.

The second part (and middle, since the first part is repeated after the psalm section of the chant) of the last example is essentially syllabic; that is, there is basically only one note per syllable of text.[2] The result is a simpler, faster, more regular rhythm that permits psalm recitation by larger, less cohesive groups (such as a congregation).

The unmetrical rhythm of Gregorian chant gives to it a flexibility that is matched by no other style, and creates a framework for the closest relationship of text and music in all Western culture.

**EX. 5.2(a)** *Ibid.* Gregorian notation

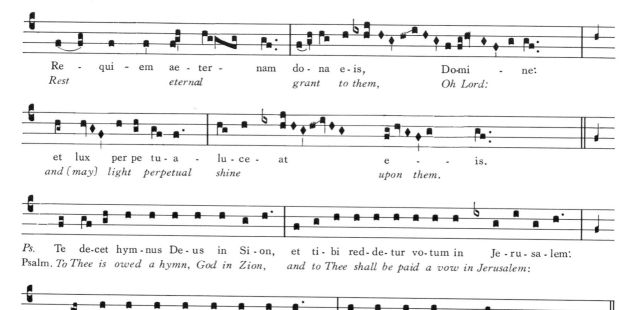

Re - qui - em ae - ter - nam do - na e - is, Do-mi - ne:
*Rest eternal grant to them, Oh Lord:*

et lux per pe tu - a - lu - ce - at e - is.
*and [may] light perpetual shine upon them.*

*Ps.* Te de-cet hym - nus De - us in Si - on, et ti - bi red-de-tur vo-tum in Je - ru - sa - lem:
*Psalm. To Thee is owed a hymn, God in Zion, and to Thee shall be paid a vow in Jerusalem:*

ex - au - di o - ra - ti - o - nem me - am, ad te om - nis ca - ro ve - ni - et.
*hear my prayer, to Thee [may] all flesh come.*

[Repeat *Requiem* as far as Psalm]

The *Agnus Dei* of Palestrina's *Missa Brevis* provides another example of unmetrical rhythm, for it gains its rhythmic stresses from the natural accents of the words, rather than from consistent, preordained patterns of stressed and weak beats. Palestrina's music was unbarred; when modern editions insert bar lines, a kind of metric accent is implied which completely destroys the natural flow of text and music. Note in the first example (5.3) that the *x*'s mark the natural accents of the text. In the

---

[2]When chants use two or three notes per syllable (e.g., *ae* [ter] *nam, et, lux*), the style is called *neumatic*; more florid settings (*eis,* [luce] *at*) are melismatic.

printing of the same notes with bar-lines, the *x*'s are placed where a metric scheme would have them, with a resultant distortion of the text:

**EX. 5.3 PALESTRINA**
*Agnus Dei*, from *Missa Brevis*, unmetrical version

The metric example is taken from an actual publication. The metric version would be better if the bar line were moved to the left by two beats, but would still result in some problems of prosody, especially on the word *mundi* and the final syllable of *peccata*, which would tend to get a secondary accent in a four-beat measure.

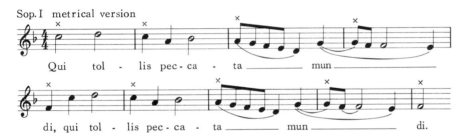

**EX. 5.3(a)** *Ibid.* metrical version

**Syncopation**

A more purposeful rhythmic alteration is *syncopation*. It, too, concerns misplaced accents, but syncopation results in rhythmic excitement and tension. Normally, meter provides regular groups of two or three beats. Because the first beat of each group is more strongly accented than the others, any occurrence of a strong accent on a beat other than the first will be felt as a contradiction of the meter. This unexpected upsetting of the "rhythmic applecart" may result from having a silence on the normally accented beat, as is shown in a passage taken from the piano part at the beginning of the third verse of Schubert's *Im Frühling*. In the example, *s* identifies the place where the accents are *expected* to be heard.

**EX. 5.4 SCHUBERT**
*Im Frühling*, bars 33–35

There is a similar effect when there is placed on the strong beat of a measure a note which has a value shorter than the type of note which normally gets the beat. If this shorter note is then followed by a longer one, a syncopation results. In the quartet from Verdi's *Rigoletto*, the quarter note gets the beat, but in the last measure of the example an eighth note comes on the first beat, thus shoving the quarter note into a syncopated pattern.

**EX. 5.5 VERDI**
Quartet, "Bella figlia dell' amore," from *Rigoletto*, bars 22–25

Syncopation occurs also when a note on a strong beat is tied to a previous note of the same pitch; its individual stress is negated because it is not sounded separately but rather is heard as an extension of the duration of the pitch to which it is tied. This may be heard often in the second movement of Brahms's horn trio. Its first appearance is at bar 41, in the violin and horn parts. The syncopation follows immediately in the piano part as well.

**EX. 5.6 BRAHMS**
Trio in E-flat, Op. 40, 2nd mvt., bars 41–46

Another technique used to achieve syncopation is simply to ask the performer to stress the weak beats over the strong ones. In the fragment from the opening theme of Berlioz' *Fantastic Symphony*, one will note the crescendo markings ( ‹ ) in bars 73 and 81. It is clear from the composer's directions that the second and fourth notes in these bars

**EX. 5.7 BERLIOZ**
*Fantastic Symphony*, 1st mvt., bars 72–86

are to be louder than the first and third, yet it is the latter two that ordinarily receive stress. The crescendo in bar 75 illustrates a combina-

tion of this syncopative device with the device of tying across the bar line
—one looks and listens in vain for a strong pulse in this bar, especially
because there is an increase in volume toward it, but the tying of the
first note of this measure to the last note of the previous one pulls the
rug from under it.

The rhythmic excitement of syncopation is a particularly vital element
in jazz, although all musical styles have made consistent use of it, especially in the twentieth century.

Two other types of rhythmic displacement are frequently encountered
and both may be heard in Brahms's horn trio. The first of these is the
sudden switch from a series of pulses in groups of three to pulses in groups
of two. The *scherzo* is in triple time, and one hears at the outset of the
movement the driving motion of the piano, whose 3 beats to the bar are
unmistakable.

**Rhythmic change
within a meter**

**EX. 5.8 BRAHMS**
Trio in E-flat, Op. 40,
2nd mvt., bars 1–4

In bar 14, however, this dynamic pulse suddenly changes into *duplets*, a
change made especially potent by the first appearance in the movement
of the horn and violin.

**EX. 5.9** *Ibid.*
bars 11–16

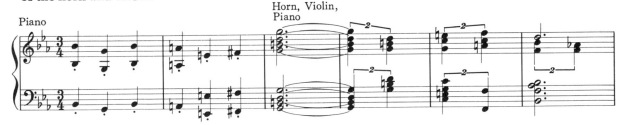

The second type of displacement, *hemiola*, may be defined in two ways:
(1) a broadening of the rhythm so that the pulse seems to extend over
several measures; (2) the playing of a duplet rhythm at the same time
that one hears a triplet rhythm. In the next example, the reader will note
in the horn and violin part that the tie ( ⌢ ) across the measure line
between bars 47 and 48 causes two notes to sound as but one; the first
note of bar 47, a half note, receives two beats, the tied notes receive two

*Aspects of rhythm*   **63**

beats, and the last note of bar 48 also receives two beats, with this rhythm as a result: . In bar 50, there is the other type of hemiola, the horn and violin pulsing in groups of two, while the piano maintains the triplets from bar 46 on.

**EX. 5.10** *Ibid.*
bars 42–51

**Tempo**

*Tempo* refers to the speed at which a composition is performed, and is usually measured in terms of beats-per-minute as indicated by a metronome marking found at the beginning of a composition or a section of it.

♩ = MM 80 means that the quarter note is the beat note and that there should be eighty of them per minute as measured on the Maelzel Metronome.[3]

Tempo may also be indicated by such words as "fast," "slow," and many others. Tempo markings are always considered more as suggestions than outright orders, for all the factors that affect interpretation will invariably cause deviations from the composer's markings. As a result, tempo becomes a highly important aspect of interpretation and is subject to criticism and disagreement among composers, performers, and listeners. Although many such arguments end up as tempests in teapots, there may be some validity to them, for a change in tempo causes a composition to become a different piece of music. When played at the proper tempo, the

[3]The Maelzel Metronome is a mechanical device which may be adjusted to sound specified numbers of beats per minute either as ticks or single bell strokes. Maelzel, although not the inventor of the device, popularized the metronome and it was thus named after him.

familiar march *Stars and Stripes Forever* is lively and exciting; a performance at a slow and languorous pace would give it a deadened or morbid character.

## Aspects of melody

Melody is a result of many factors. Since its character varies with treatment and purpose, there is a certain vocabulary necessary to its understanding.

**Motive, theme, and subject**

A *motive* is the shortest musical fragment perceivable as a unit. Many melodies utilized for the purposes of symphonic development may be fragmented into significant motives. Here are some of the motives derived from symphonic melodies recorded on the records accompanying this text; in the examples, the main motives are bracketed.

**EX. 5.11(a) MOZART**
Symphony No. 40 in G minor, 1st mvt.

**EX. 5.11(b) BEETHOVEN**
Symphony No. 5 in C minor, 3rd mvt.

**EX. 5.11(c) BARTÓK**
Piano Concerto No. 3, 1st mvt.

Motives need not be part of a larger melody; they may also be highly concise musical ideas free of any larger context. This is true of the various motives devised by Wagner for his opera *Die Walküre*, a detailed discussion of which may be found in Chapter 8. Wagner's motives serve a dual function: their constant repetition and variation provide a basic source of musical unity over long periods of constantly unfolding music, and they clarify the action and dialogue by being associated with characters, events, objects, and concepts. Although the term *Leitmotiv* (German, "leading motive") is most often applied to this use of motives in Wagner's music, it is appropriate also to any composition in which short musical ideas serve this two-fold function.

**EX. 5.12 WAGNER**
Some motives from
*Die Walküre*

A melody used as a source of development or variation in an instrumental work is known as a *theme* or *subject*. It would be convenient if there were a clear distinction between the two terms, but composers, historians, and theoreticians alike have used them sometimes as synonyms, sometimes as contrasting concepts. The main melody of a fugue is always called its *subject*, never a *theme*. The main melody of a set of variations is always called a *theme*, never a *subject*. The main melody or melodies of first movements of symphonies or concertos may be referred to by either term.

Such words as *tune, air, lay, strain,* or *measure* are used colloquially and poetically as synonyms for *melody*, but all connote a certain lightheartedness and prettiness foreign to most examples of theme and subject. *Theme* and *subject* most often imply breadth, significance, seriousness, power, and similar portentous qualities, although the innocence of the theme from the fourth movement of Schubert's *Trout Quintet* or the

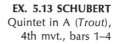

**EX. 5.13 SCHUBERT**
Quintet in A (*Trout*),
4th mvt., bars 1–4

sprightliness of the subject of the second fugue from Bach's *The Well-Tempered Clavier*, Book 1, are well-known examples of the many exceptions to be found.

**EX. 5.14 BACH**
*The Well-Tempered Clavier,*
Book 1, bars 1–2

**Harmony**  Melody is often defined as the "horizontal" element of music, since its notes are placed side by side on a page, and are sounded one after the other. *Harmony* is defined as the "vertical" element, since its basic component, the *chord*, consists of several pitches that are sounded simultaneously, and are written one above the other:  . In a larger sense, harmony also refers to that relationship of chords within a musical structure that helps to determine the feeling of tonality and movement toward a tonic note or a moment of pause. Harmony can enrich a melody, give it direction, and can lend it a strong sense of finality by the use of chains of related chords called *cadences*.

It is quite possible for a melody to suggest a harmonic feeling or direction without its being accompanied by chords. The first four notes of the familiar *A Bicycle Built for Two* outline a G major chord (G B D), for example.

**EX. 5.15**
*A Bicycle Built for Two,*
bars 1–4

The first five pitches of the principal theme from the first movement of Berlioz' *Fantastic Symphony* give the profile of a C major chord (C E G).

**EX. 5.16 BERLIOZ**
*Fantastic Symphony,* 1st mvt.,
bars 72–74

One of the most perplexing aspects of harmony is the relationship between the two concepts known as *consonance* and *dissonance*. Aesthetically, *consonance* refers to a combination of pitches that is pleasing and wholly satisfying; *dissonance* refers to a combination that produces tension, and calls for a following consonance. Historically, however, the combination identifiable as consonant has so altered over the centuries that the definition is pointless, unless one has reference to a particular historical period. In the tenth century, the middle section of *Chopsticks* would have been thought very dissonant, yet to the modern listener it seems very consonant, in fact bland.

**EX. 5.17**
*Chopsticks,* "B" section

To many modern composers, all combinations of sound are equally satisfying, hence distinctions between consonance and dissonance are irrelevant to them. Thus, it may be said simply that any combination of pitches that excites tension may be regarded as dissonant; any which provides relief from tension may be described as consonant.

Examination of a familiar melody will illustrate how it may be conditioned by various harmonic styles. In the next example, *A Bicycle Built for Two* is harmonized in simple chordal patterns in waltz style, all the chords being consonant. The melody is written in the top part of the example (to be played at the piano by the right hand); the accompanying chords, designed to support the melody without in any way detracting from its importance, are to be played by the left hand.

**EX. 5.18**
*A Bicycle Built for Two,*
with waltz accompaniment

In the next example, virtually every note is harmonized in a way that invites tension and demands forward movement until a point of rest is reached. All chords except the fifth one are dissonant. The song is no longer a simple, sociable melody; it is now packed with some kind of emotive quality that requires more serious attention from listener, player, and composer.

**EX. 5.19** *Ibid.*
with a dissonant
harmonization

In the following example, the song is harmonized in a wholly different fashion. The melody, still in the topmost voice, is accompanied by another part that not only moves in the same rhythm as the melody but remains five notes below it throughout the example. The use of the harmonic interval of a fifth gives the melody a somewhat ancient quality similar to the music of the ninth and tenth centuries.

**EX. 5.20** *Ibid.*
with harmonization in
parallel fifths

This parallel style of harmonization may be maintained, but, by changing the interval at which the voices are harmonized, the song is given a softer, more "social" character. The use of parallel sixths and thirds livens many a party song session and characterizes the middle section of *Chopsticks.*

**EX. 5.21** *Ibid.* with harmonization in parallel sixths

Still another method of altering the nature of a melody is by varying its relationship to what is being played or sung simultaneously with it. This relationship is known as *texture.*

**Texture**

The simplest sort of texture offers the listener a melody with no notes sounding other than those of the melody itself. This sort of "one-voiced" music is called *monophony* and is most easily exemplified by plainsong (*Requiem aeternam*).

If chords are added, whether broken up throughout a measure as in the first harmonization of *A Bicycle Built for Two* (Ex. 5.18) or moving in block rhythms with the melody as in the dissonant harmonization in Ex. 5.19, the texture becomes *homophonic. Homophony* is the most frequently encountered texture; music written homophonically is often called "chordal," since the listener tends to hear a progression of sounds supporting, that is, *accompanying,* one basic melody in patterns implying harmonic progressions. The pitches of chords need not be sounded simultaneously to be heard as part of a harmonic sequence. By sounding the notes of a chord in succession, one produces an *arpeggio,* so called because its sound is so characteristic of the harp.

C E G C G E C

**EX. 5.22** Arpeggio

While this may look like a melody, the repetitiousness of the pattern produces a purely background effect, although pleasant, and results in a harmonic sound rather than a melodic one. Here are some other chordal patterns often used as accompaniment figures.

UM pa  UM pa    UM pa pa pa UM pa pa pa    UM ta ta pa pa UM ta ta pa pa

If one listens to the Quartet from Verdi's *Rigoletto,* he will hear the pattern labeled *a* accompanying the tenor melody heard right at the beginning; pattern *b* is used when the tenor repeats the melody somewhat later in the ensemble.

Accompaniments may employ melodic or rhythmic patterns or figures rather than (or perhaps along with) chordal ones. In the opening measures of Schubert's *Erlkönig,* one may detect both chordal and figural patterns; the pattern labeled *a* in the example, played by the pianist's right hand, is a purely rhythmic figure; pattern *b* is a melodic figure; pattern *c* is a chordal figure, since the pitches D, B-flat, and G comprise the tones of a G minor chord.

**EX. 5.24 SCHUBERT**
*Erlkönig,* bars 1–3

Another example of a figural accompaniment is easily heard at the beginning of Bartók's Piano Concerto No. 3 where sextuplets in the violins and violas rustle quietly prior to the piano's entrance.

**EX. 5.25 BARTÓK**
Piano Concerto No. 3,
1st mvt., bars 1–2

The third kind of texture, *polyphony* ("many voiced"),[4] is the most demanding in music, for the composer is required to fit together two or more parts sounding simultaneously, each with its own feeling of melodic or rhythmic independence.

[4]*Counterpoint* and *contrapuntal* are frequently used terms which are generally synonymous with *polyphony* and *polyphonic.*

The melodic material heard at different times in the various parts may be the same (as in *Row, Row, Row Your Boat*), similar (as in Bach's complex *Little Fugue in G minor*), or entirely different. The combination of *A Bicycle Built for Two* and *Oh Dear, What Can the Matter Be?* provides an example of the last.

**EX. 5.26**
*A Bicycle Built for Two and Oh Dear, What Can the Matter Be?*

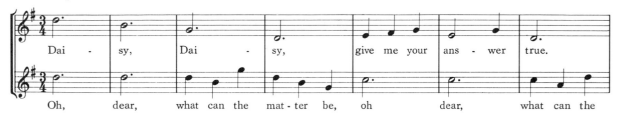

One song has become a *countermelody,* or *descant,* to the other. A more sophisticated countermelody may be heard in the "Moonlight: Nymphs' Dance" sequence from Smetana's *The Moldau* where, as the melody of the violins floats mistily over the murmuring woodwinds, a new melody in the horns announces the coming of day.

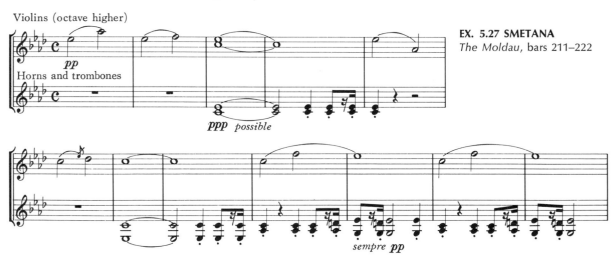

**EX. 5.27 SMETANA**
*The Moldau,* bars 211–222

Two kinds of texture can be heard in the excerpts from Handel's *Messiah.* The recitatives are homophonic. In the first recitative, "There were shepherds ..." the accompaniment is played only by instruments sustaining quiet chords while the singer declaims the text. The accompaniment for "And lo! the angel of the Lord ..." is more enriched, yet still subordinate to the music given to the soprano soloist. Here the strings play decorative figures or rhythmic patterns. Although these patterns are highly suggestive of the beating of the wings of an angel, they have no melodic importance of their own. The chorus, on the other hand, has both polyphonic and homophonic passages. The words "Glory to God in the highest and peace on earth" are sung chordally by the various voices of the choir over a decorative explosion of notes in the violins; the rest of the strings are joined by the trumpets in reinforcing the rhythmic and melodic movement of the choir.

The texture of "Good will towards men" is polyphonic, for the four voices of the choir (doubled by various instruments of the orchestra) are treated as independent parts.

**Tonality**     The tendency of a piece of music to center around, and conclude on, a particular pitch is called *tonality*. The note on which the composition tends to end is called the *tonic*. When a composition is tonal, its harmonies, whether sounded or implied, are most often arranged in such a way that they guide the listener toward the tonic note and toward the chord based on it. Cadences play an important role in this procedure and are essential building blocks for much of the music based on the tonal system, although many contemporary works establish their tonality by virtue of reiteration of a note or chord, or by highlighting it in some sort of climactic fashion.

Cadences, often easily recognized as formulas by the untrained listener, are used characteristically to punctuate phrases, a quality readily perceivable in the two phrases of the familiar *Row, Row, Row Your Boat*. The first of these, ending "... gently down the stream," has a quality of momentary pause which, because of the "cliff-hanging" nature of its harmonic/melodic cadence, demands the resolution provided by the final phrase, "merrily, merrily, merrily, merrily, life is but a dream."

Not all music is tonal. In fact, much of the attention of present-day composers has been directed toward music that is *atonal* and almost completely free of any sort of cadence structure or melodic pattern designed to guide the listener to a predetermined final pitch. The first major achievements in the field of wholly atonal music were the compositions of Schoenberg, a composer who developed the technique of *serial* composition and urged that all pitches and combinations be regarded as equal in importance, beauty, and usefulness.

Before actually composing a work, a serial composer will arrange some or all[5] of the twelve semitones within the octave in an order (or *series*)

[5]Music in which all twelve tones are serialized is sometimes referred to as *dodecaphonic* music.

that will usually avoid the repetition of any single pitch before the others are sounded. A basic *set*, or *row*, might read F, E, C, A, G, D, A-flat, D-flat, E-flat, G-flat, B-flat, B. Such a tone row—the one that was actually used by Berg for the first movement of his *Lyric Suite*—becomes the basis of the composition, in which it appears in various forms. It can be used backwards (*retrograde* motion: B, B-flat, G-flat, A-flat, and so forth), upside down (*inversion*, or changing the successive intervals to move in the exact opposite direction: F, G-flat, B-flat, D-flat, and so forth), or upside down and backwards (*retrograde inversion*). Each row may be transposed to start on any pitch. Any of the rows, their variants, or any fragments of them can be made into melodies by the application of rhythmic patterns, and harmonies can occur when several pitches in a row occur simultaneously.[6]

As Boulez has demonstrated in his second piano sonata, it is possible to serialize not only melodic intervals, but also sequences of dynamic changes, note durations, methods of playing, and timbres, the result being *total serialization*.

Schoenberg's system of twelve-tone serialism is not the only one that arrives at atonality. Other composers, such as Berg in his opera *Wozzeck*, have also created atonal music by simply avoiding traditional melodic, harmonic, and cadential sounds.

Atonal music, represented on the recordings accompanying this book by the first movement of Berg's *Lyric Suite*, knows no consonance or dissonance in the traditional or tonal sense, nor is there any principle of cadencing that draws the melody to points of rest or phrase. Listening to it requires that the music be approached on its own terms, an appreciative principle applicable to the music of every era.

The uses of tone-row composition are intricate and varied, and not all the devices of serial technique are easily heard. Successful listening is based on an acceptance of a type of composition that is melodic in inspiration, rather than harmonic. When atonal composers rely in addition on familiar patterns of composition, such as the theme and variations, the fugue, or the passacaglia (discussed in Chapter 6), listening is, of course, made much easier.

It is possible, too, for a composer to deal in more than one tonality at a time. This compositional style is known as *bitonality* or *polytonality*

---

[6]The techniques of serial composition are set out clearly and in detail in George Perle, *Serial Composition and Atonality—An Introduction to the Music of Schoenberg, Berg, and Webern*, 2nd ed. (Berkeley and Los Angeles: University of California Press, 1968).

and is found often in the music of Stravinsky, Bartók, Hindemith, William Schuman, and many other modern composers.

**Mode**     A number of other factors are as important as those already discussed, even if they are less easily identified by the untrained ear. One of these is the kind of scale upon which the melody is based. A scale is a series of pitches arranged in ascending or descending order, the pitch names remaining the same in each octave. The most familiar of all the scales is the so-called *major* scale, or, as it is sometimes known, *major mode*. The mode influences not only the nature of the melody, but also the harmonies used, inasmuch as the notes of both chords and melody are drawn from those notes found in the mode. An examination of the piano keyboard in the next example will make the ensuing discussion of scales and modes clearer.

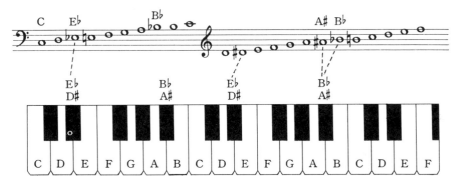

**EX. 5.28**
A portion of the
piano keyboard, with
written notes above

The major mode can be sounded by playing the white keys of the piano from C up or down to the next C. If, while playing the C mode, one should play the black key marked E-flat instead of the white key E, a markedly different kind of sound results. The interval or distance from C up to E-natural is larger than the distance from C up to E-flat; the former is called a *major* interval, the latter a *minor* one. A scale or mode which uses the smaller interval from its first note to its third note may be called a minor mode; one which uses the larger interval from its first—or *tonic*—note to its third is called a major mode. The contrast between these modes can be heard easily by listening to Schubert's *Im Frühling*. The first two verses are in the major, the third is in the minor.

The major and minor modes can be reproduced (or *transposed*) at any pitch level, no matter which key of the piano one starts on, provided one keeps in mind the basic distances between the first note of the scale and the others. For various expressive and theoretical purposes, composers vary their treatments of the minor mode by raising or lowering either the sixth or seventh step (or both). Jazz composers alternate between the major and minor treatment of the third and seventh steps, while singers and players of jazz and blues treat them with even greater freedom, using pitches that fall "between the cracks," so to speak.

There are many other modes. If one plays just the black keys of the piano, one will produce a *five-tone*, or *pentatonic* mode, which reproduces itself easily in each octave. The *whole-tone* scale, another of the so-called "exotic" modes, is also frequently encountered.

A particularly illuminating example of the effectiveness of these exotic modes may be found in Debussy's short prelude for the piano, *Voiles*. The opening phrase is a rapid splash of notes spelling out the whole-tone scale, G-sharp, F-sharp, E, D, C, then up to a B-flat (theoretically a whole step down from C, but here written in a higher octave).

**EX. 5.29 DEBUSSY**
*Voiles*, bars 1–2

In the middle portion of *Voiles,* a pentatonic mode is employed in an upward rush of notes, E-flat, G-flat, A-flat, B-flat, D-flat.

**EX. 5.30** *Ibid.*
bars 42–43

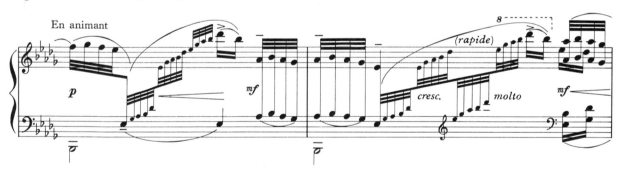

The last musical fragment from Debussy's prelude is again based on the whole-tone scale; it occurs at the end of the composition after the motive that opened the prelude is briefly recalled (Ex. 5.31).

Many compositions dealing with exotic subject matter utilize the whole-tone and pentatonic modes. Two of Puccini's operas, *Madame Butterfly* and *Turandot,* are familiar works which make use of them.

Another favorite mode is the *chromatic,* in which all twelve pitches within the octave are available. When arranged in scalar form, it proceeds in half steps: C, C-sharp, D, D-sharp, E, F, F-sharp, and so on. Chromaticism has often been used to suggest suspense, sensuality, fear, rage, and other passionate qualities.

**EX. 5.31** *Ibid.*
bars 58–64

In the sextet from Mozart's *Le Nozze di Figaro*, the passage in which Susanna expresses her anger is a good instance of a composer's use of chromaticism. In the following example, the brackets mark the half-step intervals.

**EX. 5.32 MOZART**
Sextet, "Riconosci in questo amplesso," from *Le Nozze di Figaro*, bars 40–44

Già d'a-cor-do col-la spo-sa? Giu-sti Dei, che in-fe-del-tà che in-fe-del-tà!
*In agreement with a wife already? Just God, what treachery, what treachery!*

The *Habanera* from Bizet's *Carmen* is a famous example of a melody based on the chromatic mode; its pitches descend in a regular series of half steps. Although the following example is not recorded on the discs accompanying this text, it is perhaps familiar enough to be recalled by the reader.

**EX. 5.33 BIZET**
*Habañera*, from *Carmen*,
bars 4–7

L'a-mour est un oi-seau re-bel-le que nul ne peut ap-pri-voi-ser
*Love is a rebellious bird whom no one can tame*

Of particular historical importance is a group of scales called "church modes," which served as the theoretical basis for the music of the Medieval era and the Renaissance, as well as for some of the music of the twentieth century. Each mode spans an octave with a different pattern of whole and half steps. There are 12 of them, each of which uses only the notes found in the C major scale. The most striking feature of these church modes is that the final ascending interval for most of them is not a half step, as is found in the major and most often in the minor modes, but rather a whole step. To many modern listeners this lends the church mode a somewhat ancient flavor.

The church modes have a stress that is quite different from the modern major and minor modes, for the lowest and highest notes of a church mode are not necessarily the tonic notes, but merely delimit its range. These modes may be differentiated by melodic formulas as well as by the name of their tonic pitch.

## Factors that condition the nature of melody

**The composer's purpose**

A person's understanding of melody will be much more sophisticated if he realizes that the nature of a melody depends on its purpose. A song meant to be sung by relatively untrained singers in a more or less social setting must necessarily be simple and rhythmically uncomplex so that it can be easily taught and learned. A melody meant to be developed in a symphonic composition will tend to include one or more fragments or motives—short melodic entities which are immediately grasped and remembered. Some melodies have extramusical purposes, such as providing pictorial description, supplying the music for a prayer, or creating a dramatic characterization in an opera. In such cases, the melody must not only conform to the *prosody*, or word accents (if a text is involved), but also must incisively suggest the personality and situation to which it relates.

The next few examples are of melodies which serve these different purposes. The first one is a song for social situations—*Greensleeves* (Ex. 5.34). The most notable aspect of this famous folksong is its singability. Although its range is a bit more than an octave, it lies comfortably for all types of singers, and is easily sung in unison by mixed groups of men and women. There is a basic rhythmic group (　♩　♪♩.♩♪　) found in eight of its sixteen measures; of the other measures, all but the last use either the first part of the group ( ♩ ♪ ) or the second part ( ♪. ♪ ♪ ). Two other factors make this song easy to learn and remember: (1) the same music is used for all the verses, or strophes, and (2) the refrain at the end of every verse uses not only the same music but also the same words.

**EX. 5.34**
*Greensleeves*

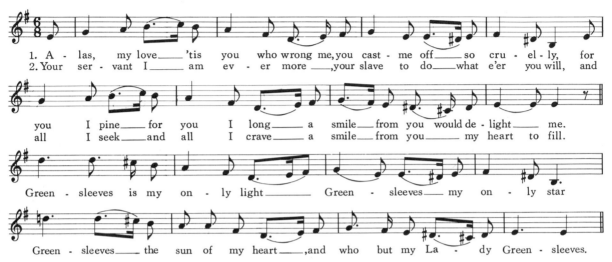

1. A - las, my love____ 'tis you who wrong me, you cast - me off____ so cru - el - ly, for
2. Your ser - vant I____ am ev - er more ____your slave to do____what e'er you will, and

you I pine____ for you I long____ a smile____from you would de - light____ me.
all I seek____and all I crave____ a smile____from you____ my heart to fill.

Green - sleeves is my on - ly light____ Green - sleeves____ my on - ly star

Green - sleeves____ the sun of my heart____,and who but my La - dy Green - sleeves.

The next example is of a melody designed to reflect textual meaning. The extended *melisma* (a group of many notes sung to a single syllable of text) on "exalted" clearly removes this melody from the area of easy singability. More important, the music illuminates the text, which concerns the prediction in the Book of Isaiah that, at the coming of the Lord, all the earth will be changed—the valleys uplifted, the high places made low, and so on. The upward surge of the melody and the florid setting of "exalted" suggest both the joy to be occasioned by the coming

**EX. 5.35 HANDEL**
"Every valley," bars 21–32, from *Messiah*

Shall be ex- alt -

- ed and ev - ry moun-tain and hill____made low; the crook - ed____

straight, and the rough plac - es plain, ____

of the Messiah and the idea of the physical raising up of the valleys (and, one interprets, of bringing new life to depressed and wretched people).

The next measures are exactly the opposite. The abasement of the mountains and the humbling of the haughty are expressed concisely and bluntly in a brief arch of melody (bars 24–26) that ends with an abrupt descent. Note how the word "crooked" is suggested by a melody that wiggles back and forth between two adjacent pitches, while the smoothing out of the "rough places" is intimated by a long, elegant phrase. Although there is in this long phrase a movement of pitches similar to that underlying "crooked," the longer note values and the general extension of the phrase give the listener a wholly different feeling.

Mozart's Symphony No. 40 provides an example of a melody that is meant to be developed.

**EX. 5.36 MOZART**
Symphony No. 40, in G minor, 1st mvt., bars 1–16

The first movement of a typical symphony from the Classical period is concerned mostly with manipulating a motive; it is not concerned with beautiful melody per se. Of the sixty-three notes in this melody, Mozart's concern is focused on the first three; more particularly, he is interested in the rhythmic profile that shapes not only these three notes, but the rest of the melody as well ( ♪♪ ♩ ). Although there is a second melody later in the movement, it is less important as far as the substance of the movement is concerned; one is made aware, instead, of the many permutations of this one rhythmic motive.

In the next example, the motive is used in the bass as a rhythmic accompaniment for a different motive heard in the oboes and flutes.

**EX. 5.37** *Ibid.*
bars 16–20

In the following example, this germinal motive is the subject of a dialogue among the clarinets, the bassoons, and the violins.

In a final example, various instruments play the motive as a transition
from one section to another.

The principal theme of Berlioz' *Fantastic Symphony* is a melody that is used for an extramusical mood or description.

The *Fantastic Symphony* is an orchestral composition concerned with the opiate dreams of a lover who attempts to forget an unrequited love by taking narcotics. Instead of forgetting his beloved, however, he sees her in ever more lurid pictures, until he imagines that he murders her, is himself executed for the crime, and eventually becomes a spectator at a witches' sabbath dominated by the satanic presence of the girl's spirit. The first movement presents a long melody (**Ex. 5.40**) that is suggestive of "dreams and passions." The many notes tied across the bar line give this melody a rhythmic vagueness that is perfectly suited to the idea of an anguished dreaminess. This purpose is realized also by the length of the melody itself, for it is difficult to remember the beginning of it by the time the end has been reached. Phrase lengths (some of the phrases are bracketed in the example) vary to such an extent that the melody seems diffuse and unpredictable. The increasing incidence of sharps, flats, and naturals near the end of the melody causes the tonic note to be less clearly felt than it was at the start of the melody, and the feeling of indefiniteness is reinforced.

In the last movement of the symphony, this melody is given a dancelike transformation that suggests the appearance of the beloved in the form of a witch. The melody is now played by a clarinet, with a fairly regular long-short rhythm ( ♩  ♪ ), decorated by grace notes ( ♪ ) in such a way as to suggest a wholly bizarre image.

**EX. 5.41** *Ibid.*
5th mvt., bars 21–29

Example 5.42 is a melody that is used for extramusical characterization. In the final act of Verdi's *Rigoletto*, the profligate and fickle Duke of Mantua is in a tavern flirting with the sensual Maddalena. Outside the tavern (see Colorplate 5) are Gilda, a girl who has been wronged by the Duke, and her father, Rigoletto, a hunchbacked jester determined to gain vengeance. Verdi presents all four simultaneously, each with a melody that characterizes him or her with a few telling strokes. Even the visual appearance of the printed music (Example 5.42) reveals the differences in characterization. The top line of the score is given to the youthful Gilda. Her melody is in groups of two notes, as if her grief were expressed in gasping sobs. The second line is Maddalena's; her laughter at the obvious flattery of the Duke is suggested by detached, short notes. More important, her groups of two notes are on one pitch, in marked contrast with the two-pitch groups of Gilda. The Duke's amorous advances are in slower note values and are written in a series of suave melodic arches, each with a gentle high point. Rigoletto is a monomaniac here, hence his utterances are rapid repetitions of one pitch, providing the whole quartet with a demoniac rhythmic impetus.

**Qualities of performance**

The character of a melody depends not only on the pitches and durations specified by the composer, but also on the manner in which they are played. *Dynamics*—the degree of loudness—is an obvious factor influencing the impact of a melody, and so is the quality of tone employed by singers or instrumentalists.

In addition, composers often indicate the nature of each note by connecting it to its neighbor or neighbors with a slur mark or by separating it or by accenting it, and so on. The examples from Debussy's *Voiles* (pp. 75–76) reveal how concerned the composer was with intensity and quality as well as with speed and loudness. Almost every note has a mark under or over it, and various performance directions indicating mood or quality abound. (Some of the more frequently used words and symbols indicating quality may be found in the *Glossary*.)

**EX. 5.42 VERDI**
Quartet, "Bella figlia dell' amore," from *Rigoletto*, bars 33–36

The next two examples (5.43 and 5.44) are a nineteenth-century score by Wagner and an eighteenth-century score by Bach. Compare the proliferation of performance directions in Wagner's music with the almost bare page of Bach's concerto. Since the modern conductor or performer is given little to go on as far as the nature of performance of Bach's music is concerned, he must rely greatly on his knowledge of style and on his taste and imagination. Should the notes of the trumpet parts be smooth and flowing? Detached? Brittle? It is clear from the comparison with Wagner's music that Bach was less concerned with instructions for dynamic change than Wagner, yet should a conductor avoid any changes from loud to soft? If he may change, where should he do so? These

**EX. 5.43 BACH**
*Brandenburg Concerto No. 2, in F,* 1st mvt., bars 1–10

**EX. 5.44 WAGNER**  *Tristan and Isolde*, Act III, excerpt

remarkably different pages of music reveal how approaches to melody and other aspects of musical sound have changed with the passage of time and direct one's attention to the importance of interpretation.

**Phrasing**     A musical *phrase* is not unlike the phrase in written or spoken language. It is essentially a thought or musical entity that gives a feeling of completeness and tends to pause at its end. The pause may be caused by a cadence, but, just as often, the phrase is defined by the manner of performance—the singer or player provides a degree of change in tempo, dynamics, or emphasis which marks the end of one phrase and the start of another. The performer is often guided in this by the cadences, or, as in the following example, by the slur marks, which group all the notes of the phrase into a visible unit.

**EX. 5.45 DEBUSSY**
*Voiles*, bars 15–18

In many cases, however, phrasing is a matter of taste and imagination on the part of the performer, and there is ample room for originality and interpretation.

Phrasing will often affect the emotive quality of a melody; long phrases may communicate a sense of breadth and majesty, while the same melody broken up into many short phrases may become restless and more agitated. In many instances, composers of tonal music have achieved an extended melodic flow that does not fall comfortably into regular phrases; the theme of the first movement of Berlioz' *Fantastic Symphony*, quoted early in this chapter, is just such a melody. It is the sequence of long phrases followed by short ones, each melodic idea straining higher and higher, that lends this theme its quality of yearning and emotional anguish.

**Timbre**     Another major factor conditioning the quality of a melody is the performing medium. An air sung by a lyric soprano may have a certain ease and tunefulness; the same air played on a tuba would be ponderous, thick, and weighty. Many composers have said that their melodies are created in their imagination with a certain tone color in mind, and that alteration of this tone color causes the melody to be a wholly different phenomenon.

The technical capacity of an instrument will also affect the notes given to it. Horns sound more majestic than flutes, for example, but flutes are more agile. Melodies written for these instruments are apt to reflect these properties. Music for other instruments should similarly reflect their natures.

### *The interaction of musical materials in Ravel's* Bolero

Ravel's *Bolero* is a relatively simple composition in its use of the elements of music.

First heard in this excerpt is the rhythmic-harmonic combination of flutes, snare drums, harp, violas, and cellos. The flute and snare drum tap out the first of the two rhythmic figures that permeate the work.

The others play a second figure that stresses the last beat of a measure and the first beat of the following measure ( ♩ 𝄾 ♩ | ♩ 𝄾 ), and they also combine into a harmonic force to provide a solid sense of tonality that is unwavering.

Another element, the melodic one, is sensuous and rhythmically irregular. One gets a swaying sensation from it and is saved from a feeling of boredom with its constant repetition because of the ever-changing timbre, which lends the melody a new quality with each repeat. The hypnotic nature of the melody is due in large part to the accents, repeated notes, and irregular lengths of the phrases, while the ebb and flow and soft dynamics contribute significantly as well.

The abbreviated score on the following pages is for just part of the recorded excerpt, which is, in turn, just part of Ravel's composition. Below is the order in which the various instruments heard in the excerpt share in the melodic, rhythmic, and harmonic functions. Instruments written across the page, from left to right, occur simultaneously.

| MELODIC ELEMENT | FIRST RHYTHMIC ELEMENT | SECOND RHYTHMIC-HARMONIC ELEMENT |
|---|---|---|
| Clarinet in E-flat | Flute, snare drum | Harp, violas, cellos |
| Oboe d'amore | Bassoons, snare drum | Strings pizzicato (plucked) |
| Flute, muted trumpet | French horn, snare drum | Strings pizzicato |

| MELODIC ELEMENT | FIRST RHYTHMIC ELEMENT | SECOND RHYTHMIC-HARMONIC ELEMENT |
| --- | --- | --- |
| Tenor saxophone | Muted trumpet, snare drum | Strings pizzicato, flute |
| Soprano saxophone | Trumpet, snare drum | Strings, oboes, English horn |
| Flute, piccolo, French horn, celesta | Flute, French horn, snare drum | Strings, bass clarinet, bassoon, harp |

**EX. 5.46 RAVEL**
*Bolero,* excerpt

In the score that follows, the notes of the melody are written in larger print than those of accompanying forces.

# 6 : HOW A COMPOSER COMPOSES

THERE is a romantic notion, popularized a great deal by the movie industry, that a composer has but to sit at a piano or desk, look skyward for inspiration, and write down the melodies and harmonies that gush forth, seemingly from nowhere. The resulting compositions come neatly packaged for performance, completely orchestrated with proper balance and color, and suitable for a mighty orchestra, chorus, or soloist.

While it is certainly true that inspiration must be present in some form in every successful composer, composition is not the simple, inspired-from-above act one is often led to believe it to be. It demands complete intellectual and emotional attention and involvement and requires long and concentrated study and development. Even Mozart, to whom composition seemingly came easier than to most, once complained that it was a mistake to think that the practice of the art came easy to him. Brahms was even more to the point: ". . . there is no real creating without hard work . . ." The twentieth-century composer Ernst Toch wrote eloquently about the subject:

Nature, intuition, inspiration are one thing; analysis, study, skill are another thing. From time immemorial the human mind has tried to hitch both to the star of human progress.

The diamond, as presented by nature, would elicit little enchantment. It takes the highest skill of the cutter, practiced, cultivated and improved through many generations, to make it the coveted jewel. At the same time this accomplished

*The first manuscript page of Stravinsky's* Dumbarton Oaks Concerto in E-flat for Chamber Orchestra *(1937–1938) in the composer's hand. The performing group is small—two flutes, one clarinet in B-flat, one bassoon (fagotto), two French horns (corni), three violins, three violas, two cellos, and two double basses—and thus provides a clean, bright, intimate sound. Neatness and clarity are suggested by the composer's handwriting as well as by his choices of instrumentation. (The Dumbarton Oaks Library, Washington, D.C.)*

Beethoven's original manuscript for the Trio of the third movement of the Fifth Symphony, bars 41–46. Frequent corrections and scrawled handwriting indicate that composing was a kind of agony for Beethoven.

art of the cutter would be a pitiful waste, utterly lost and ineffectual without nature's gift of the raw diamond.

Every composer knows, and many sketches of the masters give ample proof, that there is a long and hard road from the first inspiration to its final form.[1]

Given the talent, the drive, and the inspiration, the composer still has a long way to go. There are many steps in the process of composition that may vary from composer to composer and even from composition to composition. In spite of this variation, it is safe to assume that the first step (perhaps it is even a pre-condition) is the development of the basic compositional style. Composers, either consciously or unconsciously, tend to ally themselves with schools and camps of thought and philosophy. This is a natural tendency among all creative artists. Only occasionally is an artist or composer so individualistic that he shuts himself off completely from the rest of his world. Charles Ives was possibly such a composer, but it would be untrue to say that he did not at least make himself fully aware of what was going on around him.

The basic compositional style develops as a result of many influences

[1]Ernest Toch, *The Shaping Forces of Music* (New York: The Criterion Music Corp., 1948), p. 62.

on the composer's abilities and tastes. The influences are so numerous and varied that it would be impossible to list them all. Mozart's music reflects the styles of Italian opera, Viennese classicism, German formalism, his own performing abilities, the music of Haydn and a host of other people, and the impact of events, places, and things. Smetana was influenced by romanticism, nationalism, his folk heritage, fellow composers (Liszt and Dvořák, for instance), the nineteenth-century symphonic tradition of the Austro-German countries, mental illness, and his own rather introverted nature. A composer's style is essentially his signature and is identified with him and his musical language.

In his early years, a composer often experiments with various media and writing techniques. As his style matures, he usually directs himself toward fewer media and may limit himself to one or two genres. Medium or genre can often be identified with style. Verdi, Puccini, and Rossini, for example, are known primarily as composers of opera; Wagner is known for music drama (a specialized type of opera), Chopin for piano music, Wolf for song, Beethoven and Brahms for symphonies and chamber music, and Handel for opera, oratorio, and concerto. Mozart was unique in that he was able to compose successfully for every medium and in every genre of his time. The choice of medium and genre is obviously tempered by circumstance as well as by musical personality. Before 1800, patronage was in full flower and the composer had to write what would please the patron. After 1800, the composer became increasingly independent, and the choice was left up to him and his reactions to commercial or aesthetic stimuli.

Just as style can sometimes dictate genre or medium, genre or medium can in turn dictate structure. If a composer wished to write in the genre of opera, for example, the various structures of opera ("number" opera, music drama, or *Singspiel*, for instance) would present themselves. If the symphony orchestra were the desired medium, a number of genres (such as symphony, concert overture, concerto, suite, or tone poem) would be possible and would result in the selection of such forms as sonata, theme and variations, rondo, and so on.

Some composers will start with the choice of genre, medium, and form, and then compose; others will start with the musical idea—a melody, a phrase, a rhythm, or a harmonic progression—and develop it, eventually selecting a medium and a form into which it could be placed compatibly. In either case, the composer is working with the elements of music and molding them into a cohesive whole. How he works with them is reflective of his style and his musical personality.

Since the latter part of the seventeenth century, tonality has been the principal system of pitch arrangement in music. Before then, modality was the principal system. In this century, composers have made serious attempts to break away from tonality in various ways, usually by arranging the twelve pitches of the octave scale in various nontonal patterns and even by introducing sounds into the octave that fit between the original twelve. Regardless of the system of pitch arrangement used by a composer, melody is, and always has been, the most important single element; all others revolve around it in greater or lesser degrees of importance.

Repetition of melody is the binding force in music, since it is the recurrence or contrast of melodies or melodic patterns that results in the recognition of a form when it is heard. It is this recurrence or contrast with which a composer works to build a composition.

Although form is generally dependent upon melody for its identification and definition, it is not dependent upon the simple statement of melody alone. Once a melody has been stated, the composer must work with it to extract the maximum of meaning from it. There are six basic ways of working with melody: *contrast, variation, development, imitation, expansion,* and *juxtaposition.*

**Forms using contrast**     Contrasting forms are those in which musical meaning is derived from the statement or alternation of passages or melodies that have clearly differentiated moods or qualities. In the simplest state, a contrasting form has two melodies, each with distinctive properties. Since it is customarily the practice in charting form to designate melodies or themes by letter names, the two-part, or *binary,* form is identified *AB.* The next most simple contrasting form continues one step further by recalling melody *A,* thus creating the three-part, or *ternary,* form, *ABA.* Compositions with a single melody are also possible; they are usually quite short and

**EX. 6.1**
*Greensleeves*

First part (A)

A - las  my love____ 'tis  you  who wrong  me you cast  me off____  so  cru - el - ly,

Second part (B)

Green - sleeves is my  on - ly light____  Green - sleeves__ my  on - ly star  Green sleeves____ the

are made up of contrasting phrases which may or may not be repeated. *America* is such a "through-composed" song. On the whole, most contrasting forms are binary, or ternary, or variants of each.

Songs are so often constructed in one of these simple forms that it is not at all uncommon to refer to binary and ternary structures, whether vocal or instrumental, as the two- or three-part "song forms." *Greensleeves* is a binary composition; the contrast between its two parts is easy to see in the notation and readily heard in its performance (Ex. 6.1).

The ternary structure, *ABA*, is exemplified on the records accompanying this book in the plainsong used for the opening phrases of the Mass for the Dead. The first section (*A*) is beautifully florid or melismatic (many notes per syllable of text) and is sung to the words:

> *Requiem aeternam, dona eis Domine:*
> Rest      eternal      grant to them, Lord:
>
> *Et lux perpetua luceat eis.*
> And may light perpetual shine upon them.

The middle portion (*B*) is given over to a paraphrase of part of Psalm 65. Its musical style suggests that of psalm singing by a congregation, since it is exclusively syllabic (one note per syllable), rather than melismatic. Its text is:

> *Te decet hymnus, Deus in Sion,*
> To Thee is due a hymn, O God in Zion,
>
> *Et tibi reddetur votum in Jerusalem:*
> And to Thee shall be paid a vow in Jerusalem:
>
> *Exaudi orationem meam,*
> Hear my prayer,
>
> *Ad te omnis caro veniet.*
> To Thee all flesh shall come.

The return of the *A* portion (both text and music) rounds out the three-part form.

The first obvious variant to the simple *AB* or *ABA* form would be to continue the pattern of contrast just as *ABA* is a continuation of the pattern of contrast created by *AB*. This occurs frequently in the form of the *rondo*.

Often found as the last movement of concertos, symphonies, and sonatas, a rondo is a form that continually "turns around" a recurrent musical idea. One need only see a formal scheme for a rondo to understand this. A typical rondo might have the form *ABABA, ABACA,* or *ABACADA.* Note that melody *A* returns after each contrasting section, or *episode,* is stated. Sometimes, development sections, dealing with fragments of themes, are inserted before the final return of *A.* Beethoven particularly liked this last rondo-variant and used it often. Rondo forms that contain development sections, properly named *sonata-rondos,* are sometimes colloquially referred to as "Beethoven rondos," although Haydn used them frequently and with equally great mastery.

Smetana's tone poem *The Moldau* is a rondo in which the composer took his license to rearrange the presentation of the themes slightly. Instead of following a traditional pattern, Smetana chose the pattern of *Introduction-ABCADA-Coda,* in which, in the *D* section, there is presented a development of previously stated material rather than wholly new musical ideas. Each of the sections describing a river's progress through the Bohemian countryside serves a structural function as well as a descriptive one in this famous orchestral work. The following table will aid the listener in identifying them.

| DESCRIPTIVE EPISODE | STRUCTURAL FUNCTION | MUSICAL TRAITS |
| --- | --- | --- |
| The Two Sources of the Moldau | *Introduction* | Fast figures in flutes, then clarinets |
| The River | *A* | Broad melody in violins |
| Forest Hunt | *Transition* | Fanfares in French horns |
| Peasant Wedding | *B* | Polka in strings and woodwinds |
| Moonlight: Nymphs' Dance | *C* | Fast figures in flutes and clarinets, over high, sustained melody in violins |
| The River | *A* | Broad melody in violins and woodwinds |
| St. John's Rapids | *D (development)* | Brass fanfares, percussion, short motives in strings and woodwinds |
| The River in Its Greatest Breadth | *A* | Broad theme in violins and winds, somewhat faster than before, with more extensive percussion |
| The River before Vyšehrad Castle | *Coda* | Broad chords in winds and brass, much movement in strings |

Another variant of the binary or ternary form is the addition of a second group of contrasting themes to the already existing group. A form thus constructed might be charted *AB CDC (AB)* or *ABA CDC (ABA)*. *CDC* is the second group; the *AB* or *ABA* may or may not recur, hence the parentheses. The second group of themes is traditionally called the *trio section*, because at one time (the seventeenth century) it was written for three parts and often was played by three instruments. The obligation for three parts or three players later disappeared, but the name remained.

In the eighteenth century, a popular "song form" with trio was the *minuet*, which was used for the third movement of most four-movement compositions of the Classical period. Some works, especially serenades and divertimentos, had more than four movements, and would often include two minuets with trios. Since the minuet borrowed its character from music for the dance, it is characteristically rhythmic, moderately fast, and in triple meter.

With Haydn and Beethoven, the *scherzo* and trio replaced the minuet in many multimovement compositions, especially symphonies and string quartets. The scherzo is faster in tempo than the minuet and usually is somewhat humorous in character (*scherzo* is Italian for "joke"). Beethoven's frequent use of the scherzo is exemplified by the third movement of his Symphony No. 5. (See analysis in Chapter 10.)

The second movement of Brahms's Trio in E-flat is also a fine example of the spirit and the form of the scherzo and typifies the ternary form with a trio section as an added contrasting group.[2] The trio section de-

**EX. 6.2 BRAHMS**
Trio in E-flat, Op. 40, 2nd mvt., bars 1–7, *A* theme

Piano

parts from tradition in that it has but one theme rather than two. In order to achieve balance, Brahms repeated it. The scheme for the whole

**EX. 6.3** *Ibid.*
bars 121–128, *B* theme

Horn

[2] The use of the word "trio" in both the title of the composition and the middle section of its second movement will be less confusing if it is remembered that "trio" refers in the title to the number of parts specified (three: horn, violin, and piano) and in the nomenclature of the form of the movement to a contrasting, middle section.

**EX. 6.4** *Ibid.*
bars 287–294, trio section

movement is *ABA C ABA, C* being the trio section. (See Chapter 13 for a fuller discussion of the movement.)

Forms using contrast can vary in size from a short and simple folk song to a mighty movement of a symphony. The principle of contrast as a compositional device has been used by every composer.

**Forms using variation**

The variation form generally deals directly with the whole of a melody or theme rather than its parts. Although the form was not an innovation of the Classical period, it was crystallized and made a particularly prominent *modus operandi* during that time. The Classical concept of variation included statement of a theme and alteration during subsequent restatements without losing the theme's identity. Various methods of altering included ornamentation, change of mode (from major to minor, or vice versa), change of rhythm, change of some of the actual pitches of the melody, change to a new key, addition of another melody, or combinations of several of these. The fourth movement of the *Trout* Quintet, by Schubert, is conceived as a variation form in this Classic sense.

**EX. 6.5 SCHUBERT**
Quintet in A (*Trout*), Op. 114,
4th mvt., bars 1–8, theme

After the typically unornamented statement of the folklike theme by the violin,

**EX. 6.6** *Ibid.*
bars 21–26, Variation I

Schubert's variations begin with the theme stated by the piano, its melody altered slightly.

**EX. 6.7** *Ibid.*
bars 41–43, Variation II

In Variation II, the theme is played by the viola and echoed by the piano, while a countermelody is added by the first violin.

In Variation III, the theme, in even notes rather than in dotted ones, is stated in the lower strings against a running countermelody played by the piano.

EX. 6.8 *Ibid.*
bars 61–62, Variation III

Variation IV shows a change of mode from major to minor, with the whole ensemble stating the theme somewhat dramatically.

EX. 6.9 *Ibid.*
bars 81–84, Variation IV

There is a return to the major mode in Variation V, and a modulation to a new key, while the theme is somewhat modified by the cello, ornamentation being provided by the piano.

EX. 6.10 *Ibid.*
bars 101–107, Variation V

The last variation finds the theme stated exactly by the violin and cello, alternately, with the other instruments in an accompanying role.

EX. 6.11 *Ibid.*
bars 128–136, Variation VI

99

This final variation is a synthesis of the Schubert art song *Die Forelle* ("The Trout"), in which the piano describes the darting of a fish in a brook.

Other variation forms frequently encountered are the *passacaglia* and the *chaconne*. Polyphonic in nature, both were especially popular before the Classical period. Although many theorists have tried to differentiate between these two forms, composers have used the terms interchangeably. Generally, if the form uses a slow, ternary theme of stately character, sounded first alone, then in a number of repetitions while variations are played either higher, lower, or around it, it is said to be a passacaglia. A chaconne will differ from this in that its theme will be more chordal in nature, and the variations will be written around this harmonic structure or pattern. The concept of thematic repetition is important in both; the use of constant repetition of a melody or melodic figure is known as *ostinato* technique; the repeated melody (or figure) is known as an ostinato or a *ground*.

After the Classical period, examples of variation forms show a greater freedom in dealing with melodic materials, with composers less concerned with maintaining the basic melodic identification. A variation might be written on a given melody and the following variations might vary the variation itself. After several such alterations, an original melody could easily be obliterated. Composers of the Romantic period also found that the many tone colors available in a symphony orchestra could contribute to variation forms, and several composers wrote variations that were nothing more than changes in orchestral texture. This can be heard quite clearly in Ravel's *Bolero*. Twentieth-century composers have made further adaptations of the principle of variation to fit their needs. Serial composers, especially those who work in the twelve-tone technique, have found variation to be virtually indispensable as a compositional device.

The concept of variation adapts itself well to song, especially if the song has verses (strophes). Whenever the composer modifies his melodic design to fit a text or meaning, he is in essence writing a variation. Note how Schubert does this in the three strophes of *Im Frühling*.

**EX. 6.12 SCHUBERT**
*Im Frühling*, 1st strophe, bars 5–8

Still sitz ich an des Hü - gels Hang, der Him - mel ist so klar, das

Lüft - chen spielt im grü - nen Tal, wo ich beim er - sten Früh - lings-strahl einst

**EX. 6.13** *Ibid.* 2nd strophe, bars 21–24 (note changes in melodic line in bars 23–24)

Sieh, wie der bun - te Früh - ling schon aus Knosp und Blü - te blickt! Nicht

al - le Blü - ten sind mir gleich, am lieb - sten pflückt' ich von dem Zweig, von

**EX. 6.14** *Ibid.* 3rd strophe, bars 35–38 (note change of mode and melody in bars 37–38)

Es wan - deln nur sich Will und Wahn, es wech - seln Lust__ und__ Streit, vor -

ü - ber__ flieht__ der__ Lie - be Glück, und nur die Lie - be bleibt zur - ück, die

**Forms using development**

To a composer, development is probably the most intriguing technique for working with melodies because it places great demands upon his invention and craftsmanship. In the process of development, the composer will take fragments of his melodies and work with them, putting them together in different ways, turning them upside down and backwards, and combining them with other fragments in an attempt to derive additional meaning. Development as a technique gained great popularity during the Classical era; the form which employed it the most, the *sonata form*,[3] was an innovation of that period.

The form, as the Classical composers conceived it, was one in which a melody or melodies were stated, then put through a process of working out or development, then restated. The first statement of melodies might be preceded by an introduction, and the restatement might be followed

[3]The word *sonata* (*suonare*, "to sound") has been used in a variety of contexts and can thus be confusing. Prior to the Classical period, the sonata was conceived as a somewhat lyrical work for instrumentalists, differing from the more technically demanding *toccata* (*toccare*, "to touch"), also a work for instrumentalists. The classical sonata evolved into a multimovement work for either a solo instrument or a solo instrument accompanied by a keyboard instrument. The latter was refined further into a work in which the solo instrument and the keyboard instrument had equal status rather than one accompanying the other. When reference is made today to a sonata, it is to this latter concept or to the concept of a work for one instrument. When reference is made to the sonata *form*, it is to the developmental form described above. The form is sometimes called the *sonata-allegro* form, a name disputed by a number of theorists and historians because the use of the form does not imply an allegro tempo.

by a concluding section called a *coda*. Some sonata forms have but one melody or theme that, in order to achieve unity, is repeated starting on a different pitch. More often, however, the form includes two contrasting melodies, referred to as the *principal* and *subordinate* themes. The first statement of the theme or themes is called the *exposition*; this section is often meant to be repeated. Next is the *development* section, which is followed by a somewhat freer restatement of the material of the exposition in a section known as the *recapitulation*. If an introduction and a coda are included, the form can be diagrammed thus:

| | *A* | *A* | *B* | *A* | |
|---|---|---|---|---|---|
| INTRODUCTION | EXPOSITION | REPEAT OF EXPOSITION | DEVELOPMENT | RECAPITULATION | CODA |
| | (*a*) Principal theme | Sometimes omitted in performance | Fragmentation, modulation, free treatment of *a*, *b*, and *c* | Somewhat free restatement of *a* and *b* | |
| | (*b*) Subordinate theme | | | | |
| | (*c*) Closing section | | | | |

When there are two themes, they are often given "masculine" and "feminine" properties by the composer for the sake of contrast. Usually, the principal theme is angular or dynamic, and the subordinate theme is smoother and more lyrical. The two themes from the first movement of Mozart's Symphony No. 40 in G minor have these characteristics.

**EX. 6.15 MOZART**
Symphony No. 40, in G minor, 1st mvt., bars 1–7, principal theme

**EX. 6.16** *Ibid.*
Bars 44–51, subordinate theme

The composers of the Classical period found this form a most gratifying one to use. Almost invariably, the first movements of their multimovement compositions, such as symphonies, concertos, string quartets, solo sonatas, and masses, were cast in the sonata form; in many instances, last movements were also in the sonata form. Later composers have varied the form occasionally by including more than two themes or more than one development section, but the form has generally remained intact and is still used by many composers. On the records accompanying this text, the first movement of Mozart's Symphony No. 40 and the first movement of Bartók's Piano Concerto No. 3 are complete examples of it.

Development sections are not necessarily restricted to sonata forms nor is development within a movement or composition restricted to but one section. Development sections can be inserted into supposedly nondevelopmental forms (such as the rondo, resulting in the sonata-rondo), and many composers will start developing thematic materials as soon as they are stated.

When *Row, Row, Row Your Boat* is sung as a round, one voice starts **Forms using imitation** to sing, and, at regular points of time, other voices enter, singing exactly what the other, previously heard voices have already sung. This is *imitation,* and there are certain compositional qualities associated with it.

First, there is the statement *and repetition* of a melody or theme. The repetition takes place in a voice or part other than the one making the original statement, so there must be at least two voices or parts if there is to be imitation. Second, when the repetition begins, the first voice continues; the melodic independence of the continuing and repeating parts creates a contrapuntal, or polyphonic, texture. Imitation, therefore, involves statement, repetition, and continuation in two or more voices or parts sounding contrapuntally.

When the intervals of a theme or melody are imitated exactly, the result is a *canon*, an example of which is the interaction between the two soprano parts of the *Agnus Dei II* of Palestrina's *Missa Brevis*. When the exact imitation uses not only the same intervals but also the same pitches, the result is a *canon at the unison*, or a *round*.

The technique of imitation is also used in the *fugue*.[4] In a fugue, a melody, which is called a *subject*, is stated usually without accompaniment and is then imitated by other voices or parts in close succession. This statement and its imitation, involving from two to five or six voices (most often four, however), form the exposition of the fugue. Once a voice has stated the subject, it usually continues with a melodic design different from those heard simultaneously with it. During the course of a

---

[4]According to several writers, a fugue is not a form but a procedure, since no fugue is exactly like any other. For the purposes of this text, the point is moot.

fugue, the subject will be restated a number of times in the various voices. If at any time during the progress of the fugue there is no subject statement by any voice, the passage is said to be an *episode*.[5] Episodic passages are developmental in nature, usually work with fragments of the subject, and vary in length. In some fugues there are no episodes, while in others they are quite extended. Episodic passages lead to further restatements of the subject. These restatements (which may also be known as *expositions, internal expositions*, or *re-expositions*) may be made in any voice and answered by any or all of the other voices, in any order.

Bach was a master of the art of fugal composition. His *Little Fugue in G minor* has four voices, an easily recognizable, if not already familiar, subject, and typifies the structural excellence and inventiveness for which Bach is so highly regarded.

**EX. 6.17 BACH**
*Little Fugue in G minor,*
bars 1–6, subject and
beginning of answer

In the *Little Fugue*, the subject statement is unaccompanied. The first restatement of it, called the *answer*, enters at a different pitch level (see Ex. 6.17). After the answer is heard, the two voices continue and move back to the original key for a third subject statement. The fourth statement, another answer, comes soon after, and the exposition of all voices is now complete.

Following the original four statements of Bach's subject in the exposition of the fugue, there are five restatements of it. After the last of these restatements, there is a short section that leads to the final cadence and helps to bring the music to its climax and conclusion. The illustration on p. 105 is a graph of the *Little Fugue*, showing some of the various elements of fugal writing.

No two fugues will follow the same pattern. The *Little Fugue* is comparatively short and simple, as its name implies, but other fugues may

---

[5]*Episode* is a term applicable, therefore, to both the developmental sections of the fugue and the contrasting sections of the rondo.

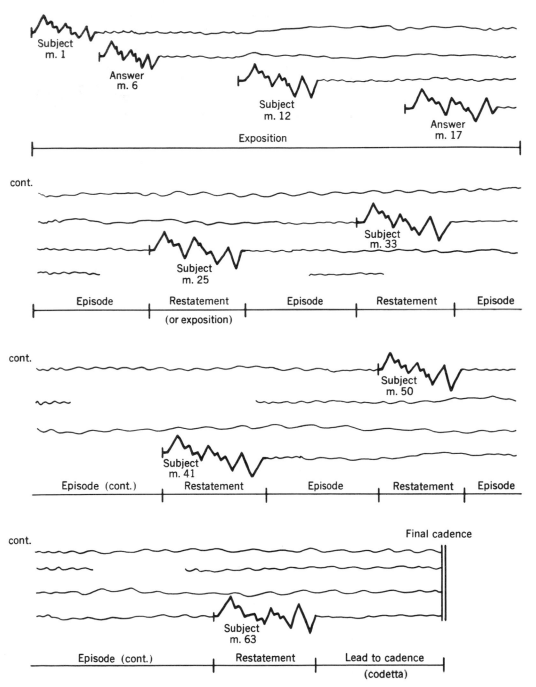

*Bach's* Little Fugue in G minor *in graph form;*
*blank spaces indicate periods of rest.*

be much lengthier and more complex. Restatements and expositions may be either less or more imitative and, in some cases, additional subjects may be introduced. An especially elaborate fugue forms part of Hovhaness' *Prelude and Quadruple Fugue,* during which not one but four subjects are introduced and developed. Double fugues, with two subjects presented simultaneously, are not unusual—the *Sanctus* from Verdi's *Requiem* and "Achieved Is the Glorious Work" from Haydn's *The Creation* are noted examples. In addition to multiplicity of subject, fugues may be extended and intensified by codas or codettas of varying degrees of elaboration, since it is the belief of most composers that the activity and continual fermentation of the fugue demands some sort of forcefully stated conclusion.

**Forms using expansion**     Expansion forms are those that have no predetermined patterns of repetition or contrast. Rather, each composition is *sui generis,* a law unto itself. Such works are free or rhapsodic in nature and are often described as *through-composed.* The most obvious examples of expansion forms are found in some genres of vocal music and in instrumental works that have extramusical reference, although neither words nor a program are by any means a precondition for their existence. As exemplified by *The Moldau,* a program work can be very neatly patterned and formally traditional.

Schubert's *Erlkönig* is an example of how text can influence the direction of the music. The dialogue of the song is divided among a father, galloping through the dark forest, his dying son, whom he is carrying in his arms, and the legendary Erl King. The Erl King, a symbol of evil and death, seductively pleads for the child to join him. The father tells the child that his visions are but mists, and the cajoling words are the rustling of dead leaves, but when they arrive home the child is dead. The music must help to portray the ride, the words of father, child, and Erl King, and the tragic end of the race with death. The text (see Chapter 7) makes it apparent that the precise repetition of any particular section of the music would interfere with the unfolding of the drama. The repeats of melodies in this song are never literal—they are changed in such a way that they continually heighten the situation.

Opera presents many examples of the expansion approach to form. The medium itself is essentially expansionist, since every opera is based on a plot that will demand individual treatment for each scene. The plot will be revealed through the stage action and the dialogue of the singers; it will be ongoing with little or no reprise of action. The music must fit into this scheme, so new musical material must be introduced continually to carry new aspects of the developing situations. It is significant in opera that, in most cases where there is an aria or ensemble in which there are very definite returns to previously stated melodies or words, the action tends to slow down or come to a halt and will not pick up again until the freer structure of the recitative returns.

The recorded excerpt from Mozart's opera *Le Nozze di Figaro* is an example of the use of the expansion technique. The plot situation is this: Figaro, valet to Count Almaviva, has borrowed some money from Marcellina and cannot repay her. She sues him and, by court order, he must either keep his agreement to pay or else marry her. The Count is delighted, for then Figaro's real love, Susanna, would be left alone and the Count could force his attentions on her. In a hilarious recitative, it is discovered that Marcellina is really Figaro's mother. Susanna, meanwhile, has raised the money for Figaro to pay Marcellina and enters just as those two are embracing, celebrating their rediscovered relationship. There is further confusion until Susanna is made to understand. The scene ends on a happy note for everyone except the Count, whose plans for the pursuit and conquest of the pretty Susanna have once again been thwarted.

Throughout this scene, there is a continual change of mood, generally and individually, starting in a spirit of vindication and satisfaction of revenge and lust, and ending in a spirit of jubilation as the parents and son are reunited and Figaro and Susanna are freed to make their own marital plans. Each situation dictates its own requirements, and, therefore, its music.

In spite of this overall expansionist approach, the listener will note that the many repeats of smaller sections and the frequent recurrence of a motive in the violins, reminiscent of an instrumental chuckle, provide a strong sense of unity throughout (Ex. 6.18).

**EX. 6.18 MOZART**
Sextet, "Riconosci in questo amplesso," from *Le Nozze di Figaro*, bars 2–3, after the recitative

This sextet is but one of many sections that make up the entire opera, each musical moment being treated on its own terms. The concept of through-composition seems to be followed in any opera as a whole, but, when one examines the separate arias and ensembles of Verdi, Mozart, and many others, one finds that they tend to fall into such types as *ABA*, sonata form, rondo, and so on. Wagner, on the other hand, rejected the concept of opera as a series of "numbers" in his later works. Instead, he developed a musical style that avoided coming to a full pause anywhere prior to the conclusion of an act in an effort to maintain the psychological continuity of the stage action. While it is possible to excerpt passages from Wagner's scores, closed forms are relatively rare in such operas as *Tristan and Isolde, Parsifal,* and the four component operas of *The Ring of the Nibelung.*

Wagner's music dramas retain structural cogency because of the frequent recurrence of easily perceived melodies or melodic fragments, each associated with an object, person, event, or idea. These *Leitmotivs,* as they are called, are treated by the expansion technique and return only when the dramatic situation demands and in such a way that they illuminate that situation.

In program music, a similar situation exists except that words are absent. The composer who writes extrareferential works, therefore, must use musical sounds to describe or narrate. Musical structure is thus often related to the progress of events or the descriptive character of the "program." In Dukas's tone poem *The Sorcerer's Apprentice,* for instance, a number of events are told in musical terms. Since each event is different from the others, it must be treated individually. Dukas ties them together by using the Leitmotiv technique, providing a motive for the apprentice, the broom, and other important features of the story.

Liszt's *Les Preludes* is also expansionist and reflects a continuous transformation of themes to meet the programmatic requirements.

Program music, however, is not by definition expansionist. It has already been pointed out that *The Moldau* is a rondo with some development, and one might point to a number of other examples of program music built on traditional forms. Richard Strauss, in particular, composed a number of symphonic poems that are free treatments of conventional structures: *Till Eulenspiegel* is a rondo with development sections; *Don Juan* and *Tod und Verklärung* ("Death and Transfiguration") are sonata forms; *Also sprach Zarathustra* ("Thus Spake Zarathustra") is essentially a theme and variations.

The technique of expansion as a compositional device has been popular for centuries. Toccatas, preludes, fantasias, and anthems (especially popular during the Renaissance and Baroque eras, but found in other periods as well) are all examples of compositions in which the technique has been employed. Electronic composers, who move beyond the traditional melodic patterns of Western musical history, often work with fragments of rhythm and pitch in ways that may be labelled as the free expansion of ideas.

Juxtaposition is the simultaneous occurrence of "layers" of melody, timbre, or key, sometimes related, sometimes not. The technique is one of the oldest in composition, and several of its varieties have been employed with vitality over the past 1,000 years.

In the Medieval era, and during much of the Renaissance, melodic juxtaposition was a major factor in the composition of virtually all forms of music other than unison songs and chants. The technique involved the composition of one or more melodic lines above or, in some cases, below a fragment of a chant or secular song. This fragment—or any melody used in this fashion—is known as a *cantus firmus* ("fixed song"; the plural is *cantus firmi*). In the Medieval era, the fragment was almost invariably drawn from plainchant; rarely was the entire melody employed in this manner. Secular songs were not used as cantus firmi until the fifteenth century, although newly composed ones were frequently employed from the thirteenth century on.

If the melodic lines were juxtaposed to a liturgical cantus firmus, the result was *organum*, of which there were a variety of types (see *Glossary*). If, on the other hand, the juxtaposition involved a newly-composed cantus firmus, the end product was a *polyphonic conductus*. In early examples of organum, the juxtapositions tended to be parallel to the cantus firmus in both pitch and rhythm, but in the latter part of the eleventh century, composers called for greater freedom among the various melodic lines. The development of more freely moving parts and the addition of text to any or all of the juxtaposed melodies eventually resulted in the *motet*, the most important sacred musical form of the Medieval era and the Renaissance. This musical structure has such a varied history that one can define it only as a polyphonic composition in which each segment of text is given its own melodic profile; that profile can be reflected in any or none of the other parts. Thus the motet, originally a major structure employing juxtaposition, eventually drew on all the constructive principles discussed in this chapter.[6]

It is quite possible for melodic parts to be combined in a manner wholly

---

[6]Such variation forms as the passacaglia and the chaconne might be described as cantus firmus works, but the melodies on which such forms are based are, in virtually all cases, composed expressly for the particular pieces in which they occur, whereas a true cantus firmus has an identity of its own before the juxtaposition technique is applied.

free of a cantus firmus. A favorite type of social singing, for example, is the *quodlibet* (or, colloquially, the "partner song"), in which two wholly unrelated songs are performed simultaneously. *Keep the Home Fires Burning* may be juxtaposed to *There's A Long, Long Trail A-winding*, while *Some Folks Do* is a pleasurable juxtaposition to *Go Tell It on the Mountain.*

The addition of one or more melodic lines above a cantus firmus is the type of juxtaposition most frequently found prior to the twentieth century. Sollberger's *Music for Sophocles' "Antigone"* uses another sort of juxtaposition, a type that the composer has described as "levels of activity."

The excerpt analyzed next is one of three recitations from the play treated by the composer with electronic sound. For Sollberger, the second of the three, the one discussed here, is a testimony to the power of love and its conflicting emotions. The text reads as follows:

STROPHE

Love, unconquerable
Waster of rich men, keeper
Of warm lights and all-night vigil
In the soft face of a girl:
Sea-wanderer, forest visitor!
Even the pure Immortals cannot escape you,
And mortal man, in his one day's dusk,
Trembles before your glory.

ANTISTROPHE

Surely you swerve upon ruin
The just man's consenting heart,
As here you have made bright anger
Strike between father and son—
And none has conquered but Love!
A girl's glance working the will of heaven:
Pleasure to her alone who mocks us,
Merciless Aphrodite.[7]

[7]From *The Antigone of Sophocles*, an English version by Dudley Fitts and Robert Fitzgerald, copyright 1939, by Harcourt, Brace & World, Inc.; renewed 1967, by Dudley Fitts and Robert Fitzgerald. Reprinted by permission of the publishers.

The first level of activity is that of pitch. It consists of a series of seven pitches ( B, D, E-flat, C, E-natural, F, F-sharp) heard in separate sine tones throughout the Strophe in its basic order, and throughout the Antistrophe in its reverse order and three half steps higher (A, G-sharp, G, E-flat, F-sharp, F, D).

The second level of activity, which occurs throughout the composition, sometimes simultaneously with the pitch level, is that of color. Sollberger uses electronic color not only to create a sort of atmosphere for each strophe (through reverberation heard at "Love, unconquerable" and "Surely you swerve"), but also to highlight specific words. Thus low, reverberated white noise gives impact to "Love" in the fifth line of the Antistrophe; the combination of square wave, filter, and reverberation provide the metallic clangor that points to "anger"; flutter (electronic switch) ending in reverberation (ring modulator and reverberator) highlights "Sea-wanderer, forest visitor"; and bell-like sine tones create the delirium occasioned at the end by mention of the goddess herself, "Merciless Aphrodite."

*Music for Sophocles' "Antigone"* is essentially a classical composition, for its use of sound is restrained, disciplined, and structured, albeit intense in expression.

The technique of sound creation is, of course, less important than is the delicacy with which the composer has captured the tenderness and passion of the goddess of love, at once sweet and uncompromising, vague, yet all-consuming. The gentle ringings follow the sway of the poetic rhythms, yet there is considerable "bite" resulting from the unpitched sounds that reinforce the affective words cited above.

Sollberger's sensitive use of new media has, then, given modern impetus to the oldest technique in Western polyphony, a technique of juxtaposition that has served not only the great Leoninus and Perotinus of the twelfth century, but also, more recently, such masters as Debussy, Stravinsky, Ives, and Carter.

### Form and the listener

At this point, a word of caution to the listener is necessary. Form is a silent element, and the search for it in a piece of music can often be frustrating. Composers are notorious for making alterations, subtle or otherwise, in formal patterns. The return of a theme may be just a suggestion rather than an entire restatement; a different use of tone color may hide a theme; a change of dynamics may well be a formal device. Recognition of structure will be the final element of music to be perceived, yet whether the form is recognized or not, the ordering of musical ideas is the only element of music that gives meaning to the interplay of timbre, harmony, and all the other facets of the art of sound.

### The test of performance

It is performance to which the composer has been pointing all along. He has brought all of his intellectual and creative facilities to bear on a work of art that he hopes will communicate his thoughts and emotions; this can be done only if it is performed. Only through performance is it decided whether the composition is a successful work of art and if the composer was a skillful craftsman able to communicate through music or just a clumsy hack with nothing to say. This decision is weighted by such factors as considerations of style, timeliness and timelessness, proper uses of elements and media, the balance between emotion and reason, depth of expression, appropriateness of form, and the impact of the work as a whole in terms of its aesthetic content.

Who makes that decision? In the final analysis, it is made by the listeners (that is, society) and often it is made long after the creation of the work. Sometimes, the decision will be changed, for not every work once considered a masterpiece has endured. Tastes will change and cause the meaning of art to have less timely value. Rossini's *William Tell*, once an immensely popular opera, is now remembered mainly for its overture and some of its vocal music, and Grieg's only piano concerto is less esteemed today than it was a generation ago. Conversely, works of art once considered questionable can gain in favor as they age. Puccini's *Madame Butterfly* was at first booed, but is now among the world's best loved operas, while Tchaikovsky's Symphony No. 6, now a favorite, failed at its first two performances.

The composer's self-satisfaction also plays an important part. Art, for its creator, is in many ways a manifestation of ego gratification, the reflection of which will vary in degree and in kind from composer to composer and from age to age. There is always an aspect of individuality in the creation of the arts, although the personality of the artist may be hidden by such factors as historical distance, changing social and artistic tastes, and the creator's need or desire to please.

## Composition in the twentieth century

The musical picture at the beginning of the twentieth century reflected two basically opposed schools of thought. On the one hand, the Germans and the middle Europeans, represented by the music of Mahler, Richard Strauss, and, eventually, Schoenberg and Berg, developed a style of composition known as *Expressionism*. It was characterized by the use of large orchestral groups, by rich textures and timbres, and by an elaborately emotional, often autobiographical quality. Directly opposed to this was *Impressionism*. Dominated by Debussy, its style was quintessentially French—objective, delicate, and suggestive, rather than obviously emotional. (See Colorplates 4, 7, and 8.)

After World War I, social and economic factors and aesthetic considerations necessitated changes in the types of music composed. Neoclassical and Neobaroque styles eventually crystallized in the music of such leaders as Satie, Stravinsky, Hindemith, and Honegger. Composers allied to this Neobaroque/Neoclassical style sought to recreate the clarity and rhythmic drive that had been a characteristic of much eighteenth-century music, although recreating these stylistic elements in twentieth-century terms. Thus, their music is also characterized by the vibrant dissonances and complex rhythms of the Modern era.

In the 1940's, there was a cultivation of lyricism and warm orchestration, although without the extravagance found in the Expressionism of earlier years. Occurring simultaneously with other stylistic currents of the century, Neoromanticism was strongest in America, where it was evidenced in the works of such men as Copland, Hanson, Harris, Moore, and others. It also manifested itself nationalistically in other countries, especially England (Vaughan Williams, Walton, and Britten) and Russia (Shostakovitch, Khachaturian, and Kabalevsky). At the same time, composers who espoused the elaborate romanticism of the late nineteenth century were also active, among them Richard Strauss, who maintained a more or less romantic bent in his music until his death in 1949, Rachmaninoff, and Sibelius.

Early in the century, Schoenberg approached composition with the premise that the tonal system was bankrupt and replaced it with serialism, a compositional style that regarded all twelve tones of the octave as equal in any composition. Although he was not the first composer to break the traditions of tonality, he succeeded to the extent that a new school of compositional thought arose based on his theories. It has been embraced by many of the important composers of the century, including his two students, Berg and Webern, and is still an important force in music.

Experimentation has also been an important factor in twentieth-century music. A major result of this has been not only the expansion of the number of pitches available for composition, but also wholly new timbres and possibilities of sound combinations made possible by all of the instruments and devices that produce sounds by electronic means.

Perhaps the most significant result of the stylistic ferment of the twentieth century and the constant experimentation with new concepts and media has been a feeling that anything in music is possible and practicable, and that only the taste of a composer may place limitations on what he may do.

Many composers have chosen to work within traditional frameworks of tonality and musical form, while others have attempted to be totally free of any strictures of the past. Traditionalists have worked with the materials of music in the various ways discussed earlier in this chapter. In essence, experimentalists and composers seeking new means of communication in music have worked in these ways, too, but the procedures and results are sufficiently different to merit special attention.

**Electronic music**     In the electronic media, composers work either with natural or traditional sounds, with sounds generated by electronic means, or with combinations of the two. Music dealing with the use and alteration of recorded nonelectronic sounds is known as *musique concrète*; all other electronic compositions come rather loosely under the heading *electronic music.*

*Musique concrète* originated in France in 1948. In the simplest terms, *musique concrète* is made up of sounds that exist in everyday life—the ringing of a bell, a street car rolling along its tracks, a truck's horn, a rattle of a chain, a steamboat whistle, the human voice, and so on. The sounds are recorded, perhaps altered, and then fitted together to make a musical composition. The ingenuity of the composer shows in the mosaic he makes of the original sounds. When a particular sound, such as a ringing bell, is altered by changing speed of the tape, by playing it backwards, by cutting off the attack of the sound and leaving only the decay (dying away), by cutting off the decay and leaving only the attack, by filtering the sound in various ways to change its timbre, or by any other means, the composer has provided himself with a highly varied group of sounds to be used in a compositional way. *Musique concrète* is, then, made up of such sounds that have been spliced together cohesively.

In *electronic music*, on the other hand, sounds are produced by synthesizers and generators and may be altered by a number of electronic sound modifiers. From these sources can come an infinite variety of pitches and tone colors, all available for the same kind of additional alteration used by the composers of *musique concrète*. The words "pitch" and "tone color" must be used cautiously, for the electronic composer does not deal with them in the same terms as the traditionalist composer who limits himself to twelve pitches to the octave and about eight octaves of total range. The electronic composer has the entire spectrum of audible sound (from about 20 to 20,000 vibrations per second) to draw from and he may further choose to work with gradations of noise rather than pitch.

The first electronic composing studio was developed in Cologne, Germany, in 1951 under the auspices of West German Radio. Its influence was quickly felt and, in the following year, the first American studio, the Columbia-Princeton laboratory, was founded in New Brunswick, New Jersey, under the direction of Luening and Ussachevsky. At first, sounds were produced by separate generators, but soon the synthesizers came into use. Since then, electronic music laboratories have been built in many places in this country, in Europe, and in Asia.

Because of the medium's newness, not many compositions have been produced that are considered by society to be "masterpieces," although several are notable. Many of the best works have incorporated sounds from both electronic and concrète sources. One of the most interesting of them is Varèse's *Poème Électronique*, which was composed to be played over the loudspeaker system of the Philips Radio Corporation's pavilion at the Brussels World's Fair in 1958. Several excellent compositions merging treated vocal sounds with electronic ones have also been produced, among them Stockhausen's *Gesang der Jünglinge* ("Song of the Youths in the Fiery Furnace," 1956) and Berio's *Visages* (1961). Taped sounds have been combined with traditional live ones with good results and have also been used to provide accompaniments and backgrounds for narratives and recitations (Sollberger's *Music for Sophocles' "Antigone,"* 1968). The medium is obviously versatile.

Why would someone choose to compose by electronic means instead of using the traditional instruments and elements? Aside from the excitement of working in a new medium, there is a need for contemporaneity, for, as many composers believe, a society that has sent men to the moon cannot truly be represented artistically by forms, instruments, and compositional concepts made popular in a time of sailing ships, sealing wax,

*Henry Moore (1898–    ). Family Group (1945). Moore's famous sculpture is another example of a contemporary work reflecting primitive simplicity. (Collection, The Museum of Modern Art, New York. Acquired through the Lillie P. Bliss Bequest)*

and powdered wigs. New sounds, media, and compositional procedures are necessary. Further, through the medium of electronic music, which uses many more pitches than the twelve notes of the traditional octave, composers can make a complete break with tonality, continuing what Schoenberg had begun with serialism. Similarly, tradition has lent musical meanings to the sounds of instruments, just as it has to the twelve tones of the octave. If these instruments are not used, those meanings are not communicated and the traditions are broken. Finally, there is a growing tendency in this century for some composers to try to take over the role of the performer as well, and nowhere can this be more easily done than in electronic music. If a composer makes a tape recording of an electronic composition and the composition is "performed" only when that tape is played, then the composer is ultimately and totally responsible for the work. It is his; no middleman may add any interpretive comment. This can bring instant condemnation for failure, but, for success, there is even greater self-satisfaction and gratification. For that reason alone, the gamble is worthwhile.

Just as there are composers who seek complete control over everything, there are composers who seek no control over anything. There is a concurrent school of composition, championed especially by Cage, dealing with "chance" or *aleatory* music, in which the composition may be the result of the actions, improvisations, discretions, and decisions of the performer. The composer sometimes merely suggests guidelines and sometimes not even those. Cage's *Piano Concert* (not "concerto") consists of a piano part, the sections of which may be played in any order desired, and orchestral parts, which may be played by any number of players who may play the sections in any desired order or play nothing at all. Stockhausen's *Piano Piece XI* similarly permits the performer to play the various sections in any order he chooses. *0'00"*, created by Cage in 1962, is to be performed in any way by anyone. An earlier work, *Imaginary Landscape*, for twelve radios, directed the performers to turn the radios on or off and to adjust the volumes of each according to a time chart; the sound of the composition was the result of chance, depending upon what each radio station was broadcasting at the time of the performance.

That in today's music there is indeed a diversity of means and a disunity of purpose should by now be clear. Thus Cage, the extreme aleatory composer, can coexist with Babbitt, the most controlled of serialists, and both can easily make room for the Stockhausens and the Berios who would work with the new or mix the new with the old. How a composer

**Aleatory music**

composes is still essentially the same—regardless of the medium or the genre, effort and genius are necessary. The new media and concepts of composition are providing exciting dimensions and, in spite of the forebodings and gloomy statements of the alarmists who would see the art in dire peril, music is probably healthier than ever.

COMPOSITIONS EXEMPLIFYING VARIOUS FORMS

*Contrasting Forms*

### Binary

Bach, J. S.:  Suite No. 2, for flute and strings, dance movements
Folksong:  *Aura Lee; Tom Dooley; Greensleeves*
Schubert:  *Ständchen* ("Serenade"), from *Schwanengesang*

### Ternary

Folksong:  *Drink to Me Only with Thine Eyes; Old Folks at Home*
Handel:  "Every Valley," from *Messiah*
Haydn:  Symphony No. 45, in F-sharp minor (*Farewell*), second movement
Plainsong:  *Requiem aeternam*, Mode VI
Tchaikovsky:  Symphony No. 6, in B minor (*Pathétique*), Op. 74, second movement

### Rondo

Beethoven:  Piano Concerto No. 5, in E-flat (*Emperor*), Op. 73, third movement
Beethoven:  Piano Sonata No. 8, in C minor (*Pathétique*), Op. 13, second movement

### Minuet and Trio

Haydn:  Symphony No. 94, in G (*Surprise*), third movement
Haydn:  String Quartet in A, Op. 20, No. 6, third movement

### Scherzo and Trio

Beethoven:  Symphony No. 9, in D minor (*Choral*), Op. 125, second movement
Brahms:  Trio in E-flat, for Horn, Violin, and Piano, Op. 40, second movement
Bruckner:  Symphony No. 6, in A, third movement

*Variation Forms*

### Theme and Variations

Elgar:  *Enigma Variations*, Op. 36
Haydn:  Symphony No. 94, in G (*Surprise*), second movement
Rachmaninoff:  *Rhapsody on a Theme of Paganini*
Ravel:  *Bolero*
Schubert:  Quintet in A (*Trout*), Op. 114, fourth movement
Webern:  *Variations for Orchestra*, Op. 30

### Passacaglia; Chaconne; Ostinato (Ground)

Bach, J. S.:  *Passacaglia and Fugue in C minor*, for organ
Bach, J. S.:  *Crucifixus*, from *Mass in B minor* (ground bass)
Brahms:  Symphony No. 4, in E minor, Op. 98, fourth movement (chaconne)
Copland:  *Passacaglia for Piano*

Hindemith: *Sonata for Cello and Piano in A minor*, Op. 11, third movement (passacaglia)

Holst: Suite No. 1, in E-flat, for Military Band, Op. 28a, first movement (chaconne)

Purcell: "When I Am Laid in Earth," from *Dido and Aeneas* (ground bass)

Stravinsky: *Symphony of Psalms*, third movement (ostinato figure)

### Modified Strophic Song

Debussy: *Fantoches*

Schubert: *Du bist die Ruh*

Schubert: *Die Forelle*

Schubert: *Im Frühling*

*Developmental Forms*

Examples from the Classical period are especially clear, since the symphonies, concertos, string quartets, and sonatas of Haydn (after 1780), Mozart, Beethoven, and Schubert almost always employ the sonata form (which has a development section) as a first movement and, in the case of symphonies, as a last movement.

### Sonata Form

Bartók: Piano Concerto No. 3, first movement

Beethoven: Symphony No. 5, in C minor, Op. 67, first movement

Mozart: Symphony No. 39, in E-flat, K. 543, first movement, fourth movement

Mozart: Symphony No. 40, in G minor, K. 550, first movement, fourth movement

Piston: String Quartet No. 2, first movement

Prokofiev: *"Classical" Symphony*, first movement

Schubert: Octet in F, Op. 166, sixth movement

Wagner: Overture to *Die Meistersinger von Nürnberg*

### Concerto Sonata Form (with double exposition)

Beethoven: Piano Concerto No. 3, in C minor, Op. 37, first movement

Mozart: Horn Concerto No. 3, in E-flat, K. 447, first movement

Prokofiev: Piano Concerto No. 3, in C, first movement (somewhat free)

### Sonata-Rondo

Bartók: *Sonata for Two Pianos and Percussion*, third movement

Beethoven: Symphony No. 8, in F, Op. 93, fourth movement

Smetana: *The Moldau*

*Imitative Forms*

### Canon

Anonymous: *Sumer is icumen in*

Beethoven: Quartet, "Mir ist so wunderbar," from *Fidelio*, Act I

Franck: *Sonata for Violin and Piano, in A*, third movement (two-part canon, with accompanying inner parts)

Mozart: Symphony No. 40, in G minor, K. 550, third movement (within structure of Minuet and Trio)

### Fugue

Bach, J. S.: *Little Fugue in G minor*

Bach, J. S.: *Passacaglia and Fugue in C minor*

Beethoven: *Seid umschlungen, Millionen* section from Symphony No. 9, in D minor (*Choral*), Op. 125, fourth movement (double fugue)

## Fugue (*cont.*)

Britten: *The Young Person's Guide to the Orchestra*, Op. 34, concluding section
Handel: "He Trusted in God," from *Messiah*, Part II
Haydn: "Achieved is the Glorious Work," from *The Creation* (double fugue)
Hovhaness: *Prelude and Quadruple Fugue*
Mozart: Overture to *Die Zauberflöte* (fugal episodes)
Schuman, W.: Symphony No. 3, second movement
Verdi: *Sanctus,* from *Requiem* (double fugue, with antiphonal choruses)
Verdi: "Tutto nel mondo è burla," from *Falstaff* (conclusion of Act IV)

*Expansive Forms*

### Tone Poem
Dukas: *The Sorcerer's Apprentice*
Liszt: *Les Preludes*, Op. 97

### Through-composed Song
Brahms: *Verrat*
Poulenc: *Main dominée par le coeur*
Schubert: *Erlkönig*
Strauss, R.: *Cäcilie*
Wolf: *Blumengruss*

### Miscellaneous Structures
Schoenberg: *Suite for Piano*, Op. 25
Stockhausen: *Gesang der Jünglinge*
Stockhausen: *Kontakte*
Varèse: *Poème Électronique*
Vaughan Williams: *Fantasia on a Theme by Thomas Tallis*

*Juxtapositional Forms*

### Parallel Organum
*Rex caeli, Domine* (see *Masterpieces of Music Before 1750,* Haydn Society Recording HSE 9038, Volume I)

### Free Organum
Leoninus: *Viderunt omnes*

### Motet with Cantus Firmus
Dufay: *Kyrie,* from *Missa Se la face ay pale*

### Quodlibet (Juxtaposition of Melodies)
Stravinsky: *Petrouchka*, Tableau IV
Sullivan: "When the Foeman Bares His Steel," from *The Pirates of Penzance*
Willson: "Pick a Little, Talk a Little," from *The Music Man*

### Juxtaposition of Keys (Bitonality)
Ives: *Psalm 67*
Stravinsky: *Petrouchka*, Tableau II

### Juxtaposition of "Levels of Activity" (e.g. timbre and melody)
Sollberger: *Music for Sophocles' "Antigone"*

part three

MUSICAL GENRES

# 7 : FOR THE SOLO VOICE ~ Song

WHILE the quotations that follow vary considerably in literary intent, the first objectively descriptive, the second and third propagandistic, and the last satiric, each sheds light on some of the approaches to song; together they reveal a basic problem in understanding the nature of song itself.

French song ... is a short lyric poem to which one adds an air to be sung on such intimate occasions as at table, with friends, mistress, or even alone, to relieve boredom for a while, if one is rich, and to help one to bear wretchedness and labor more easily, if one is poor.

Jean-Jacques Rousseau, *Dictionnaire de Musique*, 1764

[The German romanticist] ... in most cases perceives things in a natural way and expresses himself clearly and judiciously. But, when examining his works, one senses that there is something more than this lurking in the background—an attractive, unique half-light, more like dawn than dusk, which causes one to see his otherwise clear-cut outlines under an unfamiliar glow. ...

Robert Schumann, *Neue Zeitschrift für Musik*, 1837

... I should like to read in German eyes something of the dramatic situation, something of the music's joy and grief....

Robert Schumann, *Enthusiastic Letters*, 1835[1]

---

[1]Cited in Oliver Strunk, *Source Readings in Music History* (New York: W. W. Norton & Company, Inc., 1953), p. 839.

At the conclusion of the program, the first ten rows of orchestra chairs were moved back, and Signor Pancake Peti was introduced in his celebrated act with his trained voice. He first put it through such simple tricks as jumping through his hands, running to fetch a thrown ball, standing on its head, etc. Later, they developed into more difficult feats. Signor Peti broke his voice across his knees, spliced it simply with a silk handkerchief ... and ... drew his voice from the left vest pocket of Ontario Bradfield's sweater. The Signor passed from one feat to another in his dazzling Italian manner, and as the curtain fell for the last time, all united in declaring that they had spent one of the most pleasant, enjoyable and disastrous evenings of their lives.

Steven Crane, *The Pike County Puzzle*, 1894

Song is the most ancient form of musical expression, and, because of the intimate, personal, and individual nature of singing, it is also the most varied. This variety is in part a result of the differences among composers and national styles, but springs first from the diversity of man himself.

## *Types of song*

**Popular song**    The term "popular song" may refer to anything from a highly commercialized, flashy version of an ancient folk tune to the throbbing beat of a Rock and Roll lament. The specific meaning of "popular" generally refers to any style with mass appeal, as opposed to "art" music, which is theoretically more urbane and sophisticated. Distinctions of style, however, lead to so many exceptions and similarities as to make separation of the two a pointless task.

Especially attractive in popular music is its essentially youthful and vibrant character. This is reflected not only in the nature of its audience and the general age level of those who specialize in its performance, but also in the remarkably rapid changes in styles and tastes. The restlessness and enthusiasm of the young is easily perceived in much of the music of the mid-twentieth century. Although individual titles may vanish from the scene after a short time, popular music is quick to seize on inventive techniques of composition and, if the history of the interaction between art and popular music is any indication, it will eventually exert a strong influence on our major composers and will in turn continue to be influenced by them. What is especially notable in the various genres of modern popular music, especially folk rock and acid rock, is the fertilization of such techniques of composition as poly-rhythms, irregular phrasing, unusual harmonies, combinations of keys, modality, and electronic media.

*A medieval troubadour performing before a nobleman's family, guests, vassals, and adherents. Such performances were not only major sources of light entertainment in the medieval castle, but were also "newscasts" that informed the audience of outside events and reminded them of the lessons and events of history in artistic fashion. (The Bettmann Archive)*

**Folksong**

The natural way in which nations, peoples, and communities express themselves musically is through folksong. It is a melodic outpouring, often transferred from one person to another without benefit of notation; it is subject to infinite variation of text, rhythm, and pitch and, in most cases, is attributable to no one person as composer.

There are many folksongs that have such adroitly shaped melodies that they represent the most sensitive sort of artistic communication. Consider the exquisite grace of *The Ash-Grove* or *Down By the Sally Gardens*, the poignancy of *Lord Randall* and *Barbara Allen*, or the passion and intensity of *Black Is the Color of My True Love's Hair*. These are anonymous "songs of the people," but have all the sophistication and artfulness of the world's great vocal literature.

Simplicity is often a characteristic of folk music. Phrasing may be quite regular, range conveniently limited, and accompaniments kept to a minimum. Folksongs are usually *strophic*; that is, the several verses of the poetic text are set to the same music. These are some of the ways in which folksong generally reflects its amateur origins.

This is not to say, however, that a fine performer of folk music has nothing to work with, for a superior singer can forge a great emotional and artistic experience from a seemingly naive piece of music. Furthermore, complexity is by no means a sign of virtue, nor is simplicity an indication of weakness. Indeed, the way of simplicity is often the most potent and sensitive form of artistic communication. Simplicity is an apparent quality in both *Greensleeves* and *Were You There When They Crucified My Lord?*, yet the beauty and appropriateness of both text and music can scarcely be improved. *Barbara Allen*, *The Riddle Song*, and

John Jacob Niles, a famous folksinger, accompanies himself on a lute. (The Bettmann Archive)

*He's Gone Away* are other examples of apparently simple musical structures with great poetic and melodic beauty and meaning.

America's history has produced a variety of folklike songs which were formally composed but still are representatitve of a particular aspect or activity of society. Among these are cowboy ballads (*The Streets of Laredo*), narrative ballads (*Casey Jones*), minstrel songs and sentimental ballads. A nineteenth-century composer of the last two types was Stephen Collins Foster. Most of his minstrel songs have, like the minstrel shows, disappeared from the scene. A few of his songs, however, have remained to become part of American lore, among them *Jeannie With the Light Brown Hair, Nelly Bly*, and *Beautiful Dreamer*. All these possess a timeless grace and charm.

The position of composed folksong in America today is of special interest, for the idiom of the quasi-country ballad or simple song with refrain has become a major medium of social protest and comment. Such emotional vehicles as *We Shall Overcome* or *Blowin' in the Wind* are not conceived anonymously from the roots of a nation, but are compositions specifically designed to sway the hearts of men through music. This has, of course, been the main goal of song composition throughout history, but its political and social application in recent years has been made more telling because of the diffusion of these songs through various communications media.

One particular type of folksong has exerted such a potent influence in American culture that it warrants separate attention. The *spiritual*, especially the religious expression of the American Negro, although existing also as the "white spiritual," is an important example of a type of song springing from the diverse roots of a segment of a population. It is so much a part of American culture that it exists not only as an autonomous style, but also as a basic element of commercial song, jazz, blues, and various derivative works. Its poetry is dialect, its notation often uncertain, but its rhythmic ingenuity and melodic strength identify it as one of the most searching expressions of the human condition.

**The spiritual**

The essential quality of the Negro spiritual represents a combination of an inherent sense of rhythmic vitality, intensity, and zeal. Often used as a means of coordinating movements of work (*Dis Ol' Hammer*), the texts of the spirituals reveal primarily faith in a better world to come and surcease from the agonies of slavery. They are sometimes jubilant and hopeful (*Little David Play on Your Harp*), sometimes mournful and full of wretchedness (*Nobody Knows De Trouble I've Seen*).

A singer from the Kentucky mountains. Some of the most poignant and powerful folksongs are Negro spirituals. Accompanying himself on a banjo, this man sings of his memories and visions, his religion and philosophy. (The Bettmann Archive)

Response between a soloist or leader and a group or congregation is a frequent trait of these songs, as is the use of shouts and calls ("Yeah!" "Amen," etc.). Syncopation (*Little David Play on Your Harp* and *Shout All Over God's Heaven*) is frequently used, and melodies are often based on pentatonic and modal scales.

While the spiritual is basically sacred and meant to be sung in groups, its counterpart, the *blues,* is secular and soloistic. It is a strophic song in which each strophe consists of three lines of text over a twelve-measure structure. Originally the text of the three lines was identical, but the third eventually became either a variant or a conclusion of the thought expressed in the first two lines. This Afro-American folk type is the main link between Negro folk music and jazz, and thus is one of the most important types of American music. Clarity of structure, the opportunity for melodic, rhythmic, and textual improvisation provided by its soloistic character, and the use of melodies in the minor mode are characteristic of both blues and jazz and identify the genealogy of the most American of musical styles.

The position of the Negro spiritual in American musical life was enthusiastically proclaimed by the famous Bohemian composer Antonin Dvořák, who, in an article published in the *New York Herald* in May, 1893, asserted:

In the Negro melodies of America I find all that is needed for a great and noble school of music. They are pathetic, tender, passionate, melancholy, bold, merry, gay or what you will. There is nothing in the whole range of composition which cannot be supplied from this source ... I am satisfied that the future music of this country must be founded on what are called the Negro melodies.[2]

### *Art song*

*Art song* is an urbane, conscious work of a creative intellect trained in the art of music and devoted to the careful mirroring of words in a musical fabric that reveals the various meanings of the text.

The great composers of art song have lavished care on their treatments of all the elements of music that may relate to a text. Although there is much minor poetry set to music, most of the greatest songs use poetry by the leading figures of literature, including Goethe, Heine, Baudelaire, Sandburg, Frost, Ronsard, Rimbaud, and others. In general, the literary content of an art song is the original inspiration for the song itself. When set by an imaginative composer, the imagery and word-sounds of the poem are reflected in the music in such a way that they intensify the meaning of the poem. Perhaps the words of one of Schumann's biographers may best clarify the role of poetry as it developed in the nineteenth century:

... Whereas in the eighteenth century emotion was only a by-product of craftsmanship, in the nineteenth it was the sole justification for the act of creating. Poetry to the younger romantics was a means of crystallizing personal, emotional

---

[2]Quoted in Alec Robertson, *Dvořák* (London: J. M. Dent and Sons, Ltd., and New York: Farrar, Straus & Giroux, Inc., 1945), p. 170. An extended excerpt from this article may be found in David Ewen's *The World of Great Composers* (Englewood Cliffs, N.J.: Prentice-Hall, Inc., 1962), pp. 370–72.

experience, of photographing in words spontaneous individual reactions to moonlight, spring and twilight—or using these things as symbols of love and longing, hope and despair. Winds, trees, birds and streams were forever in secret communication with them, whispering messages of comfort or sorrow to their lovelorn hearts.[3]

Some composers have attempted consciously to capture in their art songs that simplicity often found in the folksong. A number of art songs have become so popular that they have become an integral part of the lore and heritage of a nation, even though their composers were representative of the intelligentsia rather than of the mass of people from whom folksongs theoretically derive. Two examples that immediately come to mind are Brahms's *Wiegenlied* ("Cradle Song") and Schubert's *Ständchen* ("Serenade").

The art song was essentially a romantic creation, and Romanticism in its earlier years was fundamentally a German expression. It should not be surprising, then, to note that the first welling of song as a significant area of musical activity came from the pens of German composers. During the last century and a half, German composers have written a flood of art songs, or, as they are also known, *Lieder* (singular: *Lied*; German: "song").

Beethoven was the first composer to devote great energy to the composition of song, making it an important field of composition. To Schubert, song was the center of musical composition, although he, like Beethoven, was a superb symphonist and composer of instrumental chamber music. The host of German song composers after Schubert included Schumann, Brahms, Franz, Wolf, Mahler, Richard Strauss, and Berg. Franz and Wolf are unusual because they are known primarily for their songs; the others achieved fame for their work in other genres as well.

German song, throughout its history, can be identified by its lyricism, emotionalism, and highly picturesque accompaniments. The rich vowels and often guttural sounds of the German language give its poetry an urgency not to be found in any other tongue, and this quality has been reflected in the music of the leading German song composers.

The majority of art songs are in a modified strophic form. That is to say there are two or more recognizable musical verses, but there are significant changes in one or more of the verses to underscore the text. These

[3]Joan Chissell, *Schumann* (London: J. M. Dent and Sons, Ltd., and New York: Farrar, Straus & Giroux, Inc., 1948), p. 132.

*Brahms accompanying a singer. One of the greatest composers of song, Brahms invested his Lieder with a rhythmic complexity and dramatic lyricism belied by his stolid appearance. (The Bettmann Archive)*

changes may be in the accompaniment or in the vocal line and may vary from the very subtle to the very obvious. Schubert's *Im Frühling* is such a song.

Franz Schubert: *Im Frühling* ("In Spring"), 1826
Poem by Ernest Schulze

*Still sitz ich an des Hügels Hang, der Himmel ist so klar,*
Quietly I sit on the slope of the hill, the sky is so clear,

*Das Lüftchen spielt im grünen Tal, wo ich beim erstem Frühlingsstrahl*
A light breeze plays in the green vale where I once in early spring's sun

*Einst, ach so glücklich war!*
Was, alas, so happy!

*Wo ich an ihrer Seite ging so traulich und so nah,*
Where I by her side walked so intimately and near,

*Und tief in dunkeln Felsenquell den schönen Himmel blau und hell,*
And deep in the dark mountain spring, I saw the beautiful sky, blue and bright

*Und sie in Himmel sah.*
And her in heaven.

*Sieh, wie der bunte Frühling schon aus Knosp und Blüte blickt!*
See how the many-hued Spring already is budded and blossomed!

*Nicht alle Blüten sind mir gleich, am liebsten pflückt' ich vom dem Zweig,*
Not all flowers are to me alike, I gathered only from the spray

*Von welchem sie gepflückt!*
Picked by my beloved herself!

*Denn alles ist wie damals noch, die Blumen, das Gefild;*
For all now is as it was then the flowers and the fields;

*Die Sonne scheint nicht minder hell, nicht minder freundlich schwimmt in Quell*
The sun shines no less brightly, no less pleasantly swims in the spring

*Das blaue Himmelsbild.*
The image of the blue sky.

*Es wandeln nur sich Will und Wahn, es wechseln Lust und Streit;*
Will and illusion are turned about, joy and discord interchanged;

*Vorüber flieht der Liebe Glück, und nur die Liebe bleibt zurück,*
The happiness of love has passed along, and only love remains,

*Die Lieb und ach, das Lied!*
Love and, alas! sorrow!

*O wär ich doch ein Vöglein nur dort an dem Wiesenhang,*
If only I were a little bird, there on the meadow's slope,

*Dann blieb ich auf den Zweigen hier, und säng ein süsses Lied von ihr*
I would stay here in these branches, and would sing a sweet song of her

*Den ganzen Sommer lang.*
The whole summer long.

This exquisite song has all the characteristics of its time. One is the poignant, longing quality of the text, which bespeaks the Romantic melancholy found throughout the arts of the nineteenth century. Another is the sweet lyricism of Schubert's melody, one of this composer's most consistent traits. Finally, one finds in almost every phrase the Romanticist's view of nature as innocent and pure.

Schubert's melody and accompaniment undergo a number of significant changes, although the division of the song into three verses (strophes), which are similar, if not exactly alike, can be easily discerned. The first noticeable example of the close relation between text and music occurs in the first strophe. The opening phrase of the voice part treats the words "Quietly I sit on the slope of the hill, the sky is so clear." The motion here is simple and calm, with but one note per syllable. Note, too, how the hillside is suggested by the easy descent of the melody.

**EX. 7.1 SCHUBERT**
*Im Frühling,* 1st strophe, bars 5–6

Still sitz ich an des Hü - gels Hang, der Him - mel ist so klar

The next phrase provides a similar melody in a descending scale, but, since the text now refers to the playing of the gentle breeze, the melody is somewhat ornamented with two notes per syllable; the result is a more capricious melodic setting.

**EX. 7.2** *Ibid.*
bars 7–8

Das Lüft-chen spielt im grü - nen Tal, wo ich beim er - sten Früh-lings-strahl

The listener should be aware of the continual change in the piano part. The first verse is consistently accompanied by a quiet, chordal background.

**EX. 7.3** *Ibid.*
bars 5–6, with accompaniment

Still sitz ich an des Hü - gels Hang, der Him - mel ist so klar

The second verse, however, which deals with the loveliness of spring, is accompanied by a delicate filigree of notes in the treble part (the top line, played by the right hand) of the piano.

**EX. 7.4** *Ibid.*
2nd strophe, bars 23–24

Nicht al - le Blü - ten sind mir gleich, am lieb - sten pflückt' ich von den Zweig,

The most dramatic alteration comes at the start of the third strophe, where the poet's bitterness comes to the fore. Here the music moves suddenly into the minor mode and the underlying rhythm changes from the gentle *um-ta-ta-ta* figure of the second strophe to a much more agitated series of chords. The listener will note that the vocal line is substantially the same as the end of the first strophe, with but minor alterations; the truly expressive change is created in the piano part.

EX. 7.5 *Ibid.*
bars 32–33

The transition to the final measures of the last strophe, with the words "If only I were a little bird," is strikingly ironic, because the impression left by the harsh chords of the beginning of this final strophe gives the lie to what is otherwise a literal return to the simple movement of an earlier part of the song.

Schubert's *Erlkönig* is an example of another type, the through-composed song (German: *durchkomponiert*), so-called because the music is shaped continually by the narrative. Goethe's poem, on which the song is based, is a stark drama, describing a wild ride of a father and child through a fearsome, dark forest. The child, deathly ill, imagines that he sees the legendary Erl King cajoling him to leave the land of the living, but the father attempts to comfort the lad by telling him he sees only the forest mists. The evil Erl King is triumphant, however, for, when they reach home, the father sees that his son has died in his arms.

The opening pounding triplets in the piano accompaniment give the listener a sense of the panic, the galloping, the urgency of the poem.

EX. 7.6 SCHUBERT
*Erlkönig*, bars 1–3

Each of the personages in the story has a melody of distinctive character. The father's melody is rhythmically solid and maintains a steady, upward direction.

**EX. 7.7** *Ibid.* bars 37–40

The child's high-pitched fear is not only higher on the staff but wavers up and down.

**EX. 7.8** *Ibid.* bars 73–79

For his last three utterances, the child starts with the words "mein Vater." Each anxious call to his father is pitched higher, increasing the tension that signifies the child's fear. The cajoling of the Erl King is equally unmistakable.

**EX. 7.9** *Ibid.* bars 58–65

The final horror—the death of the child—is for Schubert too tragic for lyric melody. Instead, he uses the blunt narrative of recitative; all the singer can do is intone the phrase, "in seinen Armen das Kind war todt" —"in his arms, the child was dead!"

Franz Schubert: *Erlkönig* ("Erl King"), 1815
Poem by Johann Wolfgang von Goethe

*Wer reitet so spät durch Nacht und Wind?*
Who rides so late through the night and the wind?

*Es ist der Vater mit seinem Kind;*
It is the father with his child;

*Er hat den Knaben wohl in dem Arm,*
He has the boy safe in his arms,

*Er fasst ihn sicher; er hält ihn warm.*
He holds him tightly, he keeps him warm.

*Mein Sohn, was birgst du so bang dein Gesicht?*
My son, why do you hide your face in fear?

*Siehst, Vater, du den Erlkönig nicht?*
Father, don't you see the Erl King?

*Den Erlenkönig mit Kron' und Schweif?*
The Erl King, with crown and robe?

*Mein Sohn, es ist ein Nebelstreif.*
My son, it is a wisp of fog.


*"Du liebes Kind, komm, geh mit mir!*
"You lovely child, come, go with me.

*Gar schöne Spiele spiel ich mit dir;*
Such pleasant games I'll play with thee;

*Manch' bunte Blumen sind an dem Strand,*
Abundant flowers are on the shore,

*Meine Mutter hat manch' gülden Gewand."*
My mother has many golden garments."


*Mein Vater, mein Vater, und hörest du nicht,*
My father, my father, didn't you hear

*Was Erlenkönig mir leise verspricht?*
What the Erl King whispered to me?

*Sei ruhig, bleibe ruhig, mein Kind;*
Be calm, stay quiet, my child;

*In dürren Blättern säuselt der Wind.*
Among the dead leaves the wind is stirring.


*"Willst, feiner Knabe, du mit mir gehn?*
"Lovely boy, will you go with me?

*Meine Töchter sollen dich warten schön;*
My lovely daughters shall wait on thee;

*Meine Töchter führen den nächtlichen Reihn*
My daughters lead nightly revels

*Und wiegen und tanzen und singen dich ein,*
And will cradle thee and dance and sing for thee,

*Sie wiegen und tanzen und singen dich ein."**
They'll sing and dance for thee and rock thee to sleep."


*Line added by Schubert.

*Schmid. A "Schubertiad" in a Viennese Home. Schubert's music was the main reason for frequent gatherings of his friends, who met in middle-class homes to hear him accompany performances of his songs, play his own piano works, or provide piano music for various party games. This engraving was quite possibly created some time after the composer's death, but the likeness of Schubert, seated at the piano, is excellent, and the type of gathering is typical of his time. (Courtesy of the New York Public Library)*

*Mein Vater, mein Vater, und siehst du nicht dort*
My father, my father, don't you see

*Erlkönigs Töchter am düstern Ort?*
The Erl King's daughters, there in that dark spot?

*Mein Sohn, mein Sohn, ich seh' es genau,*
My son, my son, I see very well

*Es scheinen die alten Weiden so grau.*
That it is only the aged willows, so grey.

*"Ich liebe dich, mich reizt deine schöne Gestalt;*
"I love you, your beautiful form charms me,

*Und bist du nicht willig, so brauch' ich Gewalt."*
And if you be not willing, I use force."

*Mein Vater, mein Vater, jetzt fasst er mich an!*
My father, my father, now he is grasping me!

*Erlkönig hat mir ein Leids gethan!*
The Erl King is hurting me!

*Dem Vater grauset's, er reitet geschwind,*
The father shudders, he gallops furiously,

*Er hält in Armen das ächzende Kind,*
He holds in his arm the failing child,

*Erreicht den Hof mit Müh' und Noth;*
Reaches the house with fear and dread;

*In seinen Armen das Kind war todt.*
In his arms, the child was dead.

**Song cycles**     There are a number of sets of songs under a common title, with or without melodies or rhythms common to several of the songs in the set. These are known as *song cycles, Lieder cycles* or, simply, *cycles.*

Beethoven's *An die ferne Geliebte* ("To the Distant Beloved"), a group of six musically related songs on poems by Jeitteles, was historically the first cycle. Schubert composed three cycles, *Die schöne Müllerin* ("The Fair Miller's Maid"; twenty songs), *Die Winterreise* ("The Winter's Journey"; twenty-four songs), and *Schwanengesang* ("Swan Song"; fourteen songs). In the first two cycles, he followed Beethoven's lead and used poetry from a single source (incidentally the same poet, Wilhelm Müller, for both). In *Schwanengesang*, three poets are represented.

The practice of cyclic composition, furthered by Schumann, Mahler, and many others, has continued into modern times; Bernstein's delightful *I Hate Music* and Barber's moody *Hermit Songs* are well-known examples.

Ordinarily, singers perform cycles in their entirety, or with most of the songs left in order and intact. Occasionally, a song or two will be lifted from its cycle context and performed separately. The most notable example of this is Schubert's famous *Ständchen*, the fourth song of *Schwanengesang*.

Cycles may be narrative, as is *Die schöne Müllerin*, or they may be simply related to a common subject. Schumann's *Dichterliebe* ("A Poet's Love"), however, is not a narrative but rather a series of intense songs on the theme of love's anguish and intensity.

**National aspects**     French vocal music is significantly conditioned by the French lan-
**of the art song**     guage's intimate, relatively closed vowels and the voicing in music of un-accented final syllables. Compare, for example, the French and German words for "week," *semaine* (suh-MEN-uh) and *Woche* (VOH-chuh, the

"ch" being guttural).[4] The French is soft, liquid, and full of closed vowels, while the German has a much more explosive sound. There are, of course, German words and expressions with lyric, gentle combinations of vowels and consonants, but as a language it has not the pliancy of French, although it can be considerably more obvious in its expression of feeling.

As a result of the qualities of the French tongue, French composers have created a body of vocal literature identified by subtle rhythmic changes, delicate harmonic colorings of word meanings, a generally restrained approach to dynamics, and an overall elegance and preciseness that may be discerned in all the French arts.

The high point of French art song was reached near the beginning of the twentieth century, when Debussy, Fauré, Duparc, and Ravel turned their attention to it. More recently the songs of Poulenc have continued the French tradition of clarity of expression and care in *prosody* (the art of setting words to music without distorting their accents or grammatical meaning).

The strong tradition of opera in Italy has so dominated vocal literature that virtually no significant art song repertoire has been created by Italian composers. There is a wondrously fertile field of folk music and composed song that has had a considerable impact on Italian opera, but the very ebullience and emotionalism of the Italian spirit has tended to give both operatic aria and folksong an expansiveness of expression quite opposed to the intense intimacy of the *Lied* or *chanson*.

In England, the art song has achieved special eminence through the compositions of Holst, Britten, and Vaughan Williams. These composers have not only written a great number of original songs in a variety of styles (see Britten's treatment of Rimbaud poems in *Les Illuminations*), but have also arranged many English folksongs in ways that give them great pungency and variety without altering their essential "Englishness."

In other European nations, art song composers have been active. Rachmaninoff, Mussorgsky, Tchaikovsky, Grieg, Sibelius, Falla, Granados, and Dvořák have all given truly beautiful expression to the spirits of their countries through the medium of song.

Art song in the United States has yet to be considered a major area of composition by leading serious composers, Barber and Ives excepted. The emphasis in twentieth-century America has been less on autonomous

---

[4]Spoken French is very different from sung French in its treatment of final syllables. The final "e" of *semaine* is silent in normal speech, but is voiced when sung.

songs or song cycles than on popular ballads and songs for the musical stage. A number of the latter, such as Kern's *Old Man River* and Rodgers' *Oh, What a Beautiful Morning*, have virtually become a part of American lore.

Just as many instrumentalists find their greatest satisfaction in instrumental chamber music, many pianists and singers turn to art songs as the epitome of vocal intimacy and sophistication. Song recitals are not the most popular of musical events precisely because of these traits. Where kindred souls meet to share the pleasures of great music, however, the art song stands side by side with the string quartet as an inexhaustible source of intellectual and emotional gratification.

# 8 : FOR THE STAGE

ANY artistic communication is in a sense dramatic in that it expresses something in as vital a fashion as possible. For the purposes of this chapter, "dramatic music" will refer to vocal music that illuminates an extended text dealing with a story or a scene enacted before an audience. This includes a variety of dramatic vehicles, ranging from the grandest of operas to simple, lighthearted entertainments. The oratorio, mass, cantata, and various choral forms, all of which harbor an element of drama, will be considered in the following chapter. Ballet, which is essentially a visually dramatic genre utilizing instrumental music, will be taken up in Chapter 12.

## Opera

Types of dramatic music written specifically to be acted and staged include *opera, musical comedy, operetta, ballet,* and *masque*. Of them all, opera has been the most attractive to the great composers, and its greater works have been the most enduring. Defined simply, opera is a theatrical vehicle in which characterization, situation, plot, and atmosphere are revealed primarily through musical means, especially in music for the voice. There are operas that use spoken dialogue, but these special types (*Singspiel* and *opéra comique,* for example) will usually resort to music for all significant situations.

The key to appreciating and enjoying opera is the understanding of its conventions and traditions. Because it relies primarily on song for the conveyance of mood, characterization, and story line, opera is necessarily different from the spoken drama. In the first place, it takes longer to sing a text than it does to speak it; second, there is the unique capacity in opera for presenting several conflicting viewpoints simultaneously through the ensemble (duet, trio, etc.), a feature that lays more stress on music than on text since clarity of text is inversely proportional to musical complexity; third, operas use choruses, which, while musically satisfactory, are dramatically awkward, since it is difficult for a large group to move about naturally. Beautiful singing requires great care in breathing, tone production, and diction, not to mention musicianship; therefore, natural stage movement is very difficult to achieve, with the result that singers often will have to sacrifice acting for the sake of musical values. In most cases, the text (called the *libretto*, literally a "little book") of an opera is not a self-sufficient play, but rather is designed to aid the music, since the music does most of the communication. Note the words, "in most cases." There have been significant moments in the history of opera when composers have considered the text to be the most important element; there have been other periods when the music was so much emphasized over the words that the latter were not infrequently reduced to the most abject doggerel.[1]

Another aspect of opera to be discussed if problems of appreciation are to be overcome is its essentially European heritage. Since its birth early in the seventeenth century, opera has been a major compositional form in all the great Western nations with the exception of England and the nations of the Western Hemisphere. The English, primarily a middle-class nation, relied on imported opera and such imported opera composers as Handel; only in the twentieth century has a native English opera been firmly established through the work of Britten. In the United States, too, a relative adolescent among nations, opera has been primarily an imported art form. The difference between the position of opera in this country and the position of other musical genres is that the latter have universally been embraced by most leading American composers, but, save for a few, opera has not. There are many reasons why this is true. For one, the last two hundred years of American history have been concerned primarily with expanding America's frontiers and building its economic muscles. There has been little time, interest, or money available

---

[1]Beaumarchais, complaining about Baroque opera, once wrote that "anything not worth saying is sung."

*Honoré Daumier (1808–1879).*
Operatic Finale *(1852).*
*A satire of emotion*
*and virtuosity in*
*Romantic grand opera.*
*(The Bettmann Archive)*

for the establishment of an indigenous operatic tradition. Also, there seems to have been a deep-seated distrust of anything that smacked of the aristocratic—which opera most certainly has during its history—hence the general populace has considered opera to be the plaything of land-barons, financial titans, social climbers, and other similar types.

There are both historical and practical reasons for the aristocratic orientation of opera. Throughout its history, opera has been the most expensive art form, requiring the services of highly trained singers, dancers, instrumentalists, stage designers, and others. The support of the wealthy has been required if opera was to exist at all. It should not be surprising then, that operatic plots have been mostly concerned with great heroes, generals, queens, goddesses, and the like. Indeed, librettos that have focused on the lower classes or on events of everyday life are notable by their scarcity and are found primarily in comic operas or in the slice-of-life compositions of late nineteenth- and twentieth-century realists such as Puccini (*La Bohême*) or Bizet (*Carmen*).

The subject matter of opera has also mitigated its "grass roots" appeal in America. The generally aristocratic characters, the historical episodes, the legends, and the stylization of their realization on the operatic stage are foreign to America's history and its lore, whereas Europeans consider these subjects to be part of their heritage. Still another reason for the relative dearth of operatic composition in America is purely economic: there are not enough opera companies able to perform new operas or to give young composers "proving grounds" to learn how to compose them. If an opera is performed, royalties are very slim, recordings are few, performances are limited in number. It is not surprising that most American composers devote themselves to more lucrative areas of composition.

And yet there is a dynamic popular interest in opera in the America of the mid-twentieth century, in spite of the fact that opera is not a basic part of its culture. Performances across the land are well attended and often sold out, recordings of noted operas enjoy voluminous sales, and the regular broadcasts of opera each Saturday afternoon from New York's Metropolitan Opera House reach more than ten million people.

Italian, French, and German operas continue to be those most frequently performed, however. Operas performed by the major companies in the United States are generally in their original language, for it is the current practice in America's relatively few opera houses to hire international stars to do the singing. These famous singers find it impractical to learn the same role in several different languages, and, if they are to be available to American opera houses, productions must be in the original language of the opera. Some European companies also follow this practice, although most often operas in Europe are translated into the language of the audience.

There is a trend toward the use of the English language, especially in smaller companies and opera workshops, but progress is necessarily slow and tentative. Good translations and singers willing to relearn their roles are hard to find. It should be remembered, too, that there is an intimate relationship between the vowels and accents of a language and the music written for it. To alter these sounds may give a melody a strikingly different character, perhaps removed from the original intent of the composer.

Opera is a flourishing, varied, exciting art form. Its enjoyment can be enhanced by acquiring a basic vocabulary of musical terms, by becoming familiar with the different things composers have tried to do, and, most of all, by becoming familiar with some of the famous operas, including their music and their stories. Although opera is usually considered a *vocal* art form, one should remember that often the orchestra is very important; in some cases, it is the major participant in the drama. This fact should be kept in mind during the following discussions that concern primarily vocal materials.

Opera utilizes several styles of solo vocal music. The first of these is **Vocal styles in opera** the *recitative*, a stylized declamation that is generally narrative, expository, or conversational. This style of singing is supported by chords or short connecting passages played by an orchestra or a keyboard instrument. Sometimes, particularly in eighteenth-century opera, the recitative is delivered very quickly with the simple accompaniment of a harpsichord; this is called *recitativo secco*, or "dry recitative." In the opera of the nineteenth century, where the orchestration is more colorful and the declamation more varied and patently emotional, one will hear the slower, yet more forceful, *recitativo accompagnato*, or "accompanied recitative." This latter type of recitative is also known as *recitativo stromentato*, or "instrumented recitative." ("There were shepherds. . .," from Handel's *Messiah*, is an example of *recitativo secco*; "And lo! the angel of the Lord. . ." is an example of the *accompagnato*.) Since the function of traditional recitative is to render events and dialogue clearly, the text is more important than the music. Note values tend to be somewhat similar, there are no regular rhythmic patterns, and the rise and fall of the melody is relatively unclimactic and small in range.

Used primarily for the exposition of the events of a story or for simple narration or dialogue, recitative attempts to stylize the accents of normal speech. It is, then, musical prose, identified often by a one-note-per-syllable setting of the words, repeated notes, irregular rhythms and accents, varied phrase lengths, a generally chordal style of accompaniment, and a continual change of melody in accordance with the text.

A second major vocal style to be found in opera is the *aria* (Italian: "song"). An aria is the musical equivalent of poetry, with a metric regularity or strong sense of pulse quite different from the unmetrical recitative. An aria has a readily perceived tune and a relatively flowing series of musical phrases (usually repeated at one point or another), often reaching a climax requiring the singer to utilize the most sophisticated of vocal techniques to meet the demands of range, phrase, and timbre. Also, there are apt to be many notes per syllable or high, sustained pitches on particularly significant words or at points of melodic climax.

The aria is used for those portions of a text that express sentiment, contemplation, outpouring of feeling, or summary of action. Particularly in operas of the seventeenth and eighteenth centuries, and in Italian and French operas of the nineteenth century, the aria has been the focus of attention for composers, singers, and listeners alike.

There is a third type of vocal style, the *arioso*, which combines elements of both the aria and the recitative. The arioso is a flowing sort of declamation with a considerable degree of melodic "arch" and enriched accompaniment, yet without the extended and repeated phrasing found in the aria. Ariosos are through-composed, although they may make some use of musical repetition. Much of Wagner's vocal melody is in this style, and the passages given to the role of Jesus in Bach's *Passion According to St. Matthew* are particularly famous examples of the arioso.

In addition to the singing styles of the recitative, the aria, and the arioso, modern composers make use of a half-spoken, half-sung technique known as *Sprechstimme* (German: "speech-song"). Its pitch is indistinct and is notated on the musical staff by crosslike symbols instead of notes.

**Baroque opera: Monteverdi and Handel**

In the late sixteenth century, a group of men gathered regularly in one of the salons of Florence, Italy, to discuss music and poetry. Known as the *Camerata* (Italian: *camera*, "room"), these poets, philosophers, and other intelligentsia were interested in reviving Greek drama, which they imagined to have been sung, in Jacopo Peri's words, "[in] a kind of music more significant than ordinary speech, but so much less so than the song as to take a middle position between them."[2]

The invention of the recitative style was their solution to the problem of revival. Save for some songs and choruses at the ends of scenes, the earliest operas were nothing but slow recitative, with the words completely dominating the music. It was Monteverdi who transformed this essentially tedious style into a passionate musical drama, using not only the recitative, but also rich orchestral music, sustained arioso, poignant arias and ensembles, powerful characterizations, and melodic variety. The great *L'Orfeo* ("The Story of Orpheus") first performed in 1607, was his first opera. *L'Incoronazione di Poppaea* ("The Coronation of Poppaea," 1642), another of his masterpieces, combines exquisite music with stunning dramatic insight in a manner timely to all ages. In the truest sense of the word, Monteverdi was the father of opera.

Handel, the greatest opera composer of the late Baroque era, is represented on the recordings accompanying this volume by excerpts from his oratorio, *Messiah* (1741). Handel was one of the foremost composers of *opera seria*, a genre typified by elaborately ornamented melodies, highly complex and artificial dramatic situations, and, most of all, by vocal

---

[2]Peri's manifesto is quoted in full in Oliver Strunk, *Source Readings in Music History* (New York: W. W. Norton and Co., Inc., 1950), pp. 373–76.

virtuosity. It is not at all strange to refer to a sacred oratorio in a section on opera, since Handel and his contemporaries imbued all their vocal music with the ornamental graces and arching curves of operatic melody, a stylistic feature which binds *Messiah*, the epitome of sacred music, with *Julius Caesar, Alcina,* and other works written for the operatic stage. "Every Valley Shall Be Exalted," an aria from *Messiah,* reflects the essence of Baroque opera in its sparkling runs of many notes per syllable (called *melismas*) and its architectural symmetry.

Handel's approach to emotion is highly stylized. As with all Baroque arias, only one or two basic *affections* (moods or emotions) are expressed, each affection prevailing for an entire segment of the aria. If the Baroque opera composer wished to reveal a character in a further dimension, a second aria based on another affection would be sung. Baroque *opera seria* was thus a series of affections, presented one at a time in a sequence of arias.

Splendor was a major aspect of opera in this period. Audiences expected the singer to improvise lavishly on the printed notes of the melody; the scenery was complex, varied, and ornate, and the plots dealt with classical mythology and history, using costuming, ballet, and theatrical effect in ingenious, if artificial, ways. Always the aim was effect, visual and aural.

Classicism, the spirit of the late eighteenth century, rebelled against the highly decorative music, the complicated plots dealing with unreal people, and the abstract emotional expression of the Baroque. This reaction was first expressed during the middle and late eighteenth century in comic opera (called by the Italians *opera buffa*), a satirical medium that stressed short, simple musical phrases, lower class protagonists, ensembles, mercurial plot developments, and stories revealing the foibles of human nature, especially of the nobility. The reform of the *opera seria*, stimulated especially by Christoph Willibald von Gluck, came somewhat later and exerted less impact.

**Classical opera: Mozart**

The pinnacle of Classical opera was reached in the music of Mozart, represented in the recordings by an excerpt from *Le Nozze di Figaro* ("The Marriage of Figaro," 1786).

Mozart's gifts, prodigious in all types of music, are noticeable in practically every work he created. *Idomeneo* is pure opera seria, *Così fan tutte* ("Women Are Like That"), an uproarious farce, *Figaro,* a brilliant satire, and *Don Giovanni*—the *Hamlet* of opera—a unique blend of the ribald and the tragic, the comic and the epic.

It is not at all a criticism of his arias to suggest that the greatest glory of Mozart's operatic music is the ensemble, for no composer before or since has been as deft as Mozart in giving several people different melodies and texts to sing simultaneously, while at the same time characterizing them and driving the story forward.

Based on a play by Beaumarchais, *Le Nozze di Figaro* is concerned with the efforts of Figaro and his fiancée, Susanna, to outwit their lecherous lord, the Count Almaviva, who has grown cold toward his lovely wife and seeks to fasten his affections on Susanna. The Count is relying on Figaro's indebtedness to the elderly Marcellina, whom Figaro has promised to marry in default of a loan, to get Figaro out of the way. In this plan, the Count is aided by a scandal-loving notary, Don Curzio, and another gentleman of the household, Dr. Bartolo. The scene recorded is the famous sextet from Act III of the opera. A *recitativo secco* precedes the sextet; the ensemble actually begins with Marcellina's unctuous greeting of her long lost son. The text follows.

RECITATIVO SECCO

| | |
|---|---|
| Don Curzio: | *È decisa la lite. O pagarla, o sposarla, ora ammutite.*<br>The case is decided; pay her or marry her. That's the judgment. |
| Marcellina: | *Io respiro.*<br>I breathe again. |
| Figaro: | *Ed io moro.*<br>I'm dying. |
| **Mar:** | *Alfin sposa io sarò d'un uom che adoro.*<br>Finally I shall be the wife of a man I adore. |
| Fig: | *Eccelenza! m'appello...*<br>Your excellency, I appeal... |
| Count: | *È giusta la sentenza. O pagar, o sposar. Bravo, Don Curzio.*<br>The sentence is just: marry or pay. Good work, Don **Curzio.** |
| Curzio: | *Bontà di sua Eccelenza.*<br>Your Excellency is most gracious. |
| Bartolo: | *Che superba sentenza!*<br>What a marvelous sentence! |
| Fig: | *In che superba?*<br>Why marvelous? |
| Bar: | *Siam tutti vendicati.*<br>We are all vindicated. |
| Fig: | *Io non la sposerò.*<br>I shall not marry her. |
| Bar: | *La sposerai.*<br>You will marry her. |

Curzio: *O pagarla, o sposarla, lei t'ha prestati due mille pezzi duri.*
Either pay or marry; she lent you two thousand silver pieces.

Fig: *Son gentiluomo, e senza l'assenso de' miei nobili parenti. . .*
I am a gentleman, and without my parents' approval. . .

Count: *Dove sono? chi sono?*
Where are they? Who are they?

Fig: *Lasciate ancor cercarli; dopo dieci anni io spero di trovarli.*
Let me look for them; in about ten years I hope to find them.

Bar: *Qualche bambin trovato?*
Are you then a foundling?

Fig: *No, perduto, dottor, anzi rubato.*
No, a lostling, Doctor. Rather, I was kidnapped.

Count: *Come?*
How?

Mar: *Cosa?*
So?

Bar: *La prova?*
Where's the proof?

Curzio: *Il testimonio?*
The evidence?

Fig: *L'oro, le gemme, e i ricamati panni, che ne' più teneri anni mi*
The gold, jewels, embroidered linen that my kidnappers found

*ritrovaro addosso i masnadieri, sono gl'indizi veri di mia*
near me in my infancy    are proofs    of my illustrious

*nascità illustre:    e sopra tutto questo al mio braccio impresso*
birth;    and above all this—on my arm there is printed a

*geroglifico.*
symbol.

Mar: *Un spatola impressa al braccio destro?*
A spatula printed on his right arm?

Fig: *E a voi ch'il disse?*
Who told *you* that?

Mar: *O Dio!    È desso.*
O God! It's he!

Fig: *È ver, son io.*
That's true, it's I.

Curzio: *Chi?*
Who?

Count: *Chi?*
Who?

Bar: *Chi?*
Who?

| | | |
|---|---|---|
| **Mar:** | (to Bartolo) *Rafaello!* | |
| | Raphael! | |
| **Bar:** | *E i ladri ti rapir?* | |
| | You say that robbers stole you? | |
| **Fig:** | *Presso un castello.* | |
| | From near a castle. | |
| **Bar:** | (pointing to Marcellina) *Ecco tua madre.* | |
| | Behold your mother! | |
| **Fig:** | *Balia?* | |
| | My wet nurse? | |
| **Bar:** | *No, tua madre.* | |
| | No, your mother. | |
| **Count,** | | |
| **Curzio:** | *Sua madre!* | |
| | His mother! | |
| **Fig:** | *Cosa sento?* | |
| | What am I hearing? | |
| **Mar:** | (pointing to Bartolo) *Ecco tuo padre!* | |
| | Behold your father! | |

SEXTET (portions are repeated)

| | |
|---|---|
| **Mar:** | *Riconosci in questo amplesso una madre, amato figlio.* |
| | With this embrace a mother acknowledges you, beloved son. |
| **Fig:** | *Padre mio, fate lo stesso, non mi fate più arrossir.* |
| | My father, do likewise, let me blush no more. |
| **Bar:** | *Resistenza la coscienza far non lascia al tuo desir.* |
| | My conscience will not let me resist your wishes. |
| **Curzio:** | *Ei suo padre?   ella sua madre?* |
| | He's his father?   She's his mother? |
| **Count:** | (aside) *Son smarrito, son stordito!* |
| | I'm confused, I'm waylaid! |
| **Curzio:** | *L'imeneo non può seguir.* |
| | The marriage cannot take place. |
| **Count:** | (aside) *Meglio è assai di quà partir!* |
| | I'd better leave, fast! |
| **Mar, Bar:** | *Figlio amato!* |
| | Beloved son! |
| **Fig:** | *Parenti amati!* |
| | Beloved parents! |
| **Susanna:** | (entering hurriedly, with a purse) *Alto, alto, signor Conte,* |
| | Wait, my Lord Count, |
| | *mille doppie son qui pronte, a pagar vengo per Figaro, ed a* |
| | here are two thousand silver pieces to ransom Figaro, and to |
| | *porlo in libertà.* |
| | free him. |

| Count, Curzio: | |
|---|---|
| | *Non sappiam com' è la cosa, osservate un poco là.* |
| | We don't know how it happened—look over there. |

| Sus: | |
|---|---|
| | *Già d'accordo colla sposa!   Giusti Dei!   Che infedeltà!* |
| | Lovey-dovey with a wife already! Just God, what treachery! |
| | *Lascia, iniquo.* |
| | Leave me, wretch! |

| Fig: | |
|---|---|
| | *No, t'arresta.   Senti, o cara...* |
| | No, stop.        Listen, dear... |

| Sus: | |
|---|---|
| | *Senti questa.* (slaps him) |
| | You listen to this! |

| Mar. Fig. Bar. | Sus. | Count, Curzio |
|---|---|---|
| *E un effetto di buon core* | *Fremo! smanio dal furore* | *Fremo! smanio dal furore* |
| 'Tis proof of a good heart | I'm trembling with rage, | I'm trembling with rage (He's trembling with rage) |
| *Tutto amore è quel che fa.* | *Una vecchia me la fa!* | *Il destino me la fa!* |
| All girls in love do thus. | An old woman does this to me! | Fate does this to me! (Fate does this to him!) |

| Mar: | |
|---|---|
| | *Lo sdegno calmate mia cara figliuola, sua madre abbraciate* |
| | Calm down, my dear little daughter, his mother embrace, |
| | *che or vostra sarà.* |
| | who now shall be your mother. |

| Sus: | |
|---|---|
| | (to Curzio, *et al.*) *Sua madre?* |
| | His mother? |

| Curzio, et al.: | |
|---|---|
| | *Sua madre!* |
| | His mother! |

| Sus: | |
|---|---|
| | (to Figaro) *Tua madre?* |
| | Your mother? |

| Fig: | |
|---|---|
| | *E quello è mio padre, che a te lo dirà.* |
| | And this is my father, he'll tell you himself. |

| Sus: | |
|---|---|
| | (to Curzio *et al.*) *Suo padre?* |
| | His father? |

| Curzio, et al.: | |
|---|---|
| | *Suo padre!* |
| | His father! |

| Sus: | |
|---|---|
| | (to Figaro) *Tuo padre?* |
| | Your father? |

| Fig: | |
|---|---|
| | *E quella è mia madre, che a te lo dirà.* |
| | And that is my mother, she'll tell you herself. |

|  | Sus. Mar. Fig. Bar. | Count, Curzio |
|---|---|---|

*Al dolce contento di questo momento*      *Al fiero tormento di questo momento*
The sweet contentment of this moment    The fiery torment of this moment

*quest' anima appena resister or sà.*     *quest' anima appena resister or sà.*
my spirit can hardly resist.        my (his) spirit can hardly resist.

**EX. 8.1 MOZART**
Sextet, "Riconosci in questo
amplesso," from *Le Nozze di
Figaro*, bars 1–5

The simplicity of every melody in this sextet is apparent, yet each is perfectly appropriate for the character who sings it. Marcellina's graciousness to her new-found son and daughter-in-law is expressed in flowing, relatively long phrases.

**EX. 8.2** *Ibid.*
bars 40–44

Susanna, first angry at Figaro's supposed infidelity, sings short bursts of melody, frequently using the tiny interval of the half step.

**EX. 8.3** *Ibid.*
bars 104–107

Only when she is apprised of the truth does her melody relax and assume the tone of a young girl melodiously in love, as reflected in the melismatic music Mozart wrote for her.

The Count and the gossip-mongering Don Curzio vent their frustration in dotted rhythms.

**EX. 8.4** *Ibid.*
bars 102–103

The parts of the Count and Don Curzio are in marked contrast with the steady, even notes sung by the still blushing Figaro, the pompous Bartolo, and the two ladies, all four of whom, united by the striking development in the plot, join in a quartet sung simultaneously with the duet sung by the Count and Curzio. Through it all run accompanying motives (Ex. 8.5 (a) and (b)) usually independent from the music given the singers, yet always supporting it, commenting on the tomfoolery, and providing an all-important sense of motion and activity that makes the scene one of the most delightful in all musical theater.

Strings, bar 2

Strings, bar 49

**EX. 8.5** *Ibid.*
bars 2–4(a) and 49–52(b)

**Romantic opera**

The nineteenth-century operatic stage was devoted primarily to a type of work known as *grand opera*. Inspired by tales of sacrifice and courage, some emanating from the French Revolution, others found in rediscovered legends and historical writings, Romantic poets contributed rambling and diffuse librettos dealing with themes of patriotism, self-denial, and other vestiges of the "stiff-upper-lip" school of writing. Composers responded with large choral sections, passionate arias, pseudo-religiosity, clichés of accompaniment, and a catalog of musical devices stressing theatrical impact rather than characterization or well-structured plot development.

It was in this milieu that Verdi and Wagner began their operatic writing, although their basic accomplishments differed in aesthetic intent. The Italian proclivity for beauty of singing, the expression of human pathos, and the development of character through vocal melody were central to Verdi's style. Wagner, on the other hand, utilized the opera as a vehicle for allegorical dramas in which the inner and hidden meanings of the action were suggested by a system of motives and an elaborate orchestration.

**Verdi and Italian Romantic opera**

Verdi's music is consistently characterized by a passionate vocal melody that soars above a subordinate yet highly atmospheric accompaniment. He used orchestrally accompanied recitative (*recitativo stromentato*), dramatic arioso, and a variety of aria forms, ranging from strophic drinking songs to through-composed prayers, in a sequence of operas that spanned a long, productive life. His earlier works show an inclination to strict alternation of recitative and aria and a tendency toward many clichés of both music and drama. A decided turn to a more unified musical style and a subtler blend of music and drama are manifested to their greatest extent in his last three works, *Aïda* (1871), *Otello* (1887), and *Falstaff* (1893), which, because of the beauty and appropriateness of their melodies and the effectiveness and importance of their orchestrations, rank as pinnacles in the history of Italian opera. *Macbeth* (1847; revised 1865), *Rigoletto* (1851), and *La Traviata* (1853) are pivotal works in this development; their mention here, along with the citation of Verdi's last three works, does not exhaust the list of Verdi operas still popular.

*Rigoletto* is the story of a wretched hunchback who is made the object of scorn and cruel humor by licentious courtiers. He gains a modicum of revenge by the use of his own sarcastic wit, shielded from the anger of the courtiers by the protection of his profligate, immoral master, the Duke of Mantua. Rigoletto is warm and loving only with his adolescent daughter, Gilda, whom he has tried to keep hidden from the avaricious, sinful world through which he must make his way. The Duke meets Gilda, however, and, with the connivance of the courtiers, dishonors her. Rigoletto, believing himself the object of a father's curse, swears to avenge this and other accumulated wrongs by slaying the Duke in a tavern to which the latter has been lured by the comely wench Maddalena.

The famous quartet from this opera occurs at a point in the final scene when Rigoletto and Gilda peer through the tavern window and observe the flirtation between the Duke and Maddalena. The quartet is a masterpiece of Italian ensemble, for it combines soaring melody with incisive characterization. In the text, which follows, portions of each section are freely repeated.

Richard Tucker, tenor, as the Duke of Mantua in Verdi's Rigoletto.

Duke:    *Bella figlia dell' amore, schiavo son de' vezzi tuoi;*
              Fairest daughter of love, I am a slave to your charms;
              *con un detto sol tu puoi le mie pene consolar.*
              with one word alone you can assuage my anguish.

| Gilda | Maddalena | Rigoletto |
|---|---|---|
| *Ah, così parlar d'amore!* Ah, thus to talk of love! | *Ah, ah, rido ben di core* Ha, ha, my heart laughs | *Taci, il piangere non vale.* Silence, thy tears are worthless. |
| *A me pur l'infame ho udito!* To me thus the traitor spoke! | *Chè tai baie costan poco.* at such insincere flattery. | *Ch'ei, mentiva or sei sicura.* Now you know he's faithless. |

**Duke:**    *Vieni, e senti del mio core il frequente palpitar.*
Come and hear how my heart beats rapidly.

*Bella figlia ...*
Fairest daughter ... (repeated while others sing)

| Gilda | Maddalena | Rigoletto |
|---|---|---|
| *Infelice cor tradito*<br>Unhappy heart betrayed | *Quanto valga il vostro giuoco*<br>The worth of your joking | *Taci, e mia sarà la cura*<br>Silence, mine shall be the concern |
| *per angoscia non scoppiar.*<br>not to die of anguish. | *mal credete, sò apprezzar'*<br>I fully appreciate, unbelieving | *la vendetta d'affrettar'.*<br>of hastening vengeance. |
| [*Perche, o credulo mio core*<br>Why, o believing heart of mine, | *sono avvezza, bel signore,*<br>I have listened, fair sir, | *Pronta fia, sarà fatale*<br>Soon it will be done, he shall die |
| *un tal uom dovevi amar!*][3]<br>did you have to love such a man! | *ad un simile scherzar'.*<br>to similar joking. | *io saprollo fulminar'.*<br>I'll be repaid in full. |

The Duke's melody, which is the very first thing heard in the score, is suave and flowing and rises to the top of the staff in such a way that it gives the singer a marvelous vehicle for lovely singing tone.

**EX. 8.6 VERDI**
Quartet, "Bella figlia dell' amore," from *Rigoletto*, bars 1–8

Duke

Bel - la fi - glia dell' a - mo - re,    Schia - vo son de' vez - zi tuo - i;    con un
*Fairest    daughter of love,    I am a slave to your    charms;    with one*

det - to,un det - to sol tu puo - i    le mie pe - ne le mie pe - ne con - so - lar.
*word    alone you can    assuage my pain*

Maddalena's response is to laugh in an earthy manner. She loves the Duke's flattery, even though she recognizes his insincerity. Verdi suggests her delighted mockery by fast notes and rapid shifts in melodic direction.

Maddalena

**EX. 8.7** *Ibid.*
bars 15–16

Ah! Ah! ri - do ben di co - re, chè tai ba - ie cos - tan po - co;
*Ha! Ha! my    heart    laughs at such    insincere flattery;*

[3]In some performances and scores, this text is omitted, and Gilda's part consists only of repeats of the previous two lines of text.

Maddalena's frivolity contrasts with the bursts of sobs from Gilda, who still loves the Duke even though she has been cruelly wronged by him.

**EX. 8.8** *Ibid.* bars 16–17

Ah!_____ co-sì_____ par-lar____ d'a-mo-re!
*Ah!* *thus* *to talk* *of love!*

Rigoletto is less concerned with comforting Gilda than with reaffirming his intent to gain his revenge. His short phrases of rage are in dramatic contrast with the blandishments of the Duke, and his tendency to sing the same pitch several times before moving up in half steps suggests a musical version of monomania.

**EX. 8.9** *Ibid.* bars 20–23

Ta-ci, il pian-ge-re non va - le; ta - ci, ta - ci, il pian-ge-re non va - le,
*Silence, thy tears are worthless; silence, silence, thy tears are worthless,*

Even when all voices are singing together, the characters remain clearly defined and contrasted. Here, for example, is a part of the quartet in which both Gilda and Maddalena are singing groups of two notes, yet Gilda's are tied in an upward, sighing effect, whereas Maddalena must sing her laughs in a detached fashion on repeated pitches. At the same time, the Duke has a flowing melody in relatively slow note values, while Rigoletto continues to hammer out his fury.

**EX. 8.10** *Ibid.* bars 33–35

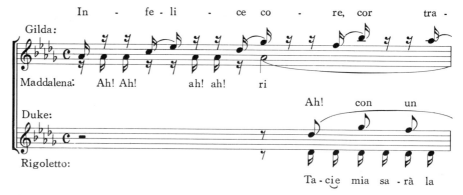

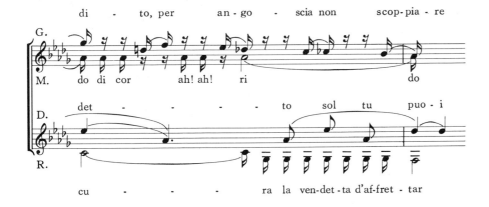

di - to, per an - go - scia non scop-pia - re

G.

M. do di cor ah! ah! ri do

D. det - - - to sol tu puo - i

R.

cu - - - ra la ven-det-ta d'af-fret - tar

| Gilda: | Unhappy broken heart, not to die of anguish. |
| Maddalena: | Ha! Ha! My heart laughs. Ha! Ha! I laugh. |
| Duke: | Ah, with one word alone you can restore me. |
| Rigoletto: | Silence, mine shall be the concern of hastening vengeance. |

One other example will show how Verdi creates dramatic order and logic within a polyphonic ensemble. In the example below, rests between each of the very short notes of both Gilda's and Rigoletto's parts suggest the agitation both feel. Yet father and daughter are not really communicating with each other, for Gilda is lost in her own sorrow, and Rigoletto is more aware of his thirst for vengeance than of his daughter's anguish. Verdi, therefore, requires Rigoletto to sing on the strong beats, Gilda on the offbeats. While this is going on, the Duke and Maddalena, both enjoying the wooing to the hilt, sing in slower, parallel rhythms.

**EX. 8.11** *Ibid.*
bars 49–51

Gilda
In - fel - li - ce cor tra - di - to per an - go - scia non scop-piar,
*unhappy heart betrayed, not to die of anguish*

Maddalena
il vo - stro gio - co sò ap - prez - zar
*your joking I fully appreciate*

Duke
sen - ti del co - re il pal - pi - tar
*hear how my heart beats*

Rigoletto
ta - ci e mia sa - rà la cu - ra la ven - det - ta d'af - fret - tar
*silence, mine shall be the concern of hastening vengeance*

The emphasis in this quartet is solely on the voice, for the orchestra does nothing but double the voices and provide rhythmic underpinnings for them.

**Other Italian opera composers**

In the last few decades of the nineteenth century, Italian opera turned from the grandiose to the veristic, following the lead of such French literary figures as Zola and Flaubert and the daring subject matter of a French opera, Bizet's *Carmen* (1875). Mascagni, Leoncavallo, and, to a certain extent, Puccini eschewed the exalted or exotic subjects of earlier librettos and focused their attentions on stories dealing with ordinary folk in inglorious situations, set in colorful but real locales. *Verismo*, as this school of opera is known, is characterized by a heightened tension, avoidance of vocal display for its own sake, brevity and simplicity of plot (many verismo operas are only one act in length), and extremes of emotion leading to deeds of violence within the context of everyday life.

Puccini was Verdi's most notable successor. There is but a degree of verismo effect in his operas, for Puccini treated his characters with affection and sentiment, even though they were rarely noble and epic in the earlier Romantic sense. The warm vocal lyricism and sensitive, if subordinate, orchestration of *La Bohème, Madame Butterfly*, and *Manon Lescaut* have made them enduring favorites of countless opera goers; *Tosca* and *Turandot*, although concerned with figures who are larger than life, deal with scenes of tremendous emotional stress in a veristic way and represent another facet of Puccini's unique blend of naturalism and romantic effusion.

After Puccini, one of the few composers who has maintained the Italian tradition in the twentieth century has been Menotti, who has dealt with modern problems in operas throbbing with powerful vocal melody. Curiously, although Menotti has never yielded his Italian citizenship, his operas have been exclusively in English.

**Wagner and German Romantic opera**

Wagner saw the voice as but one element in an opera. For him, opera was a synthesis of all the arts:[4] orchestral music was to suggest the deeper meanings of the text and to recall or foretell action; poetry was to uplift the listener by treating subjects of philosophical import and by conveying emotion through the expressive use of consonants and vowels; painting and lighting were to enrich the drama by providing the appropriate atmo-

---

[4]*Gesamtkunstwerk* ("composite art work") is a term coined by Wagner specifically to refer to this concept.

sphere and setting; the singer-actor (vocal melody and mime) was to delineate present action and express in specific terms actions, thoughts, and meanings.

Wagner considered psychological action to be a continuous force. The sharp contrast of recitative and aria, which resulted in abrupt cessations of one style in order to begin another, was anathema to him because of its intrusion into psychological continuity. He therefore developed a style of composition which resulted in "endless melody," an ongoing combination of flexible rhythms, changing harmonies, and subtle melodic phrases that avoids a final chord until one is called for by the drama.

Of special importance in Wagner's music is the *Leitmotiv* ("leading motive"), an easily recognized melodic fragment associated with a person, event, object, or idea. When such a motive is played or sung at a signifi-cant moment in the drama, the listener's attention is drawn forcefully to the relationship of present action to the past, or to some action about to occur. Of equal significance is Wagner's mutation of these motives, for the motives are continuously altered and developed as the story un-folds, character relationships change, and new meanings of the action are revealed. In brief, it is the symphonic treatment of the motives and the unceasing flow of their manipulations that are two of Wagner's most characteristic techniques.

Wagner's music represents one of the most intense peaks of Romantic expression. Its luxuriant harmonies, lustrous tone colors, and trenchant melodies combine to provide a truly emotional experience for even the most untutored listener, while at the same time they underscore a drama of far-reaching allegorical implications.

The excerpts illustrating Wagner's music are taken from *Die Walküre* ("The Valkyrie Maiden," 1854–56), the second opera of his tetralogy, *Der Ring des Nibelungen* ("The Ring of the Nibelung"). "The Ring" is a dramatic cycle dealing with mythological events concerning the trans-ference of world dominion from the Teutonic gods to man by virtue of man's capacity to sacrifice himself for the sake of love and compassion.

*Die Walküre* presents the union of a brother and sister, Siegmund and Sieglinde, both sired by Wotan, the king of the gods. Their union is a divine wedlock justified in terms of destiny, world salvation, and com-mingling of kindred, heroic spirits, even though its consummation vio-lates social law. The signal events of the opera are three: the elopement of Siegmund and Sieglinde from Sieglinde's brutish husband, Hunding; the attempt of Brünnhilde, to whom the opera's title refers, to aid Sieg-mund and Sieglinde instead of punishing them as Wotan has ordered her

*Birgit Nilsson, soprano, as Brünnhilde, in Wagner's* Die Walküre.

to do; and the banishment of Brünnhilde from the abode of the gods, eventually to become the bride of a mortal hero.

In Act I, Siegmund staggers into a mean hovel owned by Hunding, a man as coarse and unattractive as Siegmund is handsome and noble. Siegmund has lost his weapon in battle, and, as he sits alone by the fire, he remembers his father's promise to give him a great sword at the hour of darkest need. Yet his father is with him no more and he is defenseless against his enemies. Chief among them is Hunding, against whom he must defend himself on the morrow. Instead of threats, Sieglinde, Hunding's wife, has offered the stranger solace and comfort, for she sees some of herself in him. She does not at first realize that Siegmund is her twin brother, parted from her since childhood.

Sieglinde gives Hunding a sleeping potion and then joins Siegmund in the main room of the hut, one corner of which is supported by a great ash tree. She tells Siegmund that she lost her parents when but a child; later she was forced into this loveless marriage, but, at the ceremony, a stranger suddenly appeared, thrust a great sword into the ash tree, and, without a word, departed. She knows that the sword was meant for her savior, but no one has been able to extract it. Siegmund vows that he shall be that savior, and, in a famous musical passage, greets the spring night as the harbinger of his new-found love.

The first words of Sieglinde's response, "Du bist der Lenz nach dem ich verlangte in frostigen Winters Frist" ("Thou art the Spring for whom I have pined through the cold spell of Winter"), are sung to a *Leitmotiv* (Ex. 8.12) associated with Sieglinde and her love for Siegmund.

**EX. 8.12 WAGNER**
Sieglinde's love song,
from *Die Walküre* (beginning)

| Du bist | der Lenz | nach dem ich | ver-lang - te im | fro - sti-gem Win - ters | Frist |
| *Thou art* | *the Spring* | *for whom I* | *have pined* | *through the* | *cold spell of* | *Winter* |

Every expression of ecstasy by the singer is matched by an intensification of the orchestral sound, and every phrase of despair is echoed by emptiness of instrumentation or by a descending melodic motion. This is songful music, but not at all in the Verdian or Mozartian sense, for it is not set off from the rest of the action by the contrasting style of recitative. When Sieglinde finishes this episode, the orchestra immediately picks up the musical action and hastens it forward without so much as an instant's pause.

A few moments later, when Sieglinde has recognized her lover as her long-lost brother, Siegmund, she exultantly proclaims his name. Siegmund proudly accepts his name from her, recognizes the sword as the one promised by his father, names it *Nothung* ("Needed-one"), pulls it from the tree, and rushes with Sieglinde from the hut.

The dominant characteristic of this conclusion of Act I is its emotional fervor, for Siegmund and Sieglinde are swept up by love and by a sense of fulfillment of destiny. There are a number of motives, each having occurred prior to this excerpt in either the preceding opera of the tetralogy (*Das Rheingold*) or earlier in the first act of *Die Walküre*. They may be sounded sometimes only in the orchestra, sometimes only in the voice, and sometimes in both simultaneously. On occasion, only a fragment of a motive is used; at other times, the motive will occur in full, either alone or in combination with other motives.

The first important *Leitmotiv* heard is that of the *Sword* ( Ex. 8.13 a ), scored for the trumpet and piercing through the sound of the orchestra in the fourth measure of the recorded excerpt. In measures 21–29 of this excerpt, Siegmund sings of the soul's need for love to the motive known as *Renunciation of Love* ( Ex. 8.13 b ), reinforcing one of the major ideas of the "Ring" cycle: life without compassion and love is crass and empty. The motive of *Victory* ( Ex. 8.13 c ) for Siegmund's tribe, the Volsungs, is played by the brasses at measure 75, and his song of spring and love ( Ex. 8.13 d ) is recalled briefly when he calls to Sieglinde, in measure 81, to follow him to far-off places. There is a reminiscence of Sieglinde's love song ( Ex. 8.13 e ) in measures 91 and 92; the ecstasy of *Bliss* (Ex. 8.13 f ) is evoked in brief groups of three notes accompanying Sieglinde's "Bist du Siegmund, den ich hier sehe?" ("Art thou Siegmund whom I see here?") in measures 99–101.

**EX. 8.13 WAGNER**
*Leitmotivs* from *Die Walküre*

(e) Sieglinde's Love Song

(f) Bliss

(g) Valkyries

The concluding moments of Act I are also illustrative of Wagner's concept of poetry. He considered the sounds of vowels and consonants necessarily reflective of the action and of the thoughts of the characters. He also believed that words and music ought to be conceived simultaneously and interrelatedly. He wrote his own poetry, therefore, with particular reliance on a kind of alliteration called *Stabreim*. This alliterative poetry can be heard a number of times, a particularly prominent example notable in measures 81–87: "*F*ern *v*on hier *f*olge mir nun, *f*ort in des *L*enzes *l*achendes Haus. . . ."

The final Wagnerian excerpt on the recordings accompanying this book is the orchestral beginning of Act II. It is first a tumultuous description of the flight of Siegmund and Sieglinde. Although the audience does not see an actual enactment of the lovers racing fearfully through the forest, the symphonic metamorphosis of the motives of *Sword, Sieglinde's Love Song*, and *Bliss* suggests the frantic scene.

**EX. 8.14 WAGNER**
Transformed *Leitmotivs*
from *Die Walküre*

(a) Sword

(b) Sieglinde's Love Song ( beginning, transformed into *Flight* )

(c) Bliss

There is a gradual dissolution in measures 54–56 of the motives from Act I and the growing domination of the sound of the orchestra by the galloping rhythms of the Valkyries ( Ex. 8.13 g ), the daughters of Wotan and agents of his desires. The listener is thus led into Act II, in the opening scene of which Wotan and Brünnhilde sympathetically observe the escaping Siegmund and Sieglinde.

Recognition of the technique of melodic change employed here will give considerable insight into Wagner's style. There are many elements to listen for in his music; the fullest appreciation, of course, comes not only from an understanding of why he wrote as he did and the devices he used, but also from an awareness of what he was trying to communicate.

The Wagnerian influence has been potent into the twentieth century, especially in the operas of Richard Strauss, Berg, and Henze. Strauss's *Salome* (1905) and *Elektra* (1909) are continuations of the arioso melody, elaborate instrumentation, and emotional, erotic, and allegorical stories of the Wagner tradition. Some of Strauss's later works, especially the charming *Der Rosenkavalier* ("The Cavalier of the Rose," 1911) and the vivacious *Ariadne auf Naxos* ("Ariadne on Naxos," 1912), are considerably more restrained in style, the latter actually using an orchestra of the proportions of the Classical period as well as recitative-aria construction. *Arabella* (1933) is a lovely work in a romantic vein.

Berg's *Wozzeck* (1925) is a chilling, atonal opera that uses a huge orchestra, the Leitmotiv technique, and a wide variety of vocal styles, ranging from folklike songs to Sprechstimme, to set before its audience the tragedy of human cruelty and loneliness. Berg's *Lulu* (1935), written in the twelve-tone style, is similarly expressionistic.

Henze's music has borrowed freely from the Wagnerian style, from the twelve-tone idiom, and from jazz. *Boulevard Solitude* (1952) uses several contemporary types of popular dance; *Der junge Lord* ("The Young Lord," 1965) employs mixtures of tonal and atonal styles in a comic framework; *The Bassarids* (1967) stresses clarity of form and rhythm within an expressionistic type of communication.

**Eclecticism in the twentieth century**

The remarkable diversity of the Modern era is found in opera to the same extent that it is found in all the other genres of music and the other arts. Composers have borrowed freely from the several operatic traditions; only rarely, as in the case of Strauss, Menotti, and a few others, can they be linked almost wholly with a specific antecedent.

Luigi Dallapiccola's *Il Prigioniero* ("The Prisoner," 1950), for example, is a wholly twelve-tone opera with an agonizing story and an elaborate instrumentation suggesting the Wagnerian influence. The force of Verdian melody is strong, however, and the torture of a continually frustrated hope for freedom is consistently expressed in vocal terms.

Stravinsky's *The Rake's Progress* (1952) and Poulenc's *The Dialogues of the Carmelites* (1957) are both tonal operas that draw upon the heritage of previous centuries. In the Stravinsky work, the listener finds the small orchestra, the aria, *recitativo secco*, the ensemble, and the setting of an eighteenth-century *opera buffa*, vested with the biting harmonies and vital rhythms so typical of its composer. Poulenc's *Dialogues* is complete with crowd scenes, great choral episodes, powerful theatrical effects, and emotional lyricism in the manner of nineteenth-century grand opera. Like the Stravinsky work, however, it has been given contemporaneity by the composer and stands as a masterpiece of modern times.

One of the most remarkable opera composers of the twentieth century is Britten. Although he has often employed some of Debussy's suggestive devices to create "impressions" of scenes and moods, his music is strikingly individualistic in its use of English folksong or the folksong idiom, its atmospheric and appropriate orchestration, its lyric writing for the voice, and its dramatic declamation, while remaining wholly in the tonal tradition. *Peter Grimes* (1945), *Billy Budd* (1951), and *A Midsummer Night's Dream* (1960) are the most significant of his large-scale works.

**Experiments in the twentieth century**

Theatrical music in this era has often been enlivened by experimental approaches to both music and drama. Ranging from extreme simplification of the dramatic medium to the most complex mixture of such varied media as mime, electronic sounds, orchestral and vocal music, dance, narration, film, audience participation, speech, and poetry, musical theater has often manifested directions wholly removed from the traditions inherited from the eighteenth and nineteenth centuries.

Orff's *Antigone* (1949) and *Oedipus the Tyrant* (1959) represent a successful attempt to create a declamation in which rhythm and pitch combine with text and a percussive background in a manner suggesting a timeless, epochal quality.

One of the most unusual musico-theatrical experiments, described by its composer as "a variable fantasy in the manner of an opera," is Henri Pousseur's *Vôtre Faust* ("Your Faust," 1968), in which the Faust legend is recreated with a modern twist. At a certain point in the action, the curtain is lowered, and the audience is asked to determine whether Faust and Marguerite ("Maggie") should be reunited or whether Faust should take up with one of Mephistopheles' female agents. After voting during the intermission, the audience is given four other opportunities to influence the action, and is also given a voice in the selection of the final scene.

The success of this particular work has not been universally acclaimed, especially because of a bewildering variety of musical styles, including quotes and reworkings of operatic music by Bizet, Gounod, and Mozart, jazz, Medieval music, serial composition, and the use of five different languages to be both spoken and sung. It is clear, however, that Pousseur reveals a fascinatingly new attitude toward music drama.

The audience is made to feel involved also in Berio's *Passagio* (1963), in which the chorus, seated among the members of the audience, serves as brutal antagonist to the fleeing heroine.

Eric Salzman's *Verses and Cantos* (1967) uses a multimedia approach and intensified sound, the latter resulting from the placement of loudspeakers in various parts of the hall so that the audience is bombarded with sounds from all directions. Since microphones are also placed in spots other than the stage, the sources of sound are varied as well. In the composer's own words:

The performers sing and shout, they run the gamut of vocal expression from verbal to non-verbal to musical; they interact with one another, with the instrumentalists and with the audience. Their presence on stage is picked up electronically and thrown out into the space of the hall. Reality and image, clarity and confusion, abstract and emotive sound intersect and interact on many levels. ... The overall form of the work moves from controlled, predetermined experience to freer, looser, less determined means of expression; the final image is that of a controlled live improvisation clashing with a taped collage of Rock sounds pouring out of speakers at the back of the hall.[5]

**Singspiel; opéra comique**

The German *Singspiel* and the French *opéra comique* were originally light in style and mood, but some of the great composers have lifted them into the realm of potent drama or philosophical commentary and have vested them with some of their most inspired music.

The *opéra comique*, as it appeared in a more or less definitive shape in the 1750's and 1760's, was a spoken play with interspersed songs. The plots dealt with a simple peasantry, the characters expressing themselves in a tuneful fashion. There was relatively little musical complexity, in spite of frequent duets and the use of the so-called "vaudeville finale," a strophic composition for the leading characters in which, at the end of the opera, each in turn sang the verse, the others joining in for a refrain.

[5] Eric Salzman, "Something Else," *Opera News*, XXXIII, No. 4 (November 2, 1968), 13.

The *Singspiel* also assumed its definitive traits near the middle of the eighteenth century, and it too used spoken dialogue with interspersed songs. Its sentimentality, glorification of the simple life, and stress on the triumph of virtue was not unlike the *opéra comique* of the latter eighteenth century. The idiom of German folk music, however, was very strong. North German composers tended more toward a romanticized type of plot, south German composers toward the farcical and the satirical.

Both of these directions met in Vienna, where Mozart fused the serious, the sentimental, the comic, and the allegorical in one of the greatest of the type, *Die Zauberflöte* ("The Magic Flute," 1791).

In the nineteenth century, both *opéra comique* and *Singspiel* retained spoken dialogue, but became vehicles for serious subject matter. Bizet's *Carmen* and Gounod's *Faust* were originally written as *opéras comiques*, although heard most often today with sung recitatives composed after their first performances. Beethoven's *Fidelio* (1805, with revisions in 1806 and 1814) is a *Singspiel* dealing with unjust imprisonment and last-minute rescue, while a *Singspiel* by Weber, *Der Freischütz* (generally translated "The Sharpshooter," although "The Free Shot" is more appropriate, 1812), is a romantic story set in the Black Forest, where a young huntsman almost loses his soul to the devil. Both *Fidelio* and *Der Freischütz* make telling use of spoken dialogue over orchestral background music or with orchestral interludes, a device known as *melodrama*.

### Other forms of theatrical music

**Operetta**  Ever since its name was coined in 1854, *operetta* has been a play with song and spoken dialogue solely for purposes of entertainment. Tunefulness has been its most consistent trait, and its subject matter has hardly ever been serious, tending rather towards the sentimental and romantic, or, in some cases, to the purposely absurd.

The genre of the operetta, which reached its peak in Europe in the late nineteenth century and in America in the early twentieth century, used the musical forms of the opera, but never its intensity. The works of Johann Strauss (the younger), Lehár, Herbert, Friml, and Romberg have in common highly romanticized plots, gracious melodies, and lavish musical numbers, especially in finales. Offenbach and the team of Gilbert and Sullivan (Gilbert was the librettist) satirized human foibles and the institution of opera itself through bizarre turns of plot and absurd exaggerations of character, while using the musical vocabulary of grand opera.

Although operettas are revived with some frequency and enjoyed by audiences in the United States and in Europe, composers have preferred a newer genre, the *musical,* as more suited to contemporary expression.

The *musical* is a uniquely, although not exclusively, American genre **Musical** of musical expression. Included under its name are such types as the *revue* (a series of unrelated skits and musical numbers, possibly bound together by a common theme), the *musical comedy* (spoken dialogue, songs, and dances in a lighthearted vehicle, the plot of which invariably ends happily), and the *musical play* (similar to the musical comedy in construction, but dealing with subjects and emotions in a more serious fashion and with greater reliance on music for characterization and plot development). *Musical* is a term broad enough to include these types as well as offshoots or mergers of them. Spoken dialogue is common to all, as is the fact that the compositional style has most often been in close touch with popular tastes. In addition, all the types are characterized by spontaneity, informality of the idioms of speech, and dynamic and colorful production.

Musicals are primarily products of the twentieth century, although their roots are found in the pantomimes, minstrel shows, extravaganzas, and vaudeville shows of the nineteenth century. Works written prior to the late 1920's were designed solely for the purpose of entertainment, and were romantic, appealing, sentimental copies of the European operetta. Jerome Kern and George Gershwin, however, brought a more serious intent to the musical. Kern's *Showboat* (1927) was based on a serious literary work (a book by Edna Ferber) concerned with the plight of the American Negro, and Gershwin's *Of Thee I Sing* (1931) is a political satire on presidential elections (and was the first musical to be awarded a Pulitzer Prize).

By the 1940's, composers were imbuing the spirit of the musical with deftness of characterization and sophistication of plot. This had already been achieved by Gershwin in *Porgy and Bess* (1935), a successful merging of musical and opera into a real "folk opera." Kurt Weill contributed to the maturity of the musical by combining contemporary popular musical idioms with political allegory in *The Three-penny Opera* (1933; a revitalization of the eighteenth century *The Beggar's Opera*), and by providing vital melodic imagery and powerful ballet music for such works as *Lady in the Dark* (1941). His *Street Scene* (1947), based on a tragedy by Elmer Rice, approaches opera in its scope and content, as does *Lost in the Stars* (1949).

*A scene from the Broadway rock musical* Hair, *by Gerome Ragni and James Rado, music by Galt MacDermot.*

A number of works by Richard Rodgers have also marked the new depth and seriousness of the musical. Rodgers and his librettists (the most famous of whom were Lorenz Hart and Oscar Hammerstein II) paid great attention to character development and to scenes of dramatic import and weighty content. In both *Pal Joey* (1940) and *Carousel* (1945), flaws in the character of the hero were essential to the progress of the story. *South Pacific* (1949) presented the theme of racial prejudice prominently, and *Oklahoma!* (1943) showed its villain as a fully-dimensioned and understandable figure. In all of these musicals, Rodgers not only provided a host of engaging melodies but also offered an opportunity for dance as a dramatic device in a way that influenced many other composers and librettists. The increasing musical sophistication of the genre reached a high point in Bernstein's *West Side Story* (1957) by virtue of extraordinary dance sequences, melodic characterization, musical continuity, co-

A scene from Mozart's Le Nozze di Figaro ("The Marriage of Figaro"). Here Figaro introduces Susanna to his long-lost father. From left to right, Hermann Prey as the Count, Mariano Caruso as Curzio, Judith Raskin as Susanna, Gladys Kriese as Marcellina, Cesare Siepi as Figaro, and Fernando Corena as Bartolo. (The Metropolitan Opera Guild)

Rigoletto and Gilda comment on the flirtation in the tavern, a scene from Verdi's Rigoletto. From left to right, Roberta Peters as Gilda, Cornell MacNeil as Rigoletto, Rusza Pospinov as Maddalena, and Alfredo Kraus as the Duke. (The Metropolitan Opera Guild)

Siegmund hails Sieglinde as bride and sister. Jon Vickers and Gundulla Janowitz in the concluding moments of Act I of the Metropolitan Opera production of Wagner's Die Walküre. The rear part of the set suggests the great ash tree that forms part of Hunding's hut. (The Metropolitan Opera Guild)

*John Ferguson Weir (1841–1926).* Forging the Shaft. *Although a minor figure in the history of Romantic art, Weir has caught the spirit of men struggling against a great force; brilliant color, vivid action, strong feeling, and a definite nationalistic attitude mark this as full-blooded Romanticism. (The Metropolitan Museum of Art, New York. Gift of Lyman G. Bloomingdale, 1901)*

*Colorplate* **6**

hesive plot construction, and excellence of orchestration. To varying degrees, these traits are also found in recent efforts by Loesser, Loewe, and a few others.

Until the 1950's, the favorite songs of the stage were among the most popular in the land. In that decade, however, this oneness of national taste became less apparent, until a point was reached when the best-known musical comedy of the decade, Loewe's *My Fair Lady* (1956), showed no influence whatever of the most important development in popular music, Rock and Roll. It was not until 1967, with Galt Mac-Dermot's *Hair*, that an identity between the main stream of popular taste and the musical comedy was achieved once more, although this is not to say, of course, that the musical had gone into decline.

### Directions

Although there seems to be a greater rapprochement between opera and other forms of musical theater, it is quite impossible to predict the manner in which music and theater will utilize traditions and experiments in the closing decades of the twentieth century. Perhaps wholly new genres of musical theater are in the making, genres in which elements of chance, lighting, and other arts will rival if not exceed music in importance. The urge to utilize music so as to intensify narrative, characterization, and action has been one of the most consistent in the history of theater, and there is little doubt that the next few decades will bring new intensity and excitement to the lyric stage.

# 9 : FOR VOCAL GROUPS

AS with so many other definitions in music, a definition of *choral* music must be flexible. The word "chorus" implies a large group of singers, but "large" is a relative term defying precisely quantitative definition. Although some compositions for voices were originally composed for performance by one singer and/or player per part, and hence are more properly discussed under chamber music, these types, including *part song, glee, madrigal, chanson*, and others, are most often sung today by groups with many singers for each part. They will, therefore, be treated in this chapter along with the larger choral forms.

### Larger choral genres

**Oratorio**

The *oratorio* utilizes all the devices of opera except ballet. It is, however, more narrative and contemplative than dramatic, and, for the most part, is sung in concert form, without benefit of staging or costuming.

Early oratorios by Cavalieri, Carissimi, and others were indistinguishable from operatic performance save for subject matter; the oratorio was then concerned exclusively with sacred themes. Both opera and oratorio were costumed and enacted. Since then, oratorio has dealt with both sacred and secular subjects, but has lost the elements of costuming, acting, and scenery.

Oratorios that narrate the story of Easter are called *Passion oratorios*, the most famous being two by Johann Sebastian Bach, *The Passion According to St. Matthew* and *The Passion According to St. John*.

Oratorios use the operatic techniques of recitative, arioso, aria, orchestral music, and choral music, although they rely much more on the chorus than does opera. When a sacred text is used, part of it may be liturgical or biblical, part may be newly written or arranged.

Handel's *Messiah* is the most famous of all oratorios. Indeed, performance of it at Christmas time is almost a Western rite, and some choral organizations exist primarily to present this one composition. Its music is of such surpassing inventiveness and beauty, however, that it is fully capable of enduring this excessive familiarity. An examination of part of it will reveal the nature of the oratorio in general, although this particular work is somewhat less devoted to storytelling than other, less familiar compositions.

*Messiah* is in three parts, the first dealing with the Christmas story, the second with Easter, and the third with professions of religious faith. The

William Hogarth (1697–1764). A Performance of Thomas Arne's Oratorio "Judith." Bawling, disorder, and an unwigged conductor at the top of the picture show an acid view of choral performance in mid-eighteenth-century London. Arne's oratorio (1761) was the first in which women sang the soprano choral part, but no women are pictured here. Boys sing in the left foreground. (The Bettmann Archive)

excerpts recorded for this book are taken from Part I. The first of them sets the words of Isaiah predicting the blessedness of the future when the Messiah shall come. The other excerpts deal with the Nativity itself, in particular the description of the appearance of the angels to the shepherds with the first announcement of Jesus' birth. The text:

*Aria for tenor*: Every valley shall be exalted, and every mountain and hill made low; the crooked straight, and the rough places plain.

*Recitativo secco, for soprano*: There were shepherds abiding in the field, keeping watch over their flocks by night.

*Recitativo accompagnato*: And lo! the angel of the Lord came upon them, and the glory of the Lord shone round about them, and they were sore afraid.

*Recitativo secco, for soprano*: And the angel said unto them, "Fear not, for behold, I bring you good tidings of great joy, which shall be to all people. For unto you is born this day in the city of David a saviour, which is Christ the Lord."

*Recitativo accompagnato, for soprano*: And suddenly there was with the angel a multitude of the heavenly host praising God, and saying:

*Chorus*: "Glory to God in the highest, and peace on earth, good will towards men."

"Every valley" is a typically Baroque aria, in that it combines a florid melodic line with an intimate relationship between text and music. Note the rising of the melody on "exalted," the drop at "made low," the up-and-down motion of "crooked," and the long line of "made plain." Its *ABA* structure is also typical of the Baroque aria, as are the unceasing sense of motion, rhythmic drive, and solidity of bass line.

Handel's expressive touch may be heard in many places. The contrast in styles of recitative is especially apt. The simplicity of the *recitativo secco* at the start of the shepherd scene portrays a quiet mood in the dark of night.[1]

**EX. 9.1 HANDEL**
"There were shepherds abiding in the fields," bars 1–4, from *Messiah*

[1]The small notes in Ex. 9.1 were not written out in the original score, but were expected to be improvised by the harpsichordist, who was given only the bass notes and a numerical shorthand by which to "realize" the harmonies.

The sudden change to a figured violin accompaniment at "And lo! the angel..." evokes the image of the heavenly messenger's beating wings.

**EX. 9.2 HANDEL**
"And lo! the angel...,"
bars 1–2, from *Messiah*

The angel's attempt to calm the fears of the shepherds is suggested by a return to the *secco* style, but, for the brilliant appearance of a myriad of the heavenly host, Handel turns again to *accompagnato*, this time with a different figuration in the violins to suggest the beating of a multitude of wings.

**EX. 9.3 HANDEL**
"And suddenly there was with the angel," bars 1–2, from *Messiah* (accompaniment)

For the opening words of exultation, "Glory to God in the highest," Handel uses only the upper voices of the chorus (sopranos, altos, and tenors) to suggest the feeling of "in the highest," the excitement of the message reinforced by trumpets and elaborate figuration in the violins.

**EX. 9.4 HANDEL**
"Glory to God in the highest," bars 1–3, from *Messiah*

Basses and tenors, in unison, are the only voices to sing "peace on earth," the sudden turn to men's voices alone suggesting the drop of thought from heaven to earth; the solemnity of the text is emphasized by the quiet chordal accompaniment of the strings.

**EX. 9.5** *Ibid.* bars 6–9

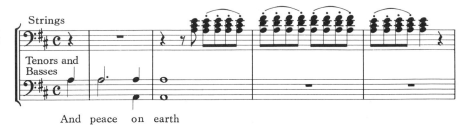

And peace on earth

The happy message of "good will" is communicated polyphonically, much as if the words were being echoed around the world.

**EX. 9.6** *Ibid.* bars 18–21

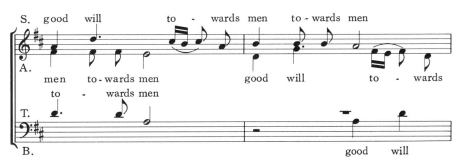

The host of angels disappears then, with a brief trill in the violins that suggests a final glimpse of them as they vanish into the clouds.

Although for most people today Handel's name lives primarily because of *Messiah*, the reader should remember that Handel was the most renowned opera composer of his day and turned to specializing in oratorios only when *opera seria* went into decline; there is no stylistic difference between his operatic arias and his oratorio arias. Thus a study of *Messiah* is in effect also an examination of some of the elements of Baroque opera.

In addition to his two famous Passion oratorios, J. S. Bach is noted for his *Christmas Oratorio* (1734) and an *Easter Oratorio* (1736?). The former is really a collection of six cantatas, a genre that will be discussed shortly; the latter is an emotionally dramatic work with little narrative. Another Baroque composer noted for work in this genre is Schütz, a master of the early seventeenth century whose *Christmas Oratorio* (1664) is a seldom-heard masterpiece.

After the Baroque era, the oratorio declined in importance, in spite of Haydn's powerful, yet charming, *The Creation* (1797) and the lovely *The Seasons* (1801). Of Romantic oratorios, only Mendelssohn's *Elijah* (1846) receives frequent performance, although works by Berlioz and Elgar are highly esteemed.

The oratorio has undergone somewhat of a rebirth in the twentieth century, although its treatment has varied widely. Honegger's *King David* (1921) largely eschews recitative in favor of spoken narration; it combines modern harmonies and instrumental combinations, the polyphonic style of J. S. Bach, simple choral songs in unison, and rhythmically complex passages in a work of powerful lyricism. Walton's romantic and colorful *Belshazzar's Feast* (1933), Stravinsky's *Oedipus Rex* (1927, performed with masked and costumed actors, narrator in modern dress, and a Latin text), and, more recently, Penderecki's atonal *Passion According to St. Luke* (1966) give strong evidence of the vitality of the oratorio on the modern musical scene.

**Cantata**

*Cantatas* may be for solo voice or voices and chorus, or for solo voice alone. The type encountered most often is that favored by J. S. Bach, in which a hymn melody (called a *chorale*) is used as a source of inventive

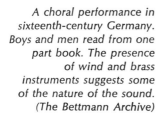

*A choral performance in sixteenth-century Germany. Boys and men read from one part book. The presence of wind and brass instruments suggests some of the nature of the sound. (The Bettmann Archive)*

writing in an opening movement for chorus and orchestra and also as a harmonized congregational hymn at the conclusion of the cantata. In between there may be one or two arias (perhaps melodic variations of the chorale), some recitatives, and occasionally a duet or trio. A particularly well known example is Bach's Cantata No. 140, *Wachet auf, ruft uns die Stimme* ("Awake, a voice calls to us"), which deals with the coming of Christ. Cantatas may be nonnarrative, too, treating such events as royal birthdays, seasons, unrequited love, or philosophical concepts through the media of aria, recitative, chorus, and orchestra. They are not staged and are shorter than the oratorio, usually lasting about twenty or thirty minutes, although some works of more expansive nature—for example Britten's *St. Nicholas* (1948), Prokofiev's *Alexander Nevsky* (1938), Schoenberg's *Gurrelieder* (1900–1), and his *A Survivor from Warsaw* (1947)—are also called cantatas.

**Mass**

CXXXII  *Sonagli adoprati nella Chiesa*

A discussion of the *Mass*, the center of the Roman Catholic liturgy, might well be undertaken in a chapter dealing with dramatic music, for it is a solemn, often emotional, reenactment of the suffering of Christ on the cross, a theme that has evoked some of the most dramatic music ever written. While the Mass is often said or sung by one person, it has been used as a major vehicle of composition ever since the time of Machaut (1300–1377).

Part of the Mass text is invariably recited or sung, without change, at every service where Mass is said; this collection of prayers and affirmations of faith is referred to as the *Ordinary* of the Mass. The remainder of the Mass uses texts appropriate to the day or event; these changeable portions comprise the *Proper* of the Mass.

Musically, the texts of the Ordinary have been most consistently divided into five portions; each portion may be divided into any number of arias, duets, and choruses as the composer sees fit. Recitative, however, is never used in a Mass setting, since its narrative or conversational style is irrelevant to the text. The opening of the Mass Ordinary is an intense prayer for mercy, the second part is a paean, the third is a profession of faith, the fourth is another laudatory and worshipful text, and the fifth a final prayer for mercy. The texts follow:

KYRIE

| | | |
|---|---|---|
| *Kyrie Eleison,*<br>Lord have mercy upon us, | *Christe Eleison,*<br>Christ have mercy upon us, | *Kyrie Eleison.*<br>Lord have mercy upon us. |

## GLORIA

*Gloria in excelsis Deo,     et in terra pax hominibus bonae*
Glory to God in the highest,     and on earth peace to men of good

*voluntatis.     Laudamus te,     benedicimus te,     adoramus te,*
will.     We praise Thee, we bless Thee,     we adore Thee,

*glorificamus te, gratias agimus tibi     propter magnam gloriam tuam.*
we glorify Thee, we give thanks to Thee for Thy great glory.

*Domine Deus,     rex coelestis,     Deus Pater omnipotens,*
Lord, God,     heavenly King, God the Father almighty,

*Domine Fili unigenite,     Jesu Christe,     Domine Deus,*
O Lord, the only begotten Son,     Jesus Christ,     Lord God,

*Agnus Dei,     Filius Patris,     qui tollis     peccata mundi,*
Lamb of God, Son of the Father, who takest away the sins of the world,

*miserere nobis;     qui tollis peccata mundi*
have mercy on us; Thou who takest away the sins of the world,

*suscipe deprecationem nostram; qui sedes ad dexteram*
receive our prayer;     Thou who sittest on the right hand

*Patris, miserere nobis.     Quoniam tu solus sanctus,*
of the Father, have mercy on us.     For Thou only art holy,

*tu solus Dominus,     tu solus altissimus,     Jesu Christe,*
Thou only art the Lord, Thou only, Jesus Christ, art most high

*cum Sancto Spiritu in gloria Dei Patris.     Amen.*[2]
with the holy Ghost in the glory of God the Father.     Amen.

## CREDO

*Credo in unum Deum,     Patrem omnipotentem,     factorem coeli et terrae,*
I believe in one God,     Father almighty,     Maker of heaven and earth,

*visibilium omnium et invisibilium.     Et in unum Dominum,     Jesum*
of all things visible and invisible.     And in one Lord,     Jesus

*Christum, Filium Dei unigenitum,     et ex Patre natum ante omnia*
Christ,     only begotten Son of God,     born of the Father before all

*saecula,     Deum de Deo,     lumen de lumine,     Deum verum de Deo vero,*
ages,     God of God,     Light of Light,     true God of the true God,

*genitum non factum,     consubstantialem     Patri,*
begotten, not made, being of one substance with the Father,

*per quem omnia facta sunt,     qui propter nos homines et propter*
by whom all things are made,     who for us men     and for

*nostram salutem descendit de coelis et incarnatus est de Spiritu Sancto*
our salvation came down from heaven and was incarnate by the Holy Spirit

*ex Maria Virgine;     et homo factus est.     Crucifixus etiam pro nobis*
of the Virgin Mary,     and was made man.     He was also crucified for our sake

[2]*Cum Sancto Spiritu in gloria Dei Patris. Amen.* is usually treated imitatively.

*sub Pontio Pilato,     passus et sepultus est.     Et resurrexit*
under Pontius Pilate,     suffered and was buried.     And He rose again

*tertia die     secundum scripturas     et ascendit in coelum,*
on the third day as told in the scriptures, and ascended into heaven,

*sedet ad dexteram Patris:               et iterum venturus est*
and sitteth at the right hand of the Father: and He shall come again

*cum gloria judicare vivos et mortuos:     cuius regni non erit*
with glory to judge the living and the dead: of whose kingdom there shall be no

*finis:   et in Spiritum Sanctum,          Dominum et vivificantem,*
end:   And [I believe] in the Holy Spirit,   Lord and Giver of life,

*qui ex Patre Filioque procedit,          qui cum Patre et*
who proceedeth from the Father and the Son, who with the Father and

*Filio simul   adoratur et conglorificatur,   qui locutus est per*
the Son together is worshipped and glorified, who spake by the

*prophetas.   Et               in unam sanctam catholicam*
prophets.     And [I believe]     in one holy     Catholic

*et apostolicam ecclesiam.   Confiteor unum baptisma in remissionem*
and Apostolic Church.       I acknowledge one baptism for the remission of

*peccatorum et expecto resurrectionem          mortuorum, et*
sins         and I look for the resurrection of the dead, and

*vitam venturi saeculi.          Amen.*[3]
the life of the world to come.     Amen.

### SANCTUS

*Sanctus,          sanctus, sanctus, Dominus Deus Sabaoth, pleni*
Holy,          Holy,   Holy,   Lord     God of Hosts,   full

*sunt coeli     et terra        gloria tua.     Hosanna in excelsis.*[4]
are the heavens and the earth of Thy glory.     Hosanna in the highest.

*Benedictus qui venit in nomine Domini.          **Hosanna in***
Blessed is he who cometh in the name of the Lord.     Hosanna in

*excelsis.*
the highest.

### AGNUS DEI

*Agnus Dei,     qui tollis     peccata mundi,          miserere nobis.*
Lamb of God, who takest away the sins of the world, have mercy on us.

*Agnus Dei,     qui tollis     peccata mundi,          miserere nobis.*
Lamb of God, who takest away the sins of the world, have mercy on us.

*Agnus Dei,     qui tollis     peccata mundi,          dona nobis pacem.*
Lamb of God, who takest away the sins of the world, grant us peace.

[3]*Et vitam venturi saeculi. Amen.* is usually treated imitatively.

[4]*Hosanna in excelsis* is usually treated imitatively.

When the musical setting of the Mass is extensive, with many repeats of words, one refers to a *Missa Solemnis* ("Solemn Mass"); a shorter setting, with relatively simple accompaniments and fewer word repetitions, is called a *Missa Brevis* ("Short Mass").

The Proper most often set to music is in the Mass for the Dead, the *Requiem Mass*. The Requiems of Mozart, Berlioz, Verdi, and Fauré are the best-known concert versions of this text. An unusual Requiem not using the standard text was composed by Brahms, whose *Ein deutsches Requiem* ("A German Requiem," 1868) utilized non-liturgical biblical texts in the vernacular, stressing comfort, hope, and defiance of death. His skillful use of contrasting textures, orchestral colors, subtle rhythmic alterations, and dynamic melodic changes reflects a remarkable dramatic instinct of a nature quite different from more traditional Mass treatments. Britten's *War Requiem* (1962) alternates the traditional Latin texts of the Requiem Mass with the intense anti-war poetry of Wilfred Owen.

**Symphonic works with chorus**

Some composers of the last 150 years have combined the medium of the multimovement symphony with that of choral music, sometimes with a liturgical text. This approach, inspired by Beethoven's Symphony No. 9, gained special attention during the last decades of the nineteenth century, especially in the music of Mahler, whose *Das klagende Lied* ("The Song of Lamentation," 1880) and second, third, and eighth symphonies call for choral, solo, and orchestral forces that produce masses of sound with many varieties of timbre and style.

Stravinsky's *A Symphony of Psalms* (1930), for two pianos, winds, lower strings, and a choir of boys' and men's voices, employs a different psalm text for each of its three movements. The first movement is in the manner of a prelude to the whole; the second is an extended fugue, beginning with austere woodwinds (suggesting the expectancy of the worshippers patiently waiting for the Lord), building to a dramatic announcement of salvation, then quietly ending; the third is a "symphonic allegro" that, while avoiding any formal label, deals with its thematic materials in a developmental fashion.

In its final movement, Beethoven's Symphony No. 9 (1817–23) uses vocal soloists and chorus as members of the orchestra in a series of variations on a simple theme. Vaughan Williams, in his *A Sea Symphony* (1910), treated voices in a romantic way, relying on masses of tone color rather than thematic manipulation. Britten's *Spring Symphony* (1949), calling for soprano, alto, and tenor solos, mixed choir, and boys' voices, draws its text from poems by various authors and concludes with a buoyant setting of the Medieval round, *Sumer is icumen in.*

### *Smaller choral genres*

**Madrigal**

The *madrigal* is a musical type that reached its greatest flowering in the late sixteenth century in Italy, where it was most often concerned with the sighings of unrequited love. Many Italian madrigals were richly dramatic, and some were narrative. In England, the madrigal took one of two forms; the *ballett* was a delightful polyphonic treatment of a pastoral text, ending with a refrain of "fa, la" or something similar; Byrd, Gibbons, Dowland, and a host of others also wrote a more sensitive kind of madrigal rivaling the Italians in depth of expression.

*Luca della Robbia (ca. 1399–1482). Choirboys. Part of a series of sculptures for the "Singing Gallery," or Cantoria, of the Florence cathedral. Robbia's bas-relief reflects the influence of Hellenism on Italian Renaissance art. (The Bettmann Archive)*

The madrigal is polyphonic; that is, each of the voices or parts is melodically and rhythmically independent. The great madrigalists of the late Renaissance, including Monteverdi, Marenzio, and Gesualdo, invested their music with daring harmonies, jagged, emotional melodies, and rhythmic freedom to an extent that is remarkable even today.

While beautiful in its own right, the madrigal is also important for historical reasons. Deeply interested in using music for storytelling purposes in the form of staged drama, composers found themselves hampered by the many-voiced quality of Renaissance music, notably the highly picturesque madrigal. It was apparent that the relationship of two characters could not be clearly established if five people were required to do the singing, and the independence of the melodic lines tended to obscure the words. The *Camerata*, concerned with this problem, as well as with reviving the spirit of the ancient Greek plays, capitalized on the melodic and harmonic intensity of the madrigal but reduced its texture to a single melodic line reinforced by harmonic accompaniment. The Italian madrigal, therefore, became an important forerunner of opera.

**Motet**

Of all the choral types, the *motet* is one of the oldest, and has gone through the greatest variety of forms. The extent of this variety is such that one must refer to such types as the Medieval motet or the Renaissance motet, rather than to one genre as if it were the same in all eras. Historically, the motet reached its greatest popularity during the Middle Ages and the Renaissance, although many Baroque, Romantic, and contemporary composers have created choral works described by this term.

The Medieval motet, as it developed in the thirteenth century, was essentially the result of adding a text (*mot* being French for "word") to a melody that originally had been vocalized, or sung on an open vowel, above a fragment of a plainsong; this fragment was sung in long note values.[5] In many cases, each of the several parts juxtaposed over the plainsong fragment, or cantus firmus, had a separate text that could be sacred or secular. Often, in liturgical motets, the added texts were paraphrases of the text of the cantus firmus.

By the time of the Renaissance, the motet had become an intricate,

---

[5]When words are added to a melody, or when a new melody is somehow inserted between segments of an old melody, or when a musical section is inserted between sections of a composition, or when both new words and music are inserted into a piece of music, the new material is said to be *troped*. The original motet, then, was a type of trope.

highly polyphonic, dramatic, and inventive sacred choral composition, second in importance only to settings of the Mass. Motet texts have been taken from both liturgical and nonliturgical sources. Some of the more frequently used religious poems are the *Te Deum Laudamus* ("We Praise Thee, O Lord"), the *Jubilate Deo* ("Rejoice in God"), the *Stabat Mater dolorosa* ("There Stood the Mother, Grieving"), *Salve Regina* ("Hail Queen"), and the *Benedicite, opera omnia Domini* ("Oh All Ye Works of the Lord, Bless Ye the Lord").

The Renaissance motet is religious, the madrigal is secular. Beyond this immediate distinction, the two are structurally similar, the madrigal being somewhat more innovative and daring, and its sections shorter and more varied. Like the madrigal, the motet treated each portion of its text as a separate section, sometimes beginning it imitatively. To avoid a constant starting and stopping, each section was begun while the previous section was ending, thus providing a sense of continuous, ongoing motion. Each of these beginnings or dovetailings of a new text in musical imitation is called a "point of imitation."

In the hands of such giants as Lassus, Palestrina, and Monte, the motet could be as powerful and as emotional as any madrigal. Palestrina's music is usually cited as the epitome of the Renaissance style. His many motets and complete settings of the Mass are identified by flowing melody and delicate interweaving of parts that produce a remarkable, intellectual complexity rendered inconspicuous by the music's sense of ineffable calm. One of his two settings of the *Agnus Dei* for his *Missa Brevis* (1570) is typical of these traits.

The first feature one can identify is the gentle progression downward in each voice; the second is the constant imitation among the five voices called for in this movement. The imitation is literal between the two soprano lines, and, in fact, these two parts sing in *canon* (that is, in strict imitation) throughout the movement. The alto, tenor, and bass parts are freer in their use of this device, as one can see in Ex. 9.7. This example shows the start of the last section of the Mass, with the canonic parts printed in large notes, the more freely moving lower parts in smaller notes. Note that there are no large skips within a phrase, and that the feeling of a descending melody is not at all a precipitous one. Note also that there is no strong sense of accent drawing attention to any one beat as more important than another. This unmetrical rhythm is a major contributing factor to the feeling of repose, discipline, and prayerfulness gained from Palestrina's music, which, as with much of the ensemble music of his time, was written without measure lines.

**EX. 9.7 PALESTRINA**   Beginning of *Agnus Dei II*, from *Missa Brevis*

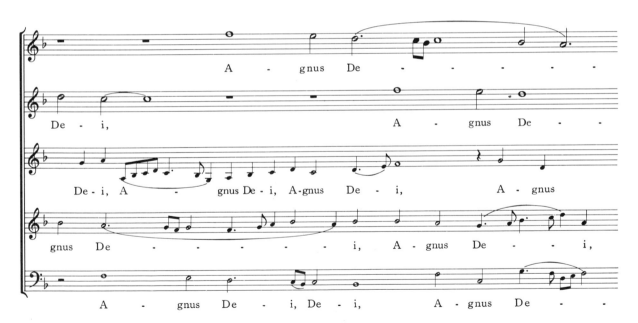

The Renaissance English composers cultivated the motet, too, but preferred to call it an *anthem*. Byrd and Gibbons worked especially in the style of the *verse anthem*, a composition alternating sections for chorus with sections for one or more solo voices. By the time Purcell and Handel

*Mathew Disel.* Choral and Orchestral Performance. *A Baroque setting in a Munich church or palace, in which architecture and decoration seem wedded to exciting sonorities and decorative melodies. Note that there are two organs. (The Bettmann Archive)*

brought the anthem to its fullest Baroque development, it had become a diverse form much like the structure of the cantata.

In the Baroque era, the motet was often in several movements, each movement being choral, rather than mixed recitative-aria-chorus as the cantata was. Bach composed six motets in this poly-movement fashion, the most famous of them being *Jesu, meine Freude* (usually translated "Jesus, Priceless Treasure" or "Jesus, Dearest Master," 1723).

Interest in the motet declined during the Classical period, but returned in the nineteenth century, especially in the work of Brahms. A number of sacred choral motets were also composed by Mendelssohn, Liszt, Verdi, and Berlioz.

Many twentieth-century composers find the motet a congenial and unrestricted area of composition for both sacred and secular texts. Schoenberg's passionate *Friede auf Erden* ("Peace on Earth," 1907), for unaccompanied eight-part chorus, is a monumental work, and Poulenc's *Stabat Mater* (1951), for soprano solo, chorus, and orchestra, infuses a modern, spiritual exuberance into an ancient sacred text. These are but two examples of many contemporary motets that display exciting rhythmic variety and melodic and harmonic expressiveness.

**Chorale**

When Luther and others began the Protestant Reformation early in the sixteenth century, the active participation by the congregation in the music of the worship service became a vital part of the new theology. Since the congregations were musically far less sophisticated than the trained choirs who had been entrusted with almost all the music prior to this religious revolution, a musical style was required that would enable the parishioners to remember the melodies of their hymns, that would make these melodies easy to sing, and that would be of a rhythmic character simple enough to keep a large group of singers together, even when they were spread along the length of the great naves of the larger churches.

Luther was himself a skilled musician and composed some of these hymns, or *chorales*, expressly for this purpose. Other chorales, equally marked by regular, clearly-defined phrases, relatively narrow melodic range, and stately, solid rhythmical motion, were reworkings of a variety of tunes, including both plainsong melodies and folksongs.[6] Thus, the

---

[6]Luther, commenting on his approval of secular melodies for sacred texts, is said to have asked, "Why should the devil have all the good tunes?"

Gregorian *Veni Creator Spiritus* ("Come, O Creator Spirit," for the Second Vespers of Whitsunday) became *Komm, Gott Schöpfer, heiliger Geist* ("Come, God, Creator, Holy Spirit") and *Veni Redemptor Gentium* ("Come, Redeemer of the Nations") became *Nun komm der Heiden Heiland* ("O Come, Thou Who Art Savior of the Gentiles").

These chorales—and there are many—were not only sung in unison by Protestant congregations, but became the cantus firmi, or foundation melodies, for more elaborate choral and instrumental compositions. Many of J. S. Bach's cantatas begin with a complex, free treatment of a chorale tune in the manner of a *fantasia*; most of these cantatas end with a four-part harmonization of the melody that seems simple to the listener, but includes some wonderfully inventive chord progressions.

Chorales were also used as cantus firmi for many organ pieces that served to introduce the congregation's unison singing of the chorale; in such a case, the terms *organ chorale* or *chorale prelude* are appropriate.

The chorale style is impressive today and is used frequently in Protestant services of worship. One of its most notable treatments may be heard in Honegger's oratorio *King David*, which concludes with the transformation of a brief recitative for soprano into a sturdy melody for the basses of the choir, over which orchestral and choral voices provide a thrilling fantasia.

**Part song**     Especially in the nineteenth century, but also very often in the twentieth century, composers have produced short lyric pieces to be sung by few singers per part, with or without piano accompaniment. These part songs tend to be simple in texture and harmony, but composers such as Schubert, Brahms, Randall Thompson (especially in *Frostiana*, 1959), and Hindemith have bestowed some of their best musical thinking upon them. Part songs, which may exist for mixed voices, men's voices alone, or women's voices alone, form the bulk of the repertoire for school choral groups in modern America, and many have moments of great charm and expressiveness well worth hearing.

**Other small choral types**     So many terms have been applied to choral compositions of varying excellence and style that the reader can be needlessly confused by a lengthy description of them. The interested student might profitably consult the *Glossary* for brief definitions of *catch, glee, ode, chanson, canzona, virelai, rondeau, conductus, ballata, ballad,* and *caccia.*

# 10 : MUSIC FOR INSTRUMENTS ~ The Symphony

THE symphony is a compound form for orchestra (and sometimes for band) in which several movements are contrasted by various means of melodic treatment as well as by changes in tempo, meter, emotional quality, texture, and dynamics. An infinite variety of tone colors and sounds exist in the symphony orchestra and each contributes to the musical whole; thus, the creator is called upon not only to demonstrate his genius as a composer but as an orchestrator as well.

There is some question whether a relationship of some sort exists between the movements of symphonies (or any other similar, multimovement compositions). In the symphonies of the Classical period, movements are related only by key. If, for example, the key of the symphony is C minor, this would mean that the first and last movements would probably begin and end in that key. The other movements might then be in related keys. (Keys are related when there are important chords common to both.)

A stronger inter-movement relationship can be established by rhythmic repetition from one to another or by using the same melodic material in more than one movement. Rhythmic repetition is a device Beethoven used in his Symphony No. 5, where the pattern of three short notes followed by a long one ( 𝄽 ♪♪♪ 𝅗𝅥 ), which is the basis for the first movement, also occurs prominently in the third and fourth movements, as will be seen in a later analysis of this work. Beethoven's Symphony

No. 9 utilizes melodic recall by quoting passages from the first three movements at the beginning of the fourth movement.

When melodic material is transferred from movement to movement, a multimovement work is said to be *cyclic*. By repeating motives or thematic material in subsequent movements, a composer can remind his listeners of previously experienced emotions and earlier thoughts, thus causing the meaning of a complete work to be cogently summarized. An example of the technique of cyclic writing in a symphony may be found in Tchaikovsky's Symphony No. 5, in E minor, Op. 64, where the theme for the introduction of the first movement becomes a harsh transitional fragment in the second, material for a coda in the third, and blossoms into a powerful main theme in the finale. Other composers who used cyclic writing to great advantage in their symphonic works were Dvořák and Franck.

### The symphony in the Classical period

The word "symphony" has its origins in the Italian word, *sinfonia*, a term used in the Baroque era to refer to any orchestral composition used as part of an opera or oratorio. In the operas of Alessandro Scarlatti, the term became more specifically relevant to his three-movement overtures. By 1740, when this type of overture (known as the *Italian overture* to avoid confusion with the two-part *French overture* of Lully, Handel, and others) was performed for audiences independently of any vocal work, the sinfonia had become a concert piece in its own right, and, eventually, the major germinal form for the Classical symphony.[1]

In mid-eighteenth century, a number of composers centering their activities around the city of Mannheim helped to establish one of Europe's first great orchestras. They, with Johann Stamitz as one of the most prominent figures, created a symphonic style characterized by the following: the use of sharply contrasted keys and themes (or groups of themes) within a single movement; simple themes made up of striking, easily separable, motives; intense melodic development; clarity of form; and a dynamic variety ranging from subtle gradations to sharply contrasted levels of sound. All these traits eventually became essential elements of the great Classical symphonies, and it was at this point that the great Austro-German symphonic tradition was firmly established.

[1]Musicologists also note the influences on the development of the symphony of several other genres, notably the *divertimento*, the *suite*, and the *concerto grosso*. For a thorough history of the symphony, the reader is referred to Homer Ulrich's helpful *Symphonic Music* (New York: Columbia University Press, 1952).

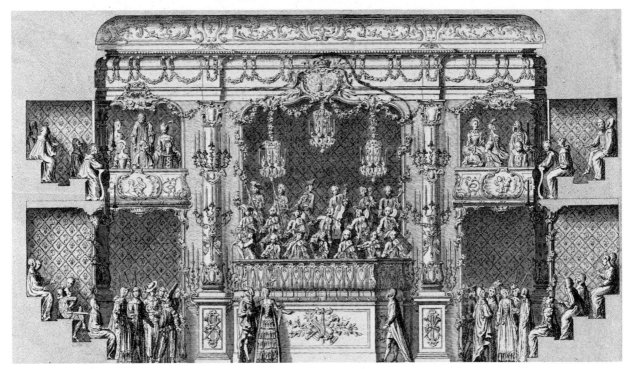

*A court orchestra in the setting of a Rococo theater. Symmetry, elegance, and refinement characterize the sound of eighteenth-century music and the environment in which it was performed. The orchestra shown is predominantly strings, save for trumpet and oboe (both in the first row, left), two bassoons (last row), and military drum (second row, right). The absence of a basso continuo group marks this as a classically conceived orchestra, while the costumes of the performers entering at the left suggest that the orchestra may be about to accompany a commedia dell' arte troupe. (The Bettmann Archive)*

By 1780, the symphony orchestra had become the single most popular vehicle for instrumental ensemble composition. Its instrumentation usually called for pairs of flutes, oboes, bassoons, horns, and trumpets as well as anywhere from fifteen to forty strings; timpani were an essential rhythmic and harmonic force of the orchestras of the period. Clarinets were not consistently employed until after 1780.[2]

One of those most responsible for the development of the symphony into a mature and meaningful form was Haydn, who during his lifetime was the most celebrated composer in all of Europe. Haydn was prolific; among his works were 104 symphonies. The earlier works, which include

---

[2]A chart of the major European orchestras and their instrumentations between 1750 and 1800 may be found in Adam Carse, *The History of Orchestration* (New York: Dover Publications, Inc., 1964), p. 171.

many gems, show an experimentation that contributed to the development of the symphony as a genre; the last thirty or so (those written after 1781) are products of Haydn at his mature best, with the last twelve, which he wrote in London, being especially noteworthy.[3] Among these are such perennial favorites as the *Surprise* (No. 94, in G), *Clock* (No. 101, in D), *Drum Roll* (No. 103, in E-flat), and the *London* (No. 104, in D). The popularity of these titles should not obscure the excellence of the others of this group of twelve nor of many of the earlier works, for musicians and audiences alike consistently find them challenging, stimulating, fascinating, and aesthetically pleasing in every way.

Haydn's younger contemporary and friend, Mozart, was also a superb symphonist, writing some forty-nine in his brief lifetime.[4] The two composers represent the highest point of attainment in Classical symphonic composition, for their symphonies reveal the most ingenious and expressive manipulation of musical ideas in terms always vital, elegant, and clear. Their capacity for seeing the possibilities of development, contrast, or variation still amazes audiences, as does the ease with which they move from simple melody and texture to complex polyphony and profound utterance.

The form of the Classical symphony, as demonstrated in the most important works of Haydn and Mozart, is in four movements, the first of which is most often a sonata form (see discussion of the first movement of Mozart's Symphony No. 40, in G minor, in Chapter 6), the second a slow movement in either a ternary form or a theme and variations, the third a gracious or zestful minuet with trio, and the fourth either a sonata, a rondo, or a sonata-rondo.

**Beethoven**     While emotional qualities were an essential part of their art, the eighteenth-century symphonists were primarily concerned that the music reflect a sense of proportion and formal balance. It remained for Beethoven to add to the symphony that element of overt, deeply felt expression that would mark the symphonies of the nineteenth and early twentieth centuries.

Beethoven was a student of Haydn for a short time and from him he

---

[3]These are sometimes referred to as the "London" or "Salomon" symphonies, the latter sobriquet taken from the name of the impresario who invited Haydn to undertake the two journeys to London and to compose for various performing groups there.
[4]Misnumbering of the earlier symphonies by publishers would make it appear that Mozart had written only forty-one, since the last in order of composition is published and programmed today with that number.

learned much about form, development, and melodic content. His early works, including the First Symphony, reveal the Haydn influence, a force somewhat less evident in the Second Symphony. The powerful Symphony No. 3 (*Eroica*) shows a distinct break from the expressive restraint which at times characterized the Classical period while retaining the Classical concern for form and development or variation. In it, Beethoven gave almost free rein to his emotions. It was to be dedicated to Napoleon but, as a result of the French general's greed for power, Beethoven angrily ripped off the title page and left instead the statement that the work was "a heroic symphony, composed to celebrate the memory of a great man."

Except for the Sixth Symphony (*Pastoral*), which has five movements, all of Beethoven's nine symphonies follow the four-movement plan. There are some changes in the types of movements, however. Beethoven moved away from the minuet, substituting the faster, more robust *scherzo* for it. The second movement of the *Eroica* is a funeral march; the finale of the Ninth Symphony (*Choral*) calls for chorus and vocal soloists. The Sixth Symphony has a distinct programmatic quality, its five movements being subtitled "Cheerful Impressions on Arriving in the Country," "By the Brook," "Peasants Merrymaking," "The Storm," and "The Shepherds' Hymn," although Beethoven stressed that this programmatic quality was meant to be "more the expression of sentiment than the painting of a picture."

**Beethoven: Symphony No. 5, in C minor, Op. 67**

Beethoven's Fifth Symphony serves as an excellent example not only of the symphonic style, but also of the Romantic-Classic dualism in music. Because of its intensity of emotional expression, its musical logic, and its structural clarity, it represents the perfect amalgam of the passion of the nineteenth century with the musical architecture of the eighteenth century.

The symphony's first movement opens with a rhythmic motive played by the whole orchestra; it is on this motive (labeled *m* in Example 10.1) that the principal theme is built. This principal theme is somewhat short and quite angular.

**EX. 10.1 BEETHOVEN**
Symphony No. 5, in C minor, Op. 67, 1st mvt., bars 1–20

The second theme is similarly short but is of a more lyric nature; it is introduced by the main rhythmic figure.

EX. 10.2 *Ibid.*
bars 59–70

The exposition of this sonata form is not too lengthy and should be repeated in performance, as was the common practice for works of the Classic period. The rhythmic intensity of the movement is the result of the continual use of the motive, which is played against itself and against fragments of the lyric second theme throughout the development section. The recapitulation brings the themes back in a more complete form and a coda finishes the movement.

The second movement is a theme and variations.[5] There is no introduction; the theme is stated immediately in the cellos and violas.

EX. 10.3 *Ibid.*
2nd mvt., bars 1–8

Violas and Cellos

It is relatively long and lyric. Although there is a great deal of orchestral color in the movement, each variation holds to the orchestration of the original theme statement.

The third movement is a scherzo, in which the rhythmic element of the main theme is directly related to that of the first movement and contributes to the feeling of intensity and cogent organization pervading the symphony as a whole.

EX. 10.4 *Ibid.*
3rd mvt., bars 1–8

Horns

[5]The theme and variations pattern of the movement is unusual and causes disagreement over the labelling of the movement's actual melodic content. Tovey, in his *Essays in Musical Analysis* (London: Oxford University Press, 1935; Vol. 1, p. 41), says that the movement has two themes, the first of which is given the most variational attention. Other writers suggest that there is one theme in two parts; still others that there is simply one long theme.

The fact that it is hammered out by the horns suggests that a bit of Beethovenian humor is involved. The older third movements—minuets—were light, graceful, and somewhat airy; the rigor of this movement is really a thunderous mockery of them. The humor shows best in the trio, however. Trios traditionally were to be played by solo instruments, creating contrast with the richer, lower sound of the full orchestra. When orchestras became larger and more proficient, more than three instruments would be playing in the trios, but trio sections were generally orchestrated a little more lightly and were, perhaps, somewhat simpler melodically than the rest of the minuet. Beethoven thumbed his nose at all of that, especially in this symphony. Not only did he turn it around and start the trio at the bottom of the orchestra in the cellos and basses, he also made the theme much more complex and stated it fugally. The result was, instead of a delicate trio, a gruff and rumbly growl behind which was a broad Beethoven grin.

**EX. 10.5** *Ibid.*
bars 141–147

The return to the main theme of the scherzo and its subsequent statement becomes one of the greatest delights in all of Beethoven's music, for here he again steps out of the ordinary. Where the theme was stated in loud sounds at the beginning of the movement, there is now muted softness. The orchestra speaks *sotto voce* for the whole theme restatement and into the coda, and it is obvious that Beethoven is building something. Only when what starts as the coda becomes a transition does his purpose become apparent; he is making a very careful and suspenseful preparation for the fourth movement. After all of the softness there comes a great crescendo that leads directly to the opening powerful chords (reinforced by the use of trombones, their first appearance in symphonic literature) of that movement's group of principal themes.

**EX. 10.6** *Ibid.*
4th mvt., bars 1–8

*The symphony in the Classical period* **193**

There is an emotional climax here. The crescendo contributes to it, as does the change from the minor tonality of the third movement to the major tonality of the fourth. Mostly, the climax comes from the stateliness and directness of the theme itself and its great contrast with what has gone before.

Very shortly the horns pronounce the majestic second theme of the principal group (like the first movement of the symphony, the fourth is in sonata form).

**EX. 10.7** *Ibid.* bars 26–33

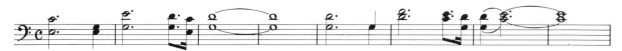

The second theme group contrasts with the first group by being somewhat less angular, more lyric, and somewhat more personal in nature. Its first member is heard in the violins.

**EX. 10.8** *Ibid.* bars 45–48

The cello countermelody, heard in measures 46 ff., is greatly exploited by Beethoven later on, in the development. The other member of the second group of themes is played by the clarinets and violas, and closes the exposition.

**EX. 10.9** *Ibid.* bars 64–72

At the end of the development section, Beethoven creates one of the most famous surprises in symphonic literature by quietly thrusting the main section of the third movement scherzo between the end of the development and the recapitulation. The tense playing of the scherzo's opening phrases, heard in violins and clarinets, provides for the triumphant appearance of the recapitulation much in the manner of the transition from the end of the third movement to the fourth, with remarkable freedom from any sort of anticlimax. The result is a structural cohesion for the entire four-movement symphony and a sense of elation and release that is psychologically and aesthetically one of the greatest moments in all music. A coda rushes the movement to a brilliant conclusion.

Beethoven's Symphony No. 5 demonstrates both the Classical and Romantic characteristics. Its form is quite obviously classically oriented:

the first movement is a sonata form, the second a theme and variations, the third a song form with trio, and the last another sonata form. The themes within each movement are clearly defined and maintain the tradition and balance of the period, although the scherzo is exceptional because of its unusual trio, its direct connection to the following movement, and because its theme returns before the recapitulation section of the last movement.

The emotional content of the work is an entirely different matter. The symphony is powerful, and this power is in sharp contrast with the stylistic elegance found in the compositions of Beethoven's immediate predecessors. It would never have occurred to eighteenth-century composers to introduce a movement as dramatically as Beethoven introduced the finale. The almost savage, motivic principal theme of the first movement would not have belonged in the music written before 1800. The excitement in orchestral color is also hardly exemplary of the eighteenth century.

In the symphonies of Beethoven can be found indications of what was to follow in the nineteenth century. In the *Eroica*, one senses a quality of extra-referential meaning, manifested by the dedicatory sentiment and the use of a title, and, more importantly, the music itself. This extra-referentialism shows even more strongly in the *Pastoral* Symphony, where, although Beethoven took great pains to explain that he was merely seeking to create impressions in the minds of the listeners, very definite program music of a descriptive nature can be found. The storm, musically depicted in the fourth movement, is as literal a description of that natural phenomenon as can be found in all of music.

In all the symphonies, there is a very direct emotional expression related to the music itself, and, with rare exception, the music displays a consummate skill in the craft of composition. Melodic design, formal structure, and textural fabric are never left without control. The symphonies thus stand as monuments for those composers who followed to look back upon and to emulate.

### The symphony in the Romantic period: Austria and Germany

There were those who thought that Beethoven's music proved the power of extra-referentialism. Berlioz was one such composer, and his *Fantastic Symphony*, written in 1831, helped to start a whole new trend in this direction.

On the other hand, there were those composers who saw in the Beethoven symphonies a successful merger of Classical form and Romantic expression and patterned their works accordingly. Among these were

Schubert (a contemporary of Beethoven), Mendelssohn, Robert Schumann, and Brahms. Although these composers span an entire century (Schubert was born in 1797 and Brahms died in 1897), there is a mutual concern for formal structure that shows in all their symphonies; with little exception, all of their works followed the traditional four-movement pattern.

Although there are no late-nineteenth-century symphonies represented in the recordings accompanying this book, the symphonic style of the period can be detected in the excerpts from *Die Walküre*. Wagner felt that Beethoven's use of a text in the final movement of the Ninth Symphony was the result of an urge to define more deeply and specifically those meanings that could only be suggested by instrumental sounds. In a sense, therefore, Wagner's music dramas (a term he preferred to "opera") are symphonies with words. The motives of *Die Walküre* are manipulated and developed in time-honored ways as well as in new ways, the latter including a uniquely wide range of keys and a rich vocabulary of harmonies. Most important is Wagner's concept of "endless melody," an ongoing musical fabric in which textures continuously change, terminal cadences are avoided, and sections, theme groups, and key areas become less well defined. The list of instruments required for *Die Walküre* is illustrative of the impact of Romantic orchestration, especially when compared with the typical orchestra of the 1780's. Wagner's score requires the following:

| STRINGS | BRASSES |
|---|---|
| 16 first violins | 8 French horns |
| 16 second violins | 2 tenor tubas |
| 12 violas | 2 bass tubas |
| 12 cellos | 1 contrabass tuba |
| 8 double basses | 3 trumpets |
| 6 harps | 1 bass trumpet |
| | 3 tenor trombones |
| | 3 bass trombones |
| | 1 contrabass trombone |
| WOODWINDS | |
| 2 piccolos | PERCUSSION |
| 3 flutes | 2 pairs of timpani |
| 4 oboes | 1 triangle |
| 1 English horn | 1 pair of cymbals |
| 3 clarinets | 1 snare drum |
| 1 bass clarinet | 1 glockenspiel |
| 3 bassoons | 1 tam-tam |
| 1 contrabassoon | |

Wagner's beliefs about the use of the orchestra were shared by at least two of the late-nineteenth-century Austro-German composers, Bruckner and Mahler. Both were primarily composers of symphonies.

Bruckner's sense of orchestration, as demonstrated in his nine published symphonies, was one of exploration of pure color. He would often call for enlarged orchestral sections, especially in the brasses and winds, to emphasize melodic lines and to enrich harmonies.

Mahler's works also reflect a concept of orchestral bigness, but he went even further in his search for meaning. By nature, Mahler was gloomy and hyperemotional and in his music he revealed a marked degree of melancholy (*Weltschmerz*) combined with an urge to embrace all of creation in philosophical and musical terms. The most diverse styles are found within the confines of single movements of works—imitations of nature, chorales, folksongs, immense climaxes, and the like. He felt that expression at times must exceed the bounds established by purely instrumental music, so in several of his ten symphonies (nos. 2, 3, 4, and 8) vocal lines were added to be sung either by soloists or choruses. For sheer magnitude in number of performers and scope, no symphony can match his Eighth Symphony, the *Symphony of a Thousand*. When Mahler died in 1911, the Austro-German symphonic tradition was essentially at an end, although many twentieth-century composers have been influenced by it.

### The symphony in the Romantic period: other countries

The symphony was popular in other countries during the Romantic era. A few French composers showed interest in the form: Franck wrote one a three-movement, cyclic symphony now considered a major item in the standard repertoire, and Saint-Saëns wrote three, the last of which is unusual in that it calls for an organ (and is sometimes subtitled *The Organ Symphony*). Russian composers also showed symphonic predilections, especially Tchaikovsky, whose fourth, fifth, and sixth symphonies are ranked among the world's favorites. Dvořák, a Bohemian (and a protegé of Brahms), is well known for his eighth and ninth symphonies, the latter bearing the title *From the New World*. The Finnish composer Sibelius must be included prominently in any list of Romantic symphonists, although he lived and worked well into the twentieth century.

### The symphony in the twentieth century

A number of modern composers have rejected the symphony as a workable form. Chief among this group who have found the symphony the least compatible to their ideas are Schoenberg, Berg, and Webern, the leaders in the school of compositional thought known as *Viennese Ex-*

*A performance of Beethoven's Symphony No. 9, in D minor, before the General Assembly of the United Nations at the celebration of its tenth anniversary in October, 1955. The New York Philharmonic-Symphony Orchestra and the Schola Cantorum are under the direction of Leonard Bernstein. The large number of singers and musicians only hints at the massiveness and dramatic impact of Beethoven's conception; the ingenuity of variation and development, expressiveness of melody and harmony, and appropriateness and power of timbre and dynamic change can be communicated only aurally, not visually. (Courtesy of the New York Philharmonic-Symphony Orchestra)*

*pressionism*, a school dedicated to the use of atonal, twelve-tone serialism as a basis for composition. Webern was the only one of the three to compose a symphony, and his lone two-movement contribution (*Symphony*, Op. 21) does not adhere to the Classical design. Twelve-tone serialism has become a most important compositional device since its beginnings (circa 1924) and a number of composers in this country and elsewhere have adopted it. None, at least since they made the adoption, have been major symphonists.

Those composers who work with the electronic media have also tended to avoid the symphonic forms. One reason for this could be the medium itself; electronic music does not need a symphony orchestra for performance, although some composers have combined the two media.

Other composers have simply used forms other than the symphony. The shifting, atmospheric harmonies and unpredictable cadences used by Debussy (and to a certain extent, other Impressionistic composers) seemed to be best suited for freer, rhapsodic forms. Ravel also chose the freer forms. Bartók, when he wrote for the orchestra, generally favored the concerto over the symphony. A number of American composers have turned to ballet music and the resultant suites.

Even so, there is a large group of composers who have used the symphonic form in this century, although with some modifications. Some of these have written tonally, others atonally, and still others somewhere in between. For those in the last two categories, there has been a relaxation of the principles of key relationships as they were inherited from the nineteenth century. Atonality is approached and even reached in a number of symphonic works. Other adaptations are related to the forms of the various movements. Instead of the sonata/theme and variations/ scherzo (or minuet) with trio/sonata (or rondo) scheme for four movements usually found in the nineteenth-century symphonies, composers have used other patterns of forms for their movements. William Schuman chose for his Third Symphony a scheme of passacaglia/fugue/chorale/ toccata, thus causing his working out of musical materials to be done in different ways. Even the accepted idea of four movements was changed. Harris' Third Symphony and Schuman's Sixth Symphony are one-movement works. Creston's Second Symphony is in two movements and a number of composers have written three-movement works, including Stravinsky (*Symphony of Psalms, Symphony in Three Movements*) and Hanson (Symphony No. 2, *Romantic*).

The instruments required for performance vary considerably from the usual complement of the symphony orchestra. Stravinsky's *Symphony of Psalms* calls for chorus and orchestra with an abbreviated string section; Schuman and Persichetti have composed symphonies for strings alone; Webern's symphony calls for clarinet, bass clarinet, two horns, harp, and a very small string section. Symphonies for the concert band have been written by Hindemith, Creston, Giannini, and others.

Although there are some who claim that the symphony is no longer a viable art form, present-day symphonic works have been as exciting and satisfying to hear and to know as traditionally conceived ones from previous centuries. The reasons for their being written are the same, but since some of the constructional details have been changed, the listener can have that often enjoyable experience of searching for aesthetic meaning through a new vocabulary of sound.

### *The concerto in the Baroque period*

ALTHOUGH the symphony was not recognizable until the mid-eighteenth century, the early types of the concerto date from the 1680's, the mid-point of the Baroque era. The concerto is said to have its source in the sixteenth-century practice of antiphonal singing by church choirs, notably in Venice's St. Mark's Cathedral. This practice, the alternation of two opposing choirs within a single piece of music, was first modified by the replacement of one of the choirs with a group of instruments. The next step, taken by Giovanni Gabrieli late in the sixteenth century, was to eliminate the voices altogether and leave the alternation to equally-sized groups of instruments. In the seventeenth century, Corelli and others introduced further refinements by reducing the size of one of the groups of instruments and elevating it in importance. The result was an instrumental composition known as the *concerto grosso*, which called for a small group of players, the *concertino*, to be alternated with a large group, the *ripieno*. Most first and last movements called for the *ripieno* to play similar material for each of its passages; this returning material is called the *ritornello*. The soloists were given contrasting and varied materials.

It was another logical step to reduce the concertino to a single player, thus creating contrast in sound between one player and an orchestra. The first such work is attributed to Torelli, who, like Corelli, was a celebrated violinist.

There were thus three distinct concerto types in existence during the

*Georges Rouault (1871–1958).* The Old King *(1916–1937).*
*Rich in color and emotion, this famous painting*
*bears a striking resemblance to Gothic stained*
*glass, the apparent source of Rouault's inspiration.*
*(Museum of Art, Carnegie Institute, Pittsburgh)* Colorplate **7**

*Edvard Munch (1863–1944).* The Scream *(1893). This
depiction of a nameless terror, so real it is indefinable
and beyond reality, is an example of the emotional intensity
typical of Expressionism. (The National Gallery, Oslo)*

Baroque era—the *orchestral concerto*, which alternated balanced groups of instrumentalists, the *concerto grosso*, and the *solo concerto*. All flourished during the period and it was from them that the modern concerto evolved. Few of the Baroque concertos have survived to the present as far as frequently encountered repertoire is concerned. Among those that have survived are J. S. Bach's six *Brandenburg* concertos,[1] in which each of the three types of Baroque concerto is represented: the Fourth Brandenburg Concerto is essentially a solo concerto for violin and orchestra (with important passages for two flutes); the Third and Sixth are orchestral concertos, and the others are all *concerti grossi* with each having a different set of instruments for its concertino. Several other concertos by Bach (some of them transcriptions of works by other composers) are still being performed. Some are for solo instruments, usually violin or keyboard, some are for two solo instruments, and some for larger concertino groups. Also quite notable are a number of concertos by Bach's contemporary, Handel, and the famous set of four solo concertos for violin and orchestra, *The Seasons*, by Vivaldi. Corelli's *Twelve Concerti Grossi* (Op. 6), are also performed from time to time.

### *The concerto in the Classical period*

The Baroque concertos, regardless of type, usually made less technical demands on their soloists than did the concertos of later periods. As the Baroque period ended and the Classical era began, the solo concerto became the most important, the other forms falling into virtual disuse until a revival of sorts in this century by Bartók, Bloch, and others. The *sinfonia concertante*, which blended several soloists with the orchestra rather than relying on alternation, was a modified form of the *concerto grosso* that gained some popularity in the eighteenth and nineteenth centuries. Several were written by Haydn and Mozart; a triple concerto by Beethoven (for piano, violin, cello, and orchestra) and a double concerto by Brahms (violin and cello) are important nineteenth-century vestiges of this form.

The concerto as conceived by the Classicists was cast in three movements. The first was usually a sonata form, the themes of which were to have some emotional strength. The second was usually slow and lyric, with the themes being highly ornamented by the solo instrument. The third movement was most usually a rondo. The minuet and trio, a fixture

---

[1] The name is derived from Bach's dedication of them to the Margrave of Brandenburg.

in Classical symphonies and string quartets, was not used in concertos.

It was an early practice for the first statement of the exposition of the first movement to be made by the orchestra, the solo instrument taking advantage of its own particular abilities and limitations, then entering and repeating the exposition. This "double exposition" came to be regarded as an unsatisfactory practice because it kept the soloist from participating in the establishment of an emotional climate and deprived him of a thematically dramatic entrance. It was Beethoven who made the complete break with the tradition. In his Piano Concerto No. 4, for instance, the pianist opens the first movement with no orchestral prelude at all, and, in his one violin concerto, the solo instrument enters dramatically within the first exposition.

As the concerto developed and matured through the late eighteenth century, the nature of the solo instrument increasingly affected the nature of the themes. A piano, for instance, could accompany itself and could ornament a melody with great ease. Passages requiring great technical facility could thus be written for it as could passages in which there was no orchestral accompaniment. A French horn, however, could play but one note at a time, had less flexibility, and, since the player's lips needed frequent rest, had to have extended pauses every once in a while. A concerto for horn would by necessity, then, have to have thematic content which, by being geared to the horn's qualities and requirements, would differ from that of a concerto for a piano. Thus, the idiomatic qualities of solo instruments became an important consideration for concerto composers.

**The cadenza**     The added subjectivity that resulted from the attention being paid to the qualities and natures of instruments, coupled with the ever-increasing emphasis on technical virtuosity, led to the inclusion of the *cadenza* in the concerto. Near the ends of first movements, and often third movements as well, the orchestral music would be brought to a halt and the soloist would be given an opportunity to improvise freely on the thematic material of the movement without any orchestral accompaniment. Such an improvisational passage (used also in many operatic arias) is known as a *cadenza*.

Since many concertos of the Classical period were written for the composer himself to play, the cadenza was almost never written out, but rather was indicated by a fermata sign ( $\frown$ ), or "hold," above a certain chord. The composer was, of course, familiar enough with the music to extemporize without getting too far afield or losing sight of his musical goals. With the gradual appearance of performing virtuosos who relied on the concertos of composers other than themselves, composers began to write out the full cadenza as a guard against bad taste or over-elaboration. Beethoven was the first composer to consider the cadenza as an integral, fully composed part of a concerto movement, and most composers since have followed suit.

Like the symphony, the concerto became a highly favored form during the Classical period and composers created a great number of them. Haydn wrote over thirty, including about fifteen for piano; Mozart wrote twenty-five for the piano and twenty-seven for various other instruments; Beethoven composed five piano concertos, a violin concerto, and the triple concerto.

The Classical concerto is an accurate reflection of the styles and traditions of its time. There is delicacy and elegance to be found in the handling of the musical elements as well as a highly refined interplay between the soloist and the orchestra. Thematic manipulation is easily perceived, and the themes themselves, especially in late period works, are so constructed that they show the idiomatic nature of the solo instrument. Form and balance were important and the traditions of key relationships within and between movements were rarely, if ever, violated.

### The concerto in the Romantic period

As the Classical period gave way to the Romantic period in the first decades of the nineteenth century, many of the traditional forms and styles, including the concerto, underwent metamorphosis. The Romanticists generally retained the Classic forms for their concertos but not with nearly as much rigidity. The changes made by Beethoven in the first movements opened new doors and allowed other changes. In his Piano Concerto No. 5, he tied the last two movements together (as he did in his Fifth Symphony), a procedure used by Robert Schumann in his one piano concerto.

Romantic composers placed increasing emphasis on virtuosity, many concertos becoming display pieces of extreme technical difficulty. Some of the violin concertos written by Paganini were so difficult that for years only he could play them, and Tchaikovsky's Violin Concerto was summarily dismissed by more than one violinist as being virtually unplayable. Richard Strauss's first horn concerto precipitated a crisis between him and his father, one of Europe's most noted horn players, because of its extreme difficulty. Liszt's two piano concertos also present many problems of technique for the performer.

At the same time, composers became interested in the orchestrational possibilities made available by the Romantic orchestra. Tone color became an important factor for the soloist and the orchestra. Going hand in hand with this was a fascination for beautiful melody of a highly individual and original character. Many of the concertos of the nineteenth century (and those of the twentieth century that have continued the Romantic tradition) are remembered for the haunting beauty of their themes. One may call to mind exquisite fragments of melody from piano concertos by Robert Schumann, Tchaikovsky, Brahms, and Rachmaninoff, from violin concertos by Mendelssohn and Tchaikovsky, and from Dvořák's Second Cello Concerto. Concertos by Barber and Bartók occasionally recall this lyric urge, even though written during a different stylistic epoch.

Many concertos of the Romantic period became intensely subjective statements of emotion, capitalizing on the spirit of the century. Attempts at expressing nationalistic ideas were rare, but the possibility of using the form (or a variant of it) programmatically seemed attractive. Berlioz' *Harold in Italy* is a programmatic concerto for viola and orchestra. Richard Strauss's *Don Quixote*, although not strictly a programmatic concerto, casts a solo cello in the role of the hero.

Because of their sometimes overriding concern for emotional expressivity, the Romantic composers felt that content could be more important than form and structure and, as a result, new, more serviceable forms (for example, the *tone poem*) were created. Also, they would transfer a concept to other forms if they felt it was necessary for expressive reasons. The *Konzertstück*, or "concert piece," a single-movement form for soloist and orchestra, became popular, especially in the works of Weber, Robert Schumann, and Liszt; the theme and variations was enlarged to concerto length and used by Franck, Tchaikovsky, and others.

### The concerto in the twentieth century

Twentieth-century composers, except for those who have continued in the Romantic tradition (such as Rachmaninoff and Richard Strauss), have lessened subjectivity in their concertos, but their attack on technique has been, if anything, even more relentless. Violin concertos by Berg, Stravinsky, and Schoenberg present formidable challenges to the performer, and they are beyond the capabilities of all but the most proficient players. Carter's piano concerto, written in 1964, is exceedingly complex for the orchestra as well as for the soloist.

This continuing demand for technical virtuosity has changed the format of the concerto in that the cadenza is no longer considered an essential part, such technical display now being incorporated into the work. This change can be noticed first in several nineteenth-century works without cadenzas; generally, these and similar contemporary works are either of exceptional difficulty for the performer or tend to emulate symphonies in which musical logic is more important than bravura and showiness.

There has been no universal dissatisfaction with traditional concerto forms by contemporary composers. Those who are considered Neoclassicists have, in fact, written concertos that are more rigidly structured than many nineteenth-century compositions. The sonata form is still used with relative frequency as a first movement in the concertos of Hindemith, Reger, Barber, Bartók, Prokofiev, and many others.

The *concerto grosso* has been revived and used to good advantage by the composers of the Modern era. Bloch's *Concerto Grosso for String Orchestra and Piano Obbligato* is a fine example; there are also *concerti grossi* by Křenek, Richard Strauss, and others. Bartók's *Concerto for Orchestra* is an especially interesting and important contemporary work. In it, the various instruments of the orchestra (except for some of those in the percussion section) at some time during the five movements become soloists or members of soloistic groups. The work is thus reflective of both the *concerto grosso* and the Baroque orchestral concerto.

The most popular solo instruments for concertos are the piano and the violin, with the cello third in order. Practically every instrument in the orchestra has a few concertos written for it, including the timpani (a work by Weinberger). A most unusual concerto is the one by Glière for soprano and orchestra (in which the soloist sings without words). Concertos are an integral part of the orchestral repertoire and many conductors do not consider a program complete without one.

### *Listening to a concerto*

In listening to a concerto, there is first of all an excitement engendered simply by watching the soloist perform in his unique and special capacity. There is really nothing quite like a concerto in any of the other arts; in its physical aspects it was once likened by an overly romantic writer to an athletic contest that pitched one against the masses—incredible odds, but, in the end, guess who won?

The idiomatic usage of the instrument is important for the concerto, especially those written after 1750. The composer had to keep himself within certain boundaries and tailor his thematic content to fit his soloist. There are particular qualities that belong to certain instruments; the cello can have a lyric, singing quality; the flute is nimble; the clarinet can play great rushes of notes over its entire range; the violin and the piano are extremely facile. When concertos for these instruments are played, listeners expect to hear these qualities. Also, certain traditions have assigned such subjective qualities as nobility to the French horn, plaintiveness to the oboe, and buffoonery to the bassoon. Although composers have often written passages in concertos that can display these meanings, they are, of course, far too limited to describe the full range of treatment given them in various works.

In the concertos of the Classical period, balance and elegance in all parts may be expected; form will be transparent. The Romantic concertos show a compositional predilection for the expressive and the subjective; there will be beautiful melodies couched in virtuoso technique. The twentieth-century concerto will most often demand great virtuosity, but the composer's attitude toward form and balance between soloist and orchestra may be either Classical or Romantic.

**Bartók:**
**Piano Concerto No. 3,**
**first movement**

The first movement of Bartók's Third Piano Concerto shows something of all the points noted above and thus can serve as an example of a somewhat universal concerto. It is cast in a strict sonata form (recalling the Classical period), has a rather hauntingly beautiful melody in its development section (Romantic), employs many twentieth-century harmonic and melodic devices, and makes strong technical demands on its soloist. In keeping with the twentieth-century idea, there is no cadenza. The movement is short in comparison to many concertos; in fact, the whole concerto is notable for its brevity.

There is a strong feeling of tonality in the movement, focused on the key of E. Both major and minor qualities are found, and listeners can detect a gypsy, folklike flavoring throughout.

The piano states the first theme almost immediately over a thinly sketched tremolo in the strings. The theme is short—only nine measures—but displays a determination, a busyness, and a striking motive (bracketed in Ex. 11.1) heard often in the movement. The timpani help to establish the triple meter. The partial descending scale (bracketed $x$ in the example) forms the basis for development, the pattern extending for several measures.

**EX. 11.1 BARTÓK**
Piano Concerto No. 3,
1st mvt., bars 2–11

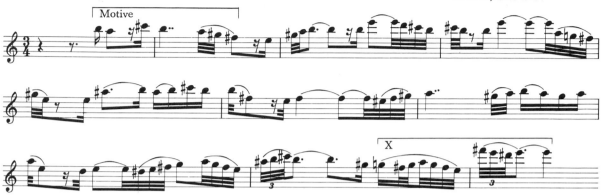

When the descending passage finally yields to an upward turn, it leads directly to a restatement of the first theme by the orchestra. The statement is interrupted by the reentry of the piano, which takes an ascending figure and works with it as it leads to the statement of the second theme.

**EX. 11.2** *Ibid.*
bar 27

There are two parts to the second theme, the first stated first by the piano (for the reader's convenience, the theme, which is rather hidden in Ex. 11.3(a), is simplified in Ex. 11.3(b) by gathering the repeated notes into a single octave).

**EX. 11.3** *Ibid.*
bars 44–45

After four measures, the woodwinds take over the theme statement during which there is some rather conversational treatment of the figure between the flutes and the piano.

Pianist Andrè Watts
in a concerto performance
with the London Symphony
Orchestra, conducted
by Hans Schmidt-Isserstedt
The intensity and
concentration demanded
by such a cooperative
effort are mirrored in
the faces of all concerned.
(Courtesy of William
Judd Concert Artists)

**EX. 11.4** *Ibid.*
bar 48

**EX. 11.5** *Ibid.*
bars 54–56

The second part of the theme follows quickly, again stated by the piano.

The orchestra enters briefly near the end of this section for a climax; the piano then works through a transition passage of a few measures, ending with another conversational moment on a two-note figure, this one with the clarinet.

**EX. 11.6** *Ibid.*
bar 71

The horn interrupts this activity with a call, based on the opening motive (see bracketed portion of Ex. 11.1) of the first theme.

**EX. 11.7** *Ibid.*
bars 73–74

The call ushers in the development section. Over strong, fast-moving, accompanying arpeggios by the piano, the woodwinds sing out with a lyrical melody based on the first theme.

**EX. 11.8** *Ibid.*
bars 76–85

The tonal center has now shifted, and Bartók includes elements of both the major and minor modes. The piano restates this evocative melody, raising the tonal center again, and, along with the orchestra, finally begins to take it apart and work with the segments, adding now and then fragments from the second theme (these are scored as solo passages for the flute, the oboe, and the clarinet). The development section is quite brief, ending with the horn calls with which it began.

The recapitulation is remarkably true to the exposition. The first theme is now harmonized (it was not in the first statement) and the conversational aspect of the second theme is removed. That quality is saved for the concluding codetta, in which the piano, the clarinet, and the flute pass the now familiar two-note figure back and forth over a rising pizzicato passage in the strings. The flute stops this to recall the first theme (Ex. 11.9); the piano ends the movement with a two note figure, harmonized and repeated.

**EX. 11.9** *Ibid.*
bars 184–186

The Third Concerto is scored for two flutes, two oboes, two clarinets, two bassoons, four horns, two trumpets, three trombones, tuba, timpani, percussion, and strings, although the tuba and two of the trombones are not used in the first movement. The movement has a light, almost transparent, texture throughout. Only occasionally is there a full orchestral sound and even then there is just a flash of it. The result is a quality of intimacy due in part to the lighter orchestration and in part to the feeling of the themes. Its clarity, personality, vitality, and interesting manipulation of musical ideas make it a concerto that is at once very representative of its age and timeless, the hallmark of great music of every era.

### Descriptive music

A bird calls to its mate at twilight; nearby a brook babbles ceaselessly over rocks and pebbles; the hunter's horn sounds in the forest; a great man states his philosophy; another man states his love and his concern for his country. What do these have to do with music? They have a great deal to do with it, for many composers have tried to make such sounds and thoughts integral parts of their compositions.

It would at first seem that music would have less of a possibility for expression of meaning than the other arts because of its abstract, nonverbal nature. Compare it, for instance, with the visual and verbal arts in which the painter and the writer can ostensibly bring meaning to the surface more readily by using apparent, representative symbols such as words and pictures. The composer has no such crutch, even when he is working with words.

Representation or description only enhance the meaning—the aesthetic meaning—of the art of music. This "secondary suggestiveness" looms importantly to many creators, however, and it is to this point that a sizeable number of composers have addressed themselves by writing music with a program, especially (but not only) during the nineteenth century.

In music, a program is simply the additional meaning (a popular term is "extramusical reference") that hopefully enriches the aesthetic one already present. The term *program* comes from the fact that accompanying the sound of the music there is a written description of what the composer intends to be suggested by his music. Some works are short enough that the program can be read before the performance and then called to mind while the music is being played. Others are so long and complex that the program must be followed during the performance if its meaning is not to be lost.

To appreciate program music fully, one must understand its strengths and weaknesses; it is in the program itself that both lie. There is truth in the statement that interest in a work can be heightened when a listener has to search for something or listen for identifiable themes and motives. It is quite enjoyable, for instance, to listen for Till's motive cavorting through Richard Strauss's *Till Eulenspiegels lustige Streiche* ("Till Eulenspiegel's Merry Pranks") or the hunters' horns and the peasant dance in Smetana's *The Moldau*. But without the program, any such work is just another composition, depending entirely upon its absolute or purely musical meaning for success.

Almost without exception, sounds in music are so abstract that they cannot be identified with people, animals, places, thoughts, events, or things unless they are designated to do so beforehand. This designation is an entirely arbitrary one made by the composer, who capitalizes on an audience's associations or who offers specific instructions pointing out the meanings to be kept in mind. Unless those instructions are understood, the whole programmatic effect can be lost, for the sound a composer had intended to represent a broom might well be interpreted by the listener to be a polar bear or a funny old lady.

There are some sounds, such as birdcalls, calls to arms, and so forth, which immediately suggest some nonmusical reference. Any time they are heard, they are likely to have the same suggstion as long as the listener's frame of reference is similar to that of the composer. But these sounds are very few indeed. The challenge to composers, then, is to use abstract, unidentifiable musical sounds and create identifiable relationships between them and extramusical ideas. Unfortunately, this can be done only when the identities are provided for the listener. It is this circumstance that has caused a number of writers on the subject to label the whole concept of program music a myth. (See Colorplates 4 and 6.)

**Types of program music**

There are three types of program music. The first of these is the narrative type, usually a musical work with some sort of plot or story outline. Typical of such compositions is *The Sorcerer's Apprentice*, by Dukas, in which the music tells of the adventures of a magician's young apprentice who is left with instructions to sweep and mop the floor. He knows enough about sorcery to make the broom come to life and carry the water from the well, but cannot remember the commands for stopping the broom and returning it to its original state. Brooms and buckets begin to multiply; soon there are hundreds of brooms, all carrying buckets of water and sweeping. The place is inundated, but the magician returns, quickly restores order, and banishes the boy.

A second kind of program music is descriptive. Debussy's *Voiles,* for example, is a brief piano work that suggests images of sailboats darting before capricious breezes. Smetana's *The Moldau* is far more literal in its pictorialization. It describes the Moldau River from its source to its mouth, following its course from rivulet to river. The Moldau begins as a tiny brook, joins another brook to become a mountain stream and eventually the river itself. It passes hunters in a forest and peasants at a wedding party. Moonlight, evoking the spirits of nymphs, dances on its waters; with the dawn, the river thunders through the raging St. John's Rapids, passes by an old castle, and rolls majestically through the city of Prague and into the distance.

The themes in *The Moldau* are simple, direct, and obvious. A figure played by two solo flutes represents the first brook.

**EX. 12.1 SMETANA**
*The Moldau,* bars 1–2

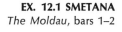

The clarinets play the melody representing the second stream.

**EX. 12.2** *Ibid.*
bars 16–17

The two streams merge, grow, and become the river.

**EX. 12.3** *Ibid.*
bars 40–47

After the theme of the river is heard, horns announce the hunt.

**EX. 12.4** *Ibid.*
bars 80–85

Horns

The polka-like music for the peasant wedding party is, of course, entirely different in character.

Strings and Clarinets

**EX. 12.5** *Ibid.*
bars 122–125

Another change in character is needed to show the moonlight on the water.

Violins

**EX. 12.6** *Ibid.*
bars 187–194

The river theme returns and leads into a turbulent passage that represents the St. John's Rapids. Following this, the river theme returns once again as the Moldau approaches Prague. As it moves past the old castle, the Vyšehrad, a chorale-like melody is superimposed.

Winds and Brasses

**EX. 12.7** *Ibid.*
bars 359–373

The river theme plays on to its conclusion, the sound dying away as the river recedes into the distance. Two short chords by the whole orchestra end the work.

Formally, *The Moldau* is a sonata-rondo. The brook motives are parts of the introduction and the river theme is Theme *A*; the hunting section is a transition leading to the wedding dance which is Theme *B*. Smetana departed slightly from tradition by stating Theme *C* ("Moonlight: Nymphs' Dance") before returning to Theme *A*. The raging rapids are a

development section (hence, the form is a sonata-rondo). A coda (the gradual dying away of the sound, representing the river sweeping off into the distance) follows the last statement of Theme *A*. The form is outlined thus: Introduction-ABCA-Development section-A-Coda.[1]

Narrative and descriptive program music can be fairly obvious. A hunter's call is a hunter's call and a storm is a storm. Birdcalls sound like birdcalls in or out of music. The third type of program music, however, is oriented to thoughts or philosophies and tends to be more elusive because there are no specific sounds that are readily identifiable. Richard Strauss's *Also sprach Zarathustra* ("Thus Spake Zarathustra") is a famous example of such philosophically oriented music. The title is the same as a major treatise by the German philosopher Nietzsche, who expounded in it his concept of the great creative human, the Superman. Strauss's music, however, is not meant to be as literal in thought as Nietzsche's book. In the composer's own words:

I did not intend to write philosophical music or portray Nietzsche's great work musically. I meant to convey musically an idea of the development of the human race from its origin, through the various phases of evolution, religious as well as scientific, up to Nietzsche's idea of the [superman]. . . . The whole symphonic

---

[1]The river theme was based on an old Czech folksong that is also the source for *Hatikvah*, the national anthem of Israel. It was adapted for that purpose by Samuel Cohen, a pioneer settler in modern Palestine.

*The Moldau River as it flows past Vyšehrad Castle, just outside Prague. The majesty of ancient fortresses, the breadth of rivers, the beauty of the countryside, and love of homeland were inspirational in shaping much of the music, poetry, and painting of the nineteenth century. Smetana's Vltava ("The Moldau") reaches its climax at the point where the scene pictured here is described in the music. (Photo by Bohumil Landisch, courtesy of Olympia Publishing Co., Prague)*

poem is intended as my homage to the genius of Nietzsche, which found its greatest exemplification in his book, *Thus Spake Zarathustra*.[2]

The titles of the eight sections of *Also sprach Zarathustra* give insight into Strauss's intent: (1) Of the Dwellers in the Rear World; (2) Of the Great Yearning; (3) Of Joys and Passions; (4) Grave Song; (5) Of Science; (6) The Convalescent; (7) The Song of the Dance; (8) Night Song. Quite obviously, if the music is to describe science, or joys and passions, it must do so only in the most indefinite of terms. Here, then, is program music refined to the most sophisticated degree.

While program music was certainly known before the nineteenth century, it remained for the composers of the Romantic century to explore its possibilities to the fullest. Beethoven was not the first of the nineteenth-century composers to write such compositions, but one may find in his output some of the first of the well-defined examples of the patterns that would be followed later in the century.

Even though he said that he did not write program music, several of Beethoven's more notable works have at least programmatic connotations. The most obvious of these is his Symphony No. 6 (*Pastorale*). In it are movements that denote pastoral scenes in the country, peasants merrymaking, a storm, and the like. Although each movement is titled and the

---

[2]Henry T. Finck, *Richard Strauss, The Man and His Works* (Boston: Little, Brown and Company, 1917), p. 181.

music contained in each is appropriate to this extrareferential title, Beethoven reminded his audience that the music was to be "more the expression of feeling than the painting of a picture."

After Beethoven there came a deluge of program music; a whole international school of composers allied themselves to its cause. The philosophy of the times was right for such a move and it was embraced enthusiastically. By mid-century, the musical world of Europe had divided itself into two camps: those who felt that music was absolute unto itself and could not profit from extramusical considerations and those who saw music as a way of deepening the awareness of life and enriching the imagination while at the same time benefiting as a communicative force from the aesthetic-emotional impact of additional, nonmusical meanings. The battle raged between the two sides for the rest of the century and is not yet completely ended, although little program music of any quality has been produced since World War II.

**Forms for program music**

Few composers of program music worked within the procedures of the eighteenth century. Berlioz' *Fantastic Symphony* is unusual in that it generally follows the symphonic design of separate movements, although he moved away from the traditional when he assigned specific extramusical meanings to musical sounds. A motive (called by him an *idée fixe*, or "fixed idea") was given specific reference and that reference was called to mind every time the motive was sounded. Thus, a musical sound had a fixed extramusical idea attached to it; the whole concept of *idée fixe* became important and was adopted in varying forms by later composers.

The most significant departure in the genre of program music was with regard to form. By mid-century, it had become apparent that the "rigid" forms of music with their predetermined patterns of contrast and repetition were not always adequate for stories or scenes that demanded constant musical change. Liszt merged the several movements of the symphony into one large, continuous, orchestral movement, which he called the *tone poem (tone poem* and *symphonic poem* are synonymous). In doing so, he was following a lead suggested by Beethoven who had merged movements in two symphonies (the Fifth and Sixth) and in a piano concerto (the Fifth, *Emperor*) and by Mendelssohn, whose Third Symphony (*Scotch*) was to be played without pause between movements. In his tone poems, Liszt applied the principle of *idée fixe* (or *Leitmotiv*) to the technique of melodic expansion, resulting in through-composed works in which themes or motives were recalled only because of the exigencies of the unfolding program.

Liszt wrote twelve tone poems, but only one, *Les Préludes*, remains in the active repertoire. More important was the influence of the form and its possibilities on such later composers as Smetana, Dukas, Saint-Saëns, Scriabin, and others, who contributed a number of tone poems to the literature. It remained for Richard Strauss to bring the form to its highest point and almost to its conclusion.

Strauss wrote nine tone poems, some of which followed rather traditional formal outlines, even though the Liszt-inspired extrareferential concept was a major force. Strauss felt so confident about his abilities to write program music that he once remarked that, if he wished, he could set a table fork to music. Time and his own maturation were to lead him to believe that the musical meaning he felt he had to express could not be said in the tone poem, so he turned from it to opera and song. When he did, Romantic program music no longer had a champion and thus lost in importance. A few examples of twentieth-century orchestral program music are in existence, one of the best-known being Honegger's *Pacific 231*, a musical depiction of a steam locomotive.

In addition to the orchestral tone poem, program music for solo instruments exists in abundance. Some of Debussy's piano preludes, for example, are short works suggesting such visual ideas as a sunken cathedral or fireworks. Mussorgsky's piano suite *Pictures at an Exhibition* describes in each movement a specific painting. *Character pieces*, short compositions usually with one main musical thought, may also be programmatic.

The whole movement of program music seems to typify the pervasive emotionalism of the arts and times of the nineteenth century. Today's society has a different set of values for which program music shows little relevance; it is no longer an issue nor a major method of communication.

## *Nationalism*

Another emotional additive was *nationalism*, which found its way into the art of most European countries during the nineteenth century. Nationalism as a factor in music varied from country to country and from composer to composer within countries. For some composers, nationalism was a subjective force resulting in deep personal involvement. For others, it was a matter of objective interest, resulting in study and reproduction of folk music, poetry, dance, and legend.

Although the romantic penchant for the exotic and the strikingly individual was a strong contributing factor, nationalism originated primarily

**Sources of nationalism**

in the military, political, and diplomatic activities that took place during the first fifteen years of the nineteenth century. Napoleon Bonaparte, who had gained power in France as a result of the revolution that had overthrown the French monarchy, was one of the most influential figures in Europe and eventually dragged most of the continent into war. The disposition of the Napoleonic Empire after his defeat in 1814 was left to the four powers who had defeated him, Austria, Prussia, Great Britain, and Russia.[3] At the Congress of Vienna (1815), those nations partitioned Europe so that there was a finely conceived balance of power between major and minor states, with smaller states and less important areas being appended to larger ones, in many cases without any concern for the feelings of the peoples involved. But Napoleon had done much to improve the status of the people when he was in power, granting citizens rights of equality before the law, lessening the power of the church and of the nobility, and, to some extent, granting freedom of worship and tolerance of religious beliefs. The Congress of Vienna could not force those people to return completely to the state of subjective obedience prevalent before 1800, although it tried to do so by various means, particularly by the imposition of government by absolute monarchy.

The seeds of liberalism had been sown and by mid-century they began to bear full flower. Revolutions against suppression began in France (1830 and 1848), in Italy (1848), then in most of Europe. In some countries, the revolutions were relatively peaceful; in others there was full-scale warfare. Only in France was the internal revolution completely successful, returning the Bonaparte dynasty temporarily to power. In the other major countries, the revolutions were doomed to failure, mostly through the lack of positive leadership, but the eruptions were to continue until World War I and even beyond.

Visualize the situation about a century or more ago: In some countries, which were beginning to emerge independently of the rule of others, the people were finding a national identity; other countries, areas, races, and ethnic groups were striving for recognition but were failing; several were doomed forever. For all, there could be a cause and reason for nationalistic feeling. For those intimately bound to the cause, it was a simple patriotism and love; for those watching from afar, it was a concern for people swept up by noble aspirations and engaged in desperate struggle.

---

[3]Their efforts at disposition were interrupted temporarily by the Hundred Days' War of 1815, brought about by Napoleon's escape from Elba. He took the reins of government in France and then had to be defeated again.

As the peoples of the countries involved were expressing themselves, so were the artists, the writers, and the composers. Thus we have a Tolstoy novel (*War and Peace*, 1865–72), a Delacroix painting (*Liberty Leading the People*, 1830, Colorplate 1), and a Sibelius tone poem (*Finlandia*, 1900). This particular reflection of popular emotion is known as *nationalism*. (See also Colorplate 6.)

As is the case with any social force, nationalism revealed itself in the arts in a variety of ways. One of the most readily identifiable is the act of preservation of a folk art. There are a number of such preservations, including Brahms's *Hungarian Dances* (later proved by Bartók not to be natively Hungarian but Gypsy), Dvořák's *Slavonic Dances*, Grieg's *Norwegian Dances*, Liszt's *Hungarian Rhapsodies*, Enesco's *Rumanian Rhapsodies*, and numerous Rumanian, Hungarian, and Slovakian folksongs arranged by Bartók. Chopin, too, preserved the flavor of his native land, Poland, by composing works that were based on such indigenous dances as *polonaises* and *mazurkas*. In Germany, Mendelssohn, Brahms, Schumann, and others not only wrote down numerous folksongs, but personally created others in the folk style.

**Nationalism in European music**

Thus there were two trends. Some composers went to the people not only for inspiration, but for material as well, the result being compositions that included folk and national music as melodic and thematic material; on the other hand, some composers used original material, but nonetheless they expressed intensely patriotic feelings through their compositions. The first trend was developed in Eastern Europe, the emerging countries of Scandinavia, and in Russia. The second was discernible mostly in countries where a national art had already been established, primarily Italy and Germany.

The works of Dvořák and Smetana typify nationalism in Eastern Europe. Smetana's *My Fatherland*, a group of six tone poems (of which *The Moldau* is the second), describes musically the people, the land, and the folklore of Bohemia (now a section of Czechoslovakia, but then a part of the Austrian Empire). His opera *The Bartered Bride* is one of several that carry a similarly nationalistic theme. In Norway, Grieg's mood of nationalism was reflected in his *Wedding Day at Troldhaugen* (for piano), the *Norwegian Dances*, and the incidental music to Ibsen's *Peer Gynt*, now performed as two orchestral suites with the same name. Finland's great composer Sibelius was inspired by the Finnish national epic poem, the *Kalevala*, and some of his early music revolved around it. *Finlandia* was so fervent a nationalistic expression that it was banned from performance by the Russian government, then Finland's overlord. The first two of Sibelius' seven symphonies also have a decidedly nationalistic character.

In Russia, nationalism was expressed in the arts with the greatest of enthusiasm. The first significant Russian nationalist composer was Glinka and after him came a group of composers known as the "Russian Five" (Balakirev, Borodin, Cui, Mussorgsky, Rimsky-Korsakov) who devoted themselves to developing an art by and for Russians. Notable works from the "Five" are Rimsky-Korsakov's overture *The Russian Easter*, Mussorgsky's opera *Boris Godunov* (probably the greatest opera ever written about Russia), and Borodin's opera *Prince Igor*. Although Tchaikovsky claimed to be an internationalist composer, he did create some works with a nationalistic flavor. His *Overture 1812* is both programmatic and nationalistic. *Marche Slav*, which Tchaikovsky felt to be one of his least artistic works, must also be considered nationalistic. The wave of nationalism in Russia died with the "Five," only to be revived forcibly by the Communist government. During the decades in which Communism has been a ruling force in Russia, its control of the arts has fluctuated from moderate to extreme. At one time or another all of the composers of any stature have had to write propagandistic music, and much of it has been bad. (One might honestly raise the question whether such propaganda is in truth nationalism.) Two of the twentieth-century musical leaders in Russia, Shostakovitch and Prokofiev, have been the most successful in creating works of any artistic merit under such circumstances. Indeed, when Shostakovitch is free of bureaucratic pressures, he proves himself to be one of the great composers of the century.

As was noted earlier, composers who used original material to express patriotic feelings (or at least something beyond objective commentary) were found in countries where a national art had already been established. It would be patently incorrect to say that nationalism and national art are the same thing. Italian opera and German orchestral music are not by themselves manifestations of a nationalistic impulse. Italian opera, for instance, began as an attempt to revitalize Greek drama—hardly a nationalistic rationale for starting something in Italy. As the wave of nationalism swept over Europe, it eventually affected the composers who were the producers of the national, as well as the nationalistic media. In both Italy and Germany, where the art of opera was by now the art of the people, composers used the medium nationalistically. In his operas, Verdi expressed his dislike of Austrian tyranny and concern for the prevailing political situation in Italy. In Germany, the music drama became a forum for nationalistic expression. Weber's *Der Freischütz* was an early nine-teenth-century work with its origins in German legend and much of its musical freshness in German folksong. As one commentator wrote, Weber set the Black Forest to music. Later in the century, Wagner used music drama to explore German legend and mythology (*Lohengrin* and *The Ring of the Nibelung*) and, later, simply to state his pride in being a German (*Die Meistersinger*). For these composers, the medium and con-tent was national, and the intent was nationalistic.

In England, Spain, and France, a well-established national identity precluded any early invasion of the arts by a sense of nationalistic feeling, even though there might have been political activity amounting to revolu-tion. England was proud of its attainments and its empire, but, remark-ably enough, there were so few English composers of any note during the nineteenth century that nationalistic English music seems not to have existed at all, in spite of the innate Englishness of Parry, Stanford, and Sullivan. Elgar's music seems only partially national in spirit.

In France, as in England, there was a national egotism based on the country's eminence. For three centuries, France had been the ultimate leader in elegance, sophistication, and worldliness. It was said during the eighteenth century that when Paris sneezed, all of Europe held the hand-kerchief. The revolutions in France did little to change this, although they did help eventually to do away with the monarchy and its attendant nobility and, even more important, to break the almost absolute power of the clergy. Nationalism as a feature in music did not appear until after all this had happened. It was introduced largely through the efforts of Debussy, who was the leader of the school of composition known as *Impressionism*, a school almost specifically French in character. His music contained little or no native material; in fact, he turned his back on such inclusion. Rather, it reflected the elegance and sophistication which, by the time of his activity as a composer (1890–1917), had sifted down from the upper classes to a now emancipated populace and had indeed become a national characteristic.

In Spain, three composers, Falla, Albéniz, and Granados, stand out as nationalists. Falla, the youngest, and perhaps the most talented of the three, tended to be more international in scope. He involved himself with Impressionism and, in works such as *Nights in the Gardens of Spain*, translated some of his native music into that idiom with novel and charm-ing results. Albéniz and Granados created works of a more purely na-tional character.

**Nationalism in the United States**  Save for the efforts of a few nineteenth-century composers, notably Foster and Gottschalk, nationalism in the music of the United States is almost exclusively a twentieth-century phenomenon. It is best represented in the works of Ives, whose *Three Places in New England* and Symphony No. 2 typify his truly distinctive American flavor. Similarly, one can find nationalistic content in some of the works of Copland, notably *Appalachian Spring* and *Rodeo*. Gershwin is also included in lists of American nationalists because he incorporated elements of the jazz idiom into such serious works as *An American in Paris* and the *Rhapsody in Blue*.

The reasons that caused nationalism to bloom in the works of composers of other countries did not and do not prevail in the United States. For one thing, much American folk music and art is not indigenous, having come with those who migrated from other countries. Further, the thought of rebelling against existing national styles and media and establishing native ones has not occurred to American composers. Finally, it seems that the days of jingoistic nationalism are gone forever. America's citizenry has become so involved with problems of international concern and so aware of needed improvements in its own national condition, that unabashed adoration of country appears to be at least controversial.

**Problems of composing nationalistic music**  Nationalistic art finds its life and death in itself; it is at once self-creating and self-consuming. Its inspiration lies in the folk heritage of a people; its success lies in its immediacy or its association with known media, idioms, or activities; its death lies in its tendency to become overly familiar. When folk rhythms and melodies are brought to serious composition, their basic shape must be maintained or they cannot be recognized. The composer is therefore penalized on two counts: first, he may not bend the rhythms or melodies too much in an aim for aesthetic and compositional improvement or he will lose the effect of the folk element's inclusion and, second, the emotional content of the folk material may be so familiar to his audience that he will not be able to make it into a vehicle for a strongly personal communication. Composers of nationalistic music have recognized these truths and have either tried to get around them in the best way possible or surrendered to them, hoping that the immediate emotional reactions to the works produced would satisfactorily offset any lack of enduring values.

### *Other orchestral types*

**Transcription**  The orchestral repertoire includes a number of types of music other than symphonies, concertos, and tone poems, some composed originally for the medium and some not. Those that are not orchestral in their original conception but are rearranged for the orchestra or band are called *transcriptions*, an excellent example of which is the orchestral setting by Ravel of Mussorgsky's *Pictures at an Exhibition*, originally written for piano. Transcriptions are found infrequently today on the programs of performing orchestras, since there is a general feeling that transcription can alter the character of a work beyond acceptable limits. Transcriptions are important to the concert band, however, since original literature for it is considerably underdeveloped, at least in quantity.

The term *overture* has meant many things in the past, including an orchestral introduction (to an opera, an oratorio, a ballet, or incidental music to a play), the beginning movement of a collection of dances, a whole collection of dances scored for orchestra (notably those by Bach), or an independent orchestral composition with some sort of extramusical association. The term *prelude*, when applied to orchestral music, generally implies a shorter, atmospheric introductory piece, although some are extensive.

**The overture and the prelude**

The overture was originated primarily to serve as an introduction to an opera. In the very early operas (those written before 1640), there was either no overture or at best a sketchy instrumental fanfare or introduction. After 1640, a formal overture became a firm and permanent fixture. By 1700, there were two distinct types, the French and the Italian.

The French overture, brought to perfection by Lully, has two movements. The first is homophonic and rather pompous and has a characteristic rhythm (long-short, long-short). The second is faster and is polyphonic in texture. Although the form did not survive beyond the Baroque period, it was important during its time. Handel used it almost exclusively (only his opera *Athalia* uses the Italian type).

Early Italian overtures had four movements (fast, slow, fast, slow) but by the end of the seventeenth century, composers (led by Alessandro Scarlatti) had modified this to a more satisfying three-movement form (fast, slow, fast), with a greater variety of texture, sentiment, and melodic treatment.

Neither of the two overture forms of the Baroque era had much relationship to the opera or ballet to which they were introductions; it was not the practice at that time to use any of the thematic material from the main work in the overture. One of the first overtures to include such material was the one for *Castor et Pollux*, an opera by Rameau written in 1735. This idea, however, did not become popular until the nineteenth century.

Rather, a more subtle relationship was established between the overture and the major work by the composers of the Classical period; they tried musically to set a mood in the overture that would be reflected later in the main work in a more dramatic way. Gluck's overture to *Iphigénie en Tauride* describes the storm experienced in the opening scene of the opera and leads into that scene without pause; the overture to Mozart's *Le Nozze di Figaro* is a marvelous bit of froth which prepares the listener for the plot developments in the opera; the restless diminished chords that follow one another in the overture to Haydn's *Creation* serve to set the emotional climate for that great oratorio; Mozart's *Don Giovanni* begins with a symphonic treatment of several musical episodes to be heard later in the opera.

By the Classical period, the overture had unified itself into a one-movement work, and, by the time the Romantic era had dawned, Rameau's idea of including thematic material (especially in opera overtures) had become consistently observed. Thus, in Weber's overtures to *Der Freischütz*, *Oberon*, and *Euryanthe*, a true merger between the overture and the opera was accomplished. This new type of overture not only represented the mood of the opera, but also contained musical elements of the opera itself, and thus the overture became a sort of musical summary of the action that was to follow.

The nineteenth century saw a continuation of both types of opera overtures, and often one composer would indulge himself in both. Verdi's prelude to *Rigoletto* is mood setting, while the prelude to his *La Traviata* is related to what follows in a dramatic and thematic way.

The idea of thematic relationship was so simplified in some instances that it became nothing more than a medley of the tunes or themes that were to be heard later. Such an overture is known as a *potpourri* and was especially popular with French composers of *opéra comique* in the nineteenth century and with American composers of musicals in this century. Such overtures do not ordinarily reflect the genius for composition found, for example, in the overtures of Wagner, in which the thematic materials that will be heard later are woven into masterful compositions. Potpourri overtures tend to be simple recitations, usually of simple (athough possibly quite listenable) tunes.

Also in the nineteenth century, the *concert overture* became a rather popular form. The concert overture is an orchestral movement designed for the concert hall and is free of any association with a staged work. There is almost always some sort of nonmusical concept connected with the concert overture, but such a concept is not always as detailed as that associated with a tone poem. Brahms's *Academic Festival* Overture exemplifies the concert overture: the listener is summoned to the halls of academe through the inclusion of several student drinking songs, but there is no picture or story line beyond this. The concert overture has not been too popular as a compositional form for the orchestra in the twentieth century. Many have been written for the concert band, however, usually without programmatic connotations.

Similarly, operatic overtures seem to be on the decline. There are not too many composers today who work in the field of opera, and these composers tend to avoid using extended overtures.

**The suite**

The *suite* is a collection of shorter works, often dances, bound together as a multimovement composition. Except for a few isolated works from the Baroque period, among which are the four orchestral suites by Bach and the *Water Music* and *Royal Fireworks Music* by Handel, the suite had little orchestral relevance until the nineteenth century. In the Classical period, the multimovement forms of the symphony and the concerto were by far the most popular for orchestral use. *Divertimentos, cassations,* and *serenades*—stylized Classical period suites for instruments (the last two especially for winds)—were primarily chamber music since they were written for small numbers of players.

In the Romantic and Modern periods, the suites have been drawn from music written for other media, including dramas, ballets, and films. Music for the spoken theater might include an overture, songs, choruses, entr'acte music, and character pieces that would enhance moods and actions portrayed throughout the drama. Such music is known as *incidental* music, and, in order to make it stand as a concert work, the composer has to rearrange it into a suite of several movements, as Mendelssohn did with his music for Shakespeare's *A Midsummer Night's Dream.* Tchaikovsky's *Nutcracker* Suite and Shostakovitch's *Golden Age* Suite are similar extractions from ballets. Prokofiev's suite *Lieutenant Kije* was written as the score for a film.

Occasionally, composers have created suites as independent compositions. Noteworthy are several written for the concert band by the English composers Holst, Vaughan Williams, and Jacob.

**Miscellaneous types**

There are many compositions written for orchestras and bands that do not fit into any of the structures thus far discussed. A concert program might include a bolero (Ravel), a theme and variations (by either Brahms or Rachmaninoff), and a funeral march (by Mozart). Some forms are particularly indigenous to a medium—the march seems to belong to the band —but there is no rule that there must be exclusive and rigid relationships.

There are also compositions, especially by contemporary composers, bearing titles that do not relate to any category. Typical of such works are Takemitsu's *November Steps*, a 1967 work for ancient Japanese instruments and a modern symphony orchestra, and Hovhaness' *Mysterious Mountain*, an orchestral work written in 1955. Each composition, regardless of the origin of the title, will have its own logic and reason for being. The search for that logic and reason can provide the listener with much intellectual and aesthetic enjoyment.

### *Ballet*

Since this chapter includes mention of music for the ballet, it is a good place to include some notes on the medium itself. Ballet, which may include autonomous dance works or dances incidental to a stage piece (such as an opera), has had a rich and illustrious history and many fine moments in music have been created for it.

A stylized form of the dance known as ballet was popular in the courts during the Renaissance, but it was during the first half of the Baroque period that it gained its first true eminence. Lully, court composer to Louis XIV at Versailles, had much to do with its development.[4] Lully's first formalizations were a merger of poetry, music, and dance; the form, known as the *ballet de cour* ("ballet of the court"), was brought to a high degree of perfection through the combined efforts of Lully and the French poet-dramatist, Molière, and it was from the *ballet de cour* that both ballet as a separate, structured form and the French opera were developed. In the ballet of the seventeenth century, the costuming was elaborate and the garments were heavy; the steps were carefully patterned and gliding. The idea of a narrative dance with leaps and other virtuoso steps was unknown.

Ballet suffered from the same excesses of grandeur that affected opera during the late Baroque period. Through the efforts of Noverre, a reform movement began about 1760, coinciding almost exactly with the one in opera, and, by 1810, most of the modern aspects of the medium had been introduced. The greatest name in ballet during the nineteenth century

[4]Louis XIV, like many of the members of his court, was an accomplished ballet dancer and performed often to Lully's compositions, a number of which were written specifically to feature the king as soloist.

*Edgar Degas (1834–1917).* The Dancing Class *(1871–1872). An Impressionist's view of other interpreters: dancers and their accompanist. Degas considered dancing to be the most graceful and delicate of the arts; he saw its ephemeral quality as most in harmony with the Impressionist's conception of reality. (The Metropolitan Museum of Art, New York)*

was that of Marie Taglioni, whose talent and daring brought to fame many of the steps and motions made possible by the new hard-toed sandal (including the "on point" stances). The most important aspect of this style was levitation—the quality of motion that utilized lifts, leaps, and dancing in such a way that created the impression that the dancer was floating across the stage. As a result of the activities of Taglioni and her contemporaries, a number of works were created featuring the prima ballerina. Among them was *La Sylphide* (not to be confused with an arrangement of some of Chopin's music, known as *Les Sylphides*), which became the most famous dance for the great Taglioni and eventually a landmark for the century. A combination of circumstances, including the introduction of the hard-toed sandal and the great interest in the new

*A Romantic artist's conception of Act I of Tchaikovsky's* Swan Lake.
*The sense of magic, vestiges of an ancient fortress, the soft glow*
*of the moonlight, and the ambience of nature are familiar Romantic images.*
*and seem totally appropriate to the moment in the story when Siegfried*
*first sees the transformation of the swan-maidens. (The Bettmann Archive)*

steps possible with it, lowered the status of the male dancer, who, because of the shape of his instep, simply could not stand on his toes and do the newer steps. The nineteenth century saw the development of the cult of the ballerina, a cult that has continued to the present although it is no longer as overbearing.

In the nineteenth century, the three centers of activity in ballet were France, Italy, and Russia, the first two placing stress on the ballerina, the Russians delighting in both male and female virtuosity. Although French and Italian composers did write works specifically for ballet, they were not nearly as prolific as were the Russian composers. Russian ballet was late in coming to maturity, but, by the time Tchaikovsky was active as a composer, it had reached artistic heights. He composed several ballets, three of which, *Sleeping Beauty, Swan Lake,* and *The Nutcracker,* are still in the active repertoire. Delibes' *Sylvia* gained great attention in Russia as did the works of several other notable Western composers. Opera scores by the Russian composers, especially Tchaikovsky and Rimsky-Korsakov, contained ballet music just as did practically all operatic scores of the Italian and French composers.[5]

By the end of the century, the quality of ballet in the Western countries had lessened considerably, the popularity of the ballerina overshadowing choreographic originality. Interest in the male dancer had dropped so much that the male part in a ballet would often be danced by a ballerina dressed as a man. In the first decades of the twentieth century this was abruptly changed by Michael Fokine, who brought to ballet a new philosophy and approach, and by an amateur-turned-impresario from Russia, Sergei Diaghilev, who reintroduced the male soloist to French audiences. The first of such dancers was Vaslav Nijinsky, also a Russian, whose abilities and artistry had an electrifying effect on audiences. Nijinsky sacrificed grace for strength and agility and brought a virile animalism to an almost sterile art. It was said that Nijinsky could leap halfway across a stage and seemed to hang in the air as if defying the law of gravity. Diaghilev commissioned a number of works featuring Nijinsky

---

[5]Indeed, no opera could be presented in Paris without a ballet sequence, preferably in the second act. Wagner's *Tannhäuser* failed as an opera in Paris twice because of the ballet requirement. The first time, it did not have a ballet at all and was immediately unsuccessful. The second time, Wagner included one, but, in order to preserve the plot, he incorporated it into the overture. Paris society, especially the influential Jockey Club, did not arrive at the opera until the second act. They missed Wagner's ballet and doomed the opera to failure again. The ballet music still exists and is known as the "Venusberg" music. The overture may be played with or without it.

to be written for presentation in Paris; the most successful of these were the *Firebird* (1910) and *Petrouchka* (1911) by the then young Russian composer Stravinsky. With his later *The Rite of Spring* (1913), these works brought a fresh perspective to ballet.[6]

Ballet has never enjoyed greater success than it is having today. New ballet companies (the Harkness, for instance) are springing up every year, especially in this country. The older companies, Sadlers-Wells, the Ballet Russe de Monte Carlo, the Bolshoi of Moscow, and the New York City Ballet are finding themselves in continual international demand. A new generation of stars, including Rudolf Nureyev, Edward Villella, Suzanne Farrell, and others, are stirring excitement by bringing to life new works and revisions of old ones. Of particular note is the choreography of George Balanchine. Working with the New York City Ballet Company, Balanchine has created works of austere simplicity, devoid of the elaborate scenery and hyperemotional plots of nineteenth-century dance, and remarkably appropriate to the restraint and clarity of such a composer as Stravinsky. Balanchine has also created dance patterns for the atonal music of Webern, the Neoromantic music of Britten, and for many others.

The tradition of operatic ballet, which began with Lully, grew ever stronger through the Classical period and into the Romantic nineteenth century. The French or Italian composer of the last century would hardly dare leave the ballet out of his opera if he sought any kind of success. In some operas of the period, the inclusion would be almost incidental; Verdi's *La Traviata* has a very minor ballet scene in the third act, for instance. In others the ballet sequence would be a major spectacle, lavish in music, costume, and motion. "The Dance of the Hours," a ballet sequence in Ponchielli's *La Gioconda*, the "Walpurgis Night" from Gounod's *Faust*, and several scenes in Verdi's *Aïda* are examples of the large sections of operas devoted to the ballet. In most cases, the ballet scene will be incidental to the plot, the idea of the inclusion being more diversionary than contributory to the action.

The medium of ballet provides both aural and visual excitement as an art. It is primarily motion set to music and guided by a plot or a staged sequence of events that tie various dances together into a cohesive whole. Ballets now considered to be part of the standard repertoire, usually those

[6]A fresh perspective was brought also to composition in general; some of the compositional techniques used by Stravinsky were considered quite radical at the time and the ballets helped to establish him as one of the pre-World War I avant garde composers of Paris.

*The Alvin Ailey Dancers in* Revelations, *danced to gospel music. (Courtesy of Columbia Artists Management)*

from the nineteenth century (for example, Tchaikovsky's *Swan Lake*), are best enjoyed when the viewer is familiar enough with the traditional motions of the ballerina to be able to appreciate the solo dancer in her performance. In such cases, the plot will quite likely be primarily a subordinate framework for the dancing. Ballet lovers search for perfection in motion and when it is found in a dancer, there is instant stardom.

The newer trends in ballet by dancers and choreographers (among the latter are Balanchine, Jerome Robbins, Alvin Ailey, and Paul Taylor) are characterized by much originality and innovation. When Martha Graham first danced in *Undertow*, she was feted not for her classic perfection, but for the uniqueness and appropriateness of her choreography and the remarkable new dramatic qualities she brought to the stage. Miss Graham's styles typify the striking departure from the traditional story line and choreographic movement of classic ballet. *Modern dance*, the result of this departure, has become a type of ballet in its own right. Ballet lovers at first regarded modern dance as an outright danger to the art. This attitude has softened considerably, and in many instances, classic ballet and modern dance have been merged successfully.

Costuming in the newer works has gained in importance and changed in character. Those costumes worn in classical works, tights, *tutus*, and tiaras for the ballerinas and tights for the males, have given way often to outfits that contribute to the dramatic aspects of the dance. In Bernstein's *On the Town*, for instance, the sailors are dressed as sailors and the work has a more direct meaning as a result.

Costuming, plots, and staging notwithstanding, the statement may be repeated that ballet is motion set to music and is best appreciated as such.

## 13 : MUSIC FOR INSTRUMENTS ~ Solo and Chamber Music

*CHAMBER music* is one of the many musical terms that are centuries old, yet its origin has not been obscured by the passage of time. In the Renaissance period the term applied to that music designated for, and performed in, the chambers of the castles and manors of nobility, separating it from music for the church, the theater, or ceremonial occasions. Present definitions of chamber music specify a small performing ensemble with each member having his own part to play. Popular combinations are for three, four, or five players, although the term refers also to duets and to compositions for larger groups, as well as to works for "chamber orchestra" (as opposed to "symphony orchestra"). The term in its original sense was more broadly inclusive than it is now and referred to all instrumental music that was played in princely chambers regardless of the number playing it. The present definition—music for small ensemble with one player per part—came into use about 1700.

Although the accepted definitions of chamber music do not include music for one performer, such literature is being included in this chapter, primarily because the intimacy found in chamber music performance is equally present in the performance of solo literature.

*Schmutzler.* The Joachim Quartet. *Josef Joachim (1831–1907)
was a foremost nineteenth-century violinist and a close friend
of Brahms, whose music he championed. (The Bettmann Archive)*

## The nature of chamber music

It is the characteristic of one player on a part with its attendant ramifications that makes chamber music unique. In a symphony orchestra, large numbers of players will often play the same part, and solo passages are relatively rare. In a chamber ensemble, all the players are essentially soloists, each working with the other members of the ensemble as an equal. The composer can place emphasis on the various soloistic sounds, fading them in and out with subtle shadings. As a general rule, tone color means less in a chamber group than in an orchestra, even in those ensembles (such as a woodwind quintet, made up of flute, oboe, clarinet, bassoon, and horn) in which there is a colorful group of instruments. Rather, variety comes from the manipulation of elements *other* than color; a composer may pass fragments and designs of melody and rhythm from one instrument to another with relatively little regard for much change in the basic sound.

When listening to large groups, the listener has to "back away" from the performance, so to speak, in order to hear and see everything. An orchestra or band is best heard and viewed from a sufficient distance to allow the sound to meld and present itself evenly. Similarly, one needs to be able to hear and see an opera from sufficient distance to allow simultaneous comprehension of sound and activity. As a result, there is by necessity a spatial wall of impersonality between the performers and the listener.

With chamber music, this wall can be removed, and the listener invited into the musicians' inner sanctum. Devotees of chamber music are sure that this brings them closer to the actual art of music; they can approach a melodic idea without having to search it out in the vastness of an orchestral or operatic space and sound. "Intimacy" becomes a key word here; it derives from a small number of players working together without a director, each trying to read the others' musical minds so that parts can be fitted together with precision and expressiveness. Chamber music is best heard in small halls, for, in larger places, this intimacy is too often dispelled when the audience cannot be close to the players.

There is quite a wealth of chamber literature, especially because works for solo instruments are included.[1] The most widely known solo instru-

[1]The organ and its literature are included in this chapter only because a single performer is involved. The organ is not really a chamber music instrument, being located primarily in such large halls as churches, theaters, and concert auditoriums.

ment today is the piano; there is so much music written for it that no pianist can get to all of it. There is also much solo literature for the violin and for the cello, but not as much as for the piano. Earlier composers wrote for the lute, the virginal, the harpsichord, and the guitar. Only the last two have survived as popular instruments.

Music for two players is plentiful, since there are so many combinations possible. For instance, there is music for violin and piano, two violins, two pianos, viola and piano, violin and viola, violin and cello, cello and piano, clarinet and piano, flute and piano, oboe and flute, clarinet and flute, and so on through almost the entire list of instruments including percussion. The combinations are almost endless and even include works for two snare drums.

Trios first gained popularity in the Baroque period, and there are many in varying combinations. However, the most popular chamber music group is the quartet, the most important instrumentation being two violins, one viola, and a cello. The string quartet emerged in the middle of the eighteenth century and has been a focal point for chamber music ever since. Quartets of wind instrument combinations and of three strings and piano (called piano quartets) are also common. The woodwind quintet ranks second in popularity to the string quartet and is the only chamber ensemble that does not include strings or piano to gain major status. Instrumentations with more than five players are not standardized; composers call for specific instruments when they require them. An octet by Stravinsky is scored for flute, clarinet, two bassoons, two trumpets, and two trombones. The Beethoven Octet needs two oboes, two clarinets, two horns, and two bassoons, while the one by Mendelssohn requires only strings. Works requiring more than eight performers are even more diverse; Richard Strauss wrote a serenade for one set of thirteen instruments and a suite for another group of thirteen. He wrote two sonatinas for sixteen instruments, which, in present terminology, stretch the definition of chamber music to its limit.

An examination of some music for one player and for several combinations of players will reveal some key points about the medium.

**Music for one instrument: Debussy's Voiles**

Debussy's *Voiles* ("Sails") is an apt example of music for the piano as a solo instrument (see Chapter 5 for a fuller description of its melodic content). Here, even on a recording, the listener can comprehend the individualistic meaning inherent in chamber music. In this case, there is but one performer and there is no competition for him from an orchestra or even other instruments. One may listen to *Voiles* and feel that there is nothing between the pianist and the ear but the music. The attention is not called elsewhere for a thematic statement or a dramatic movement. There is the pianist, the music, the listener—nothing more. The result is an intimacy with an art that allows the soloist total freedom of tempo, dynamic shading, and so on without concern for values other than those of the music itself.

Compare *Voiles* with Bartók's Piano Concerto No. 3; in the Bartók work one must listen for many things in addition to the piano, including a melody in the strings, a horn call, solo woodwind passages, or an orchestral *tutti*. All of these may distract the listener from the piano and cause the total work to be more generally impersonal. While this impersonality is a known factor to the composer and is by no means a deterrent to his creating a fine work of art, it results in an aesthetic experience quite far removed from that of chamber music.

One finds in most music for two players aesthetic qualities similar to those found in that for one player, especially in those works that are for a soloist with an accompanist. Sonatas for two instruments imply equal parts, but even so, distractions from attentiveness to an individual musical idea can be kept minimal.

**Music for two instruments**

The advantage gained for a solo instrument may be continued into chamber ensembles, provided they are not too large or diverse. For example, in Brahms's *Trio in E-flat, for Horn, Violin, and Piano*, Op. 40, there is no loss of intimacy. The listener knows that there will be the three instruments, and he can quickly learn to recognize their sound qualities. Although attention may not be riveted to any one sound or instrument, those that are present are few enough and direct enough not to be overwhelming. The listener can find great enjoyment in discovering how Brahms is able to manipulate his materials between the three instruments and how the timbre of each contributes individually and cohesively.

**Music for three instruments: Brahms's Trio in E-flat, for Horn, Violin, and Piano, Op. 40**

In spite of the vibrant rhythmic departures from expected patterns (see Chapter 5) and the obvious experimentation in the use of timbre, Brahms's trio shows how the conservative nature of the composer prevents any personal idiosyncrasy or coloristic device from interrupting the on-going musical thought. There is a departure from the traditional plan of movements in that the first movement is a moderately paced, rather lyric rondo, the second movement a scherzo, the third a moody adagio, the fourth a lively sonata form. Note that the order is the reverse of the pattern usually used for four-movement works.

The scherzo is one of the liveliest Brahms ever wrote. It bounces along happily throughout; even the minor key in which the trio section is cast cannot dampen its gaiety. As is typical of Brahms's compositions, rhythmic displacement is a characteristic feature. Its form is quite simple: the main portion is in an *ABA* form and the trio has but one theme that is repeated. The main section is repeated entirely after the trio, giving a pattern of *ABA* (scherzo)/ *CC* (trio)/ *ABA* (scherzo).

There is no introduction. The piano opens the movement with the first theme (*A*) in octaves.

**EX. 13.1 BRAHMS**
Trio in E-flat, Op. 40,
2nd mvt., bars 1–7

The triple-noted metric evenness of the theme is quickly broken up by the entrance of the violin and the horn with a different rhythmic pattern.

**EX. 13.2** *Ibid.*
bars 13–20

Brahms's use of the two-note pattern to break the rhythmic drive of the three-note rhythm is most effective. Some developmental treatment of the first theme follows and then a partial repeat of it by the horn and the violin occurs, with the piano providing a simple accompaniment.

The more lyric second theme (*B*) is given to the violin.

**EX. 13.3** *Ibid.*
bars 121–128

Both horn and piano subside in importance here, the former playing simply harmonic tones, the latter accompanying arpeggios. The lyricism is short-lived, however, for Brahms returns quickly to the first theme, again subjecting it to some developmental processes that lead to a final cadence. A short passage modulates to the key in which the trio is heard.

The trio theme (*C*) is lyric and in the minor mode, although by no means is it somber. It is given to the horn at first.

**EX. 13.4** *Ibid.*
bars 287–300

After this the piano repeats the theme and extends it. The theme is restated, begun by the horn and ended by the piano. The trio modulates back to the key of the main section (*ABA*), which is then repeated exactly.

It is easy to hear the interplay between the instruments throughout the movement. Each has its own character, which Brahms brings out sometimes subtly, other times obviously. Although one instrumental part may be momentarily more important, there is no one timbre dominating. The players have to view each other as partners rather than as assistants or superiors, and this partnership demands greater reliance on one another's abilities. This is a quality essential for success in any chamber music performance involving more than one player, regardless of the number.

*Haydn leading the rehearsal of a string quartet. More than any other composer, Haydn established the Classical quartet as an ensemble with homogeneous sound, all four parts equally sharing thematic material in an intimate, refined, charming, dynamic way. Haydn is the violinist at the right. (The Bettmann Archive)*

In the *Lyric Suite*, Berg calls for the traditional instrumentation of the string quartet. Once again, intimacy is preserved, although in this case the similarities of timbres of the various instruments are in sharp contrast with Brahms's horn trio. The cello's upper notes have sounds similar to those in the viola's lower range, and the viola's higher range sounds much like the violin. The two violins have the same sound, although it is usually the first violin that plays prominent solo passages (thus giving rise to the bittersweet references made to the "second fiddle").

The *Lyric Suite* is typical of twentieth-century chamber compositions, in that it employs modern compositional devices (in this case, tone rows and serial systems; see Chapter 5) and is technically demanding of the performers. The first and last of the six movements are completely serialized, and portions of other movements involve rows. The *Lyric Suite* also has a historical interest, for it was only the second composition in which Berg used a tone row and the first in which he used a row as basic material for a complete movement, thus foreshadowing later works in which a row served for an entire composition.

The first movement resembles a sonata form without a development section. Largely because the *Lyric Suite* is atonal, Berg deliberately avoided using the sonata form in its classic concept. The exposition is considerably abbreviated and miniaturized, consisting of a two-measure introduction, an eleven-measure principal theme, a bridge passage of ten measures, a ten-measure second theme, and a three-measure coda. Then there is a very free return of the same pattern.

Here is the row on which the movement is based:

| Pitch name: | F | E | C | A | G | D | A♭ | D♭ | E♭ | G♭ | B♭ | B |
|---|---|---|---|---|---|---|---|---|---|---|---|---|
| Order in row: | 1 | 2 | 3 | 4 | 5 | 6 | 7 | 8 | 9 | 10 | 11 | 12 |

In the first measure, Berg sounds all twelve notes in four rather blunt and harsh chords. These he considered the "source" of his material. Note that Berg's arranging of the order of the notes of the row is wholly free of any tonal implications. F-sharp equals G-flat, hence F-sharp may be considered the tenth note of the row.

EX. 13.5 BERG
*Lyric Suite*, 1st mvt.,
bar 1, the "source"

The first violin then plays a rapid, ascending, six-note passage (the first six notes of the row), which leads into the principal theme, bracketed as *P.T.* in the following example. The theme starts on the seventh note of the row and is accompanied.

**EX. 13.6** *Ibid.*
bars 2–4

The row is stated either wholly or partially several times in the principal theme and is stated once in the *inverted* form (the intervals or distances between the pitches remain the same, but in a direction opposite to the original version of the row).

**EX. 13.7** *Ibid.*
bars 18–19, inverted row

The second theme is another statement of the row, this time given to the cello in its lowest range. The tempo of the movement is slowed to a more tranquil pace, in keeping with the time-honored treatment of subordinate themes in the classical sonata. The smooth quality of the melodic line adds to its lyricism.

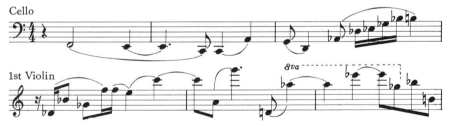

**EX. 13.8** *Ibid.*
bars 22–27

The row is repeated by the first violin immediately after the cello passage, again smoothly and lyrically.

After a very free return of the two themes, a brief coda follows. In the last measure of the movement, all twelve notes appear as they did in the first measure, but are not sounded in such a harsh and complex manner. Here, there is a strong flavor of cadence and finality, and the repeated chord that finishes the movement has a satisfyingly consonant quality.

The first movement of the *Lyric Suite* has an ebullience and joyfulness even though its overall sound is somewhat muted and dynamically understated. Although it does use the serial system—thus implying a certain complexity—it is also, as its name obviously implies, quite tuneful. Themes of considerable lyrical quality are rare in later serial compositions, which often rely on a highly intellectual "pointillism," a style concerned with a delicate interrelationship of isolated pitches.

**Music for five instruments: Shubert's Quintet in A, (Trout), Op. 114, fourth movement**

Schubert presents a somewhat different aspect of chamber music in the *Trout* Quintet. Here, the piano is cast almost in the same light as in a concerto (see Chapter 6 for a complete thematic analysis), thus creating an illusion that the work is for a soloist and accompaniment. He dispels this illusion by often using the piano as an ensemble instrument or as an accompaniment, as well as a prominent solo instrument. Other times, he will pit the piano against the strings, setting up countermelodic ideas that are equal to one another in importance. The intimacy of the chamber sound is not lost, for, even in the most elaborate passages, there are still only five instruments playing, and the astute listener can delight in their sharing of thematic material and the various roles of accompaniment, melodic statement, and variation.

When the number of instruments goes beyond five or six, musical composition becomes decidedly more complex, although it can be true to the spirit of chamber music even with the larger numbers if it retains that signatory delicacy of sound. One does not feel overwhelmed in the Stravinsky *Octet*, for instance, or even in the larger chamber works of Richard Strauss.

### Chamber music before Haydn and Mozart

Before 1750, the amateur played an important role in chamber music. In the houses of royalty and nobility where composers lived and worked under patronage, they were often called upon to write music that the members of the household could perform. Instrumentation was usually an uncertainty, depending on who was present and which instruments they could play. The trio was a popular combination, calling for two soprano instruments and basso continuo. The soprano instruments were not specified, and thus could be either two flutes, two oboes, two violins, or combinations of any two of these or other soprano instruments. There is a wealth of this music available, and many amateur players, especially those who play recorders, enjoy performing it. Notable composers of trios

*Frederick the Great playing the flute at Sans Souci. One of the most
significant military figures of the eighteenth century, Frederick was also
a composer and an accomplished flutist. He is apparently in the midst
of a cadenza, for the accompanying violins and basso continuo are silent.
The cellist and harpsichordist read from the same part. (The Bettmann Archive)*

*Antoine Jean Duclos (1742–1795). The Concert. This print reveals the aristocratic spirit and intimacy of eighteenth-century chamber music. Note the central position of the harpsichordist, who not only improvised harmonic passages in accordance with* basso continuo *practice, but also served as the "maestro" of the performance. The cellist reinforces the bass line and reads from the same part as the harpsichordist. (The Metropolitan Museum of Art, New York. Harris Brisbane Dick Fund, 1933)*

were Telemann, Corelli, Vivaldi, Purcell, Couperin, and Rameau, as well as others. Solo keyboard literature by Rameau and Domenico Scarlatti also has had lasting value.

The trio gave way to the quartet in the early years of the Classical period and the role of chamber music began to change. No longer was it written only for the amateur performer in the royal household, for fewer composers were being patronized as the eighteenth century waned. To be sure, there were those who still were under patronage (Haydn was one), but secular music—chamber music included—was gradually becoming a public art performed in public halls. Chamber music eventually became less popular, but its quality of intimacy among the performers intensified. It was now an introspective art, the music for musicians.

## Chamber music of the Classical period

Even so, chamber music reflected the styles of the times. No one can listen to a string quartet by Haydn or a Mozart piano sonata without acknowledging that he is hearing the very essence of Viennese Classicism. In fact, the chamber music of the Classical period was able to reflect the style of the period in the purest sense possible, since it could be written without commercial influences. Haydn turned the string quartet from its Baroque past and made it into a classic jewel. He loved the quartet, completing some eighty-three between his first in 1755 and his death in 1809.[2] The later quartets were in the four-movement plan, which had become the pattern for most of the multimovement instrumental compositions written after 1780.

Mozart, who wrote twenty-three quartets, had an almost equal fondness for them. During the 1780's Mozart and Haydn were both in Vienna and occasionally played together in a string quartet; their marked influence on each other as composers dates from this time. Mozart worked with combinations other than the string quartet and wrote several works for strings plus such wind instruments as the flute, the clarinet, the oboe, the bassoon, or the horn. He also explored the piano trio and piano quartet combinations and has often been said to be the father of both. Haydn and Mozart both wrote for solo instruments (especially sonatas for piano) and both contributed numbers of *divertimentos, serenades,* and *cassations* for various small combinations of winds and strings.

What Haydn and Mozart had begun was continued by Beethoven and Schubert in the late years of the Classical period. Beethoven wrote thirty-two piano sonatas, sixteen string quartets (the last few of which were astonishingly introspective), a number of chamber works involving wind instruments, and fifteen so-called *ensemble sonatas* for piano and either violin or cello. The Beethoven chamber music encompasses every facet of its creator's imagination. In these works, there is consistently the remarkable amalgam of musical invention and strength of personality that not only brought to a new summit all that had gone before but also provided inspiration for the musical thinking of those who followed. Schubert's chamber music, identified by intense lyricism, includes solo works and quartets, but his quintets for piano and strings are more important.

---

[2]Authorities disagree as to the number of Haydn quartets, some accepting only seventy-six, others claiming as many as eighty-four.

During the nineteenth century, chamber music remained a medium primarily for the performer and the musical sophisticate. It adopted such basic Romantic notions as the emphasis on instrumental color, which had become so important in symphonic composition. On the other hand, such romanticisms as grandiosity and programmaticism were minor reflections in ensemble writing. The woodwind quintet gained in stature and there was some interest in slightly larger ensembles—quintets, sextets, octets, and the like. The forms which Haydn and Mozart had perfected were basically retained (especially in the string quartets of Brahms and Dvořák) except that they became larger and more diffuse. There was the typically romantic emphasis on longer, more lyric and colorful melodic lines, which at times would cause an imbalance in the equality of the voices in an ensemble. Practically every composer of the era wrote some chamber music, but there was none who matched the output of the men of the Classical period. The French composers generally showed little interest in the medium except for solo works and Italian composers even less (Verdi's beautiful string quartet notwithstanding). The art song, a vocal form of chamber music (discussed in Chapter 7), matured in the nineteenth century. Occasionally, there were mergers of other instruments with the voice and piano (by Brahms, Schubert, Berlioz, Richard Strauss, and others). These were so successful musically that there is cause to wonder why more such works were not written.

In the nineteenth century, chamber music felt the impact of the increasing interest in virtuosity and striking individuality. Both of these characteristics were particularly manifested in literature for the solo instrument, the piano and the violin being the media most exploited.

Of special interest was the expanding popularity of the *character piece*, a short composition, often with a programmatic title, which sometimes stood alone, but was also often one of many similar pieces within a collection (with or without musical relationships to other pieces in the collection). Beethoven's *bagatelles* and *écossaises* for piano were among the first of the genre.

The character pieces of Chopin, Schumann, and Liszt deserve special mention, for they are among the most notable compositions in the keyboard literature of the period. Chopin's works range from the grandiose to the intimate and demand from the performer delicate shadings of dynamics and subtle inflections of tempo and rhythm that identify an important manner of piano performance. Schumann's character pieces

*Mihaly de Munkácsy (1844–1909). The Music Room. Chamber music of the Victorian era often took the form of a character piece, a short, highly atmospheric, frequently descriptive composition, written usually for the piano. The ladies in the painting may very likely be listening to such a composition. (The Metropolitan Museum of Art, New York. Bequest of Mrs. Martha T. Fiske Collard, 1908, in memory of Josiah M. Fiske)*

also vary widely. Some are cycles of pieces meant for the concert virtuoso, others are individual pieces or collections of varying difficulty. All, however, are rich in atmosphere and melodic invention.

The piano music of Liszt, like Chopin's, not only epitomizes a style of performance but represents an outstanding originality. Liszt's piano music makes frequent use of rapid runs and ornaments and full chords in both hands and requires the performer to play over the entire keyboard with great bravado, agility, and, at the same time, expressiveness. His adventurous harmonies and unique melodic and structural patterns are often overlooked by the modern student but provide a source of great interest to composers and to anyone willing to pay more than casual heed to them.

Brahms, too, was a major composer of solo and accompanied chamber music. His list of compositions includes major pieces of all types, all of them characterized by inventive rhythms, unusual phrasing, clarity of form, and richness of color.

The accompanied sonata, the solo sonata, and the character piece reflected the rise of the virtuoso by placing ever greater demands upon the performer. Many composers continued the tradition of writing music for their own concert appearances, among them Liszt and the violinist Paganini. There appeared a number of musicians, however, whose fame rested on their ability to perform music not of their own composition, and such figures as violinists Joseph Joachim and Leopold Auer and the pianist Clara Schumann influenced the composition of many works that were either commissioned by them or written with their specific talents in mind.

### Chamber music in the twentieth century

As the Romantic century ended and Europe stumbled toward World War I, composers turned away from the huge symphony orchestra to the more controllable chamber-sized ensemble. Social history and economics played no small role in this metamorphosis. The Europe that had fostered the huge orchestral and dramatic compositions of Wagner, Richard Strauss, Bruckner, and Mahler in the last decades of the nineteenth century was in a state of turmoil by 1912 and in a full-scale war two years later. The society that had produced the Romantic giants during the nineteenth century was to undergo great change, although vestiges of the old world remained until after World War II.

The effect of this change on a composer may be seen in the case of

Stravinsky, who in the years between 1910 and 1913 wrote his three famous ballets, *Firebird, Petrouchka,* and *The Rite of Spring.* Each called for a large orchestra, corps de ballet, and several solo dancers. In 1918, however, Stravinsky wrote the ballet *L'Histoire du Soldat,* which called for an "orchestra" of seven players plus conductor, three dancers, and a narrator, a total of twelve performers. Some of his other works from the same period were similar in size: *Ragtime* calls for eleven instruments and *Les Noces* is scored for small chorus, soloists, four pianos and seven-

Joseph Wolins (1915–    ). Chamber Music Group. A dynamic modern conception of a string quartet. The highly personal idiom, strong accents of light and dark, and the unusual interplay of line and shape are strongly suggestive of Alban Berg's Lyric Suite. (The Metropolitan Museum of Art, New York)

teen percussion instruments—highly unusual, but not massive. Stravinsky noted at the time that not only did he feel a kindred relationship with the small-sized performing group, but also that he knew his use of small groups made performances more likely.

Other composers were doing exactly the same thing; chamber music again became an economically viable medium. Composers found themselves in sympathy with its size, its possibilities for clarity in design and expression, and its popularity.

Chamber music has found favor with all the schools of twentieth-century composition, and works using both new and traditional combinations are being produced. Neoclassicist Stravinsky called for violin, double bass, trumpet, trombone, clarinet, bassoon, and percussion in the score to *L'Histoire du Soldat*, while Neoromanticist Bartók and Expressionists Schoenberg and Berg found the traditional string quartet suitable. The Postimpressionists in France, including Ravel and the "French Six," all worked with new sizes and sounds. Honegger's oratorio *King David* (1921), and Milhaud's ballet *The Creation of the World* (1923) both call for chamber orchestras with unusual instrumentations.

Some composers have added electronic sounds to small groups, in many instances gaining startling and successful results. Varèse's *Déserts* (1954) was a pioneering work in this direction. Chamber works by Babbitt (*Philomel*, 1968) and Sollberger (*Music for Sophocles' "Antigone,"* 1968) mix voices and electronic sounds. In other directions, Carter and Kirchner have both written concertos for chamber-sized groups, Carter's for harpischord, piano, and two chamber orchestras, Kirchner's for violin, cello, ten winds, and percussion.

The role of the chamber music performer has changed in the twentieth century. For one thing, the professional chamber music ensemble, particularly the string quartet, has become a regular part of the concert world. The original purpose of these professional ensembles was to play the works of past composers, but, as these groups gained in number, stature, and ability, they began to include works of contemporary composers in their repertoire. The fact that professional groups do exist often seems to encourage composers to write as they please, regardless of the technical problems that they might create.

At this point in the Modern era, chamber music is enjoying a robust good health. A number of writers on the subject believe that the small ensemble is the medium of the future, and that it will eventually replace the symphony orchestra as the major medium of instrumental music.

### Organ literature

The organ is one of the very few musical instruments which requires the use of both hands and both feet for playing. It is a complex machine, and its playing problems are equal to its construction. There is the initial problem of making one's four limbs do different things simultaneously: for the feet, there is a pedal board, expression pedals, and several buttons that change the set of timbres (*registration*) of one or more of the manuals; for each hand, there are keyboard passages to play plus the pushing and pulling of buttons that add or subtract ranks, change registrations, and the like. (With all the exercise, it is no wonder that one sees so few obese organists.)

Of the many musical problems that present themselves to the organist, perhaps the most pressing one is that of registration. Registration is the combining of the sounds from several ranks; these combinations provide the player with a variety of timbres to suit various passages in compositions and the various styles of the organ repertoire. Registration is complicated not only by the choice of ranks, but also by the choice of octaves; by adding new sounds that are an octave or more above or below the pitch desired, new dimensions of richness can be obtained. Brilliance can be increased when sounds other than the octave (for example, the third or fifth) are added to the basic sound. Registration, then, is an important matter of taste and perception.

In some compositions, registration is carefully spelled out, but in others there will be no markings at all, registration being left to the discretion of the performer.[3] Registration can become a problem when a work composed for a Romantic organ is to be performed on a Baroque instrument, which has fewer stops. The organist must make arbitrary choices and hope that they will suit the music.

Composers usually think polyphonically when they write for this instrument. A glance at the literature written for it will show that the fugue, for instance, an inherently polyphonic type of music, is most popular with organ composers. As an example, listen to Bach's *"Little" Fugue in G Minor* and note that the polyphonic style is the essence of the composition. The subject is an active one.

**EX. 13.9 BACH**
*Little Fugue in G minor,*
bars 1–5

As the fugue progresses, note the number of "imitations" or repetitions of the subject and the ingenuity with which they have been woven into the fabric of the composition. Note also that the busyness of the voices

[3]Because he wrote primarily for himself, Bach rarely indicated registrations; the lack of them has caused more than one argument over how his works should be registered. Franck, on the other hand, although he also wrote for his own performance, had an eye for publication and indicated all his registrations with care. Generally, nineteenth- and twentieth-century compositions come with registrations clearly indicated.

as they keep moving against one another maintains a sense of unrest and determination that is resolved only at the end of the composition. (A graph of the entire fugue may be found in Chapter 6.)

Most of the music written for the organ has to be played in churches, primarily because they house the best instruments, employ the finest organists, and provide regular audiences via their congregations. However, the fact that organ literature is played in churches does not mean that it is inherently sacred. The location of the performance is really incidental; music is music, and it will be aesthetically rewarding, in or out of the church or temple, in direct proportion to its purely musical worth. Some compositions may have powerful sacred connotations regardless of where they are played because they may be based on works that originally had religious texts or because of special familiarity within a sacred framework.

There is not a vast amount of organ literature from the great composers whose names are familiar to most music lovers, for, after the Baroque era, not too many of them have approached the instrument as a major medium of expression. There is, of course, Johann Sebastian Bach, and organists will argue that for no other instrument was there a composer so prolific and so consistently great as Bach was for the organ, although such earlier composers as Frescobaldi, Sweelinck, Buxtehude, Pachelbel, and Böhm produced many fine works for organ. It is from the Baroque period that the greatest amount of organ music comes, with such famous Bach compositions as the *Passacaglia and Fugue in C minor*, the *Toccata and Fugue in D minor*, and any number of chorale preludes as monumental examples.

Despite some fine music by Mozart, there is very little significant organ music from the Classical period. During the nineteenth century, however, several French composers, especially Franck, evinced a new interest in the medium. Franck, like Bach, was himself an organist, so his interest was naturally pointed in that direction and was revealed not only in his famous *Prelude, Chorale and Fugue*, but also in a shifting kind of chromaticism in his one orchestral symphony which suggests the not-so-subtle influence of an organist moving his fingers from chord to chord. Brahms wrote several works, including eleven chorale preludes, and the Mendelssohn organ music is also significant.

During the first half of the twentieth century, other French composers continued the composition of fine works for this instrument. The organ symphonies of Vierne and Widor, Messiaen's *Le Banquet céleste* ("The Heavenly Banquet"), and music by Duruflé and Langlais all figure importantly. The French composers came the closest to establishing a national school or tradition of composition for organ, but this has faded in recent years.

In the post-World War II period, there has been a decline in the number of compositions written for organ, a movement which has become more distinct since 1960. Organists think that there may be two reasons for this. First, many of the modern compositional techniques do not fit the instrument too well. Second, it is hard to imagine a more conservative audience for a musical composition than a church congregation, and such conservatism is not usually appreciated by avant garde composers who feel that their works ought best be directed toward more radically inclined listeners.

# POSTLUDE

This book has compressed much important information and a number of admittedly difficult conceptualizations into its few hundred pages. Many names and titles have been mentioned and many styles have been discussed, yet the wealth of music of the Western world has been but hinted at and the art of composition explained but briefly.

If the reader feels that his grasp of the art of sound is still inadequate, let him take heart from some essential truths: the greatest of artists never cease to learn about their art, and finding meaning or beauty in new things or new meaning in familiar things is one of the great joys of life.

The world of the arts is a world of perpetual discovery. How much one finds in it is, in the long run, entirely up to himself.

# APPENDICES

# A : THE HISTORY OF MUSIC IN CHART FORM

*THE MEDIEVAL ERA: 850–1450\**

| Key figures | Musical | Historical | Cultural |
|---|---|---|---|
| | Gregory I (540–604) | Charlemagne (742–814) | Abelard (1079–1142) |
| | Guido d'Arezzo (ca. 997–ca. 1050) | Barbarossa (ca. 1123–1190) | Eleanor d'Aquitaine (ca. 1122–1204) |
| | St. Martial school (fl. 1150) | St. Francis of Assisi (ca. 1182–1226) | Cimabue (ca. 1240–1302) |
| | Notre Dame school (late 12th century) | St. Louis (1215–1270) | Dante (1265–1321) |
| | Leoninus (12th century) | Aquinas (ca. 1225–1274) | Giotto (ca. 1267–1337) |
| | Perotinus (1155/60–1200/05) | Duns Scotus (ca. 1265–ca. 1308) | Boccaccio (1313–1375) |
| | Troubadours (fl. ca. 1100–1300) | Henry V (1387–1422) | Chaucer (ca. 1340–1400) |
| | Trouvères (fl. ca. 1150–1300) | | Jan van Eyck (ca. 1370–1440) |
| | De la Halle (ca. 1240–1287) | | |
| | Minnesänger (fl. ca. 1150–1300) | | |
| | De Vitry (1291–1361) | | |
| | Machaut (ca. 1300–1377) | | |
| | Landini (1325–1397) | | |
| | Dunstable (ca. 1380–1453) | | |
| | Burgundian school (fl. early 15th century) | | |
| | Dufay (ca. 1400–1474) | | |
| | Binchois (ca. 1400–1460) | | |

## Key events

| | |
|---|---|
| Great Schism (1054) | Seventh Crusade (1245–50) |
| Battle of Hastings (1066) | Polo's first trip (1271–75) |
| First Crusade (1096–99) | Avignon Papacy (1305–75) |
| Second Crusade (1146–48) | Burning of Joan of Arc (1431) |
| Magna Carta (1215) | First printing press (1440) |

**Attitudes and characteristics**

All life and art in service of church, and in church's shadow • Earthly life a brief moment in time • Mixture of pagan, secular, and sacred • Music a major tool for apperception of God's works • Passionate self-abasement and search for perfection mingled with sensuality and secular pleasure • Love of romance and adventure • Brilliant, clearly separated colors • Soaring, vertically accented architecture • Feudalism • Theoretical acceptance of past—that is, Classical—learning, social order, concepts of beauty • Emotional aspiration for life to come

**Melody and texture**

Monophony in plainsong (A), secular songs of Troubadours, Trouvères, Minnesänger

Texture linear, not harmonic (A, but less so in E)

Plainsong cantus firmi (A)

Cantus firmi in tenor (lowest) part, in long note values (B, C)

Dronelike lowest parts, either played or sung (B, C, D)

\*Note: Characteristics listed in this table do not apply equally to all stages of the Medieval era. Hence they are keyed by letters referring to historical sub-divisions as follows: (A) all stages; (B) 850–1000 (period of early polyphony); (C) 1000–1150 (Romanesque; period of staff notation); (D) 1150–1300 (early Gothic; Ars Antiqua); (E) 1300–1450 (late Gothic; Ars Nova).

Clarity of texture (A)

Homophony in polyphonic conductus (D)

Top voice quasi-soloistic; lower parts likely to be played rather than sung (E, late D)

Parallel movement (B)

Frequent crossing of parts (D)

Free counterpoint among smoothly flowing melodies (E)

Melismas and ornaments often improvised (A)

Hocketing (D, E)

Freer motion, melodic character in tenor (E)

Secular composition free of cantus firmus (E)

Modal melodies of relatively narrow range (A, less so in E)

Changes of vowel from one melisma to another, plus changes in texture and from solo to choral performance result in sharply contrasted sections (D)

Approach to tonic note from 6th degree of scale—"Landini" cadence: 7-6-8 (E)

---

Basic consonances are unison, octave, 5th, 4th (A)

Dissonances found in passing notes (A)

Parallel 5ths, 4ths (B)

Triads at unstressed points (D)

Triads, parallel 3rds, 6ths, 10ths (late E, but late D in England)

Music linear, not harmonic; little sense of chords as parts of a series (A, but less so in E)

**Harmony**

---

More frequent use of faster note values (D, E)

Dance rhythms (A, although often conjectural)

Dynamic variety a result of change in instrumentation, texture (A)

Great rhythmic complexity, syncopation, written-in rubatos, rhythmic variety (late 14th, early 15th centuries)

Unmetrical rhythm; mixture of binary and ternary groups (B, C)

Measured rhythm based on poetic modes (D)

Ternary rhythm dominant (B, C, D)

Duple rhythm as acceptable as ternary (E)

Moderate tempi (A)

**Rhythm, tempo, dynamics**

---

Balanced sound made up of heterogeneous colors rather than blending ones (A)

Light, thin, bright sound ideal, probably more nasal and penetrating than modern concepts (A)

Little vibrato; boys' voices, not women's (A)

Instruments regarded as doublers or as substitutes for voices, especially for slow tenors

Frequent drone basses; frequent percussion

Little distinction of idiom between voices and instruments, both probably always together; untexted or vocalized parts may have been performed on instruments

Falsetto often used (A)

Strings: vielle, rebec, harp, psaltery, lute, guitar

Winds: bagpipe, recorder, shawm

Brass: trumpet (buizine), sackbut

Percussion: drums, bells, cymbals of many types

Keyboard: several types of organ

**Performing media**

---

Plainsong (A) • Trope (B, C) • Parallel organum (B) • Free organum (C, D) • Monophonic conductus (C, D) • Polyphonic conductus (D) • Liturgical drama (C, D) • Clausula (D) • motet (D, E; isorhythmic, E) • Lauda (Italy, D) • Bar (D) • Ballade (D, E) • Strophic song with refrain (C, D) • Virelai (E) • Rondeau (E) • Madrigal (E) • Caccia (E) • Ballata (E)

**Vocal structures**

---

Dance types • Fanfares

**Instrumental structures**

---

*Requiem aeternam*, Mode VI (plainsong)

**Accompanying recording**

| Key figures | Musical | Historical | Cultural |
|---|---|---|---|
| | Dufay (ca. 1400–1474) | Savonarola (1452–1498) | Bosch (ca. 1450–1516) |
| | Ockeghem (ca. 1425–1495) | Lorenzo de Medici (1449–1492) | Da Vinci (1452–1519) |
| | Obrecht (ca. 1450–1505) | Copernicus (1473–1543) | Grünewald (ca. 1470–1528) |
| | Des Prez (ca. 1450–1521) | Luther (1483–1546) | Dürer (1471–1528) |
| | Willaert (ca. 1490–1562) | Henry VIII (1491–1547) | Michelangelo (1475–1564) |
| | Monte (1521–1603) | Calvin (1509–1564) | Ronsard (1524–1585) |
| | Palestrina (ca. 1525–1594) | Elizabeth I (1533–1603) | Brueghel the Elder (ca. 1525–1569) |
| | Lassus (1532–1594) | Galileo (1564–1642) | Cervantes (1547–1616) |
| | Byrd (1543–1623) | | Shakespeare (1564–1616) |
| | Victoria (ca. 1549–1611) | | |
| | Marenzio (1553–1599) | | |
| | G. Gabrieli (ca. 1554–1612) | | |
| | Monteverdi (1567–1643) | | |

**Key events**  First printing press (1440)  Luther's 95 theses (1517)
Fall of Constantinople (1453)  Council of Trent (1545–63)
Columbus' first voyage (1492)

**Attitudes and characteristics**  Classical attitude: restraint, self-control, calm • Interest in Hellenism • Humanism, scientific inquiry • Man as most glorious of God's creatures • Classical subject matter, horizontal lines in painting and architecture • Culture universally pursued, both within and without the church • Protestant ideal: man in direct contact with God • Sophistication in the South, fundamentalism in the North • Chiaroscuro, softly modeled figures

**Melody and texture**  Use of modal scales  Madrigals richly chromatic (especially
Imitation as consistent trait (after Des    in Italy)
    Prez, except for frottola, madrigal)  All parts equally important melodically

Melodic smoothness, especially in sacred music

Prevailingly polyphonic; although some accompanied song, some homophony (e.g., frottola)

Some polychoral writing

Cantus firmus technique used, but secular sources; many works wholly free of it

Chords by-products of interacting melodies

Dissonance for word settings, rather than for voice leadings or chord progressions

Bass line gains harmonic role

Open 5ths and octaves used in cadences by early composers or later conservatives

**Harmony**

Moderate tempi; half note at speed of heart beat

Dynamic variety not indicated in score; some gradations, but moderate and unobtrusive

Unmetrical rhythm; tactus principle; unbarred

Accents those of text, not regular rhythmic groups

**Rhythm, tempo, dynamics**

One idiom for voices and instruments

Instruments as doublers or substitutes for voices

Some idiomatic writing for lute and keyboard; canzona, ricercare are transcriptions of vocal forms

Strings: viol, lute (many types)

Winds: shawm, recorder, cornetto

Brass: zink, trumpet, trombone

Keyboard: organ, harpsichord, virginal

**Performing media**

Madrigal • Motet • Mass • Chanson • Chorale • Frottola

**Vocal structures**

Fantasia • Ricercare • Toccata • Canzona • Prelude

**Instrumental structures**

Palestrina: *Agnus Dei*, from *Missa Brevis* (motet, Mass)

**Accompanying recording**

| Key figures | *Musical* | *Historical* | *Cultural* |
|---|---|---|---|
| | Monteverdi (1567–1643) | Galileo (1564–1642) | El Greco (ca. 1548–ca. 1614) |
| | Schütz (1585–1672) | Harvey (1578–1657) | Shakespeare (1564–1616) |
| | Lully (1632–1687) | Richelieu (1585–1642) | Rubens (1577–1640) |
| | Buxtehude (ca. 1637–1707) | Descartes (1596–1650) | Bernini (1598–1680) |
| | Corelli (1653–1713) | Cromwell (1599–1658) | Milton (1608–1674) |
| | Pachelbel (1653–1706) | Mazarin (1602–1661) | Rembrandt (1606–1669) |
| | Purcell (ca. 1659–1695) | Spinoza (1632–1677) | Molière (1622–1673) |
| | A. Scarlatti (1660–1725) | Louis XIV (1638–1715) | Racine (1639–1699) |
| | Couperin (1668–1733) | Leibnitz (1646–1716) | Swift (1667–1745) |
| | Vivaldi (ca. 1675–1741) | Frederick the Great (1712–1786) | Watteau (1684–1721) |
| | Rameau (1683–1764) | | Fielding (1707–1754) |
| | J. S. Bach (1685–1750) | | |
| | D. Scarlatti (1685–1757) | | |
| | Handel (1685–1759) | | |

| Key events | First opera (1597) | Pilgrims land in America (1620) |
|---|---|---|
| | Thirty Years' War (1618–1648) | Newton's *Mathematical Principles* (1687) |

**Attitudes and characteristics**   Conviction of enlightenment and consequent desire to classify and assimilate all knowledge • Splendor; elaboration of classical models and subjects • Effect for its own sake; theatricality • Stylization; ceremony • Emotionalism • Counter-reformation versus elaborate secularism • Belief in divine right of kings; later in conflict with ideas of universal rights of man • Emergence of modern European nations

| **Melody and texture** | Melody highly ornamental; ornamentations often improvised or interpolated in performance | Texture generally consistent for section or movement |
|---|---|---|
| | Continuous motion, especially in lowest voice | Melody spun out, highly sequential |
| | | Intimate relation between melody and pictorial aspects of text (affections) |

Stress on outer voices; basso continuo
  fills in alto, tenor
Clarity of parts

Moving bass line gives feeling of polyphony, even in homophonic works
Reliance on major and minor modes

Chords viewed functionally in tonal
  rather than modal sequences; strong
  sense of harmonic direction
Rapid chord changes (i.e., harmonic
  rhythm)

Strong bass line; use of basso continuo
Dissonance used for both harmonic
  direction and affective word setting

**Harmony**

Doctrine of Affections: one basic mood,
  tempo for a complete movement or
  section
Terraced dynamics in concerted works;
  graded and free for soloists

Propulsive, restless, even in slow tempo
Strong sense of motion, although in
  early Baroque uncertain and frequently changing

**Rhythm, tempo,
dynamics**

Basso continuo accompanies all media
No standard orchestra; strings main
  melodic force in concerted groups
Modern violin family dominant; trumpet
  a favorite melodic instrument
Winds used primarily as melodic
  doublers
Clarity, brilliance

Contrast of groups by size, timbre
Strings: modern violin family
Winds: recorder, flute, oboe, bassoon
Brass: clarin trumpet, horn, trombone
Percussion: timpani
Keyboard: harpsichord, clavichord,
  organ

**Performing media**

Opera seria ● Intermezzo ● Da capo aria ● Oratorio ● Cantata ● Chorale ● Mass
● Recitative ● Motet

**Vocal structures**

Concerto grosso ● Solo concerto ● French overture ● Italian overture ● Trio sonata
● Toccata ● Prelude ● Suite

**Instrumental structures**

Fugue ● Fantasia ● Binary and ternary patterns ● Passacaglia ● Chaconne

**Structures common both
to voices and instruments**

Bach: *Little Fugue in G minor*
Handel: Excerpts from *Messiah* (ABA aria, chorus, *recitativo secco* and *accompagnato*)

**Accompanying recordings**

| Key figures | *Musical* | *Historical* | *Cultural* |
|---|---|---|---|
| | Pergolesi (1710–1736) | Franklin (1706–1790) | Pope (1688–1744) |
| | C.P.E. Bach (1714–1788) | Frederick the Great (1712– | Voltaire (1694–1778) |
| | Gluck (1714–1787) | 1786) | Fielding (1707–1754) |
| | J. Stamitz (1717–1757) | J.J. Rousseau (1712–1778) | Goya (1746–1828) |
| | Haydn (1732–1809) | Kant (1724–1804) | David (1748–1825) |
| | J.C. Bach (1735–1782) | Washington (1732–1799) | Goethe (1749–1832) |
| | Mozart (1756–1791) | Watt (1736–1819) | Stuart (1755–1828) |
| | Beethoven (1770–1827) | George III (1738–1820) | Blake (1757–1827) |
| | Schubert (1797–1828) | Napoleon (1769–1821) | Schiller (1759–1805) |
| | | | Turner (1775–1851) |

**Key events**

Seven Years War (1756–63)
Wincklemann's *History of the Art of Antiquity* (1764)
Declaration of Independence (1776)

French Revolution (1789–92)
Reign of Napoleon I (1804–15)

**Attitudes and characteristics**

Restraint, self-control • Elegance • Simplicity, naturalness • Profundity and seriousness masked by element of playfulness • Graciousness • Objectivity • Age of Reason: search for order, propriety, taste • Standardization of behavior, dress, procedures of both manners and artistic forms • Subordination of detail to whole, unobtrusive decoration • Veneer of sophistication and well-being over deep social unrest

**Melody and texture**

Symmetrical, balanced phrasing, well marked by cadencing
Repeated cadence formulas
Feminine endings, gracious ornamentations
Free mixture of homophony and polyphony in a single movement or section
Melodies often built of chord tones
Interest in short, concise motives

Interest in development, fragmentation, variation
Transitions often developmental
"Symphonic counterpoint": all parts share equally in development
Alberti bass and other accompaniment figures; early period prevailingly homophonic, but with vestige of moving bass line of Baroque

| | | |
|---|---|---|
| Repeated cadence formulas<br>Strong bass notes, but little sense of bass "line" in middle and late period | Clear key relationships, strongly felt even if not recognized by listener<br>Harmonies simple, change slowly | **Harmony** |
| Clear, precise patterns; repeated figures of accompaniment suggest motion even if harmony does not change<br>Rhythmic motives used for development<br>Syncopations, especially at climaxes | Elegance often created by feminine endings<br>Graded dynamics<br>Some flexibility of tempo, especially slow movements | **Rhythm, tempo, dynamics** |
| Small, balanced orchestra, free of continuo<br>String quartet, piano trio, sonata<br>Piano replaces harpsichord<br>Brasses used as fillers; woodwinds melodically important and independent<br>Strings: modern orchestral quintet | Winds: pairs of flutes, oboes, bassoons, clarinets, English horn (rarely)<br>Brass: French horn, trumpet, trombone (especially in church and opera orchestras)<br>Percussion: timpani<br>Keyboard: piano, organ | **Performing media** |
| Opera seria • Opera buffa • Singspiel • Opéra comique • Art song • Folklike song • Mass • Oratorio • Cantata • Motet • Expansive ensemble | | **Vocal structures** |
| Symphony • Solo concerto • Sinfonia concertante • Sonata • String quartet • Divertimento • Cassation • Serenade • Fantasia • Minuet with trio • Scherzo with trio | | **Instrumental structures** |
| Sonata form • Rondo • Theme and variations • Fugue • Sonata-rondo • Ternary patterns | | **Structures common both to voices and instruments** |
| Beethoven: Symphony No. 5, in C minor, 3rd movement (scherzo and trio) and 4th movement (exposition of sonata form)<br>Mozart: Symphony No. 40, in G minor, 1st movement (sonata form)<br>Mozart: Sextet, "Riconosci in questo amplesso," from *Le Nozze di Figaro*, Act III (expansive ensemble, preceded by *recitativo secco*)<br>Schubert: Quintet in A major (*Trout*), 4th movement (theme and variations) | | **Accompanying recordings** |

|  | German | French | Italian |
|---|---|---|---|
| **Major composers** | Beethoven (1770–1827)<br>Weber (1786–1826)<br>Schubert (1797–1828)<br>Mendelssohn (1809–1847)<br>Schumann (1810–1856)<br>Wagner (1813–1883)<br>Bruckner (1824–1896)<br>Brahms (1833–1897)<br>Wolf (1860–1903)<br>Mahler (1860–1911)<br>R. Strauss (1864–1949)<br>Schoenberg (1874–1951) | Berlioz (1803–1869)<br>Gounod (1818–1893)<br>Franck (1822–1890)<br>Saint-Saëns (1835–1921)<br>Bizet (1838–1875)<br>Fauré (1845–1924)<br>Debussy (1862–1918) | Rossini (1792–1868)<br>Donizetti (1797–1848)<br>Bellini (1801–1835)<br>Verdi (1813–1901)<br>Puccini (1858–1924) |

**French**

**Russian**

Borodin (1833–1887)
Mussorgsky (1839–1881)
Tchaikovsky (1840–1893)
Rimsky-Korsakov (1844–1908)
Rachmaninoff (1873–1943)

**Other**

Chopin (1810–1849)
Liszt (1811–1886)
Smetana (1824–1884)
Dvořák (1841–1904)
Grieg (1843–1907)
Janáček (1854–1928)
Elgar (1857–1934)
Sibelius (1865–1957)

|  | Figures | Events |
|---|---|---|
| **Historical figures and events** | Napoleon I (1769–1821)<br>Manzoni (1785–1873)<br>Lincoln (1809–1865)<br>Kierkegaard (1813–1855)<br>Bismarck (1815–1898)<br>Victoria (1819–1901)<br>Franz Josef (1830–1916)<br>Nicholas II (1868–1918) | Revolutions of 1848<br>Marx's *Communist Manifesto* (1848)<br>American Civil War (1861–1865)<br>Darwin's *Origin of Species* (1862)<br>Unifications of Italy and Germany (1871) |
| **Cultural figures** | Turner (1775–1851)<br>Hoffman (1776–1822)<br>Irving (1783–1859)<br>Corot (1796–1875)<br>Heine (1797–1856)<br>Hugo (1802–1885)<br>Daumier (1808–1879)<br>Poe (1809–1849)<br>Dickens (1812–1870)<br>Thoreau (1817–1862)<br>Whitman (1819–1892) | Dostoevski (1821–1881)<br>Dumas *fils* (1824–1895)<br>Ibsen (1828–1906)<br>Manet (1832–1883)<br>Whistler (1834–1903)<br>Homer (1836–1910)<br>Rodin (1840–1917)<br>Van Gogh (1853–1890)<br>Mann (1875–1955)<br>Jeffers (1887–1962)<br>O'Neill (1888–1953) |

**Attitudes and characteristics**   Desire to express the self; autobiographical content in the arts • Individualism • Nationalism • Rich description and imagery • Overt emotional expression, free of restraint • Fascination with nature, inner self, supernatural, exotic, bizarre, unusual • Escapism • Interest in the past • Free reign to the imagination • Paradoxes: grandiose vs. intimate; desire to communicate on grand scale vs. communion with kindred spirits • Mixture of diverse elements within single structure • Rejection of restraints of tradition, academicism, old ways of doing things ● Tendency to long or large structures or very intimate ones ● Longing, melancholy, search for better life ● Virtuosity, uniqueness of the artist as a creator or performer ● Notion of transcendental inspiration for the creative act

| | | |
|---|---|---|
| Long, asymetrical phrases<br>Striking melodic phrases; melody an end in itself<br>Variety of melodic styles, from folklike to highly chromatic | Affected by frequent change of tempo, dynamic gradation, change of instrumentation<br>Melody apt to be highly varied within single movement | **Melody and texture** |
| Rich chromaticism; dramatic chord changes<br>Especially in late part of era, indistinct keys, frequent key changes | Cadences deceptive, delayed, obscured<br>Dissonances resolved in unexpected ways or to other dissonances<br>Modulations to distant keys | **Harmony** |
| Wide gradations within single movement<br>Extreme, and often sudden, contrasts<br>Irregularity and unpredictability | Cultivation of exotic and nationalistic rhythms<br>Frequent subtle gradations of speed, thus affecting rhythmic consistency | **Rhythm, tempo, dynamics** |
| Tone color an end in itself and an emotional force<br>Large, rich, varied instrumentation<br>Many types of large and small ensemble<br>Extensive solo literature for almost all media, although piano and violin dominant<br>Frequent solo passages within concerted works<br>Many voice types (dramatic, lyric, spinto, etc.) | Exotic, unusual instruments; use of instruments for nationalistic or highly picturesque effects<br>Cultivation of complete families of instruments (including sopranino, alto, contra members)<br>Exploitation of virtuosity of performers, both solo and orchestral, although concerto primarily a medium for the soloist | **Performing media** |
| Grand opera ● Music drama ● Operetta ● Opéra comique ● Oratorio ● Mass ● Motet ● Cantata ● Part song ● Anthem ● Scena ● Cabaletta ● Art song | | **Vocal structures** |
| Tone poem ● Symphony ● Concert overture ● Solo concerto ● Character piece ● Rhapsody ● Fantasia ● Prelude ● Suite ● Sonata ● Chamber ensembles | | **Instrumental structures** |
| Sonata ● Rondo ● Theme and variations ● Through-composed form ● Scherzo and trio ● Fugue ● Binary and ternary forms | | **Structures common both to voices and instruments** |
| Beethoven: Symphony No. 5, in C minor, 3rd movement (scherzo and trio) and part of the 4th movement (exposition of sonata form)<br>Berlioz: Fragments from *Fantastic Symphony* (program symphony)<br>Brahms: Trio in E-flat, 2nd movement (scherzo and trio)<br>Schubert: *Erlkönig* (through-composed art song)<br>Schubert: *Im Frühling* (modified strophic art song)<br>Smetana: *The Moldau* (tone poem)<br>Verdi: Quartet, "Bella figlia dell'amore," from *Rigoletto* (operatic ensemble, Italian)<br>Wagner: Excerpts from *Die Walküre* (music drama, with leitmotivs) | | **Accompanying recordings** |

| | Historical | Cultural |
|---|---|---|
| **Key figures** | Freud (1856–1939) | F.L. Wright (1869–1959) |
| | Wilson (1856–1924) | Picasso (1881–     ) |
| | Dewey (1859–1952) | Chagall (1887–     ) |
| | Churchill (1874–1965) | Eliot (1888–1965) |
| | Stalin (1879–1953) | Cummings (1894–1962) |
| | Roosevelt (1882–1945) | Hemingway (1898–1961) |
| | Hitler (1889–1945) | H. Moore (1898–     ) |
| | Oppenheimer (1904–1967) | Calder (1898–     ) |
| | Von Braun (1912–     ) | Giacometti (1901–1966) |
| | Salk (1914–     ) | Dali (1904–     ) |
| | M.L. King (1929–1968) | Balanchine (1904–     ) |
| | | Pollock (1912–1956) |
| | | J. Robbins (1918–     ) |
| | | Bergman (1918–     ) |
| | | Mailer (1923–     ) |
| | | Yevtushenko (1933–     ) |

| | Pre-1950 | Post-1950 |
|---|---|---|
| **Key events and discoveries** | Powered flight | Korean War |
| | World War I | Television |
| | Great Depression | Electronics |
| | World War II | Antibiotics |
| | Atomic bomb | Race crisis |
| | United Nations | Population crisis |
| | | Space exploration |
| | | Heart transplants |
| | | Vietnamese War |
| | | Manned lunar landing |

**Accompanying recordings for all schools**

Bartók: Piano Concerto No. 3, 1st movement (Neoromantic, sonata form)
Berg: *Lyric Suite*, 1st movement (twelve-tone, serial)
Debussy: *Voiles* (Impressionist, character piece)
Ravel: *Bolero*, fragment (Neoromantic, variation)
Sollberger: *Music for Sophocles' "Antigone,"* second section (electronic, juxtaposition)

## LATE-ROMANTIC SCHOOL

Mahler (1860–1911) • R. Strauss (1864–1949) • Sibelius (1865–1957) • Rachmaninoff (1873–1943)   **Major composers**

Passionate expression • Deeply personal • Autobiographical • Allegorical • Programmatic • Overt emotionalism   **Attitudes and characteristics**

19th-century forms   **Structures and styles**

Long, irregular phrases • Chromatic melodies • Complex textures   **Melody and texture**

Lush chords • Tonal, but key often unclear • Wagnerian cadences   **Harmony**

Varied, flexible • Changes frequent, often extreme   **Rhythm and dynamics**

Huge orchestra; mixture of voices and instruments • Thick dark sounds, but sharp contrasts   **Performing media**

## IMPRESSIONIST SCHOOL

Debussy (1862–1918) • Ravel* (1875–1937) • Griffes (1884–1920)   **Major composers**

Purposeful vagueness • Objectivity • Subtly atmospheric • Beauty is in the eye of the beholder • Suggestive symbolism   **Attitudes and characteristics**

Tone poem • Character piece • Through-composition   **Structures and styles**

Fragmentary melodies • Highly chromatic • Essentially homophonic • Glissandos • Pedalpoints • Frequent parallel motion   **Melody and texture**

Parallel chords • Key and harmonies often obscure • Overlapping cadences   **Harmony**

Vague rhythms • Disguised pulse • Dynamics restrained, although extremely soft dynamics are used   **Rhythm and dynamics**

Large orchestra, but rarely massed • Intimate media important, especially piano and song • Divided choirs   **Performing media**

*Partly.

*The history of music in chart form*   **267**

EXPRESSIONIST SCHOOL

| | |
|---|---|
| **Major composers** | Schoenberg (1874–1951) • Stravinsky* (1882–    ) • Webern (1883–1945) • Berg (1885–1935) • Dallapiccola (1904–    ) • Carter* (1908–    ) • Rochberg (1918–    ) • Henze (1926–    ) • Penderecki (1933–    ) |
| **Attitudes and characteristics** | Searing emotionalism • Dissonance an end in itself, and, in theory, as self-sufficent as consonance • Lurid or extreme subject matter |
| **Structures and styles** | Both through-composed and 18th-century forms • Variation important |
| **Melody and texture** | Serialism • Tone rows • Angular, chromatic, irregular melodies • |
| **Harmony** | Extremely dissonant • Atonal, noncadential • Clusters, not chords |
| **Rhythm and dynamics** | Varied dynamics and tempo • Pulse subject to fluctuation • Rhythm important in identifying motives, but not propulsive |
| **Performing media** | Very large or very small • Extreme demands on both voice and instruments • Often thick sounds and clusters |

NEOCLASSICAL AND NEOBAROQUE SCHOOLS

| | |
|---|---|
| **Major composers** | Satie (1866–1925) • Ravel* (1875–1937) • Stravinsky* (1882–    ) • Piston (1894–    ) • Poulenc (1899–1963) • Honegger (1892–1955) • Milhaud (1892–    ) • Hindemith (1895–1963) |
| **Attitudes and characteristics** | Clarity • Preciseness • Objectivity • Understatement • Frequently satirical • Economy of means |
| **Structures and styles** | 18th-century symphony, opera, chamber music |
| **Melody and texture** | Diatonic • Angular • Phrasing unpredictable, but always clear • Frequent fugue • Developmental |
| **Harmony** | Pungent dissonance • Clear cadences • Polytonal and tonal |
| **Rhythm and dynamics** | Strong syncopation • Propulsive • Vital • Strongly metrical • Dynamics restrained, but frequent sudden contrasts |
| **Performing media** | Small groups made of sharply contrasted timbres • Frequently percussive • Unusual combinations • Clear sonorities |

*Partly.

## NEOROMANTIC AND NEONATIONALIST SCHOOLS

| | |
|---|---|
| *American*   Ives (1874–1954) • Hanson (1896–      ) • Sessions (1896–      ) • Gershwin (1898–1937) • Copland (1900–      ) • Barber (1910–      ) • Dello Joio (1913–      ) | **Major composers** |
| *Others*   Vaughan Williams (1872–1958) • Ravel* (1875–1937) • Bloch (1880--1959) • Bartók (1881–1945) • Kodály (1882–1967) • Prokofiev (1891–1953) • Shostakovitch (1906–      ) • Britten (1913–      ) | |
| Emotional • Tendency toward lyricism and use of folk or folklike materials • Interest in national subject matter • New ways of expressing human and national values within traditional frameworks • Nationalism often unconscious | **Attitudes and characteristics** |
| 18th- and 19th-century forms | **Structures and styles** |
| Warm lyricism • Essentially homophonic, although polyphony not avoided • Phrases clearly marked • Textures mixed in sections | **Melody and texture** |
| Tonal • Dissonance is frequent, but is used as part of harmonic sequence | **Harmony** |
| Meters are clear and change often • Dance rhythms | **Rhythm and dynamics** |
| Fairly large orchestra that is warm and rich • Virtuosity required, but extremes are avoided | **Performing media** |

## AVANT-GARDE AND ELECTRONIC SCHOOLS

| | |
|---|---|
| Varèse (1885–1965) • Cowell (1897–1965) • Ussachevsky (1911–      ) • Cage (1912–      ) • Babbitt (1916–      ) • Ginastera (1916–      ) • Rochberg (1918–      ) • Stockhausen (1928–      ) | **Major composers** |
| Search for new sonorities and new means of communication • Rejection of past • Often satirical and dadaesque • Intellectual • Complex | **Attitudes and characteristics** |
| Through-composition • Aleatory | **Structures and styles** |
| Use of notes not found on conventional media • Electronic textures may be very complex • Melody may be fragmentary or nonexistent | **Melody and texture** |
| Not a consideration | **Harmony** |
| May be complex or irrelevant • Flexible • Irregular | **Rhythm and dynamics** |
| Unlimited • Combinations of traditional media with new media • Percussive effects • Sounds classified electronically • Traditional sounds used in wholly new ways, or sounds themselves are wholly new | **Performing media** |

*Partly.

# B : A BASIC RECORD LIBRARY

This book has presented the names of many composers, compositions, genres, and styles. Assuming the reader's interest has been stimulated, the following suggestions for building a record library are offered. At best, the groups of titles are over-brief. Many superb works and composers, some of whom may be the reader's favorites, have been necessarily passed by. Emphasis has been placed on the music of the eighteenth, nineteenth, and twentieth centuries, although others are represented. Consultations with librarians and teachers will be helpful in filling in wherever there are omissions.

The following assumptions have been made: (a) the record library should include works of varied types, composers, and styles; (b) the budget available for record purchases will be moderate; (c) the listener will want to begin with works that are relatively easy to grasp, and with which he will be likely to have some familiarity as a result of a semester's study of music.

Each of the following groups represents an expenditure of about fifty dollars. In arriving at this figure, it was estimated that works which occupy one side of a twelve-inch recording or less would cost as little as two dollars, those which take up both sides would cost about five dollars, and multi-record albums would range in cost from twelve to fifteen dollars. In a case such as Rossini's overture to his opera *Il Barbiere di Siviglia* ("The Barber of Seville"), the composition will be one of several on the disc; one such recording includes this overture plus seven others. Thus, although the buyer may spend five dollars for the recording, he may get a stimulating variety of works for his money.

In some cases, more than one group will be represented on the same recording (one record now available includes both Beethoven's Fifth Symphony and Schubert's Eighth Symphony (the *Unfinished*). Judicious buying and careful thought about how one's library should take shape will be rewarding, even though the task may not be easy.

It is suggested that the beginner start with Group 1, then move to Group 2, and so on. All of the works listed here are masterpieces, and most can be appreciated at several levels of sophistication. The placing of a composition in Group 1 does not make it less great than one in Group 6, only perhaps more immediately grasped.

# GROUP 1

Beethoven: Symphony No. 5, in C minor, Op. 67

Dvořák: Symphony No. 9, in E minor (*From the New World*), Op. 95, formerly cataloged No. 5

Shostakovitch: Symphony No. 5, Op. 47

**Symphonies and large orchestral works**

Smetana: *The Moldau*

Sibelius: *Finlandia*, Op. 26

Ravel: *Bolero*

R. Strauss: *Till Eulenspiegel's Merry Pranks*, Op. 28

**Overtures, suites, tone poems, etc.**

Rachmaninoff: Piano Concerto No. 2, in C minor, Op. 18

Bach: *Brandenburg Concerto No. 2*

**Concertos**

Bizet: *Carmen*

Handel: *Messiah*

An anthology of motets and madrigals by such composers as Gesualdo, Monteverdi, Palestrina, Lassus, Byrd, and Gibbons

**Choral and large-scale vocal works**

Schubert: Such *Lieder* as *Erlkönig*, *Im Frühling*, or the cycle *Die schöne Müllerin*

Haydn: String Quartet in C major, Op. 76, No. 3

Debussy: *Images*, Book I (for piano)

Brahms: Trio in E-flat major for Horn, Piano, and Violin, Op. 40

**Chamber music**

# GROUP 2

Schubert: Symphony No. 8, in B minor (*Unfinished*)

Tchaikovsky: Symphony No. 6, in B minor (*Pathétique*), Op. 74

Sibelius: Symphony No. 2, in D major, Op. 43

**Symphonies and large orchestral works**

Rossini: Overture to *Il Barbiere di Siviglia*

Rimsky-Korsakov: *Capriccio Espagnol*, Op. 34

Mendelssohn: *Overture and Incidental Music for "A Midsummer Night's Dream,"* Op. 21

Tchaikovsky: Suite from *The Nutcracker*, Op. 71a

**Overtures, suites, tone poems, etc.**

Beethoven: Piano Concerto No. 5, in E-flat major (*Emperor*), Op. 73

Tchaikovsky: Violin Concerto in D major, Op. 35

**Concertos**

| | |
|---|---|
| **Choral and large-scale vocal works** | Verdi: *Aïda* |
| | Moore: *The Ballad of Baby Doe* |
| | Mendelssohn: *Elijah* |
| **Chamber music and organ literature** | Bach: *Passacaglia and Fugue in C minor* (for organ) |
| | Bartók: String Quartet No. 4 |
| | Brahms: Such *Lieder* as *Wie Melodien zieht es, Wie bist du meine Königin, Der Tod das ist die kühle Nacht* |
| | Beethoven: Piano Sonata No. 14, in C-sharp minor (*Moonlight*), Op. 27, No. 2 |

*GROUP 3*

| | |
|---|---|
| **Symphonies and large orchestral works** | Haydn: Symphony No. 94, in G major (*Surprise*) |
| | Brahms: Symphony No. 2, in D major, Op. 73 |
| | Hovhaness: *The Mysterious Mountain* |
| **Overtures, suites, tone poems, etc.** | Beethoven: *Overture to Goethe's "Egmont,"* Op. 84 |
| | Liszt: *Les Preludes*, Op. 97 |
| | Copland: Suite from *"Appalachian Spring"* |
| | Stravinsky: *The Rite of Spring* |
| **Concertos** | Brahms: Violin Concerto in D Major, Op. 77 |
| | Bartók: Piano Concerto No. 3 |
| **Choral and large-scale vocal works** | Puccini: *La Bohême* |
| | Bach: Cantata No. 140 (*Wachet auf, ruft uns die Stimme*) |
| | Haydn: *Die Schöpfung* ("The Creation") |
| **Chamber music** | Schubert: Piano Quintet in A major (*Trout*), Op. 114 |
| | R. Strauss: Such *Lieder* as *Zueignung, Cäcilie, Morgen, Allerseelen* |
| | Beethoven: String Quartet in F major (*Rasumovsky*), Op. 59, No. 1 |
| | Chopin: Various Preludes and Nocturnes for piano |
| | Cage: *Fontana Mix* (with or without aria) |

*GROUP 4*

| | |
|---|---|
| **Symphonies and large orchestral works** | Mozart: Symphony No. 41, in C major (*Jupiter*), K. 551 |
| | Beethoven: Symphony No. 7, in A major, Op. 92 |
| | Hindemith: *Symphony, "Mathis der Maler"* |

Wagner: Overture to *Tannhäuser* (with or without *Venusberg* music)  
R. Strauss: *Don Juan*, Op. 20  
Stravinsky: Suite from *The Firebird*  
Tchaikovsky: Overture, *Romeo and Juliet*

**Overtures, suites, tone poems, etc.**

Tchaikovsky: Piano Concerto No. 1, in B-flat minor, Op. 23  
Dvořák: Cello Concerto No. 2, in B minor, Op. 104

**Concertos**

Wagner: *Lohengrin*  
Mozart: *Die Zauberflöte*, K. 620 ("The Magic Flute")  
Bach: *The Passion According to St. Matthew*

**Choral and large-scale vocal works**

Beethoven: Trio in B-flat major for Clarinet (or Violin), Piano, and Cello, Op. 11  
Debussy: *Sonata for Cello and Piano*  
Mozart: *Eine kleine Nachtmusik*, K. 525  
Varèse: *Poème Électronique*  
Duparc: Songs such as *Phidylé, Extase,* or *Invitation au Voyage*

**Chamber music and electronic music**

## GROUP 5

Haydn: Symphony No. 101 in D major *(Clock)*  
Berlioz: *Fantastic Symphony*, Op. 14

**Symphonies and large orchestral works**

Beethoven: Overture, "*Leonore,*" No. 3, Op. 72b  
Rimsky-Korsakov: Symphonic Suite, *Scheherazade*, Op. 35  
Wagner: *Siegfried's Rhine Journey,* from *Götterdämmerung*  
Schubert: *Overture and Incidental Music for "Rosamunde,"* Op. 26

**Overtures, suites, tone poems, etc.**

Mozart: Piano Concerto in C minor, K. 491  
Mendelssohn: Violin Concerto in E minor, Op. 64  
Bartók: *Concerto for Orchestra*

**Concertos**

Mozart: *Don Giovanni*, K. 527  
Verdi: *Rigoletto*  
Honegger: *Le Roi Davide* ("King David")

**Choral and large-scale vocal works**

R. Schumann: Such *Lieder* as *Widmung, Die beiden Grenadiere,* and *Mondnacht,* or a cycle, such as *Dichterliebe*  
Chopin: *Ballades,* for piano  
Debussy: *String Quartet*  
Stravinsky: *Octet*

**Chamber music**

| | |
|---|---|
| **Symphonies and large orchestral works** | Mozart: Symphony No. 40, in G minor, K. 550 |
| | Brahms: Symphony No. 3, in F major, Op. 90 |
| | Prokofiev: *Classical Symphony*, Op. 25 |
| **Overtures, suites, tone poems, etc.** | Wagner: Overture to *Die Meistersinger* |
| | Debussy: *Prélude à l'Après-midi d'un Faune* ("Prelude to the Afternoon of a Faun") |
| | Webern: *Six Pieces for Orchestra*, Op. 6 |
| | Borodin: Ballet music from *Prince Igor* |
| **Concertos** | Rachmaninoff: *Rhapsody on a Theme by Paganini* |
| | R. Schumann: Piano Concerto in A minor, Op. 54 |
| **Choral and large-scale vocal works** | Puccini: *Madame Butterfly* |
| | Menotti: *The Consul* |
| | Brahms: *Ein deutsches Requiem*, Op. 45 ("A German Requiem") |
| **Chamber music and electronic music** | Wolf: Such *Lieder* as *Verborgenheit, Mignon, Fussreise*, or a cycle, such as the *Spanisches Liederbuch* |
| | Berg: *Lyric Suite* (for string quartet) |
| | Brahms: Sonata No. 2 for Clarinet and Piano, in E-flat major, Op. 120 |
| | Grieg: such *Lieder* as *Ein Schwann, Ich liebe dich*, and *Solvejgs Lied* |
| | Stockhausen: *Gesang der Jünglinge* ("Canticle of the Hebrew Children in the Fiery Furnace") |

# C : SHORT BIOGRAPHIES

**Adam de la Halle** *(ah DAMH du lah HAHL; damh is nasal) ca. 1240–1287* A famous trouvère gifted as a poet and a composer; considered to be one of the first secular composers of consequence.

**Albéniz, Isaac** *(ahl BAY niss; also ahl BAY neth) 1860–1909* Spanish nationalist composer of the Romantic period, whose music reflected both the flavor of Spain and the Impressionistic influences extant in France. Some operas are performed still in Spain, but other countries know only works for piano or piano and orchestra.

**Babbitt, Milton** *1916–* American composer whose music, often utilizing computers and synthesizers, is abstract and non-tonal. Twelve-tone systems and work with electronic media form the bases for much of his music. His compositions have been highly influential in the area of total serialization, and his influence has been keenly felt in electronic music.

**Bach, Carl Philipp Emanuel** *(BAHCH; ch is guttural) 1714–1788* Son of the great Johann Sebastian Bach, and a famed composer and theorist. A major figure in the turn from the Baroque style to the Classical, he cultivated a refined style of sensitive performance known as the *Empfindsamer Stil.*

**Bach, Johann Christian** *(BAHCH; ch is guttural) 1735–1782* German composer of the early Classical period. Son of Johann Sebastian Bach, he was often called the "London Bach" because he spent his last twenty years in that city. Prolific and gifted, he is unfortunately less known for his gracious and elegant compositions than for his influence as a classicist on Mozart and other later composers, although most of the traits of their music can be found in his works.

**Bach, Johann Sebastian** *(BAHCH; ch is guttural) 1685–1750* German organist-composer of the late Baroque period. As a contrapuntist, he has no peer; his fugues are still the models of polyphonic perfection. Famous for many keyboard compositions, cantatas, Passion oratorios, concertos, and chamber works, he devoted most of his professional life to the Lutheran church, yet still produced much secular music. Bach's style of composition serves as a summation of the Baroque—elegant and rich polyphony couched on a firm bed of disciplined, highly inventive harmony and profound expression.

**Balakirev, Mily Alexeyevitch** *(bal lah KEE reff) 1837–1910* One of the *Russian Five,* he spent much of his musical life editing, collecting, and using Russian folk material, some of which is revealed in the extremely difficult piano work, *Islamey.* Notable also as a teacher of Mussorgsky and Borodin.

**Barber, Samuel** *1910–* American Neoromantic composer. He has achieved considerable acclaim for several of his works, especially those for voice, although he is well esteemed for orchestral music as well. His *Antony and Cleopatra* was commissioned for  the opening of the new Metropolitan Opera House in Lincoln Center, New York City, in 1967.

**Bartók Béla** *(BAR tawk) 1881–1945* Hungarian composer now regarded as one of the most important and influential musical figures of the twentieth century. Bartók's music reflects a fascination for primitive and folk rhythms and melodies. Although he employed dissonances and chromaticism freely, he rarely left systems of tonality completely, choosing rather to employ exotic scales and polytonality. In 1940, to escape Nazism, Bartók fled to New York where he spent his last years in poverty and ill-health.

**Beeson, Jack** *1921–* American composer specializing in operas characterized by lyricism, gracious singing lines, and native American themes.

**Beethoven, Ludwig van** *(BAY toe ven) 1770–1827* German composer, late Classic and early Romantic periods. In their formal construction, his works reflect a culmination of the elegance and clarity of Viennese classicism. In their emotional content and use  of instrumental color, they indicate the direction which German music was to take during the nineteenth century. Probably no composer has been as influential in so many directions. Wagner and his followers found inspiration in Beethoven's orchestration and powerful, emotional statements, while Brahms was guided by his formal concepts and developmental processes.

Beethoven's compositional life is usually divided into three periods. The first ends about 1800 and includes the first two symphonies, three piano concertos, and various works for piano. The second period (1800–1815) was the happiest and most productive: Symphonies 3–8, an opera *(Fidelio)*, the *Egmont* music, the ballet *Prometheus*, the last two piano concertos (including the famous *Emperor*), and numerous chamber works. By 1815, Beethoven was almost totally deaf and became more and more introspective, a trait that was reflected in the music of his third period (1815–1827). The Ninth Symphony, the *Missa Solemnis*, five piano sonatas, and five string quartets came from this period. His total output includes nine symphonies, five piano concertos, a violin concerto, eleven overtures, thirty-two sonatas for piano, sixteen string quartets and many other chamber works.

**Bellini, Vincenzo** *(bell LEE nee) 1801–1835* Italian opera composer, Romantic period, noted for graceful, ornate vocal melodies that represent the lyricism of early Romantic Italian opera at its best.

**Berg, Alban** *(BAIRG) 1885–1935* Austrian composer, student of Arnold Schoenberg and ardent disciple of the atonal method of composition. Berg applied twelve-tone serial systems successfully to several media, including opera, chamber music, and the orchestra, although *Wozzeck*, his greatest work, is atonal without being extensively serial.

**Berger, Jean** *(bair ZHAY) 1909–* American composer, German-born and once a French citizen. He is especially noted for choral works characterized by vibrant rhythms and pungent harmonies, expressed with lyricism and not infrequent wit.

**Berio, Luciano** *(BER ee oh) 1925–* Italian avant-garde composer (now living in the United States) who has experimented in new sounds, new notations, and electronic music.

**Berlioz, Hector** *(bairl yowes; equal stress) 1803–1869* French composer, Romantic period, noted for development of the compositional device known as the *idée fixe*— the assignment of extramusical meanings to musical themes and motives. Influential also as an  orchestrator, Berlioz brought new ideas and instruments to the orchestra. He was not financially successful as a composer and supported himself as a music critic and writer. *Evenings in the Orchestra* is a collection of some of his best essays, often in a delightfully humorous vein, and his treatise on orchestration is still timely and informative.

**Bernstein, Leonard** *(BURN styn) 1918–* American composer, conductor, pianist, and educator, whose vitality has gained for him considerable acclaim in several directions. As a pianist, he has made numerous solo appearances with major symphony orchestras. He is regarded as one of the world's finest and most exciting conductors and his work as music director of the New York Philharmonic Symphony Orchestra from 1957 to 1969 attests to this. His inherently American compositions, some of which reflect the influence of jazz, are performed with regularity.

**Billings, William** *1746–1800* American composer, one of the first of any stature. He is noted for hymn-tunes *(Chester, When Jesus Wept,* and others), often with fugal episodes.

**Binchois, Gilles** *(banh SCHWAH)* *ca. 1400–1460* Burgundian composer, especially noted for his polyphonic *chansons*. Although little is known of his life, his contemporaries and those who have sung his music (mostly secular) regard him as the equal of Dunstable and Dufay.

**Bizet, Georges** *(bee ZAY; no diphthong)* *1838–1875* French composer in the Romantic period whose opera *Carmen* is one of the world's most popular. Striking rhythms, picturesque melodies, and originality of timbre and harmony mark his best music. His *Symphony in C* and the *L'Arlésienne* suite are popular works for orchestra.

**Bloch, Ernest** *(BLAWCH; ch is guttural)* *1880–1959* Swiss-born composer, who, from 1917 on, lived and wrote in the United States. Much of Bloch's music reflects a rich Jewish heritage and inspiration.

**Borodin, Alexander** *(bor oh DEEN)* *1833–1887* Russian Romantic composer. With Rimsky-Korsakov, Mussorgsky, Cui, and Balakirev, he was a member of the *Russian Five*. The philosophy of *The Five* was intensely nationalistic, as typified by Borodin's opera *Prince Igor*. The first two of Borodin's three symphonies are in the standard orchestral repertoire.

**Boulez, Pierre** *(boo LEZ)* *1925–* French composer and conductor, a member of post-World War II avant-garde groups. His compositions range from those that include aleatory passages to those in which every element is controlled and often serialized. He is presently music director of the New York Philharmonic-Symphony Orchestra.

**Brahms, Johannes** *1833–1897*
German composer who stands as supreme champion of absolute music of the Romantic nineteenth century. Brahms's compositions are noted for their depth of expression and feeling as well as for their clarity of form. They show  a complete mastery of the craft of composition. Brahms was at home in several media, four symphonies, two piano concertos, a violin concerto, and two overtures remaining in the standard repertoire. *A German Requiem* is one of the great large vocal works of the nineteenth century. His numerous *Lieder* are superb, as are his chamber works (for solo piano, various trios and quintets, and three string quartets). Brahms's firm stand on the absolute qualities of music led to a sometimes acerbic verbal battle between the "absolutists" who allied with him and the "referentialists" who found their leader in Richard Wagner. The battle raged for most of the last half of the nineteenth century and into the twentieth.

**Britten, Benjamin** *1913–* English composer who has done much to restore England to a position of musical eminence. Britten's style of composition, which ranges through Neoclassicism, Impressionism, and Neo-romanticism, with emphasis on the last, uses compositional devices which are somewhat more conservative than some of his European and American contemporaries. Major works include several operas, which are performed regularly in England and on the Continent, and many vocal and choral works, among which is the profound *War Requiem*, a deeply moving testament to the struggles of our times.

**Bruch, Max** *(BROOCH; ch is guttural)* *1838–1920* German composer, a late Romantic. His violin concertos, a setting of *Kol Nidrei* for cello and orchestra, and the *Scottish Fantasy* (for violin and orchestra) are important concert fare.

**Bruckner, Anton** *(BROOK ner)* *1824–1896* Austrian composer who stood firmly on Wagner's side in the Romantic-period philosophical battle between Brahms (and the absolutists) and the referentialists. His nine symphonies are performed by the world's larger orchestras—the instrumental requirements are too great for smaller groups—while many choral compositions are highly esteemed.

**Buxtehude, Dietrich** *(books tuh HOO duh)* *ca. 1637–1707* German organist and composer of the middle Baroque period. He had a profound influence on J. S. Bach, both as an organist and a composer. Compositions are mainly for organ or voice.

**Byrd,** (or **Bird**) **William** *1543–1623* English composer of the late Renaissance known for his expressive English madrigals, anthems, and music for the virginal and for viols. A typical collection of his works was published under the title *Psalmes, Sonets, and Songs of Sadness and Pietie.*

**Caccini, Giulio** *(kah CHEE nee)* *1546–1618* Italian composer of the late Renaissance sometimes called the "father of a new style of music" because of the enthusiasm he displayed in composing and performing (as a singer) in the monodic style, a style that evolved during the late sixteenth century. A member of the Florentine *Camerata*, he was one of the first composers of opera and one of the early users of the *basso continuo,* as revealed in his influential collection of arias and madrigals entitled *Le nuove musiche* ("The New Music," 1602).

**Cage, John** *1912–* Modern American composer whose style is probably best defined as "Dadaism in music." Cage's compositions are often for specially prepared musical instruments (for example, a piano with screws, copper coins, paper, and so on, placed on and in the strings) or for nonmusical devices. *Imaginary Landscape* is for twelve radios dialed to prescribed wave lengths and intensities. *4 Minutes 33 Seconds* is a work for piano in three movements during which the pianist sits at the piano and never makes a sound. *0'00'* is "to be performed in any way by anyone." The wave of cynicism and sarcasm that has swept the arts during the 1960's has brought Cage, who has provided some of the philosophical background for much of our new music, to a new peak of popularity.

**Carter, Elliot** *1908–* American composer whose style of composition leans toward density and complexity. Not a serial composer, he seems to have followed paths started by Ives.

**Cavalieri, Emilio del** *(kah vahl YAIR ree)* *ca. 1550–1602* Italian composer of the late Renaissance who is credited with being one of the innovators of the *monodic* style and the *basso continuo*, both of which were to become functional aspects of seventeenth-century composition.

**Chausson, Ernest** *(cho SAWNH; last syllable nasal)* *1855–1899* French Romantic composer noted for lyric melody and rich orchestration as typifed by *Poem of Love and the Sea.*

**Chávez, Carlos** *(SHAH vez)* *1899–* Mexican composer. His works are distinctly modern and original. They reflect a strong nationalism because of the inclusion of Central American Indian and Spanish-Mexican influences, although these are rarely quoted directly.

**Chopin, Frederic** *(sho PANH)* *1810–1849* Polish-born pianist and Romantic period composer. Most of his compositions are miniatures for piano–études, nocturnes, preludes, ballades, etc. He acknowledged his Polish background by composing several  mazurkas and polonaises in the style of the dances of that country. Besides these "character pieces," some of which are found on virtually every piano recital performed in the Western world, two piano concertos are given frequent hearings. His use of subtle gradations of tempo and dynamics as well as his inventive chromaticism mark him as one of the great innovators in Romantic piano music.

**Copland, Aaron** *(KOPE land)* *1900–* American composer whose strong nationalistic tendencies are reflected in many of his early works. Later compositions show a moderate interest in twelve-tone systems. *Connotations* for orchestra was commissioned for a first performance during the inaugural concerts of Philharmonic Hall in New York's Lincoln Center in 1962. Books include *What to Listen for in Music, Music and Imagination*, and *Our New Music.*

**Corelli, Arcangelo** *(kaw RREL lee)* *1653–1713* Italian violinist and composer of the mid-Baroque. Corelli was not a prolific composer, yet is important historically for formal developments in trio sonatas and *concerti grossi*, exerting considerable influence on Vivaldi, J. S. Bach, and Handel. He is also considered as the founder of the modern school of violin technique.

**Couperin, François** *(KOO puh ranh; final syllable nasal, with a as in hat)* *1668–1733* French organist and mid-Baroque composer who was given the name "Le Grand" during his tenure as a court organist to Louis XIV. Although much of his creative life was devoted to composing religious works, he is best known for his highly decorative compositions, especially for keyboard.

**Cowell, Henry** *1897–1965* American composer who has championed several contemporary causes for music, especially the avant-garde. Cowell's compositions are striking and reflect his somewhat quixotic humor. Favorite techniques include the creation of tone clusters, playing the piano with the forearm, and strumming its strings.

**Cui, César Antonovitch** *(KWEE)* *1835–1918* A Russian nationalistic composer, one of the *Russian Five*, especially noted for work in small forms.

**Dallapiccola, Luigi** *(dahl lah PEEK koh lah)* *1904–* Italian-born composer noted for his extensions of the atonal systems developed by Schoenberg. Dallapiccola is especially gracious to the voice, even when using serial technique.

**Davidovsky, Mario** *(dah vee DOHFF skee)* *1934–* Argentinian composer who has studied extensively in the United States. Works include those for traditional and electronic media.

**Debussy, Claude** *(duh byu SEE)* *1862–1918* French composer and founder of the school of French Impressionism, a somewhat nationalistic attempt to counter the oppressive hegemony of German Romanticism. Debussy's music is marked by the use of veiled, unresolved exotic harmonies, pentatonic and whole-tone scales, a

generally ethereal and suggestive feeling, and an often delicate beauty. Debussy was first considered to be a somewhat enigmatic composer, but now is given his proper due as one of the most influential musical figures of the early twentieth century. He is known for songs, intimate piano works, orchestral music, and one great opera.

**Delibes, Léo** *(duh LEEB)* *1836–1891* Famed principally as composer of the lovely ballets *Sylvia* and *Coppelia,* his music is notable for melodiousness and refinement of instrumentation.

**Delius, Frederick** *(DEEL yuhss)* *1862–1934* English composer, one of the few of international stature since Purcell. Some orchestral works (for example, *Brigg Fair*) draw upon Impressionistic devices, elaborate instrumentations, and folk elements.

**Dello Joio, Norman** *(DEL loh JOY oh)* *1913–* American composer whose style is generally Neoromantic. Compositions include *New York Profiles* for orchestra, *A Jubilant Song* for chorus, and an opera, *Blood Moon.*

**De Monte, Philippe** See Monte, Philippe de

**Des Prez, Josquin** *(day PRAY, zhohs KANH*; no diphthongs; final syllable nasal) *ca. 1450–1521* Franco-Flemish composer of the early Renaissance who was considered by his contemporaries to be the greatest of his times. His works reflect a balance between the imitative Franco-Flemish art of contrapuntal writing and the more homophonic style then prevalent in Italy. His *Missa Pange Lingua,* many motets, and numerous small secular works are among the great achievements of the Renaissance.

**D'Indy** See Indy, Vincent d'

**Dohnányi, Ernst von** *(dohch NAHN yee; ch is guttural)* *1877–1960* Hungarian composer, generally with romantic inclinations. His best-known works are for piano, alone or with orchestra.

**Donizetti, Gaetano** *(dawn ee TZET tee)* *1797–1848* Italian composer, Romantic period, one of the last (with Bellini and Rossini) of the great *bel canto* composers who emphasized vocal ornamentation. His works are characterized by floating lyricism over the most simple of accompaniments.

**Dowland, John** *1562–1626* Irish-born English lutenist and composer of the late Renaissance, known primarily for his solo songs with lute accompaniment.

**Dufay, Guillaume** *(du FAH ee)* *ca. 1400–1474* Burgundian composer famed for his masses, although he composed in every form popular during his time. He was one of the great lyric composers as well as a master of polyphony.

**Dukas, Paul** *(du KAH)* *1865–1935* A Romanticist whose best works were in the area of opera or tone poem. *The Sorcerer's Apprentice* is in the repertoire of every major orchestra; the opera *Ariane et Barbe-bleu* is one of the few successful post-Debussy Impressionist operas.

**Dunstable, John** *(DUN sta bl)* *ca. 1380–1453* Late Medieval English composer. Little is known of his life except that his compositions indicate the remarkably advanced state of music in England at the time. Certain liberties that he took regularly with modal tradition are not noted in European composers until almost a century after his death. He included great expressiveness in his highly intricate compositions, most of them motets.

**Duparc, Henri** *(du PAHRK)* *1848–1933* French Romantic composer, mainly of songs, many of which have evocative melodic lines. Especially well known are *Invitation au Voyage, Extase,* and *Phidylé.*

**Dvořák, Antonin** *(DVOAR zhahk)* *1841–1904* Romantic period Bohemian composer who exhibited a strong nationalism in his many symphonic and vocal compositions. Dvořák was a great melodist; lyricism pervades practically all of his works (to the advantage of some and the detriment of others). A protégé of Brahms, he  gained quick fame for his compositional ability. From 1892 to 1895 he was in the United States as the director of New York's National Conservatory. His Ninth Symphony *(From the New World),* and the *American* String Quartet date from this period but, although influenced by American folk melodies and spirituals, they do not contain any specific tunes, as is often erroneously averred. Recataloging of Dvořák's symphonies has caused a renumbering. The *New World* was No. 5 and is now No. 9, while the *G minor,* now No. 8, was No. 4, and No. 7 was No. 2.

**Elgar, Edward** *1857–1934* One of the first major English composers since Purcell. Elgar's four *Pomp and Circumstance* marches represent but a minor, if famous, aspect of his career. Strong melodies, firm yet rich orchestration, and well-worked-out developments characterize his most significant works, the *Enigma Variations* for orchestra and the oratorio *The Dream of Gerontius.*

**Enesco, Georges** (e NESS koh) 1881–1955 A modern Romanticist, famous as a violinist, conductor, and composer, whose two *Rumanian Rhapsodies* and various vocal and symphonic works are richly laden with folk material.

**Falla, Manuel de** (FAH yah) 1876–1946 Spanish composer, who, along with several other Spanish composers of his time, merged nationalism and Impressionism with successful results. A piano work, *Nights in the Gardens of Spain*, and a ballet, *El Amor Brujo*, are especially typical of his vibrant rhythms and colorful instrumentation.

**Fauré, Gabriel** (faw RRAY; no diphthong) 1845–1924 French composer whose *Requiem*, choral music, and songs foreshadowed the Impressionism of his younger contemporary, Debussy. He was master of piquant, lyric expression, with a strikingly original sense of color and harmony.

**Floyd, Carlisle** 1926– American composer whose musical dramas, *Susannah* and *The Passion of Jonathan Wade*, have shown him to possess considerable lyric talent and dramatic ability.

**Foster, Stephen Collins** 1826—1864 American composer of songs, several of which have become a part of American folklore.

**Franck, César** (FRAHNK) 1822–1890 Belgian-born French Romantic period composer who revived instrumental music in an operatically-minded Paris. Not a prolific composer, however, he wrote only one symphony, in D minor (at the age of sixty-six), four symphonic poems, the *Symphonic Variations for Piano and Orchestra*, some chamber music, and a rather important list of compositions for organ now considered standard fare for any serious organist.

**Franz, Robert** (FRAHNTS) 1815–1892 German composer of the Romantic period who wrote and published over 350 songs and is today considered one of the great composers of the *Lied*.

**Gabrieli, Giovanni** (gah bree EH lee) ca. 1554–1612 Italian composer of the late Renaissance whose polychoral and idiomatic innovations in both vocal and instrumental music were influential and long lasting. A number of motets and madrigals, a mass, and several works for instruments are significant.

**Gershwin, George** 1898–1937 American composer most talented as a song writer (*The Man I Love, They Can't Take That Away From Me, I Got Rhythm*). Excursions into other media (the ballet *An American in Paris*, the *Concerto in F*, and *Rhapsody in Blue*) met

with varying degrees of success in fusing jazz with traditional idioms. The folk opera *Porgy and Bess* was quite successful and is now in the repertoires of several European opera houses.

**Gesualdo, Carlo** (jeh zoo AHL doh) ca. 1560–1613 Late Renaissance Italian composer whose madrigals are considered among the very best of his time. Gesualdo's music was extremely complex and chromatic, with some almost bizarre devices for word-painting. Even today, some of his compositional habits, especially in the area of harmony, seem so unusual that he sits rather enigmatically in the mainstream of music.

**Giannini, Vittorio** (jyahn NEE nee) 1903–1966 American composer who tried to revive interest in opera as a compositional medium, although he achieved excellence in orchestral and band music as well.

**Gibbons, Orlando** 1583–1625 English composer and organist of the Chapel Royal, the chapel of the king of England. Gibbons is known now for his choral music, in particular his developments of the English derivative of the Latin motet, the *verse anthem*.

**Ginastera, Alberto** (hee nah STAIR ah) 1916– Argentinian composer who, in the 1960's, turned to opera with success (*Bomarzo* and *Don Rodrigo*). A choral work, *The Lamentations of the Prophet Jeremiah*, is an earlier work of note.

**Glinka, Mikhail** (GLINK ah) 1804–1857 The first of the great Russian Romantic composers. He was widely emulated and imitated by those who followed.

**Gluck, Christoph Willibald von** (GLOOK; rhymes with "took") 1714–1787 Austro-Bohemian composer of the Classical period whose importance is based not only on the beauty of his music but also on the reforms he and his librettist, Calzabigi, made in the style of operatic composition and performance. Three important

works reflect these reforms toward simplification, stateliness, and dramatic cogency: *Orfeo ed Euridice, Iphigénie en Tauride*, and *Alceste*. In a preface to *Alceste*, Gluck and Calzabigi stated a famous manifesto on opera.

**Gottschalk, Louis** *1829–1869* American composer-pianist, world famous as a virtuoso. His charming character pieces are regaining favor.

**Gounod, Charles** *(GOO noh;* also *goo NOH) 1818–1893* French composer of Romantic operas, of which *Faust* and *Romeo and Juliet* remain in the repertoire. His setting of one of J. S. Bach's keyboard preludes as an *Ave Maria* is famous, as are several of his masses.

**Granados, Ernesto** *(grah NAH dohss) 1867–1916* Spanish composer who reflected nationalistic feelings, although not as intensely as his contemporaries, Falla and Albéniz. His series of piano pieces, *Goyescas*, was inspired by the famous Spanish painter Goya. Granados used the themes for a similarly named opera premiered in 1916 by the Metropolitan Opera Company in New York. Having attended the premiere, the composer was killed when the boat on which he was returning to Europe was sunk by a torpedo.

**Gregory I, "The Great"** *540–604* Pope from 590 to 604. Gregory was not a composer but was largely responsible for encouraging the collection and codification of the music being used in the mass services in many of the various Christian churches and its revision and reorganization into a universal, stylized liturgy which could be used in all church services, Much of the plainsong of the Roman Catholic mass is known as Gregorian Chant.

**Grieg, Edvard** *(GREEG) 1843–1907* Norwegian composer of the Romantic period who is remembered for his piano concerto and the *Peer Gynt* suites. Neither reflects the genius and ability shown in his songs, many of which are considered by cognoscenti to be jewels.

**Griffes, Charles Tomlinson** *1884–1920* American composer whose early death cut off a promising flow of Impressionistic works.

**Guido d'Arezzo** *(GWEE doh dah REDZ soh) ca. 997–ca. 1050* Italian. Guido is known in the history of music for his development of the nomenclature of syllabic singing (ut, re, mi, fa, sol, la) and also for the codification and improvement of staff notation, both contributing immeasurably to precise notation and polyphonic composition.

**Handel, George Frideric** *1685–1759* German-born Baroque composer who spent most of his adult life in England. Handel, along with J. S. Bach, represents the summation of the Baroque. His major efforts were in the medium of opera, and more and more of them are being performed today. Handel is especially remembered  for his oratorios, a number of *concerti grossi*, and other orchestral works. Handel's music is characterized by a warm, florid lyricism which, while typical of Baroque extravagance, is strikingly individual and affecting. He accomplished his lyricism while staying well within the bounds of the styles and forms typical of his period.

**Hanson, Howard** *1896–* American composer whose Neoromantic style is typified by his Second Symphony *(Romantic)* and many choral works. In 1924, he became director of the Eastman School of Music where he was quite influential in the training and develop-  ment of American musicians and composers.

**Harris, Roy** *1898–* American composer who, during the 1930's, gained considerable fame as a promising talent. His style included pan-diatonic writing, a then novel way of causing all the notes in a major scale to sound equally in relation to the key tone, thus eliminating the process of singling out tones that have tendencies to lead to or from points of rest. Since World War II, Harris has existed rather quietly but competently in the stream of American music.

**Hassler, Hans Leo** *(HAHSS ler) 1564–1612* German composer of the late Renaissance. Motets, psalms, and other religious works, most often in the vernacular in keeping with his Protestant faith, constitute the major portion of his music.

**Haydn, Franz Joseph** *(HIDE n) 1732–1809* Austrian composer who, with Mozart, represents the highest point of Viennese Classicism. While Haydn "invented" neither forms nor media, he is responsible for the maturation of several: the sonata form, which became the first movement pattern for several of the multimove-

ment instrumental forms of the Classical period; the symphony, which under Haydn's hand became a major form in style and content; and the string quartet, which he made into a medium of supreme intimate expression. He was a prolific composer, at home in practically every medium. In his output are at least 104 symphonies, 83 string quartets (total number is subject to disagreement and varies from 76 to 84), 3 oratorios, at least 30 concertos for various solo instruments, 60 piano sonatas (of which 8 are lost), 19 operas, and hundreds of chamber works and songs. Haydn was one of the last composers to spend most of his professional life under patronage. His fame was widespread and he travelled over all of Europe to compose and perform. An element of humor abounds in his music and it was this which caused critics of the nineteenth and early twentieth centuries to consider him a composer of lesser stature. He has now been placed in perspective and is properly considered to be one of the greatest composers of all time.

**Henze, Hans Werner** *(HEN tzuh) 1926–* German composer whose forte has been in the area of opera, where he has used a lyric twelve-tone system to underscore libretti that have passionate political and social implications. His short symphonies reveal a more recent tendency to concise expression, although his major efforts continue to be for the stage.

**Herbert, Victor** *1859–1924* Irish-born American composer of lighter music, notably operettas. Herbert was a cellist and wrote two cello concertos that get occasional hearings.

**Hindemith, Paul** *(HIN duh mith) 1895–1963* German-born composer who spent several years in the United States. Primarily a Neoclassicist, he was one of the most outstanding and influential composers of the century. He borrowed concepts of constructivism  from his contemporary painters and applied them to musical composition with admirable results. Hindemith believed that composition, in order to be successful, had to be based on a firm knowledge of craft and technique and that all music should be written to be playable by amateurs *(Gebrauchsmusik)* as well as for concert use. A common characteristic of his music is dissonant counterpoint punctuated by cadences that consist of a simple major triad. An author and teacher, his texts, *Traditional Harmony* and *The Craft of Musical Composition*, are in wide use.

**Holst, Gustav** *1874–1934* English composer and teacher, one of the few in the last two centuries to gain world repute. Two suites for the military band and an orchestral suite, *The Planets*, are among his better-known compositions.

**Honegger, Arthur** *(awn e GAIR; hard g; also pronounced HAHN uh gur) 1892–1955* French composer, one of the group of Postimpressionist composers known as *Les Six*. At a relatively young compositional age, he displayed his ability as a creative artist in *King David*, a powerful oratorio with strong Neoclassical traits. *Pacific 231*, a popular work that describes a locomotive starting, gaining full speed, and then slowing to a stop again, is typical of the strong rhythmic drive in Honegger's music.

**Hovhaness, Alan** *(ho VAHN ness) 1911–* American composer, strongly Neoromantic, but also influenced by the Baroque. Hovhaness incorporates the rhythms and melodic designs of his Armenian heritage into much of his music. A fascination with Indian and Oriental music also manifests itself.

**Ibert, Jacques** *(ee BAIR) 1890–1962* French composer, whose post-Impressionist *Escales (Ports of Call)* is typical of his many orchestral works.

**Indy, Vincent d'** *(danh DEE; a as in hat, but nasal) 1851–1931* French composer who tried to apply the Germanic principles of Romanticism to French music, eventually causing a furor between his disciples and those of the Impressionist Debussy. He has come out second best in this ideological struggle, so his music does not get the performance it deserves, although some piano pieces are given recital hearings, and the *Symphony on a French Mountain Air* is esteemed.

**Isaac, Heinrich** *(ee ZAHK) ca. 1450–1517* Flemish-born composer who spent most of his compositional life under the patronage of the Medici family in Florence. He is best known for his lovely, poignant, polyphonic *Lieder*, especially the exquisite *Innsbruck, Ich muss dich lassen*, and his religious works.

**Ives, Charles** *1874–1954* American composer whose music was virtually ignored during his lifetime, but which now has gained fame and is exerting tremendous influence. Ives as a young man was a church organist in New York City. He entered the insur-  ance business and was most successful at it, although he continued to compose. Many of his works he never heard and some were still being premiered in the 1960's, a full half-century after they had been composed. A nationalist, his works are dotted with snatches of American folk and patriotic songs, especially those of New England; the Second Symphony is based entirely on such material. Although his influence on other American composers was negligible during his lifetime, he is now considered to be one of the most important and influential men of the century.

**Jacob, Gordon** *1895–* English composer whose *Original Suite* and *Music for a Festival* are familiar parts of concert band literature.

**Janáček, Leos** *(yahn AH chek) 1854–1928* Czech composer who stylistically encompasses Smetana, Dvořák, Bartók, and Kodály, in that he was an eastern European nationalist as well as a most original and dynamic composer. He is entirely underrated as a composer by all except the relatively small number of audiences who have heard his operas (notably *Jenufa*) and chamber music.

**Janequin, Clément** *(ZHAN nuh kanh) ca. 1475–ca. 1560* French Renaissance composer of *chansons*, especially noted for his onomatopoetic effects as well as contrapuntal brilliance.

**Josquin Des Pres** *See* Des Pres, Josquin

**Kabalevsky, Dmitri** *(kah bah LEFF skee) 1904–* Russian composer who reaches eminence especially through his piano music. *The Comedians*, a suite for orchestra, is also important.

**Kay, Ulysses** *1917–* American composer, some of whose works are programmatic, but most of which are generally Neoclassic. He was a winner of the Prix de Rome (1949), of a Fulbright Scholarship for the study of composition, and of the Gershwin Memorial Award. Notable works include a cantata, *Song of Jeremiah*, the film score for *The Quiet One*, and a serenade for orchestra.

**Kern, Jerome** *1885–1945* American composer of songs and musical comedies. An example of the latter was the production *Very Warm for May*, from which came the very popular song *All the Things You Are*. His most famous musical was *Showboat* (songs: *Old Man River, Bill, Why Do I Love You*, and others), one of the finest and most lasting of its type.

**Khachaturian, Aram** *(kah chah toor ee AHN) 1903–* A major Russian nationalist, whose *Masquerade Suite, Gayane* (from which the famous *Sabre Dance* is taken), and various concertos and chamber works show harmonic originality and orchestral/melodic verve.

**Kodály, Zoltán** *(KO dah ee; also ko DAH ee) 1882–1967* Hungarian composer who, with Bartók, devoted years to collecting and editing Hungarian folk music. Not a radical composer, his works are marked by mild dissonances and gentle departures from tonality, as well as by a strongly romantic mode of expression. His methods for teaching music to the young are now widely respected in Europe and in the United States.

**Křenek, Ernst** *(KREN ek) 1900–* Austrian-born composer who resided in the United States after 1937. A post-Wagnerian composer, he naturally became attracted to Schoenberg's teachings, but not before his early opera, *Jonny spielt auf* ("Johnny Strikes Up," 1927), about a jazz musician, reflected the popularity of American rhythms and tonal music in the post-World War I era. A gradual commingling of tonal and twelve-tone elements began, with the latter style dominating his expressive and influential compositions in spite of some clear evidence of the contrapuntal clarity of Hindemith.

**Lalo, Édouard** *(LAH loh) 1823–1892* French composer of the Romantic period. Success and fame came primarily from a violin concerto and the *Symphonie Espagnole* for violin and orchestra, both guided in their creation to some extent by Sarasate.

**Landini, Francesco** *(lahn DEE nee) 1325–1397* Italian composer of the Ars Nova period. Landini was a blind organist whose compositions and playing were famous during his time. He is noted now for his *ballatas*, an important musico-poetic form.

**Langlais, Jean** *(lahn GLAY; no diphthong) 1907–* French organist and composer, blind from a very early age. Although he has written for other instruments and groups, his organ compositions are best known.

**Lassus, Orlandus** *(also known as* Roland de Lassus *[lah SSU]* and Orlando di Lasso *[LAH sso]) 1532–1594* Flemish Renaissance composer noted for his exceptionally beautiful motets and madrigals. Compositions also include masses, *chansons*, and *Lieder*.

**Leoncavallo, Ruggiero** *(leh awn kah VAHL loh) 1858–1919* Italian Romantic composer of opera whose fame rests primarily on one work, *Pagliacci*, an opera of the *verismo* style.

**Leoninus** (or Léonin) (*lay oh NIGH nus; LAY oh nanh*) *12th century* French organist and composer, probably the first major figure of the Notre Dame School in Paris, who compiled the *Magnus Liber*, a cycle of liturgical settings, mostly in two parts, for use throughout the church year.

**Liszt, Franz** (*LIST*) *1811–1886* Romantic Hungarian pianist and composer of great fame during his lifetime. Although Liszt's compositions have been attacked for being overly exaggerated and affected, his harmonies have influenced many modern composers,

and a number of his works are still in active repertoire. Liszt is credited with developing the symphonic poem as a vehicle for extra-musical expression. In the ideological battle of the nineteenth century, he was allied completely with Wagner (who married Liszt's daughter). In spite of several "Don Juan" escapades, Liszt was feted in courts and concert halls all over Europe and was considered to be the greatest piano virtuoso of his century. Compositions include twelve symphonic poems, two piano concertos, numerous other works for piano, and a great variety of transcriptions for the piano of works by other composers.

**Luening, Otto** (*LOO ning*) *1900–* American composer, a pioneer in the development and use of electronic means for composition.

**Lully, Jean-Baptiste** (*lool LEE*) *1632–1687* Italian-born Baroque composer of the court of Louis XIV at Versailles. Lully is credited with several innovations, including the development of the "Lully," or "French," overture. His most important accomplishments were in the *ballet de cour* and in the composition of recitative that was especially adapted to the qualities of the French language.

**MacDowell, Edward** *1861–1908* American Romantic composer, the first of this country to gain international stature. The *Indian Suite* is heard occasionally, and the second piano concerto is highly regarded.

**Machaut, Guillaume** (*mah SHOH; no diphthong*) *ca. 1300–1377* French organist and composer of the Ars Nova, and probably the first composer of secular music whose works are still being performed. Machaut brought French medieval polyphony to its highest point and was the first composer in history ever to compose a complete mass as a single musical unit (all others before were compilations). Besides the mass, works include a number of motets, ballades, and other four-teenth-century types.

**Mahler, Gustav** (*MAH ler*) *1860– 1911* An Austrian, who, with Richard Strauss and Bruckner, was one of the great Viennese Romantic composers. He was spiritually allied to Wagner, although he did not indulge in extra-referentialism to any great degree.

Most of his nine symphonies, each with many diverse styles, are gigantic works. The eighth is the largest requiring choruses, soloists, and a greatly enlarged orchestra; it is aptly named *Symphony of a Thousand*. Especially poignant are his several song cycles, some of which are with orchestra. From 1909 to 1911, he was conductor of the New York Philharmonic.

**Marenzio, Luca** (*mahr REN tsee oh*) *1553–1599* Italian composer of the late Renaissance, creator of exquisitely beautiful madrigals characterized by striking harmonic daring.

**Mascagni, Pietro** (*mahss KAHN yee*) *1863–1945* Italian Romantic opera composer who at the age of twenty-five completed his most famous opera, *Cavalleria Rusticana*, but was never again able to write a work of comparable worth.

**Massenet, Jules** (*MAHSS in ay; no diphthong on the last syllable*) *1842–1912* French Romantic composer whose operas *Manon* and *Werther* are still heard with some frequency. The *Meditation* from the opera *Thaïs* is also an orchestral favorite.

**Mendelssohn, Felix** (*MEN del sown*) *1809–1847* German composer of the Romantic period, who, in addition to being a creative genius, was a superb conductor, and, as such, was largely responsible for the resurrection of J. S. Bach's *St. Matthew Passion*. Highly imaginative, his works are often marked by impressions of travel. His music is character-

ized by a restrained but romantic lyricism, with orchestrations that are often wonderfully light and always colorful. Works include oratorios, five symphonies, incidental music to *A Midsummer Night's Dream*, an overture for band, many excellent piano pieces, and a famous violin concerto.

**Menotti, Gian Carlo** *(meh NAWT tee)* *1911–* Italian-born composer, presently residing in the United States. A Neoromantic, Menotti has devoted his compositional career to opera and has not only composed the music for several successful ones *(The Consul, The Medium, Amahl and the Night Visitors)* but has also writ-

ten the libretti for his own operas as well as for those of several other composers.

**Messiaen, Olivier** *(meh see YANH; no diphthong on first syllable)* *1908–* French composer and organist. Although presently considered primarily for his works for organ, Messiaen has been influential in French music as a pedagogue and theorist, especially on those composers who lean towards the atonal.

**Meyerbeer, Giacomo** *(MY uhr bair)* *1791–1864* German composer, resident in Paris, especially noted for grand operas. None of these operas are in the modern repertoire, although excerpts from *Le Prophète* (Coronation March), *Les Huguenots*, and *L'Africaine* are occasionally heard.

**Milhaud, Darius** *(mee YOH)* *1892–* French composer, one of *Les Six*. In his younger years, his attraction to jazz was revealed in a ballet, *The Creation of the World*, which was based on jazz rhythms, melodies, and orchestrations. A prolific composer, he has written in practically every medium and genre.

**Mimaroglu, Ilhan** *(mim ahr OG loo)* *1926–* Turkish composer noted for electronic compositions.

**Monte, Philippe de** *(MAWN tay; no diphthong)* *1521–1603* Flemish composer of the late Renaissance. He wrote masses, motets, and madrigals. His madrigals are outstanding for their word painting and startling harmonies.

**Monteverdi, Claudio** *(mawn teh VAIR dee)* *1567–1643* Italian composer now considered to be not only an important founder of opera but also one of its greatest masters. He is responsible for the development of the overture and most of the distinctive features of opera as it is known today. His madrigals also represent the highest points in that genre. Early works connect him with the Renaissance, but most of his compositions are reflective of the early Baroque tradition.

**Moore, Douglas** *1893–1969* American composer, for many years professor of music at Columbia University.

His songful music has nationalistic flavors, especially of a regional nature (for example, the operas *Ballad of Baby Doe* and *The Devil and Daniel Webster*). Also a writer, his *Listening to Music* is a respected explanation of the art of music in layman's terms.

**Mozart, Wolfgang Amadeus** *(MOH tsahrt)* *1756–1791* Austrian composer of prolific and ultimate genius and one of the greatest creators in Western civilization who, along with Haydn, represents the very best in Viennese Classicism. He was a child prod-

igy, playing in the courts of Europe at the age of six, and his first published compositions appeared in 1763, when he had just turned seven. In his early years, Salzburg was his home, but in 1779, he moved permanently to Vienna. During the 1780's he and Haydn became friends and each influenced the other in styles and systems of composition. Mozart was at home in every genre of music, producing a variety of masterpieces in each. His operas are in the repertoires of every significant opera house, and several of his symphonies, especially Nos. 36, 39, 40, and 41, are performed regularly, along with a number of piano concertos and violin concertos. His sonatas are musts for pianists and violinists. During his short lifetime, he produced a voluminous amount of music, including forty-nine symphonies, over forty concertos for a variety of soloists, sixteen operas, a great amount of chamber music (including twenty-six string quartets, forty-two violin sonatas, and seventeen piano sonatas), a requiem, fifteen masses, and a Magnificat. He had the ability to compose a work completely in his mind and then simply "copy" it on paper (Symphony No. 36 was composed, orchestrated, copied, rehearsed, and performed in only four days). While influential in many directions, Mozart perhaps made his greatest mark in opera. While some earlier works were in the style of Italian *opera seria*, his later ones fused German profundity, Italianate melody, and French elegance into deeply human works in the finest Classical tradition.

**Mussorgsky, Modest** *(moo SORG skee* *1839–1881* Russian Romantic composer, one of the *Russian Five*. He had an education and career as an officer of the Imperial Guard but gave it up to become a composer. He showed great talent, but, because he was raw and untrained through most of his musical life, his frus-

trations overwhelmed him and he died an alcoholic. His daring harmonies and unusual timbres exerted a powerful influence on Debussy and Stravinsky. *Boris Godunov* is his greatest masterpiece and is now considered the greatest Russian opera of the nineteenth century. The most often performed versions of this opera are those edited by Rimsky-Korsakov and Shostakovitch. A programmatic piano piece, *Pictures at an Exhibition* (scored for orchestra by Ravel) and an orchestral work, *A Night on Bald Mountain* (rescored by Rimsky-Korsakov) are other well-known works.

**Obrecht, Jacob** *(OH brecht; ch is guttural)* ca. *1450–1505* Flemish composer of the early Renaissance. Primarily a church composer, his prolific output consists of masses and motets, all in a highly imitative and deeply expressive style.

**Ockeghem, Johannes** *(AWK kay gem; hard g)* ca. *1425–1495* Flemish composer of the early Renaissance. A consistent and imaginative use of imitation is a characteristic of his compositions (masses, motets, chansons).

**Offenbach, Jacques** *(AWF fen bahch; ch is guttural)* *1819–1880* German-born French Romantic composer of comic operas that are highly tuneful and often tongue in cheek. Late in life, he wrote one fine serious opera, *The Tales of Hoffman.*

**Orff, Carl** *1895–* German composer whose scenic cantata, *Carmina Burana,* is one of the best-known choral works of the century. Orff is also an educator whose methods of teaching and special educational instruments are widely respected. He is important as an opera composer, and his music is always characterized by rhythmic variety, clarity of texture, and emotional excitement.

**Paganini, Niccolò** *(pah gah NEE nee; hard g)* *1782–1840* Italian violin virtuoso and composer, early Romantic period. One of the first great violin virtuosos, his was an ability few if any have equaled. All his compositions are for the violin and are specifically intended to show the instrument's technical extremes.

**Palestrina, Giovanni** *(pal eh STREE nah)* ca. *1525–1594* Italian composer, late Renaissance. One of the greatest composers of church music, he spent most of his musical life in church posts. His motets and masses (for example, the *Pope Marcellus* Mass) represent a high and a concluding point in modal polyphony. His compositions are not only studied for their contrapuntal excellence and for their summation of three centuries of compositional style, but they are also performed because of their suave beauty and profound expressiveness.

**Penderecki, Krzystof** *(pen der ET skee, SHISH tawff)* *1933–* Polish composer now recognized as one of the leaders of the expressionist avant-garde. His *Passion According to St. Luke,* which has caused great excitement wherever performed, combines a wide variety of styles and devices, ranging from plainsong to serial technique.

**Pergolesi, Giovanni** *(pehr goh LEH zee)* *1710–1736* Italian composer whose few works show that his untimely death deprived the world of a great master. *La Serva Padrona* is a comic jewel and exerted a strong force in the turn away from the elaborate Baroque *opera seria* toward the simpler, mercurial character of Classical *opera buffa.*

**Peri, Jacopo** *(PEHR ee)* *1561–1633* Italian composer of the late Renaissance and early Baroque eras. He was a member of the *Camerata,* the group that attempted to revive the drama and style of declamation of ancient Greece. His *Dafne* (1597), in the then new monodic style, was the first opera.

**Perotinus** (or *Pérotin*) *(pair oh TIE nus; PAIR o tanh)* *1155/60–1200/05* French composer who followed Leoninus as master of the Notre Dame School in Paris. He made extensive revisions of Leoninus' *Magnus Liber,* providing significant contributions in the area of measured rhythm and in the composition of *organa* and *clausulae.*

**Persichetti, Vincent** *(purr si KET tee)* *1915–* American composer whose compositions have a compact, Neoclassical quality. Several excellent works are for band. *The Hollow Men,* for trumpet and strings, is also an interesting and popular work. A composer of seven symphonies, most of his compositions are for instruments in small or large combinations.

**Piston, Walter** *1894–* Prolific American composer, also outstanding as a teacher. He is formally a Classicist but uses interesting Neoromantic sonorities with some frequency. Three of his books—*Harmony, Counterpoint,* and *Orchestration*—are standard texts.

**Poulenc, Francis** *(POO lanhk; also poo LANHK)* *1899–1963* French composer, one of *Les Six.* Humor is often laced through his works, most of which are for piano or voice. A Stabat Mater and a Gloria are frequently performed, as is his great tragedy, *The Dialogues of the Carmelites.* Poulenc's lyricism is always supported by a significant and atmospheric accompaniment and by harmonies which, while always tonal, are spiced with interesting dissonances and chord relationships.

**Powell, Mel** *1923–* American composer and jazz pianist; has interest in electronic music.

**Prokofiev, Sergei** *(proh KOH fee eff) 1891–1953* Russian composer, one of the two leaders (with Shostakovitch) in the music of that country during the twentieth century. Prokofiev's early works were sharply sarcastic, but this sarcasm later mellowed into a rather ironic humor that is a part of many of his mature compositions. He toured extensively, coming to the United States to perform, lecture, and conduct. Criticisms were leveled at him by the Communists during their artistic purges, but he managed to survive aesthetically. His famous *Classical Symphony* indicates his nature as a Neoclassical formalist, yet his music can be starkly emotional (the Third Piano Concerto is an example).

**Puccini, Giacomo** *(poo CHEE nee) 1858–1924* Italian Romantic period composer who was the successor to Verdi as master of Italian opera. Consummately lyrical, his operas are filled with gorgeous, soaring melodies. He understood his medium completely from both musical and dramatic standpoints, and many of the memorable moments in opera today are in his works. All the major opera companies in the Western world keep Puccini's operas regularly in their repertoires.

**Purcell, Henry** *(PURR sl) ca. 1659–1695* English composer of the mid-Baroque, the last of any stature in that country until the late nineteenth century. A highly inventive composer, Purcell infused his music with a strong sense of drama touched with humor. He was known to his contemporaries for his craftsmanship and his originality. One opera, *Dido and Aeneas*, has had lasting fame, as has some of his instrumental music.

**Rachmaninoff, Sergei** *(rach MAHN in off; ch is guttural) 1873–1943* Russian composer and pianist of the Postromantic school of the twentieth century. Rachmaninoff was a moody and brooding person, and his character seems to be reflected in his haunting, melancholy melodies, many of which are world-famous.

**Rameau, Jean-Philippe** *(rrah MOH) 1683–1764* French composer, organist, and theorist of the late Baroque (Rococo) period. He is remembered not only for his operas, ballets, and keyboard works, but also for his definitive treatises on music theory as well. Attacked when first published, the *Traité de l'Harmonie* and the *Nouveau système de musique théorique* both were soon recognized as invaluable and are now considered indispensable for those who would study music history or theory.

**Ravel, Maurice** *(rrah VEL) 1875–* *1937* French composer, Impressionist in some works, Classical or Romantic in others. During his lifetime, Ravel was considered "ultra modern"; now he appears in a logical succession of stylists from Debussy to the present. His

earlier works are markedly Impressionistic, but later compositions became more dissonant, witty, and strongly rhythmic. His output includes many important works for piano, as well as songs and orchestral music.

**Respighi, Ottorino** *(ress PEE gee; hard g) 1879–1936* Late Romantic Italian composer known primarily for two symphonic poems, *The Pines of Rome* and *The Fountains of Rome*, which demonstrate orchestral virtuosity and the influence of Impressionism.

**Riegger, Wallingford** *(REE ger; hard g) 1885–1961* American composer who for most of his life was neither recognized nor accepted as a major force in American music. By 1950, however, an overdue recognition did come, and in retrospect his works take on a more important character. His Third Symphony was an award-winning composition, and *Dance Rhythms* has become popular for both band and orchestra. His mature works combine vital rhythms with a wholly individual atonality, often couched in highly polyphonic terms.

**Rimsky-Korsakov, Nicolai** *(RIM skee KOR sah kohff) 1844–1908* Russian composer of the Romantic period and an important member of the *Russian Five*. A cadet in the Russian Imperial Navy, he resigned his commission to take up a career in music. He had an exceptional knowledge of orchestration, and his treatise on the subject is still important. He was an ardent nationalist, choosing subject matter and musical materials native to Russia as sources for many of his compositions.

**Rochberg, George** *(RAHCH burg; ch is guttural) 1918–* American composer of considerable prestige. Rochberg works in twelve-tone systems, although not exclusively. A symphonic poem, *Night Music*, won the George Gershwin Memorial Award. His *Apocalyptica* is a major atonal essay for band.

**Rodgers, Richard** *1902–* American composer of popular songs and music for Broadway musicals. *Carousel, South Pacific, Oklahoma!, The King and I*, and *The Sound of Music* are not only melodious in a natively American way but combine dance and song with subject matter based on themes important to the present.

**Rossini, Gioacchino** *(rrohss SEE nee; rolled r)* *1792–1868* Italian composer of the Romantic period and one of the last of the *bel canto* opera composers. His compositional style was melodic and lyric, if sometimes flippant and predictable. *The Barber of Seville* is his most famous work, although in his own day he was as famous for his grand operas (especially *William Tell*) as for his comedies. Overtures from his other operas are often played. At the age of thirty-seven, he inexplicably quit composing and, except for a very few religious and humorous pieces, wrote nothing for publication for the rest of his life.

**Saint-Saëns, Camille** *(sanh SAHN; both syllables nasal; first a as in hat, second a as in father)* *1835–1921* Versatile French Romantic composer. A contemporary of Debussy and Wagner, he was essentially a conservative and combined careful form and development with rich sonority and flowing melody.

**Sarasate, Pablo** *(sahr ah SAHT teh)* *1844–1908* Spanish violin virtuoso and composer for the violin.

**Satie, Erik** *(sah TEE)* *1866–1925* French composer with Dada proclivities, an example of which is his direction that the short piano piece *Vexations* is to be repeated 840 times. In spite of such comments and other purposefully absurd performance directions, Satie's music is highly regarded and was most influential in establishing the modern Neoclassical movement. His studied simplicity and lack of sentimentality was in striking contrast with the elaborate appurtenances of late nineteenth-century German Romanticism.

**Scarlatti, Alessandro** *(skahr LAHT tee)* *1660–1725* Italian opera composer of the mid-Baroque period, said to be the founder of the Neapolitan school. He wrote at least 115 operas, a number of which are still available, although rarely performed, and many beautiful solo cantatas. Some chamber music gets occasional performance.

**Scarlatti, Domenico** *(skahr LAHT tee)* *1685–1757* Late Baroque Italian composer and harpsichordist, son of Alessandro. His sonatas for harpsichord are in the standard repertoire for pianists of the present day, but he is remembered much more as the developer of the modern playing technique for keyboard. Crossing of hands, changing fingers on a rapidly repeated note, and leaps larger than an octave are among his contributions.

**Schoenberg, Arnold** *(SHURN bairg; r of first syllable is silent)* *1874–1951* Austrian-born composer who, after 1933, lived in the United States and was one of the most influential and controversial composers of the twentieth century. Very early works

showed a marked influence of Wagner (for example, *Gurrelieder* and *Verklärte Nacht*), but by 1907, his works were showing decidedly extreme tendencies and complete, consistent atonality. As early as 1912, he was experimenting with twelve-tone serial techniques; he based the fifth of his *Five Pieces for Piano*, Op. 23 (1923) on it, but it was not until 1924 (in the *Suite for Piano*, Op. 25) that he used it as a basis for the composition of a complete work. In spite of the limits to which he took his experimentation, he remained a romantic, and his compositions always reveal deep emotional involvement. His violin concerto is highly regarded, although its technical requirements limit it to performance by only the very best violinists. *Moses and Aaron*, a biblical drama, is provocative and of great importance. A fine painter, Schoenberg had an early association with the great nonobjectivist Wassily Kandinsky, who was to become to art what Schoenberg was to become to music.

**Schubert, Franz** *(SHOO burt)* *1797–1828* Austrian composer of the late Classical and early Romantic periods, and, with Beethoven, one of the first to make song an important area of composition. Schubert had little schooling as a musician, yet demonstrated genius in all he composed. In most of his 600 or

more *Lieder*, of which he is perhaps the ultimate master, he was able to effect the perfect balance between melody, accompaniment, and poem. There are eight symphonies (a misnumbering in some sources makes it appear that there are nine), of which the fifth (in B-flat), the seventh (in C), and the eighth (*Unfinished*, in B minor) stand out. None of his operas has withstood the test of time, in spite of many beautiful passages. The overture and incidental music to *Rosamunde*, however, is ranked with the *Unfinished* Symphony as part of the world's most loved orchestral repertoire. Schubert was financially unsuccessful as a composer; only near the end of his life were any of his major works published or performed, and it is likely that he never heard any of his symphonies performed by an orchestra. (The *Unfinished* Symphony was not performed until 1865.) His vocal and instrumental chamber music fared better, largely through the efforts of his friends. His songs, part songs, and piano works were also heard, but provided little remuneration from their publication. Schubert's music is as memorable for his atmospheric and original harmonies as for his unmatched gift of lyricism.

**Schuller, Gunther** *1925–* American composer who, in a style known as "the third stream," has tried to merge jazz and the procedures of "serious" music. A recent opera, *The Visitation* (1967), shows a move away from the third stream toward a more consistent and personally mature style.

**Schuman, William** *1910–* American Neoclassical composer, and first president of the Lincoln Center of the Performing Arts, New York City. Nine symphonies, the third being the most popular, an opera, three ballets, and numerous other works for various performing media receive frequent performance.

**Schumann, Robert** *(SHOO mahn)* *1810–1856* German composer and journalist of the Romantic period. He showed promise as a concert pianist, but in 1832 an injury to his right hand, accidentally self-inflicted, ended that career. He turned to composition and writing. In 1840 he married Clara Wieck, who was to become one of the renowned piano virtuosi of the century. A mental aberration, which first appeared when Schumann was still in his youth, finally overwhelmed him and he spent his last two years in an asylum with only rare moments of lucidity. Schumann's genius is reflected best in the passionate songfulness, rhythmic instability, and harmonic originality of his *Lieder* and piano works, although the first two of his four symphonies, his piano concerto, and the cello concerto are certainly masterpieces.

**Schütz, Heinrich** *(SHUHTS;* vowel as in *foot) 1585–1672* German composer of the early Baroque period. He composed the first German opera *(Dafne)* on Italian models. Through his teachings and compositions, he had a profound effect on J. S. Bach if for no other reason than his creation of an atmosphere and tradition of German music in which Bach could exist and thrive. Most of all, his music has a power and beauty that mark him as one of the greatest of early Baroque masters.

**Scriabin, Alexander** *(skree AH bin) 1872–1915* Russian composer, a late Romantic. Scriabin was an experimenter and tried to relate color and sound spectra in a single musical instrument. Some of his compositions are based on a scale which he derived from a "mystic" chord of six notes (C, F♯, B♭, E, A, D). He was influential in that he caused other composers to consider the possibilities of sounds based on devices other than the major and minor scales. *The Poem of Ecstasy* and a piano concerto are among his most often played works.

**Sessions, Roger** *1896–* American composer whose early music is romantic; more recently his works show a Neoclassical clarity and even an austerity. His Fifth Symphony and an opera, *Montezuma*, are notable. Both were premiered in 1964.

**Shostakovitch, Dmitri** *(shahss tah KOH vitch) 1906–* Russian composer who has already taken his place as one of the great geniuses of the twentieth century. His music is markedly Romantic, harking back at times to nineteenth-century traditions, but it is always honest and original. Some works produced during times of great propagandistic pressure from the controlling forces in Russia are weak in aesthetic content, but those works he created when he was allowed to work freely reflect his greatness to the fullest extent. His Fifth Symphony is his most popular orchestral work (there are now thirteen symphonies). A ballet, *Golden Age*, includes some exceptionally delightful and humorous passages, the *Polka* in particular. The humor reflected there and in his Ninth Symphony has often been a part of his music.

**Sibelius, Jean** *(si BAYL yuhss) 1865–1957* Finnish composer of the late Romantic period. In his earlier years, he was an ardent nationalist. His first two symphonies are fervent expressions of love for country, but are not nearly so intensely patriotic as is the tone poem *Finlandia*. First performed in 1900, *Finlandia* was so moving that the Russian Czarist government, then Finland's overlord, would not allow it to be performed during times of political or social unrest. Sibelius turned away from nationalism after about 1905 and adopted a style that was similarly intense, but more terse and without a nationalistic label. His most important works are his seven symphonies and his tone poems. Some chamber music, mostly from his younger days, is also known.

**Smetana, Bedřich** *(SMET ta na) 1824–1884* Bohemian composer, intensely Romantic and nationalistic. His major compositions are those in which his nationalistic fervor shows the best—the opera *The Bartered Bride* (1866) and the set of six tone poems entitled *My*

*Country*, of which *The Moldau* is the second. Two string quartets, one in E minor (programmatic, subtitled *From My Life*) and the other in D minor, are performed.

**Smith, Hale** *1925–* American composer, primarily of orchestral works. He draws on a variety of styles, and his craftsmanship and imagination have brought him wide respect.

**Sollberger, Harvey** *1938–* American composer gaining recognition for his electronic compositions and for works mixing electronic and traditional sounds. Some of his instrumental works reflect his virtuosity as a flutist.

**Sousa, John Philip** *(SOO zuh) 1854–1932* American bandmaster and composer, primarily of marches. He was conductor of the United States Marine Band from 1880 to 1892, when he resigned to form his own band. With it, he toured and conducted for the remainder of his life. Among his many appealing marches are *The Stars and Stripes Forever, Semper Fidelis, Manhattan Beach, Thunderer, King Cotton,* and *El Capitan.*

**Stamitz, Johann** *(SHTAH mits) 1717–1757* German composer of the early Classical period. One of the leading composers and conductors in Mannheim, he helped make that city's orchestra the best in Europe. He standardized and developed techniques of orchestral performance and was one of the chief developers of the element of contrast between the principal and subordinate themes of the Classical sonata form. The work of Stamitz helped to stimulate interest in developmental ingenuity.

**Still, William Grant** *1895–* American composer whose works reflect his determination to develop a symphonic type of Negro music. *Afro-American Symphony* (1931) is typical and is the first such work by a black composer.

**Stockhausen, Karl Heinz** (or Karlheinz) *(SHTAHK how zen) 1928–* German composer of the avant-garde. Stockhausen applies techniques of uninhibited dissonance in unusually free rhythmic settings and includes improvisation as a necessary part of many of his compositions. He is among the foremost users of electronic devices, and his *Gesang der Jünglinge (Canticle of the Hebrew Children in the Fiery Furnace,* 1956), using human and electronic sounds and serial techniques, is one of the major electronic works of our time.

**Strauss, Johann** (the elder) *(SHTROWSS; ow as in cow) 1804–1849* Australian military band director and conductor of court balls in Vienna. He was known as the "Father of the Waltz," although his more famous son created all the waltzes with which the Strauss name is associated.

**Strauss, Johann** (the younger) *(SHTROWSS; ow as in cow) 1825–1899* Austrian composer of operettas and lighter music, especially waltzes *(The Blue Danube, Wine Women and Song* and many others). Two operettas, *Die Fledermaus* and *The Gypsy Baron,* are favorites in Germany and receive many performances in America.

**Strauss, Richard** *(SHTROWSS; ow as in cow) 1864–1949* German composer, intensely Romantic in his early works, somewhat less so in later works. Strauss was a follower of the Wagnerian principles in form, content, and orchestration. His earlier compositions  were tone poems *(Don Juan, Don Quixote, Also Sprach Zarathustra, Death and Transfiguration,* and *Till Eulenspiegel's Merry Pranks).* He believed strongly in extra-referentialism but eventually felt that expression thus made was not complete, and so he gradually shifted to opera as a main compositional medium. A number of his operas (for example, *Elektra, Der Rosenkavalier)* have achieved great success. The *Four Last Songs,* written in his last year, represent a summation of the German Romantic *Lied,* and, for that matter, German Romanticism. When he died the tradition was ended. In addition to the works noted above and many other songs, he wrote two concertos for horn and orchestra, both excellent vehicles for the instrument.

**Stravinsky, Igor** *1882–* Russian-born composer who lived in France, Switzerland, and, after 1939, the United States. Stravinsky ranks as one of the foremost composers of the twentieth century in progressiveness, as an artist seeking new ways to express  himself. He was a student of Rimsky-Korsakov and his earlier works, at least until 1912, reflect his teacher's influence. In 1910, he went to Paris and was commissioned by Diaghilev to write a ballet. The *Firebird* was the result; it was followed by *Petrouchka* (1911) and *The Rite of Spring* (1913), in which Stravinsky finally broke with his past and used new and daring harmonies and rhythms that literally caused a riot in the audience at the first performance. During World War I he was in Switzerland, where he wrote several works that indicated a great interest in chamber-sized ensembles (*L'Histoire du Soldat* calls for seven musicians, three dancers, and a narrator). An extended period of Neoclassicism was thus ushered in, but was followed by some excursions into the Neobaroque and, more recently, serial composition. An *opera buffa* in the eighteenth-century mold, *The Rake's Progress*, was premiered in 1951. The ballet *Agon* (1957) is noted. He has influenced many composers and musicians in America and Europe and will be recorded in history as one of the musical titans of the century.

**Sullivan, Arthur** *1842–1900* English composer who, with William S. Gilbert, produced fourteen famous comic operas, completely English in character and humor. Among them are *H. M. S. Pinafore*, *The Pirates of Penzance*, *Iolanthe*, and *The Mikado*.

**Takemitsu, Toru** *(tah kuh MITT tsoo)* *1930–* Japanese. He is a brilliant young composer who has merged Eastern and Western music with successful and startling results. *November Steps*, commissioned and premiered by the New York Philharmonic-Symphony Orchestra in 1967, is typical, using as solo instruments a *biwa* and a *shachahari* (both are ancient Japanese, the former a lute-like stringed instrument and the latter a bamboo flute), floating on an orchestral accompaniment of dazzling modern harmonies. *Requiem*, for strings, has attracted considerable attention.

**Tallis, Thomas** *ca. 1505–1585* English composer and organist of the Renaissance, one of the first to set English words to music for the rites and ceremonies of the Church of England. He is known also for his motets and madrigals.

**Tchaikovsky, Peter Ilyitch** *(chy KAWF skee)* *1840–1893* Russian composer of the Romantic period. Tchaikovsky was not a member of the *Russian Five* and was in some ways opposed to their obsessive nationalism. He felt that music should be international and  thus supersede purely nationalistic feelings. Even so, a few of his works (for example, *Overture, "1812"*) show evidences of a nationalistic impulse. He was a moody and affected individual, and this moodiness and affectation is reflected in some of his music. For years, he was patronized by a wealthy widow, Nadja Von Meck, whom he never met, their only communication being by correspondence. He was one of the leading composers of the Romantic period and his music is played and loved as much as that of any composer of his time.

**Telemann, Georg Philipp** *(TAY luh mahn)* *1681–1767* German composer of the late Baroque. Telemann's list of compositions assumes almost fantastic proportions. There are over 3,000 works for the church, either with organ or orchestra, over 600 overtures, and many trio sonatas and other chamber works. Works from the last group are still played occasionally, sometimes more for their historic than their aesthetic content. He was regarded in his own day as a leading composer whose music represented the best elements of the *Empfindsamer Stil*.

**Thompson, Randall** *1899–* American composer, primarily of choral music (notably *The Peaceable Kingdom*, *Testament of Freedom*, *Alleluia*, *Frostiana*). He has a superb sense of vocal timbre and of melody, both lyric and dramatic.

**Thomson, Virgil** *1896–* American composer and music critic. His operas and film music (*Louisiana Story*, *The Plow that Broke the Plains*) demonstrate a sensitive lyric talent in an innately American Neoromantic vein.

**Toch, Ernst** *(TAWK)* *1887–1964* Austrian-born composer who lived in the United States from 1935 until his death. His compositional style was a curiously satisfying mixture of romantic emotion and highly chromatic dissonance. An experimenter, he wrote one work for speaking voice only. His book *The Shaping Forces of Music* discusses the act of composition in a very effective way.

**Ussachevsky, Vladimir** *(oo sah SHEV skee)* *1911–* Russian-born American composer who, with Luening, has been a pioneer in electronic music.

**Varèse, Edgar** *(vahr EZZ)* *1885– 1965* French-born composer who shuttled his residence between New York and Paris. After a short first period of composition, he moved in radically new directions, dismissing harmony and melody as essential elements and  considering music rather as organized sound (*Ionisation*, for 41 percussion instruments and two sirens). Later, he became involved with electronic devices, and his last years were spent composing primarily for that medium. His *Poème Électronique* is a major work and was composed for the special architecture and loudspeaker system of the Philips Pavilion at the Brussels World's Fair.

**Vaughan Williams, Ralph** *1872–1958* English Neoromantic composer, one of the leading figures in the revitalized musical scene in England during the twentieth century. Nationalistic to a certain extent, his earlier works acknowledged England's musical heritage (for example, *Fantasia on a Theme of Thomas Tallis*). A prolific composer, he is represented by many different types of music in modern repertoire, ranging from colorful symphonies to highly evocative choral works, opera, and song.

**Verdi, Guiseppe** *(VAIR dee) 1813–1901* Italian opera composer of the Romantic period, one of the great musical figures of the nineteenth century. Younger works reflected the *bel canto* style of the early Romantics. As he matured, he moved to a more subjectively lyrical style that united drama, emotion, word, and music  in a more meaningful whole, while still retaining the essential formal characteristics of the "number" opera. Although he was a supreme melodist, his sense of drama directed his attention to all aspects of music and theater, so that he became a consummate master of orchestration, characterization, etc. His operas, in whole or in part, are now familiar to all music lovers, whether or not opera buffs.

**Victoria, Tomás Luis de** *(vik TOAR ee ah) ca. 1549–1611* Spanish composer of the Renaissance. He spent much of his compositional life in Italy in the service of the Roman Catholic church, returning to Spain in 1598. A requiem mass is one of his masterpieces. His motets show the influence of his study with Palestrina, even though a strong Spanish flavor is evident.

**Vierne, Louis** *(vee AIRN) 1870–1937* French composer noted for his compositions for organ. In spite of blindness, he was famous in his time as an organist, holding that position in the Notre Dame Cathedral in Paris for 37 years.

**Villa-Lobos, Heitor** *(VEE yah LO boss) 1887–1959* Brazilian composer. He had much to do with the development of music in his own country, educationally and artistically. A nationalist, his abilities and feelings are shown in a set of eight different compositions entitled *Bachianas Brasileiras*.

**Vivaldi, Antonio** *(vee VAHL dee) ca. 1675–1741* Italian composer of the late Baroque. Although he wrote a number of operas and religious works, his genius is best reflected in his instrumental works, particularly the many concerti grossi and trio sonatas.

**Wagner, Richard** *(VAHG ner; hard g) 1813–1883* German composer, a Romantic and one of the most controversial and influential figures of music history. Aesthetically, he was directly opposed to Brahms, believing that music must seek to express deep  philosophical and extramusical meanings. He was responsible for the development of the music drama (*Gesamtkunstwerk*, "composite art work"), in which he demonstrated his conviction that opera should not exist simply as a series of short pieces, but rather should have a continuous flow of drama, emotion, and, consequently, music. His unifying feature was the *Leitmotiv*, which he used to identify characters, places, events, and abstract concepts. An intense nationalist, his greatest effort was a cycle of four music dramas, *Der Ring des Nibelungen* (*The Ring of the Nibelung*, first performed as a cycle in 1876), based on Teutonic mythology. In addition, *Tristan und Isolde* (1865), *Die Meistersinger von Nürnberg* (*The Mastersingers of Nuremberg*, 1868), and *Parsifal* (1882) are among the world's most important operas. Several others are in the standard repertoire of every important opera house of the Western world. Wagner's life was filled with political intrigues and philosophical disputes, notably with Nietzsche and the critic Hanslick. He had to flee from Dresden in 1849 to avoid political arrest and could not return until 1860. His romances were legend, the capstone being his love affair with Liszt's daughter, Cosima, who was the wife of one of Wagner's most ardent adherents, the conductor Hans von Bülow. The seamier aspects of Wagner's life and philosophy are interesting, but less significant than his cultivation of a richly chromatic harmonic and melodic palette in which reside the roots of modern atonality. His atmospheric orchestration, motivic techniques, allegorical libretti, and superb sense of theater have made his operas subjects of endless study.

**Walton, William** *1902–* English composer. He is a modern nationalist more because of his innately English wit and elegance rather than for his use of folk materials (see *Facade*, for speaking voice and small orchestra). *Belshazzar's Feast* is one of the major oratorios of the twentieth century and, as with his violin and viola concertos, reveals a Romantic seriousness expressed in contemporary terms. He has also written for films (*Major Barbara, Henry V*).

**Ward, Robert** *1917–* American composer, somewhat Neoromantic. Works include *Jubilation—An Overture* (now for concert band) and an opera, *The Crucible.*

**Weber, Carl Maria von** *(VAY ber) 1786–1826* German composer of the early Romantic period. When *Der Freischütz (The Sharpshooter,* 1821) was first performed, it was heralded as the first truly German opera because of its utilization of Germanic lore, elaborate orchestration, and a strong element of Germanic folksong. Weber stands as the most important composer of German Romantic opera before Wagner.

**Webern, Anton von** *(VAY burn) 1883–1945* Austrian composer, a student and disciple of Schoenberg and a foremost exponent of the serial system. His output was relatively small, and most of his works were short. Viewed in retrospect, Webern's works are models of restraint, intensity, serial craftsmanship, and economy of means. He was accidentally shot to death by an American military policeman in occupied Austria soon after the end of World War II.

**Weill, Kurt** *(VYL) 1900–1950* German-born composer who, after 1935, lived in America. Probably his best-known work is the folk opera *Down in the Valley* (1948), based on Kentucky mountain songs, although a number of quasi-operatic musicals (*The Three-penny Opera, Street Scene*) and lighter works (*Knickerbocker Holiday*) are well-remembered.

**Whittenberg, Charles** *1927–* American composer. Primarily a serialist, he has shown interest in electronic music and in computerized composition.

**Widor, Charles-Marie** *(VEE dor;* also *vee DOR) 1844–1937* French composer, organist, and teacher. Influential mostly as a teacher of organ at the Paris Conservatory (where he taught both Vierne and Albert Schweitzer), he is also noted for several symphonies for organ.

**Wieniawski, Henry** *(veen YAWF skee) 1835–1880* Polish composer, especially for violin.

**Willaert, Adrian** *(VILL ahrt) ca. 1490–1562* Flemish composer, establisher of the Venetian polychoral style. A master composer, he is best known for madrigals and *ricercares.*

**Wolf, Hugo** *(VOLF; o* as in *go) 1860–1903* Austrian composer whose fame and significance rest on many beautiful *Lieder,* of which there are more than 300. Wolf's abilities as a composer reflected themselves only occasionally in other media. The *Spanisches Liederbuch* and the *Italienisches Liederbuch* are two of his greatest song cycles. These and his individual *Lieder* reveal powerful melodic and pianistic passages, indelibly wedded to their poetry. Wolf's last years were spent in an asylum.

# D : GLOSSARY

The list of musical terms found below includes technical words referred to in the text, plus others which one may come across in program notes, record jackets, and other places.

## A

**Abbreviations** *(see* Symbols and abbreviations)

**Absolute music** Music that has inspiration from, and realization through, musical values only, and, as far as the composer's intent is concerned, is devoid of any extramusical reference; also referred to as "abstract," "pure," or "non-descriptive" music.

**Abstract music** *(see* Absolute music)

**A cappella** *(It., ah kah PEL lah)* Choral music without instrumental accompaniment; *lit.,* "in the chapel style."

**Accelerando** *(It., ah chel air AHN doh)* Gradually faster.

**Accidental** A sharp (♯), flat (♭), or natural (♮) sign written before a specific pitch, as opposed to those gathered into a key signature.

**Accompagnato** *(see* Recitative)

**Accompaniment** (1) Music provided as a subordinate support for a soloist or group of performers; (2) music subordinate to a melodic line or lines.

**Acoustics** The science of sound.

**Action** The mechanism of an instrument that transmits the movement of fingers or feet to the sound-producing devices.

**Adagietto** *(It., ah dah JEE-ET toh)* Slowly, but not as slowly as *adagio.*

**Adagio** *(It., ah DAH zhee oh)* Slow.

**Ad libitum** *(Lat., ahd LIB ee toom)* Freely, at will; abbreviated *ad lib.*

**Aesthetics** The study of the relationships between the emotions, the mind, and the meaning, quality, and perception of beauty.

**Affection** (1) A general mood or emotional flavor (referred to as the "basic affection") of a composition or movement as a result of consistency of dynamics, texture, tempo, instrumentation, etc.; (2) the musical reflection of the specific meaning of a word. Both meanings apply especially to Baroque aesthetics. The *Doctrine of Affections* is the basic philosophy under which the creator adds the quality of an affection to his art.

**Affektvoll** *(Ger., ah FEKT fol)* With fervor.

**Affetuoso** *(It., ah fet too OH zoh)* Tenderly.

**Agitato** *(It., ah gee TAH toh)* Agitated, restless.

**Alberti bass** A repeated accompanying figure, the notes of which outline chords. Especially popular in the Classical period, the term comes from the name of the composer who often used it as a stylistic device.

**Aleatory** By chance; descriptive of pitches, rhythms, etc., not specifically determined by the composer, but left to the taste and imagination of the performer(s).

**Alla** *(It., AHL lah)* In the style of, similar to.

**Allègre** (Fr., *ah LEHGRR*) Cheerful, fast.

**Allegretto** (It., *ahl leh GRRET toh*) Happy, easy; not as fast a tempo as *allegro*.

**Allegro** (It., *ahl LEH grroh*) Cheerful, fast.

**Allemande** (Fr., *ahl MANHND*) A moderately slow dance in duple time; with the *sarabande, courante*, and *gigue*, one of the standard dances in the Baroque suite.

**Alto** (1) The lowest type of female voice, also called *contralto*; (2) a member of an instrumental choir corresponding in range and function to the alto voice; (3) the part performed by such an instrument or voice (immediately below the *soprano* part).

**Andante** (It., *ahn DAHN teh*) Slow, but with motion; ongoing; walking.

**Andantino** (It., *ahn dahn TEEN oh*) Somewhat slow, but with lightness of motion; has been interpreted as being both slightly slower and slightly faster than *andante*, hence one of the most confusing of musical terms.

**Animato** (It., *ah nee MAH toh*) Animated, lively.

**Animé** (Fr., *ah nee MAY*; no diphthong on final syllable) Lively, animated.

**Answer** In a fugue, the restatement of the subject, but starting on a different pitch.

**Anthem** (1) Any choral selection performed as an autonomous part of a sacred or ceremonial service; (2) an inspirational song, usually with a strong nationalistic flavor; (3) in the late sixteenth century, an English motet; (4) in the Baroque period, an English version of the cantata.

**Antiphonal** (*an TIF a nul*) (1) A book containing music to be sung in the Roman Catholic church in services other than the mass; (2) an adjective referring to a style of performance or composition in which two or more groups perform in alternation.

**Arco** (It., *AHRR koh*) Played with the bow; opposed to *pizzicato*.

**Aria** (It., *AHRR ee ah*) Song, air; in opera, oratorio, and cantata, an extended passage for solo voice, easily distinguished from the music that precedes and follows it, and identified by a degree of regularity of rhythm, phrase, and form; essentially vocal, although the term is applied also to certain passages for solo instruments; important from the Baroque era to the present.

**Arioso** (It., *ah rree OH zoh*) Melodic style that is somewhat declamatory in the manner of recitative, but with some of the melodic interest of aria and song; important from the Baroque era to the present.

**Arpeggio** (It., *ahrr PEHJ gee oh*) Notes of a chord played in ascending or descending order through one or more octaves.

**Arrangement** The writing of melody, harmony, etc., for specific voices or instruments. The term usually implies the reworking of a piece to suit the demands of instruments or voices in a way not found in the original version.

**Ars Antiqua** (Lat., *ahrss ahn TEEK kwah*) (1) *Lit.*, "ancient art"; (2) a specific reference made by fourteenth-century writers to music written before 1300 (*see also Ars Nova*).

**Ars Nova** (Lat., *ahrss NOH vah*) (1) *Lit.*, "new art"; (2) term borrowed from a treatise by Philippe de Vitry (1291–1361) concerning new procedures of notation; (3) the fourteenth-century style of Machaut and Landini, characterized by secularism, delicacy, lyricism, and, in Italy, a new polyphony (*see also Caccia; Ballata; Madrigal; Virelais; Rondeau*).

**Art song** A type of vocal chamber music, usually with piano, in which text and music are intimately related, and piano and voice are of equal importance; the German term *Lieder* is sometimes used synonymously; important from the Romantic era to the present.

**Assai** (It., *ahs SYEE*) Very much.

**Assez** (Fr., *ahs SAY*; no diphthong) Somewhat; rather.

**a tempo** (It., *ah TEM poh*) A return to the original speed after a change in speed or a pause.

**Atonality** Absence of any particular pitch serving as the tonic or key note.

**Ausdrucksvoll** (Ger., *owss DROOKS fol*) With great feeling.

# B

**Ballad** (1) A tale set to relatively simple music (especially popular in sixteenth-century England); (2) a popular twentieth-century song of a commercial nature; (3) a narrative or sentimental song such as a cowboy ballad.

**Ballade** (Fr. and Ger., *bahl LAHD*) (1) A piece for solo instrument evoking some sort of narrative mood; (2) a form of poetry and music, especially in southern medieval France (*see Trouvère*), essentially in a musically *AAB* pattern (not the same as *ballata*).

**Ballad opera** A type of opera popular in eighteenth-century England, using spoken dialogue and music of varying styles; *The Beggar's Opera* (1728), with text by Gay and music arranged by Pepusch, was the first of the type.

**Ballata** (It., *bahl LAH tah*) A fourteenth-century poem treated musically in several strophes, each preceded and followed by a refrain; brought to its height by Landini *(see Ballade).*

**Ballet** *(bal LAY; al* as in pal; also *BAHL* lay; no diphthong in either case) Stylized solo or group dancing, with costumes and scenery, for aesthetic rather than social purposes.

**Ballet de cour** (Fr., *bal LAY duh KOOR*; no diphthong on final syllable of first word) Courtly entertainment in seventeenth-century France combining dance with poetry, decor, and music; predecessor of both ballet and opera in France.

**Ballett** (*BAL lett; a* as in *hat*) An English version of the madrigal, usually sprightly or amorous in text, concluding with a refrain of nonsense syllables such as *fa la* or *tra la*; popular in the late sixteenth century.

**Band** A group of woodwind, brass, and percussion instruments, often with several of each type of instrument per part; when used in procession or choreographed movement, the group is called a *marching band*; in concert it is known as a *symphonic band, concert band,* or *wind ensemble* and has a more varied instrumentation, with varying numbers of each instrument; some concert groups may also employ some lower strings.

**Bar** (*see* Measure)

**Bar form** An *AAB* song form.

**Baritone** A man's voice with a range between that of tenor and bass, combining the lightness and brilliance of the former with the warmth and richness of the latter.

**Baroque** (1) Elaborate, exaggerated, theatrical, ornamental; (2) a historical era, 1600–1750, devoted to stylized emotion, drama, and ornamentation, combined with vibrant rhythmic pulsation and colorful instrumentation. *See* Appendix A for major composers and stylistic traits.

**Bass** (1) lowest male voice; (2) lowest register of harmony; (3) an instrument that plays these notes or approximates their quality and function.

**Basso continuo** (It., *BAHSS oh cawn TEEN oo oh*) (1) In the music of the Baroque era, the bass line of a composition and harmonies improvised above that line, usually played by a low sustaining instrument (for instance a cello) and a chording instrument (for instance a harpsichord); the bass notes were underscored with numbers indicating the position of pitches above the bass note in a sort of shorthand notation called "figured bass"; (2) the instruments playing this sort of accompaniment; (3) the practice of improvising chords and melodies over a given bass line to accompany voices or instruments.

**Basso ostinato** (It., *BAHSS oh aws tee NAH toh*) A melodic figure, usually in the lowest-voiced instruments, which is repeated continually throughout a composition or a section of a composition.

**Battery** The array of percussion instruments.

**Beat** The unit of measurement of time; pulsation.

**Beaucoup** (Fr., *bo KOO*) Much.

**Bel canto** (It., *bell KAHN toh*) "Beautiful singing"; specifically, the highly ornamented style of singing characteristic of seventeenth- and eighteenth-century Italian opera and of the music of such early nineteenth-century Italian opera composers as Rossini, Bellini, and Donizetti.

**Binary** (1) Two part; a composition with two melodies or sections; (2) type of meter with pulsations in groups of two or multiples of two.

**Bitonality** A quality resulting when two tonalities occur at the same time.

**Blue note** (1) In the jazz idiom, a dissonant note added for purposes of color and richness to an otherwise consonant chord; blue notes, even though dissonant, do not require release or resolution, since they are not used primarily to create tension; (2) a pitch "area" performed by jazz singers and players in such a way as to waver between the major and the minor; primarily a nuance of performance, its exact pitch is unable to be written down; the third, fifth, and seventh scale steps are the ones most often treated in this manner.

**Bourrée** (Fr., *boor RRAY*; no diphthong) A brisk dance in duple meter, popular as a movement in Baroque suites.

**Bowing** The manner in which a bow is drawn across the strings of a member of the violin or viol families. For a down bow, the bow is drawn to the right; upbow is to the left. The bow may be hammered forcefully (*martelé*), bounced lightly (*spiccato*), or moved back and forth very rapidly, with short strokes (*tremolo*), to mention but a few basic techniques.

**Brass instruments** Wind instruments made of metal; sound is generated when the player vibrates his lips into a cup-shaped mouthpiece.

**Bravura** (It., *brah VOO rrah*) Zest, boldness, courage.

**Breit** (Ger., *BRIGHT*) Broad, flowing.

**Brio** (It., *BREE oh*) Spirit, vigor.

**Buffa** (It., *BOOF fah*) Comic.

# C

**Cabaletta** (It., *kah bah LET tah*) A fast aria that concludes a scene that had begun with a slow aria and characterized by vocal virtuosity (for example, "Sempre libera," from Verdi's *La Traviata*).

**Caccia** (It., *KAH chah*) A two-voiced canonic setting of a poem related to hunting, fishing, etc., usually over a freely moving tenor ("tenor" here referring to a lower voice with long notes); French equivalent: *chace* (SHAHSS).

**Cadence** (1) A point at which all musical activity reaches a point of rest or pause; (2) a series of chords establishing a key and a tonic chord; (3) in military and marching bands, a rhythmic pattern played by the percussion section to establish and maintain order in marching.

**Cadenza** (It., *kah DEHN tsah*) A display of the technical virtuosity of a performer, especially in opera and concerto, inserted at a point near the end of a movement or aria where all other musical activity ceases; can be written out by the composer or the performer, or improvised during performance.

**Calando** (It., *kah LAHN doh*) Weakening; getting softer and slower.

**Camerata** (It., *kah mehr RAH tah*) A group of literati who resided in Florence around the start of the seventeenth century; in their attempt to revive the musical style of ancient Greek dramas and to use music for dramatic purpose without obscuring the text, they literally invented the recitative style and, with it, the opera.

**Canon** The exact imitation of one voice or melodic line by another; these imitative entrances need not start on the very same pitch, but must retain the same melodic intervals as the original statement of the melody; when parts imitate each other using precisely the same pitches, the canon is called a *round*.

**Cantabile** (It., *kahn TAH bee leh*) In a singing style.

**Cantata** (It., *kahn TAH tah*) A composition for soloists, chorus, and accompaniment, or for just one solo voice; shorter than an oratorio, but essentially the same style, using recitative and aria, without benefit of costumes and scenery; may be either sacred or secular; especially popular in Baroque Lutheran services of worship, reaching its greatest heights in the works of J. S. Bach, although the solo cantatas of Alessandro Scarlatti and Handel were also major achievements.

**Cantus firmus** (Lat., *KAHN tooss FEER moos*) A melody borrowed for use as the basis of a new composition, a device that was particularly popular in the Medieval and Renaissance eras. In the former era, plainsong was the most often used source, usually placed in long notes in the lowest part (called the *tenor*, or "holding" part); Renaissance composers used more varied sources, many being secular songs; note that the plural form is *cantus firmi* (not *canti*).

**Canzona** (It., *kahn TSOH nah*) Prior to 1600, a vocal composition or an instrumental transcription of a vocal composition; after 1600, a vocal solo with keyboard accompaniment.

**Cassation** An instrumental composition, usually a suite, to be played out-of-doors, hence primarily for woodwinds and brasses; popular in the Classical era.

**Castrato** (It., *kahss TRAH toh*) An adult male singer whose voice had the natural sound of a soprano or alto, combined with the strength of the mature male as a result of prepuberal emasculation. The castrati were great vocal virtuosos, dominating the world of vocal music during the Baroque era.

**Catch** A round, usually for three or more voices.

**Cembalo** (It., *CHEM bah loh*) Harpsichord.

**Chaconne** (Fr., *shah KAWN*) (1) A dance in triple time, probably imported into Spain in the latter part of the sixteenth century; (2) a composition in triple time over a *basso ostinato*, usually of eight measures and in the minor mode, in which the identity of the *ostinato* pattern is kept while variations are performed above it; (3) insofar as composers have used the term, it is interchangeable with *passacaglia*; popular during the Baroque era.

**Chace** (see Caccia)

**Chamber duet** (see Duet; Trio sonata)

**Chamber ensemble** A group of performers with one player or singer per part.

**Chamber music** (1) During the sixteenth, seventeenth, and eighteenth centuries, any music to be performed in the princely chambers of the nobility; (2) from the eighteenth century to the present, chamber music is understood as any music for small instrumental or vocal groups (usually, but by no means always, for no more than eight performers), with one player or singer per part.

**Chamber orchestra** A small orchestra, usually with no more than two dozen players, with few per part; woodwinds and brasses are never more than two per part, although most often there is but one of each kind of instrument per part.

**Chamber sonata** (see *Sonata da camera*)

**Chanson** (Fr., *SHANH sonh*) (1) Song; (2) in the Renaissance, a polyphonic vocal chamber work in several sections, similar in style and artistic intent to the Italian madrigal.

**Character piece** A short composition for solo instrument with or without accompaniment, with a highly individual mood or flavor.

**Chest** (1) A type of voice production, usually resorted to in the lowest part of the range; (2) in the Renaissance, a family of instruments of similar construction, for example, a chest of viols (see *also* Consort).

**Choir** (1) A group of singers, with several per part; (2) a group of like instruments in an orchestra or band, as a clarinet choir, in which soprano, alto, tenor, and bass voices are represented; (3) a group of instruments of acoustic similarity, even if they are not exactly alike (for example, the woodwind choir), with all four voices represented; (4) that place in a church where the singers are grouped together, usually referred to as a "choir loft"; (5) a manual, or keyboard (and thus a *division*, *q.v.*) on an organ.

**Chorale** (*kawr AL; al as in pal*) (1) A hymn, particularly in the Lutheran church, composed and harmonized especially during the Renaissance and Baroque eras; (2) a group of singers, several per part; in this sense, "chorale" is synonymous with choir and chorus.

**Chorale prelude** (*kawr AL PREL yood; also PRAY lood* and *PREE lood*) A composition for organ (sometimes for orchestra) elaborating on a chorale cantus firmus; organ preludes were usually played prior to the singing of the chorale by a congregation; chorale preludes were important in the music of J. S. Bach and other Baroque composers, although Brahms also made major contributions.

**Chord** A group of pitches sounded simultaneously; although the notes of a chord are usually built up in

thirds from the root note, some twentieth-century composers utilize the fourth as a basic interval; when chord tones are played in sequence, the result is an *arpeggio*.

**Choreography** (*kohr ee AHG ra fee; hard g*) Organization of dance steps, body movements, and hand and arm positions into meaningful series or patterns; the organization of marching patterns.

**Chorus** (1) A group of singers, with several per part, as in a choir or chorale; (2) music written for such a group; (3) a refrain of a song, sometimes to be sung by a choral group, but also sung by a soloist.

**Chromaticism** (*kroh MAT i sizm; a as in hat, i's as in hit*) "Color"; the use in a composition of notes which are not found in the scale or mode on which the composition is based (see *Accidental*).

**Chromatic scale** (1) A scalar pattern of half steps only; (2) a scale in which all the notes available in the octave are used in either ascending or descending order.

**Church modes** The scale patterns on which most music of the Medieval and Renaissance eras was theoretically based; so called because they were used first and primarily to explain the construction of the music of the early Christian church.

**Church sonata** (see *Sonata da chiesa*)

**Clarino** (It., *klah RREE noh*) (1) A trumpet of the seventeenth and part of the eighteenth century; (2) the high register of the clarinet (also called *clarion* register).

**Classical era** (see Appendix A)

**Clausula** (Lat., *KLOW zhu lah*) In the twelfth and thirteenth centuries, a polyphonic vocal composition based on a segment or portion of plainsong and often substituted for a corresponding part of a liturgical composition; all parts were usually vocalized. When full texts were added to the upper voices, the clausula became the motet.

**Clavicembalo** (It., *klah vee CHEM bah loh*) Harpsichord.

**Clavecin** (Fr., *KLAHV sanh*) Harpsichord.

**Clavier** (Fr., *KLAH vyay, no diphthong*; Ger., *klah VEER*; Eng., *KLAY vee er*) (1) Keyboard; (2) an early keyboard instrument.

**Clef** A sign which, when placed on the staff, indicates the pitch name for a particular line; the most frequently used are the G clef (𝄞), the C clef (𝄡), and the F clef (𝄢).

**Cluster** In modern musical terminology, a group of several notes sounded simultaneously, the group being too dissonant to be considered a chord.

**Coda; codetta** A conclusion to a movement, but of sufficient length to be identified as a separate section, especially in a sonata form or fugue; a codetta is a short conclusion to one of the subsections of a movement, rather than to the movement as a whole, although a short coda is sometimes called a codetta.

**Coloratura** (1) Ornamentation, often by the use of *fioritura*, of melodic lines, especially in vocal music; (2) loosely, the highest female voice, particularly one trained in the performance of highly decorative music. Coloratura may be performed by any type of voice, however, as long as the singer has the required flexibility and technique.

**Comodo; commodo** (It., *kaw MOH doh*) Comfortable, easy.

**Con** (It., *KAWN*) With.

**Concert** A musical presentation to an audience by a soloist or performing group (see Recital).

**Concertino** (It., *kawn chair TEE noh*) (1) In a *concerto grosso*, the small group of soloists, as opposed to the orchestra as a whole; (2) a concerto-like composition, but smaller in size and scope than a concerto.

**Concertmaster** The chief violinist of an orchestra, who advises the conductor on certain matters of interpretation (especially bowing) and handles all incidental solos for his instrument; sometimes, the chief clarinetist in a concert band serves a somewhat similar function.

**Concerto** (*kon CHAIR toh*) (1) A multimovement composition for a solo instrument with a large group of instruments (an orchestra or band) in accompaniment or equal participation; popular from the eighteenth century to the present; (2) in a *concerto grosso* (q.v.) the term is applied to the orchestra as opposed to the small group of soloists (*concertino*).

**Concerto grosso** (It., *kawn CHAIR toh GRAWSS soh*) A multimovement concerto in which a small group of instruments (called the *concertino* or, sometimes, the *principali*) is alternated, contrasted, or combined with a larger group (called the *ripieno, concerto,* or *tutti*); *concerti grossi* were popular in the Baroque era, and some have been written in the twentieth century (see also Sinfonia concertante).

**Concert overture** An orchestral work, in one movement, usually with programmatic content (see Program (4)), free of any larger work and intended for performance by itself.

**Concitato** (It., *kawn chee TAH toh*) Excited.

**Conductor** A leader or director of a musical group, responsible for programming, interpretation, rehearsal, setting of tempo, and all other musical factors.

**Conductus** (Lat., *kawn DOOK tooss*) (1) A monophonic, Latin, strophic song of the twelfth and thirteenth centuries, possibly for processionals, although also used with other types of texts; (2) a polyphonic thirteenth-century composition in which the *cantus firmus* is original with the composer and not borrowed from plainsong; the *conductus*, identified by the fact that all parts move in the same basic rhythm, represents true choral polyphony, and was one of the first wholly original polyphonic styles in Western music.

**Consonance** Two or more pitches, sounded simultaneously, which do not create tension nor demand resolution to other pitches; the concept of what is consonant has changed so much over the centuries that it is impossible to establish definite rules as to which intervals are consonant and which are dissonant without reference to a specific era of music history.

**Consort** In the Renaissance and early Baroque eras, an ensemble of like instruments or of instruments easily blended (thus, "loud" consorts, "soft" consorts, viol consorts, and others); groups of dissimilar instruments were known as "broken" consorts.

**Contemporary era** (see Appendix A)

**Continuo** (see Basso continuo)

**Contralto** (see Alto)

**Contrapuntal** Adjectival form of "counterpoint."

**Contrary motion** Voices or parts moving in opposite directions.

**Countermelody** A melody with its own individual character sounded simultaneously with another melody of equal musical worth.

**Counterpoint** *Lit.,* "point against point" or "note against note"; the technique involved in writing polyphony.

**Courante** (Fr., *KOO rahnt*) A lively dance in triple meter; with the *allemande, sarabande,* and *gigue,* one of the standard dances of the Baroque suite.

**Crescendo** (It., *kreh SHEN doh*) Gradually becoming louder.

**Cycle** (1) A group of separate compositions, especially songs, related to a common extramusical idea, with or without recurrent melodies; (2) a group of movements with recurrent melodies or motives. Most often, when this latter meaning is intended, the term *cyclic treatment* is preferred. Not all compositions using cyclic treatment are programmatic, however.

# D

**D.** Abbreviation for *Deutsch (DOYTCH) Index*; followed by a number in the listing of Schubert's works on concert or recital programs; refers to the complete catalogue of Schubert's music by Otto Eric Deutsch.

**da capo** (It., *dah KAH poh*) (1) Direction to repeat from the beginning; (2) a section of a composition which is so repeated; (3) a type of aria in *ABA* form, the end of the *B* section marked with this term as a way of avoiding the need for writing out the repeat of the *A* section. The *da capo aria* is the type most often found in the opera, oratorio, and cantata of the Baroque period.

**dal segno** (It., *dahl SAYN yoh*) Repeat from the sign (.S.).

**D. C.** Abbreviation for *da capo*.

**Decibel** A measurement unit of loudness.

**Decrescendo** (It., *deh kreh SHEN doh*) Gradually get softer.

**Descriptive music** Music that is purposefully suggestive of stories, scenes, philosophical concepts, people, etc. (*see* Tone poem; Concert overture; *Leitmotiv*; Extramusical reference; Program; Nationalism)

**Development** Manipulation of a fragment of a melody through varying instrumentation, key, mode, rhythm, pitch, etc.

**Diatonic** (*dy uh TAHN ick*) Derived from the major or minor scales, and relatively free of accidentals.

**Diminuendo** (It., *dee meen oo EHN doh*) Gradually get softer.

**Diminution** (1) Shortening of the time values of a melody; (2) in the late sixteenth century and in the seventeenth century, the ornamentation of a melody through the use of quick-moving passages.

**Dissonance** A simultaneous sounding of different pitches which creates an aural tension and demands relief through consonance. The concept of what is dissonant has changed so much through the history

of music that further definition must be relevant to particular periods and styles.

**Divertimento** (It., *dee vair tee MEHN toh*) A form of chamber music with four to ten relatively short movements, some of which are dance-like; for woodwinds, brasses, strings, or mixed groups; popular in the latter part of the eighteenth century.

**Division** (1) Synonym for "diminution" (*see* second meaning); (2) variation, usually above a ground bass; (3) an array of organ pipes of varying pitches and timbres controlled by a keyboard.

**Doctrine of Affections** (*see* Affection)

**Dodecaphony** (*doh de CAF oh nee*) (*see* Twelve-tone music)

**Dolce** (It., *DOL cheh*) Sweetly, gently.

**Dolente** (It., *doh LEN teh*) Sorrowfully.

**Doloroso** (It., *doh lohr OH zoh*) Sorrowfully.

**Double reed** A type of woodwind instrument whose column of air is set in motion by air pressure from the player's mouth directed against a narrow space between two pieces of cane, both of which vibrate; Renaissance double-reed instruments were the krummhorn and shawm; modern double reeds are the oboe, English horn, and bassoon.

**Double stopping** (*see* Stop)

**Doubling** (1) Playing the same notes at the same time as those given to another instrumental or vocal part; playing in unison; (2) playing more than one instrument.

**Dramatic voice** A singing quality characterized by power and richness of timbre.

**D. S.** Abbreviation for *dal segno*.

**Duet** A composition for two performing parts; in the Baroque era, a group consisting of two treble singers plus basso continuo (a total of four players) was referred to as a *chamber duet*.

**Durchkomponiert** (Ger., *DOORCH kom poh neert*) (*see* Through-composed)

**Dynamics** Relationship of loud to soft, and the nature of change from one to the other. Dynamics that change smoothly and gradually are called *graded*; dynamics that change abruptly are called *terraced*. The terms "high" and "low" are often used to describe levels of loudness, but are better reserved for qualities of pitch.

# E

**Embellishment** Decoration through trills, moving notes, mordents, cadenzas, and the like; in Baroque music, embellishments were expected to be provided by the performer even though they were not written.

**Empfindsamer stil** (Ger., *emp fint ZAHM ur shtill*) The style resulting from the attempt of C. P. E. Bach and other north German composers, during the period between approximately 1750 and 1775, to combine simplicity and naturalness with the delicacy and refinement of the rococo (*see also Style galant*).

**Empfindung** (Ger., *emp FINDT doong*) Feeling, emotion.

**Energico** (It., *eh NAIR gee koh*) With vigor.

**Ensemble** (1) A sense of playing together, with ideas of timbre and interpretation held in common; (2) any group of performers engaged in a common musical endeavor; (3) in opera, two or more singers singing simultaneously; (4) a group of two or more performers of chamber music, each with his own part.

**Entr'acte** (Fr., *AHN tract*) Between the acts; music that is to be performed between the acts of a play, ballet, or opera.

**Episode** A passage in which secondary themes or motives derived from a main theme are stated and developed; especially relevant to rondo and fugue.

**Ernst** (Ger., *AIRNST*) Serious.

**Etwas** (Ger., *ET vahss*) Somewhat.

**Exotic scales** Scales other than the major, minor, and chromatic (for example, the whole-tone and pentatonic scales).

**Expansion** The free treatment of thematic material that does not follow any typical pattern of restatement, development, etc.

**Exposition** (1) The clear statement of musical materials to be developed at a later point; (2) the opening section of a sonata form or a fugue.

**Expressionism** A late nineteenth- and early twentieth-century style, especially Germanic in quality, characterized by intensity of expression, personal involvement of the composer, large performing apparatus, lugubrious subject matter, rich tone color, and allegorical meanings; an extension of Romanticism.

**Extramusical reference** Objects, persons, events, or ideas meant to be communicated in musical terms

(*see Leitmotiv;* Program; Tone poem; Concert overture; Nationalism).

# F

**Falsetto** A type of male vocal production using pitches above the normal range, which sacrifices richness for lightness and flexibility.

**Fantasia** (It., *fahn tah ZEE ah*) (Eng., *fan TAY zhah*) (1) A composition using a variety of contrapuntal devices, plus a combination of improvisation-like embellishments and unpredictable patterns of structure; (2) a type of character piece; (3) a development section of the Rococo and early Classical sonata.

**Feminine ending** A cadence in which the final chord falls on a weak beat.

**Fermata** (It., *fair MAH tah*) A musical symbol (⌢) indicating that a note, chord, or pause may be held *ad libitum;* in some cases (in arias and concerto movements), an indication of the point at which a cadenza may be inserted.

**Feurig** (Ger., *FOY rigkch;* final syllable is guttural) Fiery.

**Figuration** The use of a particular harmonic, melodic, or rhythmic figure.

**Figure** A short rhythmic, melodic, or harmonic pattern intended to be repeated.

**Figured bass** A type of shorthand in which numbers and accidentals indicate what chords are to be provided above the written bass line; used particularly in basso continuo practice.

**Fioritura** (It., *fee or ee TOOR rah*) Trills, mordents, running notes, and other embellishments applied to a melody.

**Flat** A sign (♭) indicating that the note which follows is to be lowered one half step; this is applied to that pitch elsewhere in the measure unless cancelled by another accidental; when two flats are written together (♭♭), it becomes a double flat, lowering the pitch two half steps.

**Folksong** A type of vocal music, often anonymous, which springs from a culture without the application of the craft of the trained musician; words and musical elements are subject to great changes resulting from an essentially oral tradition.

**Form** Structure; the cohesive element of music which results from the application of repetition, variety, etc., to melody, harmony, rhythm, and so on.

**Forte; fortissimo** (It., FOR teh; for TEES ee moh)  Loud; very loud.

**Fragmentation**  The breaking up of a melody into short entities, or motives, which can be easily detected by the listener and followed; an essential process in development.

**French overture**  A two-part introductory sinfonia, first standardized by Lully and placed at the beginning of most operas and oratorios of the Baroque period, as well as at the start of many instrumental works; the first section is slow, homophonic, and is characterized by dotted rhythms (♩ ♪ ♩ ♪), while the second is fast and in the fugal style.

**Fret**  A strip of wood, gut, or metal across the neck of a stringed instrument, serving as a locus for the stopping of a string.

**Freude** (Ger., FROY duh)  Joy.

**Fröhlich** (Ger., FRUR ligkch; second r is silent and final syllable is guttural)  Cheerful, fast.

**Frottola** (It., FRAHT toh lah)  A composition for three or four voices, chordal in texture, with the melodic stress on the top part, which is of fairly simple range and rhythm; texts are amorous or sprightly in character; popular in northern Italy in early sixteenth century.

**Fughetto** (It., foo GET toh; hard g)  A short fugal passage.

**Fugue** (FYOOG; hard g)  A compositional procedure in which a subject (or principal melody) is stated by each of the voices or instruments in succession, each voice continuing with subsidiary material while succeeding voices imitate it. Fragments of the subject are developed in episodes. The frequency of the imitative entrances and the tendency for each vocal or instrumental part to retain its melodic identity make the fugue the most contrapuntal musical style.

**Fundamental**  (1) The lowest note (more commonly called the root note) of a chord; (2) the lowest natural sound produced by a vibrating column of air (see also Overtone).

# G

**Gavotte**  (gah VAHT)  A rather fast dance of French origin, frequently found in eighteenth-century dance suites.

**Gesamtkunstwerk** (Ger., guh ZAHMT koonst vairk)  (see Music drama)

**Gebrauchsmusik** (Ger., guh BROWCHS moo zeek)  Lit., "useful music"; music which is designed to be played by amateurs rather than professionals. This style is identified by shorter forms, simpler technical requirements, and to a certain extent, equality of parts in small ensembles. The term was first used by Hindemith.

**Gesangvoll** (Ger., guh ZAHNG foal)  Songful.

**Gewidmet** (Ger., guh VID met)  Dedicated.

**Gigue** (Fr., ZHEEG; hard final g)  Lively dance in 6/8 time, originally English in character (jig); with the allemande, sarabande, and courante, a standard movement of the eighteenth-century suite.

**Giocoso** (It., joh KOH zoh)  Playful, joyous.

**Giusto** (It., JOO stoh)  Appropriate.

**Glee**  A part song for men's voices.

**Glissando** (It., glih SAHN doh)  A rapid sliding of a finger up or down a keyboard, set of keys (as on a flute), or strings (as on a harp or violin).

**Goliard** (Fr., goh LYARD; hard g)  A wandering student or young cleric (tenth to thirteenth century); goliard songs, often parodistic or satirical, were part of the earliest secular repertoire of the Medieval era.

**Grace note**  A very rapidly executed ornamental note, usually adjacent in pitch to the note it ornaments.

**Grand opera**  A term coined in nineteenth-century France to differentiate the more serious opera from the lighter opéra comique; grand opera was sung throughout, dealt with historical and heroic subject matter, stressed spectacle and vocal virtuosity, and generally subordinated drama and structure to musical effect. Major composers were Rossini, Meyerbeer, Halévy.

**Grave** (It., GRAH veh; Fr., GRAHV)  Serious, solemn, slow.

**Gregorian chant**  The plainsong of the Roman Catholic church; the term is derived from Gregory I, the last of several popes who encouraged the classification and ordering of the many melodies used in the Roman liturgy.

**Ground bass**  A short melody in the bass, repeated any number of times while the upper parts provide varying melodies and harmonies; same as basso ostinato (see Division 2).

**Gusto** (It., GOOS toh; hard g)  Taste, appropriateness.

**Gymel** (GIM ml; hard g)  Singing in parallel thirds; primarily a medieval English practice.

# H

**Half step** The distance between two immediately adjacent notes as they are represented on the piano keyboard.

**Harmonic** (1) Same as overtone ("harmonic series" is synonymous with "overtone series"); (2) a sound produced on a stringed instrument by touching a string lightly with the finger while bowing; (3) a sound produced on wind instruments by subtle techniques of blowing and fingering.

**Harmony** The vertical structure of music; the simultaneous sounding of different pitches in groups called "chords," and the ordering of these chords into sequences that lend tonal direction. Harmony may not only be specific as a result of chords, but may be implied by the notes of a melody, whether or not chords accompany it (see also Cadence).

**Heldentenor** (Ger., *HELD en ten or*) Lit., "heroic tenor"; a special type of male voice with great stamina, depth, and brilliance of sound; required particularly in the Wagner roles.

**Homophony** *(hah MAH fah nee)* A musical texture in which one melody is accompanied by subordinate chords or musical figures; also the result of simultaneous and similar motion in subordinate or accompanying parts.

**Hymn** A religious song of adoration or praise.

# I

**Idée fixe** (Fr., *ee DAY FEEX*; no diphthong on *day*) (see *Leitmotiv*)

**Imitation** Repetition of a melodic idea in another voice or part while the previous voice or part continues with different material.

**Impresario** One who arranges concerts, plays, performances, and the like, for public presentation, hopefully for profit.

**Impressionism** A late nineteenth-century style, led in music by Debussy; created in painting (Monet, Manet, and others), poetry (Verlaine, Baudelaire, Maeterlinck), and music as a reaction against German Romanticism; identified in music by delicate instrumentation, exotic scales, glissandos, pedal points, bell sonorities, divided choirs, fragmentary melodies, overlapping chords and sonorities, and parallel chord progressions.

**Improvisation** Extemporization; insertion of chords, melodies, or decorations over a given bass line, harmonic progression, or melody; a major aspect of jazz, *basso continuo* accompaniment, and Baroque solo vocal and instrumental music.

**Instrumentation** The instruments called for in a piece of music (see also Orchestration).

**Intermezzo** (It., *in tair MEDS oh*) (1) An orchestral passage or complete composition serving as a bridge or transition from one scene or act of a theatrical presentation to another scene or act; (2) in the eighteenth century, a comic or light-hearted dramatic entertainment performed between the acts of an *opera seria*; in this form, the intermezzo is an important harbinger of the *opera buffa* and is represented most significantly by Pergolesi's *La Serva Padrona* ("The Maid Mistress," 1733); in the sixteenth century, a musical interlude between the acts of a stage play, in which form the intermezzo is better known as an *intermedio (in tair MAY dee oh*; no diphthong), a collection of solo and choral madrigals and dances, all with instrumental accompaniment; (3) a character piece for piano.

**Interval** The distance between two notes. Intervals are called *major, minor, perfect, augmented,* or *diminished* according to the number of half or whole steps in them and in accordance with certain acoustical theories. In the key of C, the intervals measured upward from C are as follows: C-D-flat, minor second; C-D, major second; C-E-flat, minor third; C-E, major third; C-F, perfect fourth; C-F-sharp, augmented fourth (C-G-flat is a diminished fifth); C-G, perfect fifth; C-G-sharp, augmented fifth (C-A-flat is a minor sixth); C-A, major sixth; C-B-flat, minor seventh; C-B, major seventh; C-c, perfect octave.

**Intonation** The degree of accuracy of pitch in performance.

**Inversion** (1) The sounding of a lower note of an interval (or the root note of a chord) higher than the upper note (or notes); (2) turning the notes of a melody exactly upside down.

**Istesso tempo** (It., *ee STESS oh TEM poh*) The same speed, even though there may be a different time signature.

**Italian overture** A three-part instrumental composition used to precede an opera of the late Baroque period, standardized by Alessandro Scarlatti; the first movement, in fast tempo, is somewhat polyphonic, the second is slow and songful, the third is fast and dance-like; an important forerunner of the Classical symphony because of its homophonic tendencies as well as its frequent use for concert performance as a *concerto ripieno* (a concerto for orchestra without solo instruments as featured players).

# J

**Jazz** An aspect of innately American, especially Negro, chamber music in which players improvise on a melody in a highly personal and idiomatic way, utilizing such devices as syncopation, blue notes, and swinging; reflected in such styles as dixieland, ragtime, bebop, as well as in a number of "classical" compositions by Gershwin, Milhaud, Schuller, Stravinsky, and others (*see also* Third stream).

**Jongleur** (Fr., *zhawn GLUR*) (1) An entertainer, particularly one who is an acrobat, juggler, etc.; (2) throughout the Medieval era, an instrumentalist and minstrel; particularly in the eleventh and twelfth centuries, a trained musician who assisted and accompanied the more nobly born Troubadour or Trouvère.

# K

**K.; K.v.** Abbreviation for *Köchel Verzeichnis* (*KUR chul fair TSYCH nis*; guttural *ch*), the index of Mozart's compositions published by Ludwig von Köchel in 1862.

**Key** (1) A mechanism which, when depressed, causes a string to be struck (piano) or plucked (harpsichord), a stream of air to be directed through a pipe (organ), a hole to be covered or uncovered (woodwind instruments), or a bar to be struck (celesta); (2) the specific tonality of a piece of music.

**Key signature** (*see* Signature)

**Klagend** (Ger., *KLAH gent*; hard *g*) Mournful, dolorous.

**Klavier** (*see* Clavier)

**Konzertstück** (Ger., *KAWN zairt shtuhk*) Concertpiece; a work for one or more solo instruments and orchestral accompaniment, usually less structured or developmental than a concerto, and more devoted to the display of virtuosity.

# L

**L.** Abbreviation for *Longo Index*, the catalog of Domenico Scarlatti's harpsichord music prepared by Alessandro Longo.

**Langsam** (Ger., *LAHNG zahm*) Slow.

**Larghetto** (It., *lahr GET toh*; hard *g*) Slow, but not as slow as *largo*.

**Lauda** (It., first syllable rhymes with *cow*) A strophic, monophonic hymn of praise (with refrain) that was important in Italy from the thirteenth through the nineteenth centuries.

**Lebhaft** (Ger., *LAYP hahft*) Lively.

**Legato** (It., *lay GAH toh*) Smooth, connected.

**Leger line**; also **ledger** A short line added above or below a staff for purposes of writing pitches higher or lower than the normal five lines and four spaces.

**Leggiero** (It., *lehj JAIR roh*) Lightly.

**Leitmotiv** (Ger., *LIGHT mo teef*) A brief melody associated with a person, object, event, or idea; *Leitmotiv* is particularly associated with Wagner's music drama, although also used by Weber, Richard Strauss, Verdi, Puccini, and a host of others to varying degrees.

**Lent** (Fr., *LANH*) Slow.

**Lento** (It., *LEN toh*) Slow.

**Lesson** British word for suite.

**Libretto**; plural, **libretti** Lit., "a little book"; the text of an opera, oratorio, or cantata; the author of a libretto is the librettist.

**Lied** (Ger., *LEEDT*); plural, **Lieder** (*LEED ur*) (1) Song; (2) a polyphonic song of the Renaissance era, brought to its peak by Isaac and Lassus (*see also* Art song).

**L'istesso tempo** (*see Istesso tempo*)

**Liturgical** Referring to church services, particularly those rubrics or texts prescribed as part of the worship service.

**Liturgical drama** In the Medieval era, a collection of chants, conductus, hymns, and so forth, sung in Latin and so arranged as to narrate and enact stories associated with major festal days. By the fourteenth century, the plays were free of liturgical texts and had become anonymous entertainments, sometimes with spoken dialogue; eventually they were written in the vernacular, with secular music as well as sacred melodies.

**Luftpause** (Ger., *LUHFT powzuh*) Lit., "air pause," or "air space"; a feeling of momentary pause at the end of a phrase, but without a break in rhythmic flow.

**Lustig** (Ger., *LOOST igkch; ch* is guttural) Cheerful.

**Lyric** (1) Melodious or tuneful; (2) a type of singing voice, light in timbre and pleasant to hear, with a great deal of flexibility, and especially adapted to pitches of medium and high range; (3) the words to a song.

**Lyric opera** *(see Opéra lyrique)*

# M

**Madrigal** (1) In the fourteenth century, an amorous or idyllic poem set to music in several strophes and a refrain; (2) in sixteenth-century Italy, a highly dramatic, polyphonic work, marked with daring harmonies and chromaticism, both of which were used for affective word-setting rather than chord sequences within a tonal framework; (3) in sixteenth-century England, the English equivalent of the Italian model was composed by Byrd, Gibbons, and others, although madrigal also referred to a type more properly known as the *ballett (q.v.)*.

**Mässig** (Ger., *MESS igkch; ch* is guttural) Moderately.

**Maestoso** (It., *my STOH zoh*) Majestic.

**Maestro al cembalo** (It., *MY stroh ahl CHEM bah loh*) Lit., "conductor at the keyboard"; in the Baroque era, the conductor was the *basso continuo* player, and directed from his place at the harpsichord; although the *continuo* practice declined in the Classical era and conducting duties were shared with the first violinist *(see* Concertmaster), the term was still applied, especially in the church and the opera house.

**Major** (1) A mode or scale in which the intervals from the tonic note follow the pattern of two whole steps, a half step, three whole steps, and a final half step; the major scale is the same ascending and descending, unlike some versions of the minor scale *(q.v.)*; (2) a key or tonality based on such a scale. *(see also* Interval)

**Mannheim school** *(MAHN hym)* A mid-eighteenth-century group of composers, most notably Stamitz, Cannabich, and Richter, important in the evolution of the symphony of the Classical era. The dominance of the violins, general celerity and buoyancy of motion (often called the "singing allegro"), a variety of dynamic devices (crescendo, decrescendo, orchestral rest, sforzando), triadic motives (often called "rockets"), elimination of the *basso continuo* in favor of written-out inner parts, and a generally homophonic, developmental character instead of Baroque counterpoint identify both their manner of playing and a style of composition.

**Manual** A keyboard of any type of keyboard instrument, but especially that of the harpsichord and organ (a keyboard operated by the feet is better known as a *pedalboard*, although *pedal manual* is occasionally noted); organ manuals are identified by the names *great, swell, choir, solo,* and *echo*.

**Marcato** (It., *mahr KAH toh*) Strongly accented.

**March** A composition in duple rhythm, accented strongly enough to guide the steps of people in a procession; the march is usually divided into sections, the main theme alternating with contrasting themes; these latter themes are in sections called *trios (q.v.)*.

**Marching band** *(see* Band).

**Marcia** (It., *MAHR chyah*) March.

**Martelé** (Fr., *mahr tell LAY*; no diphthong) Hammered. *(see* Bowing)

**Mass** The principal form of service in the Roman church, and some Protestant denominations *(see* Mass ordinary; Mass proper).

**Mass ordinary** That portion of the Latin liturgy which is the same at every service; the Mass ordinary is divided into five basic sections, each titled by the opening words of the section–*Kyrie eleison* ("Lord have mercy upon us"), *Gloria in excelsis Deo* ("Glory to God in the highest"), *Credo in unum Deum* ("I believe in one God"), *Sanctus* ("Holy"), and *Agnus Dei* ("Lamb of God") *(see also* Mass proper).

**Mass proper** That portion of the Latin liturgy which changes from day to day or is appropriate to special occasions.

**Mazurka** A moderately fast Polish dance in triple time.

**Measure** A group of beats, clearly organized into strong and weak accents, which is separated from similar groups on the printed page by vertical lines; also called a *bar*; the vertical line is called a *bar line* or *measure line*; measures are also audible groups, although varied rhythmic groups within a composition may alter the clarity of beats.

**Medieval era** *(see* Appendix A)

**Medley** A composition, usually an overture, made up of several songs or melodies which are unrelated musically, although they may all come from a single source, such as an operetta, opera, musical comedy, etc.; segments of a medley are usually linked by brief and obvious transitions; the favorite overture form of the operetta and the musical comedy. *(see also* Potpourri)

**Mehr** (Ger., *MAIR*) More.

**Meistersinger** (Ger., *MY ster zing er*) (1) Lit., "master singer"; (2) a member of a musical craft guild, especially in the fifteenth and sixteenth centuries; songs by composers of these guilds were usually in the *bar form (AAB)*, were monophonic in texture, and highly florid; (3) an opera by Wagner, first performed in 1868 (full title: *Die Meistersinger von Nürnberg*, "The Mastersingers of Nuremberg").

**Melisma** *(meh LIZ muh)* A group of three or more notes for a single syllable of text.

**Melody** (1) Any series of pitches played or sung in succession and given some sort of identity through patterns of pitch and duration *(see* Rhythm); (2) the horizontal element of music, harmony being the vertical element *(see also* Tone row).

**Meno** (It., *MEH noh*) Less.

**Mesto** (It., *MEH stoh*) Sad.

**Meter** The scheme of accented and unaccented beats in music and poetry, such a scheme being described by the time signature. Music with regularly stressed and unstressed beats is known as *metrical* music; when all the beats are evenly stressed, or not apparent to the listener, the music is *unmetrical.*

**Mezzo** (It., *MEDS zoh*) Lit., "half" or "middle"; thus, *mezzo forte* means half-loud, or moderately loud.

**Mezzo-soprano** (It., *MEDS zoh soh PRAHN noh*) "Middle soprano"; a female voice with a wide range combining the qualities of both alto and soprano, without the extreme pitches of their ranges, but with great warmth and dramatic potential.

**Microtone** A fraction of a half step.

**Miniature** A term applied to a composition, usually of the Romantic era, but also appropriate to many rococo works, just long enough to contain only one or just a very few musical or aesthetic statements.

**Minor** (1) A mode or scale in which the intervals from the tonic note include a minor third rather than a major third; the sixth and seventh scale steps of such a mode vary according to the type of scale used: if the sixth and seventh are natural ascending but flatted descending, the scale is called the "melodic minor"; the use of a flatted sixth and natural seventh both ascending and descending results in the "harmonic minor"; (2) a key (or tonality) or chord based on such a scale.

**Minnesinger** (Ger., *MIN nuh zing er*); plural, *Minnesänger* (*MIN nuh zeng er*) Noblemen of the twelfth through fourteenth centuries who devoted themselves to poetry and the music written for it. Neithart von Reuenthal's songs are similar to those of the French Troubadours and Trouvères, but Walter von der Vogel-

weide (ca. 1170–1230), Tannhäuser (mid-thirteenth century), and Frauenlob (Heinrich von Meissen, d. 1318) wrote primarily moralistic, devotional, or narrative poetry.

**Minstrel** (1) A generic term used today with reference to such poet-musicians as the Troubadours, Trouvères, Jongleurs, Minnesänger, and Meistersänger; (2) the black-faced, imitation-Negro type of amusement, or a performer in such an amusement, popular in the United States during the nineteenth and early twentieth centuries, but now justifiably in disrepute.

**Minuet** A dance form, moderately fast, light, and gracious in character and in triple meter; used by eighteenth-century composers as a movement of most multimovement instrumental compositions; in form, an overall *ABA.*

**M. M.** Abbreviation for Mälzel's Metronome (*MEL tzuhl*); followed by a note and numbers, an indication of the quantity of that note per minute; thus, M.M. ♩ = 80 means that there should be 80 quarter notes per minute.

**Modality** The use of modes as a system for composition, especially the church modes (*q.v.*).

**Mode** (1) Any ordering of pitches into a scale pattern *(see* Major; Minor); even though it is wholly correct to refer to the major and minor scale patterns as modes, the use of the word is popularly reserved for the scale systems on which most music written before 1600 was based; (2) a pattern of rhythm, particularly when applied to polyphonic music by Léonin, Pérotin, and their contemporaries, and to the monophonic music of the Troubadours and Trouvères.

**Moderato** (It., *mohd air AH toh*) Moderately.

**Modéré** (Fr., *mod air AY*; no diphthong) Moderately.

**Modern era** *(see* Appendix A)

**Modulation** The process of shifting from one key or tonality to another.

**Moins** (Fr., *MWANH*) Less.

**Molto** (It., *MOL toh*) Much.

**Monody** A single melody that dominates the very simple accompaniment provided for it; any early Baroque or late Renaissance song of this type.

**Monophony** *(mah NAH fah nee)* A single, unaccompanied line of music; unisonal performance, with no accompaniment.

**Morendo** (It., *mor EHN doh*) Dying away.

**Mosso** (It., *MOHSS soh*)  Moving faster.

**Motet**  (1) A polyphonic, vocal (usually choral) composition, with or without accompaniment, with a religious text; instrumental transcriptions of Renaissance motets were known as *ricercares*; like the madrigal, the history of the motet is so varied as to forbid elaborate summary here; (2) the fourteenth-century *isorhythmic* motet utilizes repeated rhythmic and/or melodic patterns in its tenor and/or all other parts.

**Motive**  The shortest recognizable melodic unit; in program music, motives often carry extramusical associations (*see Leitmotiv*).

**Moto** (It., *MOH toh*)  Motion.

**Musical**  A type of lyric drama, especially popular in America, using spoken dialogue, song, and dance. In the early twentieth century, the music was generally simple, with little care given to expressive instrumentation, ensemble, or melodic characterization; since the late 1920's, subject matter has become more varied (often serious) and musical content more meaningful.

**Music drama**  A type of operatic composition developed by Wagner in which the flow of music is uninterrupted by autonomous "numbers"; all arts are considered equally important, hence the term *Gesamtkunstwerk* ("collected" or "composite" art work) is applied. Essentially opposed to the "number opera," music drama utilizes continuous orchestral music to suggest the deeper meanings of the stage action and text which is sung in the manner of the arioso (*see also Leitmotiv, Heldentenor*).

**Musicology**  The scholarly examination of musical literature, notation, pedagogy, and other aspects of music in all cultures and historical eras.

**Musique concrète**  (Fr., *moo ZEEK kawn KRETT; kawn* is nasal)  Taped and electronic music, the source of the sounds being "real" sounds rather than electronically generated ones.

**Mute**  A device used to change or soften the sound of an instrument, particularly the sound of brasses and strings.

# N

**Nationalism**  When spoken of with reference to the arts, nationalism signifies a reflection of conscious or unconscious feelings of patriotism and love of country and can be found especially in music in the nineteenth century. Nationalistic content may be programmatic or may be the result of the use of national materials (for instance, folk tunes, national instruments).

**Natural**  A sign (♮) which indicates that the note following is not to be made sharp (♯) or flat (♭), regardless of previous indications to the contrary; after a note has been made natural, it remains that way for the rest of the measure, unless other directions are given (*see Accidental*).

**Neo-**  A prefix meaning "new" or implying the conscious cultivation of a bygone style or genre in a new way (for instance, Neobaroque, Neoclassic).

**Neume** (*NYOOM*)  A medieval notational symbol, or group of symbols, a type of which is still in use for plainsong notation; there were several systems of symbols used from the eighth through the fourteenth centuries.

**Number opera**  A type of opera in which the music consists of a succession of independent compositions (arias, dances, choruses, an overture or prelude, etc.), as opposed to the "endless" melody and seamless style of Wagner's music drama.

# O

**Obbligato** (It., *awb blee GAH toh*)  (1) Obligatory parts that must not be omitted; (2) an accompanying melody or decorative passage offered as a foil for a more prominent melody heard simultaneously in another part.

**Octave**  The distance (interval) between a note and the next note with the same pitch name, either higher or lower than the first.

**Octet**  (1) A group of eight performers; (2) a composition for eight performers.

**Ode**  A vocal composition, similar in construction to the cantata, usually commemorative of a person, event, or occasion.

**Op.**  Abbreviation for *opus (OH pus;* plural, *opera).*

**Opera**  (1) A composition which merges vocal and instrumental music with drama and stagecraft to form a cohesive whole, the music being the focus of attention for purposes of characterization and dramatic impact. (*see Singspiel; Opera buffa; Opera seria; Opéra comique; Ballad opera; Number opera, Music drama*); (2) plural of *opus*.

**Opera buffa** (It., *OH pair ah BOOF ah*)  Comic opera, originating in the eighteenth century primarily as short diversions, or *intermezzos*, between the acts of the longer, epic *opera seria*. Eventually it developed into an operatic genre in its own right with the popularity of Pergolesi's *La Serva Padrona* ("The Maid Mistress," 1733).

**Opéra comique** (Fr., *oh pai rah kaw MEEK*) Opera with spoken dialogue; sentimental comedy in the eighteenth century, but any sort of story in the nineteenth century; Bizet's *Carmen* and Gounod's *Faust* were originally of this type, but recitatives were written for them after their first performances.

**Opéra lyrique** (Fr., *oh pai rah lee REEK*) Lyric opera in nineteenth-century France, usually sentimental and tragic, centering on the brief and unhappy lives of young women (typical is Massenet's *Manon*); lyric opera used the devices of grand opera, but not its excesses.

**Opera seria** (It., *OH pair rah SAY rree ah*; no diphthongs) A type of opera, particularly of the Baroque era, devoted to the glorification of the singing voice, especially by means of the *da capo aria*; a particularly gorgeous art form, dealing with figures of classical history or mythology, with Handel and A. Scarlatti as major composers (*see also* Affection).

**Operetta** Light-hearted, sentimental opera with spoken dialogue, with relatively simple music for both voices and orchestra; major composers include Sullivan, Herbert, Romberg, Friml, and Kern.

**Opus** (Lat., *OH pus*; plural, *opera*) Composition, or work; usually followed by a number indicating the chronological position of the composition in the composer's output; may have several complete compositions within it; Beethoven's Opus 1, for example, consists of three piano trios, each with several movements.

**Oratorio** A composition devoted to the merging of music and drama, but without staging, costuming, etc. (although some early Baroque oratorios were staged); choral work is especially significant and religious texts predominate; an oratorio based on the Easter story is a *Passion Oratorio*.

**Orchestra** (1) A group of instrumentalists, of which the string section is the most numerous, with more than one player per part; various synonymous names are applied to large orchestras: *symphony orchestra, philharmonic orchestra, philharmonia, philharmonic-symphony*, etc.; small orchestras, with but few players per part, are *chamber orchestras*; (2) that section of seats on the main floor of a concert hall or theater.

**Orchestration** An arrangement of a composition that an orchestra (or, more loosely applied, a band) plays; the act of arranging such a composition.

**Ordre** (Fr., *AWRDRR*) French word for *suite*.

**Organum** (Lat., *OR gahn oom*) A method of composition originating in the Medieval era as an added part to plainsong. At first, the organal parts ran parallel to the plainsong (*strict*, or *parallel, organum*), but later became a freely moving, ornate part above the plainsong *cantus firmus*, and thus was one of the first major forms of Western polyphony (*free organum*).

**Ornament; ornamentation** Embellishments used to decorate melodies or the individual notes of a melody; may include trills, rapid figures, mordents, etc.

**Ostinato** (It., *awss stee NAH toh*) A musical phrase or figure repeated consistently throughout a composition (or a section), while other parts or voices change around or above it; this usually, but not always, takes place in the bass.

**Overblowing** In wind instruments, the practice of playing on any of the partials of the overtone series other than the fundamental.

**Overtone; overtone series** One of a series of notes or the series itself created by the sounding of a fundamental; the physical arrangement of overtones, in which some are weaker or stronger than others, is the determining factor of the timbre of an instrument (*see* Harmonic 2).

**Overture** (1) An instrumental composition that precedes an opera, play, ballet, or oratorio, with or without musical materials drawn from it (*see* French overture; Italian overture; *Sinfonia*; Prelude; Potpourri; Medley); (2) a concert piece in one movement, usually with some sort of extramusical reference (*see* Concert overture); (3) a rather misleading term for the Baroque suite.

# P

**P.** Abbreviation for *Pincherle Index* (*panh CHERL*), the catalog of the works of Vivaldi compiled by Marc Pincherle.

**Pandiatonic music** Twentieth-century music that is diatonic, but free of the strictures of "traditional" harmony, that is, harmonic procedures based on eighteenth-century principles.

**Parallel motion** Music in which the notes of chords or simultaneously sounding parts move in the same direction and remain at the same interval from one another.

**Part** (1) Music for a single instrument or voice (for example, the soprano part, first violin part, and so on);

(2) music for a group of instruments or voices of the same type; (3) a melodic line, also called a *voice*, within an orchestral, choral, or solo musical complex; (4) a section of a composition.

**Partial**  An overtone.

**Partita** (Ger., *pahr TEE tah*)  German word for *suite*.

**Part song**  A type of vocal chamber music with various types of accompaniment, popular in the early Romantic era and characterized by lyricism and varying degrees of polyphony; notable are those works for men by Schubert and for mixed voices by Mendelssohn and Brahms.

**Passacaglia** (It., *pahss ah KAHL yah*)  (see *Chaconne*)

**Passion oratorio** (see *Oratorio*)

**Pathétique** (Fr., *pah tay TEEK*; no diphthong)  Pathetic, sorrowful.

**Patronage**  Financial support and moral encouragement of the arts.

**Pedal**  (1) A foot-operated device used to alter the dynamics or sustaining quality of some instruments, particularly the piano; (2) a foot-operated device used to make all the notes of the same pitch names either sharp, natural, or flat (harp); (3) a type of keyboard operated by the feet (see *Manual*); (4) a loosely used term for a low pitch (see *Pedal point*).

**Pedalboard** (see *Manual*)

**Pedal point**  The sustaining of a pitch in one part while other parts move freely above, below, or around the held tone; need not be a bass tone, as might be implied by the term "pedal" (*q.v.*).

**Pentatonic**  A type of scale in which the first five notes may involve any intervals desired, but the sixth tone is a repetition an octave above or below the first tone.

**Percussion**  (1) A type of instrument that is struck with the hand or an object; (2) music that is so created.

**Pesante** (It., *peh ZAHN teh*)  Heavy, ponderous.

**Peu** (Fr., *PUR*; silent *r*)  Little.

**Philharmonic** (see *Symphony orchestra*)

**Phrase**  A melodic fragment, longer than a motive, with a sense of lift or pause at its end.

**Piacere** (It., *pyah CHEH reh*)  Pleasure; *a piacere*: "freely," "at your pleasure."

**Piano; pianissimo** (It., *pee AH noh; pee ah NEESS ee moh*)  Soft; very soft.

**Piano quartet**  A chamber ensemble consisting most often of piano, violin, viola, and cello.

**Piano trio**  A chamber ensemble consisting most often of piano, violin, and cello.

**Pitch**  A musical tone, variable in duration and intensity, but fixed as to frequency of vibration; pitch degree is usually referred to as "high" or "low," terms often misapplied to dynamics.

**Più** (It., *PYOO*)  More.

**Pizzicato** (It., *pits ee KAH toh*)  Plucked; usually abbreviated *pizz*.

**Placito** (It., *PLAH chee toh*)  Pleasure; *a bene placito*: "as you please."

**Plainchant; plainsong**  A monophonic style of sacred song used in Western Christian worship, most often with Latin texts in the Roman ritual; characterized by unmetrical rhythms and modal scale structure; known somewhat inaccurately as *Gregorian chant*, the style may range from simple, strophic chants, with one note per syllable of text, to through-composed, highly melismatic compositions.

**Plectrum**  A small device made of metal, ivory, horn, plastic, etc., and used to pluck stringed instruments; the harpsichord plectrum, made of quill or leather, is held in place by a wooden jack that is activated by the key.

**Plus** (Fr., *PLU*)  More.

**Poco** (It., *POH koh*)  Little.

**Pointillism** (*PWANH tee yizm*)  (1) In painting, a technique by which the entire painting is composed of small dots of color, dots that are fused by the viewer into recognizable, if somewhat indefinite, forms; an outgrowth of Impressionism; (2) in music, a melodically fragmentary style cultivated in particular by Webern, whose short works place tremendous importance on each individual pitch and the sonority used for it, to the point of utmost conciseness and intensity of expression.

**Polka**  A moderately quick dance in duple time that originated early in the nineteenth century; popular as a social dance in eastern Europe and the United States.

**Polychoral**  Simultaneous combination and/or opposition of separate groups of instruments and/or voices; especially notable in the Renaissance and Baroque eras.

**Polyphony** (*pa LIF a nee*)  Many-voiced music; the simultaneous sounding of two or more melodic parts; fugue and canon are, by definition polyphonic although the madrigal, motet, and the sonata form also make extensive use of it; *counterpoint* is the technique involved in composing polyphonic music.

**Polytonality** The simultaneous sounding of two or more keys (*i.e.*, tonalities).

**Potpourri** (*po poo REE*) A medley, or collection of diverse musical materials, usually as an overture to a stage piece.

**Prelude** (*PREL yood*; also *PRAY lood, PREE lood*) (1) A short introduction to a stage play or opera, or to an act of one, usually to set its mood; (2) an autonomous composition for piano or orchestra, highly atmospheric in character, with or without extramusical reference; (3) the earliest type of keyboard music, designed for various liturgical purposes, written especially in fifteenth and early sixteenth centuries, with the particular idiom of the keyboard in mind (*see also* Chorale prelude).

**Presto; prestissimo** (It., *PRESS toh; press TEESS ee moh*) Fast; very fast.

**Program** (1) An array of compositions presented in a concert; (2) a concert or recital; (3) the printed list of the compositions of a concert or recital, or the cast and other data as printed for an opera, ballet, etc.; (4) a story or other extramusical reference suggested by, explicit in, or lying at, the source of an instrumental composition; (5) the type of music concerned with extramusical reference.

**Prosody** (*PRAH sa dee*) The relation of words and music with regard to the natural accents of the words and the stress given them in spoken language.

**Purfling** (*PER fling*) A decorative strip around the outline of the members of the violin family, designed for ornament and to prevent chipping of the edge.

# Q

**Quartal harmony** Harmonic progressions in which the chords are built of fourths (*see* Tertian harmony).

**Quartet** (1) A group of four players or singers, the most common being the string quartet; (2) a composition for such a group.

**Quasi** (Lat., *KWAH zee*) As if; resembling.

**Quintet** (1) A group of five players or singers; (2) a composition for such a group.

**Quodlibet** (Lat., *KWAHD lib et*) Lit., "what you will"; a simultaneous combination of two unrelated, autonomous melodies, each perhaps familiar to the listener; the combination of two unrelated texts in a similarly incongruous manner; somewhat loosely applied to a potpourri treatment.

# R

**Ragtime** A style of dance music popular in the nineteenth and early twentieth centuries, marked by its syncopation and ebullient improvisation; a forerunner of jazz.

**Rallentando** (It., *rahl en TAHN doh*) Slowing down.

**Range** (1) The span of notes available to an instrument, or performable with a voice; (2) in a piece of music, the highest and lowest pitches called for in a given part.

**Rank** A group of organ pipes of similar timbre.

**Recapitulation** (*see* Sonata (3))

**Recital** A performance of chamber music by one singer or player, with or without accompaniment, for an audience; the term is rarely applied to performances by larger combinations.

**Recitative** (*ress ih tah TEEV*) (1) Stylized declamation sung with a usually subordinate, chordal accompaniment and used for narration or dialogue in an opera, oratorio, or cantata; stress is on clarity of text and through-composition, musical values being secondary; (2) *recitativo secco* (*retch ih tah TEEV oh SEK koh*), or "dry" recitative, is accompanied only by *basso continuo* or a keyboard instrument; found in *opera seria* of the Baroque era and in *opera buffa*, it is characterized by a rapid, speech-like delivery; (3) *recitativo accompagnato* (*ah kawm pahn YAH toh;* "accompanied") and *recitativo stromentato* (*stroh mehn TAH toh;* "instrumented") are synonyms referring to orchestrally accompanied recitative; these are slower in delivery than the *secco*, more dramatic and effusive in style, and are found mostly in the opera (both serious and comic) of the Romantic era, although they are not unknown by any means in the previous eras.

**Reed** (1) A piece of cane which, when attached to a mouthpiece and blown over, vibrates to produce a tone; (2) colloquially, any of the instruments which use this principle; (3) a stop on an organ in which the reed principle is applied, although the reed in this case is made of metal.

**Referential** (*see* Extramusical reference)

**Refrain** A part of a song that recurs, usually both musically and textually, at the end of each strophe.

**Register** (1) A set or rank of pipes in an organ which is controlled by a single stop; (2) a part of the range of an instrument or voice which may have a quality of sound peculiar to itself; thus, the lower register of the clarinet, called the *chalumeau* register, has a bigness of sound and mellowness quite in contrast to the highest register, called the *clarino* or *clarion*.

**Registration** A combination of stops on an organ or harpsichord producing the particular timbre called for by the composer or the performer.

**Renaissance era** (*see* Appendix A)

**Requiem** A mass for the dead.

**Retrograde** Backwards; the sounding of a melody in reverse order.

**Revue** A type of variety entertainment employing dance, song, and spoken comedy, loosely organized around an extramusical idea, rarely a plot.

**Rhapsody** An expansive composition, especially favored in the nineteenth century for works of programmatic or nationalistic intent; the freedom of structure exhibited in these works led to the application of the term in the twentieth century to works not necessarily programmatic or nationalistic (for example, Gershwin's *Rhapsody in Blue*) and to the use of *rhapsodic* as synonymous with *expansive*.

**Rhythm** The temporal organization of music. There are so many ways in which notes of varying durations can be combined into meaningful sequences that no other simple definition may be applied (*see* Meter; Melody).

**Ricercare** (It., *ree chair KAH ray*, no diphthong; also pronounced *ree chair KAHR*; plural: either *ricercari* or *ricercares*) The instrumental equivalent (often a transcription) of a motet; highly imitative, usually with several sections, each section with its own subject treated in imitation; forerunner of the fugue.

**Riff** A jazz *ostinato*.

**Ripieno** (It., *ree pee EH noh*) "Filler"; in a *concerto grosso*, the large group of players, as opposed to the small group of soloists (*concertino*).

**Ritardando; ritenendo; ritenuto** (It., *ree tahr DAHN doh; ree ten EHN doh; ree ten OO toh*) Slowing down, held back.

**Ritornello** (It., *ree tohr NEL loh*) (1) A recurrent instrumental passage, alternating with contrasting episodes; (2) the orchestral music in a Baroque *concerto grosso*; (3) instrumental episodes in Baroque arias or operatic scenes; (4) the final portions of fourteenth-century Italian madrigals.

**Rococo** (1) A style characterized by highly refined and extravagant ornamentation, usually expressed in intimate terms; (2) a historical subperiod, contemporary with the end of the Baroque era and the beginning of the Classical era, thus usually dated 1720–1770; major composers include Rameau, Couperin, Telemann, D. Scarlatti; elements of the rococo are also found in major composers of the Classical era (*see Style galant*).

**Romantic era** (*see* Appendix A)

**Rondeau** (Fr., *rawn DOH*; no diphthong; plural, *rondeaux*) A secular song form with refrain, with numerous repeats and alternations of both text and music; popular as monophonic song form of the Trouvères and as a polyphonic form of the fourteenth and fifteenth centuries.

**Rondo** (It., *RAHN doh*) A musical structure in which a principal theme *(A)* is played in alternation with contrasting sections or episodes (*B, C, D*, etc.); when one of these sections is developmental, the hybrid term *sonata-rondo* is more appropriate.

**Root note** A note upon which a chord is based, thus giving the chord its name; this term is not synonymous with *bass note*, for the root of the chord need not be the lowest note heard.

**Round** (*see* Canon)

**Rubato** (It., *roo BAH toh*) A slight variation of tempo for expressive purposes.

**Ruhig** (Ger., *ROO igkch*; final *g* is guttural) Calm, peaceful.

# S

**S.** Abbreviation for *Schmieder Index (SHMEE dur)*, the catalog of the works of J. S. Bach published by Wolfgang Schmieder.

**Sarabande** A dance in slow triple time; with the *allemande, courante,* and *gigue,* one of the standard movements of the Baroque suite.

**Scale** A pattern of pitches, in either ascending or descending order, which is repeated in each octave (*see* Whole-tone scale; Chromatic scale; Major; Minor; Pentatonic; Mode).

**Scherzo** (It., *SKAIR tzoh*) (1) *Lit.*, "joke"; (2) an *ABA* movement in very fast tempo, usually referred to as a *scherzo and trio*; (3) a musical style identified by lightness of timbre and celerity.

**Schleppend** (Ger., *SHLEP pent*)  Dragging.

**Schnell** (Ger., *SHNEL*)  Fast.

**Schwer** (Ger., *SHVAIR*)  Heavy, harsh.

**Score** (1) The printed music showing what every instrument or voice is performing at a given moment, each part being written out individually or together with parts for similar instruments; (2) to arrange a composition for specific instruments or voices.

**Secco** (It., *SEK koh*)  Dry (*see* Recitative).

**Sehr** (Ger., *ZAIR*)  Very.

**Semitone**  Half step.

**Sempre** (It., *SEM preh*)  Always; consistently.

**Sequence** (1) A melodic or harmonic pattern repeated at a higher or lower level; (2) an addition or insertion of text or music (or both) in a melisma over the word "Alleluia" (*see* Trope).

**Serenade** (1) A type of chamber music, in several movements of varying styles and forms, for outdoor performance, hence with stress on wind instruments; (2) a love song, usually strophic, usually with a light accompaniment.

**Serialism**  The technique of building a composition on a *tone row* (q.v.), treating the notes of the row as a melody, as parts of chords or clusters, or as reverse or upside-down versions of the original row. Time values can be altered and the tone row can be transposed or combined with new material or with different versions of itself. Serial technique has been used particularly in atonal music, although it is possible in theory to write tonally with it.

**Sforzando; Sforzato** (It., *zfor TZAHN doh; zfor TZAH toh*)  Suddenly accented.

**Sharp** (1) A sign (♯) indicating that the note which follows is to be raised one half step; (2) to raise a note one half step. When a note is sharped, it remains sharp for the rest of the measure, unless directions to the contrary are given (*see* Accidental); a double sharp (✕) raises a pitch two half steps.

**Signature** (1) Sharp or flat signs placed at the left of a staff, indicating which pitches are to be raised or lowered from their natural position throughout the composition or until a new signature is indicated; this group of sharps or flats is called the *key signature*; (2) a letter or numerical fraction, the top number indicating the number of beats in a measure, the bottom one indicating the type of note to be given the beat; this fraction is called a *time signature*.

**Sinfonia** (It., *sin foh NEE ah*) (1) In the Baroque era, the generic term for any orchestral composition used as an introductory piece to an opera, oratorio, cantata (*see* Overture; French overture; Italian overture); (2) the Italian word for *symphony*; (3) a term loosely used for any independent orchestral or instrumental composition (as Bach used it for his three-part inventions).

**Sinfonia concertante** (It., *sin foh NEE ah kawn chair TAHN teh*)  A concerto-like composition, popular in the Classical era and somewhat popular in the Romantic era, which calls for two or more soloists and orchestra.

**Singspiel** (Ger., *ZING shpeel*)  A German operatic genre using spoken dialogue with arias and ensembles. In the eighteenth century, they were humorous, sentimental, and moralistic (Mozart's *Die Entführung aus dem Serail,* "The Abduction From the Seraglio"); in the nineteenth century, they became serious and melodramatic as well as moralistic (Beethoven's *Fidelio,* Weber's *Der Freischütz*).

**Slide** (1) A device used to lengthen the tubing and thus lower the pitch of a trombone; (2) an adjustable device on all brass instruments for the purpose of intonation adjustment.

**Slur** (1) A smooth, unbroken movement from one pitch to another; (2) a curved line above two or more pitches to indicate that they are to be played *legato*.

**Soave** (It., *so AH veh*)  Sweet, gentle.

**Solo** (1) Alone; to be played by one instrument rather than several; (2) a composition or performance by one person, with or without accompaniment.

**Sonata** (It., *so NAH tah*) (1) Any piece to be played rather than sung; (2) a composition, usually in three movements (although not always), for one instrument alone or with the equal participation of another; (3) a formal structure consisting of the statement of one or more themes (*Exposition*; in sonatas of the Classical era, the Exposition is repeated), their development, and their relatively free restatement (*Recapitulation*); the whole is sometimes preceded by an introduction and concluded with a coda; this structure is known as the sonata form (*see also* Trio sonata; *Sonata da camera; Sonata da chiesa; Sonata form*).

**Sonata da camera** (It., *so NAH tah dah KAH mehr ah*) "Chamber sonata"; a collection of dance movements, usually with an introductory movement of some kind (*see* Suite); a favorite Baroque form, usually for two or more solo instruments and *basso continuo*.

**Sonata da chiesa** (It., *soh NAH tah da kee EH sah*) "Church sonata"; a collection of diverse movements, usually four in number, the second and fourth being similar to the character of the fugue and faster than the first and third; eventually all movements became dance-like; primarily Baroque, for two or more solo instruments and *basso continuo*.

**Sonata form** A structural procedure in which a theme (or themes) is stated simply in an opening section, the *Exposition* (usually repeated once), manipulated in a *Development* section, then restated in a free way in a *Recapitulation*. When the sonata form is in fast tempo, it is often preceded by a slow introduction, and a coda often concludes it. Most first movements of sonatas (see Sonata (2)), quartets, and symphonies are written in sonata form. In a concerto of the Classical era and many later concertos, the exposition is played first by the orchestra, then by the soloists, with changes in melody and accompaniment as necessary to suit the nature of the solo instrument.

**Sonata rondo** (*see Rondo*)

**Sonatina** (It., *sohn ah TEEN ah*) A short sonata, relatively light or tender in nature, usually less demanding on both performer and listener than a full sonata; the movements of the sonatina are fewer and shorter than those of the sonata.

**Song** A single vocal melodic line with text, with or without accompaniment; usually shorter and less complex than an aria, although it is apt to be more subtle than an aria when in the style of the art song. Songs or more than one vocal part are called *part songs*.

**Song cycle** (*see Cycle*)

**Sopranino** (It., *soh prah NEEN noh*) "Little soprano"; an instrument higher than the soprano member of the instrumental type of the same basic construction.

**Soprano** (It., *soh PRAHN noh*) (1) the highest female voice; (2) the member of an instrumental choir that corresponds in range or function to the soprano voice; (3) the uppermost part of a composition in which all four basic ranges (soprano, alto, tenor, bass) are represented.

**Sostenuto** (It., *sohss ten OO toh*) Sustained.

**Sotto voce** (It., *SAWT toh VOH cheh*) "Under the voice"; whispered or hushed; in an undertone.

**Spiccato** (It., *spee KAH toh*) Bounced (see Bowing).

**Spinto** (It., *SPEEN toh*) A type of soprano or tenor voice characterized by warmth and roundness of tone, rather than by capacity for *coloratura*, great dramatic weight, or extremity of range.

**Sprechgesang** (Ger., *SHPRECH guh zahng*) (*see Sprechstimme*)

**Sprechstimme** (Ger., *SHPRECH shtim muh*) A type of declamation halfway between song and speech, in which pitches notated with a special sign ( ♩ or ♪ ) are approximated rather than actually realized; also known as *Sprechgesang* ("speech-song").

**Stabreim** (Ger., *SHTAHP rym*) Alliterative poetry, especially used by Wagner in his "Ring" cycle.

**Staccato** (It., *stah KAH toh*) Detached and short.

**Staff** The lines and spaces identifying the pitches of printed notes; although most often printed with five lines and four spaces, the staff may be expanded through use of one or more leger lines above or below it. The four-line staff is still regularly used for the notation of plainsong. The *grand staff* is an eleven-line staff encompassing both treble and bass ranges; for ease in reading, the middle line ("middle C") is omitted, a leger line being used for that pitch as needed (*see also* Clef).

**Stanza** (*see Strophe*)

**Stile** (It., *STEE leh*) Style.

**Stop** (1) A handle or piston on an organ that controls a certain pipe or group of pipes (see Rank; Register); stops are also found on some harpsichords that have more than one string for each pitch; (2) to shorten a string with the finger (as on a violin) or with a mechanism (as on a clavichord); when a violinist stops more than one string at a time, he employs *double stopping*; (3) to muffle or mute the sound of a French horn by inserting the hand well into the bell.

**Stretto** (It., *STRET toh*) (1) faster; (2) in a fugue, imitations or restatements of the subject before previous statements have been completed.

**String** (1) A piece of gut or wound wire tuned to a specific pitch; (2) a family of instruments that are bowed or plucked (lute, violin, viol da gamba, harp, and the like).

**String quartet** (1) A chamber ensemble usually consisting of two violins, a viola, and a cello; (2) a composition, usually in four movements, written for such an ensemble.

**Stromentato** (*see Recitative*)

**Strophe** (*STROH fee*)  Verse; a strophic song is one in which the same music is used for each of the verses of the poetry; synonymous with *stanza*.

**Style galant** (Fr., *STEEL gah LAHN*; nasal *n*)  The subperiod coinciding with the end of the Baroque, stressing intimacy, delicacy, playfulness, prettiness, decoration, and accompanied melody rather than massive polyphony; major figures include Telemann, Couperin, and C. P. E. Bach, the last of whom lent a vigor and expressiveness which made the *style galant* an important harbinger of the Classical era (*see* Rococo; *Empfindsamer Stil*).

**Sturm und Drang** (Ger., *SHTOORM uhnt DRAHNG*) *Lit.*, "storm and stress"; an eighteenth-century movement in German romantic drama which spilled over into the music of the Classical era, manifesting itself as agitated, emotional expression.

**Subject**  The theme of a fugue or *ricercare*.

**Suite**  A collection of miscellaneous movements, with or without relationships of key and musical material, most often (but not necessarily) of dance-like character; suites of the Baroque era utilized four dance types with great consistency–the *allemande, courante, sarabande,* and *gigue*; many other dance types were also employed.

**Swinging**  Variation of a pitch or phrase in such a way as to affect intonation, intensity, rhythm, etc.; the basic element of the jazz style of performance; the nuance of jazz (*see also* Blue note).

**Symbols and abbreviations**  Performance directions may be abbreviated or indicated by symbols. Among the more commonly used abbreviations are:

| | |
|---|---|
| *pp* | *pianissimo*—very soft |
| *p* | *piano*—soft |
| *mp* | *mezzo-piano*—half-soft |
| *mf* | *mezzo-forte*—half-loud |
| *f* | *forte*—loud |
| *ff* | *fortissimo*—very loud |
| *sfz* or *sf* | *sforzando* or *sforzato*—suddenly accented |
| ten. | *tenuto*—sustained |
| ped. | *pedal*—depress pedal (on a piano, for instance) |
| D. C. | *da capo*—return to the beginning |
| D. S. | *dal segno*—return to the sign |

Among the more commonly used symbols are

| | |
|---|---|
| ⌒ | slur or tie—connect smoothly (a slur connects notes of different pitches, a tie connects notes of the same pitch) |
| > ∧ ′ | accent marks—stress the note |
| · | *staccato*—detached; short |
| — | *marcato*—emphasize the note |
| ⌢ | *fermata*—hold |
| ↓ | spoken or struck |
| ✳ | release the pedal |
| < | *crescendo*—get louder |
| > | *decrescendo*—get softer |
| 𝄋 | sign; *segno*—point of return (*dal segno*; to the sign) |
| ‖: :‖ | repeat—repeat enclosed measures |
| ∕·∕ | repeat—repeat previous measure or notational pattern |
| *8va* - - - - | *ottava*—play an octave higher or lower, depending on where sign is placed |

**Symphonic band** (*see* Band)

**Symphonic poem**  A tone poem.

**Symphonie concertante** (Fr., *SANH fo nee konh sair TAHNT*)  Same as *sinfonia concertante*.

**Symphony**  A multimovement composition for orchestra, each movement with its own mood and structure; a sonata for orchestra; a major form of the Classical, Romantic, and Contemporary eras.

**Symphony orchestra**  A large assemblage of strings (violins, violas, cellos, double basses, harp), woodwinds, brasses, and percussion, especially devoted to the performance of instrumental concert music of the period from about 1770 to the present, although earlier works are also programmed.

**Syncopation** (*SIN koh PAY shun*)  The occurrence of an accented note on a normally unaccented portion of a measure.

# T

**Tactus** (Lat., *TAHK toos*)  (1) Beat; especially in the music of the Renaissance, an unaccented pulse; (2) measure of the time length of a note, or the basic unit of duration.

**Tarantella** (It., *tahr ahn TEL lah*) A quick dance, usually in 6/8 time.

**Tempo** (It., *TEM poh*) Rate of speed.

**Tenor** (1) The highest male voice; (2) instruments which play in the tenor range or serve the tenor function in a four-voiced composition; (3) in the music of the Medieval era and some works of the Renaissance, the lowest part, usually assigned the note of a *cantus firmus* in long time values (hence the etymology of the word: from the Latin *tenere*, "to hold").

**Tenuto** (It., *ten OO toh*) Held, sustained.

**Ternary** (*TER na ree*) (1) A kind of meter with recurrent groups of three pulses, the first of which, in metrical music, is more strongly accented than the other two; (2) descriptive of musical structure in three sections (e.g. *ABA*).

**Terraced dynamics** In the Baroque era, set levels of loud and soft which are played in alternation. Such "terraces" often result from the contrast of differently constituted instrumental groups and are an attribute of orchestral and choral performance rather than solo.

**Tertian harmony** A system of constructing chords up from the root notes using intervals of thirds; the harmonic basis for most of the music of the Western world from the late Medieval era to the present.

**Tessitura** (It., *tess ih TOO rah*) The generally maintained range of a particular part, as opposed to the extreme high or low pitch called for.

**Texture** The relation of melodic and accompanimental parts. If there is but one melody with no accompaniment, the texture is *monophonic*; one melody with subordinate accompaniment results in *homophony*; if there is more than one melodic line, each with its own musical interest, the texture is *polyphonic*.

**Theme** A melodic portion of a piece of music that is to be treated compositionally (by development, imitation, contrast, variation, expansion, or juxtaposition).

**Theme and variations** A musical form in which a melody is stated in a simple way, then restated a number of times with various ornamentations, new harmonies, different instruments, and so forth.

**Third stream** A concept of contemporary music in which the traditional media of symphonic and vocal music are fused with the improvisational and rhythmic style of jazz.

**Thorough-bass** Synonymous with *basso continuo*.

**Through-composed** Music that continually changes with the demands of text or program, rather than with a format of preconceived repeats and contrasts; German: *durchkomponiert*.

**Timbre** (*TAM ber; a as in hat*) The color of the sound of a musical instrument or voice or of any combination of them; the timbre of a single voice or instrument is the result of relative strengths of various overtones; synonymous with *tone color*.

**Time signature** (*see* Signature)

**Toccata** (It., *toh KAH tah*) (1) A "touch piece" for keyboard, involving elaborate finger work; (2) an introductory or rhapsodic work of expansive character, often improvisatory.

**Tonality** An arrangement of melody and harmony so as to stress one pitch as a tonic or key tone (*see also* Modality, Atonality); the tonal system dominated Western music during the Baroque, Classical, and Romantic eras, although in the later stages of the Romantic era and throughout the Contemporary era it has coexisted with atonality.

**Tone color** (*see* Timbre)

**Tone poem** A one-movement orchestral work with extramusical reference; also called *symphonic poem* (*see* Program 4).

**Tone row** A melody used in atonal music as the basis of a twelve-tone or serial composition; tone rows are so constructed to avoid allowing any one pitch to seem more final or important than the others (*see* Serialism).

**Tonic** (1) A note that serves as the key note of a tonality; (2) a chord based on such a note.

**Transcription** The reinstrumentation of a composition (*see* Arrangement).

**Transposition** (1) The rewriting of music at pitch levels different from the original ones; (2) transposing instruments are those which actually sound higher or lower than the notes written for them.

**Traum; träumerisch** (Ger., *TROWM, ow as in cow; TROY mair ish*) Dream; dreamy.

**Traurig** (Ger., *TROW rigkch, ow as in cow*; final syllable is guttural) Sad.

**Treble** (1) The higher voices, especially women's and boys'; (2) instruments corresponding to soprano and alto voices in their choirs; (3) a clef (𝄞) and the staff on which such a clef is placed.

**Tremolo** (It., *TREM oh loh*) (1) Trembling; (2) rapid repetition of a single pitch; (3) rapid alternation of pitches at an interval of a third or more; (4) an over-wide vibrato. (*see also* Bowing)

**Très** (Fr., *TRAY*; no diphthong)  Very.

**Triad** (*TRY ad; a as in hat*)  A chord of three pitches built up in thirds (*see* Interval) from the root note.

**Trill**  The rapid alternation of a note with the pitch a half step or whole step above it.

**Trio** (1) A group of three singers or players; (2) a composition for such a group; (3) a contrasting section of a musical form.

**Trio sonata**  In the Baroque era, a composition in several movements for two treble instruments and *basso continuo* (hence, four players); later works may call for more players, but maintain an essentially three-voiced texture.

**Trop** (Fr., *TROH*)  Too much.

**Trope** (*TROHP*)  The addition or insertion of text or music or both into a preexistent composition, especially plainsong; most often employed in medieval musical practice.

**Troppo** (It., *TROHP poh*)  Too much.

**Troubadour** (Fr., *troo bah DOOR*)  A member of the aristocracy of medieval southern France (Provence) who devoted himself to composing poetry and monophonic music for it; especially prominent were Bernart de Ventadorn (d. 1195) and Guiraut Riquier (d. 1294) (*see also* Trouvère; Minstrel; *Jongleur*; *Minnesinger*).

**Trouvère** (Fr., *troo VAIR*)  A medieval poet-musician of northern France who composed songs of varying structures; prominent were Blondel de Nesles (ca. 1150–1200) and Adam de la Halle (ca. 1240–1287) (*see also* Troubadour; Minstrel; *Jongleur*; *Minnesinger*).

**Tutti** (It., *TOOT tee*)  "Everyone"; in a composition for soloists and orchestra or soloists and chorus, an indication that all are to play or sing.

**Twelve-tone music**  Dodecaphony, or music using all twelve pitches of the octave in a tone row (*see* Serialism).

# U

**Unison**  The result when more than one part sounds the same pitch or the same melody at the same time, whether in the same or in different octaves.

**Up-beat**  The last beat of a measure, characterized by an upward motion of a conductor, so that he may move smoothly and naturally to the down-beat (that is, the first beat) of the next measure.

# V

**Variation**  The presentation of a melody in a new light, through such techniques as ornamentation, reinstrumentation, and others (*see* Theme and variations)

**Verismo** (It., *vair EESS moh*)  *Lit.*, "truth"; in opera, a tendency in the late nineteenth and early twentieth centuries to use plots that were vivid, realistic and, more often than not, violent, with characters taken from the lower walks of life (in most cases) and treated unsympathetically; although outwardly a reaction against Romanticism in opera, *verismo* opera was really a frenetic kind of Romanticism; Mascagni's *Cavalleria Rusticana* and Leoncavallo's *Pagliacci* are the two best-known examples.

**Verse** (1) A stanza of poetry or of music; (2) the solo part of an anthem, as opposed to the refrain; (3) the complete musical setting of a stanza.

**Vibrato** (It., *vee BRAH toh*)  A slight regular fluctuation of pitch or dynamics that lends richness to the timbre of an instrument or voice.

**Viel** (Ger., *FEEL*)  Much.

**Virelais** (Fr., *VEER uh lay*; no diphthong)  A medieval poetic-musical form along the lines of a strophic song with refrain.

**Vite** (Fr., *VEET*)  Fast.

**Vivace** (It., *vee VAH cheh*)  Lively.

**Voice** (1) The human instrument of song and speech; (2) part.

**Voll** (Ger., *FOAL*)  Full.

# W

**Waltz**  A gracious dance in ternary meter, characterized by a flowing, swaying motion, usually fast enough for the listener to feel as if there were but one beat to the measure; especially popular in the nineteenth century.

**Whole step**  The distance between pitches that are two half steps apart.

**Whole-tone scale**   A scale with intervals only of a whole step; starting with C, a whole-tone scale (and the melodies and chords drawn from it) would include the pitches C, D, E, F-sharp, G-sharp, A-sharp, C; a major feature of Debussy's music and the Impressionistic style.

**Wie** (Ger., *VEE*)   Like; similar to; as.

**Wind ensemble**   A small concert band.

**Woodwind instrument**   Any instrument, originally made of wood (although now metal and plastic are widely used), in which the column of air is set in motion by the vibration of a single or double reed, or by the splitting of the air against a sharp edge (as in flutes and recorders).

**Woodwind quintet**   A chamber ensemble of five instruments, usually a flute, an oboe, a clarinet, a bassoon, and a French horn.

# BIBLIOGRAPHY

Books useful for further research or for general reading about music are organized into the following sections:

  1: Reference Books
  2: Aesthetics and Criticism
  3: History of Music
  4: Composers
  5: Chamber Music (including jazz)
  6: Choral Music
  7: Dramatic Music
  8: Orchestral Music
  9: Song
10: Folk Music and Music of Other Cultures
11: Related Arts

Books relevant to a single topic should be sought in more than one section, since each bibliographical source is listed but once. The books listed here are of varying difficulty, but all are in English. This list is of books only and is not intended to be all-inclusive.

## SECTION 1: REFERENCE BOOKS

Apel, Willi, ed., *Harvard Dictionary of Music*, 2nd ed., rev. and enl. Cambridge, Mass.: Harvard University Press, Belknap Press, 1969.

Backus, John, *The Acoustical Foundations of Music*. New York: Norton, 1969.

Baines, Anthony, ed., *Musical Instruments Through the Ages*. Baltimore: Penguin Books, 1961.

Barrell, R. D., *Schirmer's Guide to Books on Music and Musicians*. New York: G. Schirmer, 1951.

Benade, Arthur H., *Horns, Strings and Harmony—The Science of Enjoyable Sound*. Garden City, N.Y.: Doubleday, Anchor Books, 1960.

Blom, Eric, ed., *Grove's Dictionary of Music and Musicians*, rev. 5th ed. New York: St. Martin's, 1961. 10 vols.

Demuth, Norman, *Musical Forms and Textures: A Reference Guide*, 2nd ed. London: Barrie and Rockliffe, 1964.

Donington, Robert, *The Instruments of Music*, 3rd ed., rev. London: Methuen, 1962.

Dorf, Richard H., *Electronic Musical Instruments*, 3rd ed. New York: Radiofile, 1968.

Feather, Leonard, *Encyclopedia of Jazz*. New York: Horizon Press, 1955.

Jacobs, Arthur, *A New Dictionary of Music*. Baltimore: Penguin Books, 1963.

Marcuse, Sibyl, *Musical Instruments: A Comprehensive Dictionary*. Garden City, N.Y.: Doubleday, 1964.

Sacher, Jack, ed., *Music A to Z*. New York: Grosset and Dunlap, 1963.

Sachs, Curt, *The History of Musical Instruments*. New York: Norton, 1940.

Scholes, Percy A., ed., *Oxford Companion to Music*, 9th ed., rev. by Nicolas Slonimsky. New York: Oxford University Press, 1965.

Slonimsky, Nicolas, ed., *Baker's Biographical Dictionary of Musicans*, rev. 5th ed. New York: G. Schirmer, 1958. With supplement (1965).

Thompson, Oscar, ed., *International Cyclopedia of Music and Musicians*, 9th ed. New York: Dodd, Mead, 1968.

Tovey, Donald Francis, *Essays in Musical Analysis*. New York: Oxford University Press, 1935–39. 6 vols.

Von Foerster, Heinz, and James W. Beauchamp, eds., *Music By Computers*. New York: Wiley, 1969.

Watson, Jack M., and Corinne Watson, *A Concise Dictionary of Music*. New York: Dodd, Mead, 1967.

Westrup, J. A., and F. H. Harrison, *The New College Encyclopedia of Music*. New York: Norton, 1960.

## SECTION 2: AESTHETICS AND CRITICISM

Allen, Warren Dwight, *Philosophies of Music History*. New York: Dover, 1962.

Aschenbrenner, Karl, and Arnold Isenberg, eds., *Aesthetic Theories: Studies in the Philosophy of Art*. Englewood Cliffs, N.J.: Prentice-Hall, 1964.

Barzun, Jacques, *Darwin, Marx and Wagner*. Garden City, N.Y.: Doubleday, 1958.
———, ed., *Pleasures of Music*. New York: Viking, 1962.

Berlioz, Hector, *Evenings in the Orchestra*, trans. Jacques Barzun. New York: Knopf, 1956.

Bernstein, Leonard, *The Joy of Music*. New York: Simon and Schuster, 1959.

Boulez, Pierre, *Notes of an Apprenticeship*, trans. Herbert Weinstock. New York: Knopf, 1968.

Buermeyer, Laurence, *The Aesthetic Experience*. Merion, Pa.: Barnes Foundation Press, 1929.

Cage, John, *Silence*. Middletown, Conn.: Wesleyan University Press, 1961.

Chase, Gilbert, ed., *The American Composer Speaks (A Historical Anthology, 1770–1965)*. Baton Rouge: Louisiana State University Press, 1966.

Copland, Aaron, *Music and Imagination*. Cambridge, Mass.: Harvard University Press, 1962.

Einstein, Alfred, *Essays on Music*. New York: Norton, 1962.

Epperson, Gordon, *The Musical Symbol*. Ames: Iowa State University Press, 1967.

Feldman, Edmund Burke, *Art as Image and Idea*. Englewood Cliffs, N.J.: Prentice-Hall, 1967.

Ghiselin, Brewster, ed., *The Creative Process—A Symposium*. New York: New American Library, Mentor Books, 1952.

Greene, Theodore Meyer, *The Arts and the Art of Criticism*, rev. ed. Princeton, N.J.: Princeton University Press, 1948.

Hanslick, Eduard, *The Beautiful in Music*, trans. Gustav Cohen. New York: Bobbs-Merrill, 1957.

Hindemith, Paul, *A Composer's World—Horizons and Limitations*. Cambridge, Mass.: Harvard University Press, 1952.

Kolodin, Irving, ed., *The Composer as Listener*. New York: Collier, 1962.

Krause, Joseph H., *The Nature of Art*. Englewood Cliffs, N.J.: Prentice-Hall, 1969.

Langer, Susanne K., ed., *Reflections on Art: A Source Book of Writings By Artists, Critics and Philosophers*. Baltimore: Johns Hopkins Press, 1958.

Lee, Harold Newton, *Perception and Aesthetic Value*. New York: Johnson Reprint Corp., 1967 (orig. Prentice-Hall, 1938).

Meyer, Leonard B., *Music, The Arts, and Ideas: Patterns and Predictions in Twentieth-Century Culture*. Chicago: University of Chicago Press, 1967.

Norman, Gertrude, and Miriam L. Shrifte, eds., *Letters of Composers*. New York: Grosset and Dunlap, 1946.

Prall, D. W., *Aesthetic Analysis*. New York: Crowell, 1967.

Rader, Melvin, ed., *A Modern Book of Esthetics*, 2nd ed. New York: Holt, 1966.

Randolph, David, *This Is Music*. New York: New American Library, Mentor Books, 1964.

Rolland, Romain, *Essays on Music*, ed. David Ewen. New York, Dover, 1959.

Schumann, Robert, *On Music and Musicians*, ed. Konrad Wolff, trans. Paul Rosenfeld. New York, Pantheon, 1946.

Shaw, George Bernard, *Shaw on Music*, ed. Eric Bentley. Garden City, N.Y.: Doubleday, 1955.

Slonimsky, Nicolas, *Lexicon of Musical Invective*, rev. ed. Seattle: University of Washington Press, 1969.

Stravinsky, Igor, *Poetics of Music in the Form of Six Lessons*, trans. Arthur Knodel and Ingolf Dahl. New York: Random House, 1947.

Strunk, Oliver, ed., *Source Readings in Music History*. New York: Norton, 1950.

Thomson, Virgil, *The Art of Judging Music*. New York: Knopf, 1948.

———, *The State of Music*. New York: Random House, 1962.

Toch, Ernst, *The Shaping Forces of Music*. New York: Criterion, 1948.

UNESCO, *The Arts and Man*. Englewood Cliffs, N.J.: Prentice-Hall, 1969.

Walker, Alan, *An Anatomy of Musical Criticism*. Philadelphia: Chilton, 1966.

Walter, Bruno, *Of Music and Music Making*, trans. Paul Hamburger. New York: Norton, 1961.

Zoff, Otto, ed., *Great Composers Through the Eyes of Their Contemporaries*. New York: Dutton, 1951.

## SECTION 3: HISTORY OF MUSIC

Abraham, Gerald, *A Hundred Years of Music*, 3rd ed. Chicago: Aldine, 1964.

Apel, Willi, *Gregorian Chant*. Bloomington: Indiana University Press, 1957.

Austin, William W., *Music in the Twentieth Century*. New York: Norton, 1966.

Blume, Friedrich, *Renaissance and Baroque Music—A Comprehensive Survey*, trans. M. D. Herter Norton. New York: Norton, 1967.

Bukofzer, Manfred F., *Music in the Baroque Era*. New York: Norton, 1947.

———, *Studies in Medieval and Renaissance Music*. New York: Norton, 1950.

Chase, Gilbert, *America's Music From the Pilgrims to the Present*. New York: McGraw-Hill, 1966.

Copland, Aaron, *The New Music, 1900–1960*, rev. and enl. ed. New York: Norton, 1968.

Crocker, R. L., *A History of Musical Style*. New York: McGraw-Hill, 1966.

Donington, Robert, *The Interpretation of Early Music*, 2nd ed. London: Faber and Faber, 1965.

Edwards, Arthur C., and W. Thomas Marrocco, *Music in the United States*. Dubuque, Iowa: Brown, 1968.

Einstein, Alfred, *A Short History of Music*. New York: Random House, 1954.

————, *Music in the Romantic Era*. New York: Norton, 1947.

Goldron, Romain, *Music of the Renaissance, the Link With Humanism*, trans. Doris C. Dunning. Paris: H.S. Stuttman, and Garden City, N.Y.: Doubleday, 1968.

Grout, Donald J., *A History of Western Music*. New York: Norton, 1960.

Hansen, Peter, *An Introduction to Twentieth Century Music*, 2nd ed. Boston: Allyn and Bacon, 1967.

Harman, Alec, *Medieval and Early Renaissance Music Up to c. 1525*. London: Rockliffe, 1958.

————, and Anthony Milner, *Late Renaissance and Baroque Music, c. 1525–1750*. London: Barrie and Rockliffe, 1959.

Heger, Theodore E., *Music of the Classic Period*. Dubuque, Iowa: Brown, 1969.

Hitchcock, Wiley, *Music in the United States*. Englewood Cliffs, N.J.: Prentice-Hall, 1969.

Howard, John Tasker, *Our American Music*, 4th ed. New York: Crowell, 1965.

Lang, Paul Henry, *Music in Western Civilization*. New York: Norton, 1941.

————, and Otto Bettman, *A Pictorial History of Music*. New York: Norton, 1960.

Longyear, Ray M., *Nineteenth-Century Romanticism in Music*. Englewood Cliffs, N.J.: Prentice-Hall, 1969.

Machlis, Joseph, *Introduction to Contemporary Music*. New York: Norton, 1961.

McKinney, Howard, and W. R. Anderson. *Music in History*, 2nd ed. New York: American Book Company, 1957.

Palisca, Claude, *Baroque Music*. Englewood Cliffs, N.J.: Prentice-Hall, 1968.

Parrish, Carl, *A Treasury of Early Music*. New York: Norton, 1958.

————, and John F. Ohl, *Masterpieces of Music Before 1750*. New York: Norton, 1951.

Pauly, Reinhard G., *Music in the Classic Period*. Englewood Cliffs, N.J.: Prentice-Hall, 1965.

Reese, Gustav, *Music in the Middle Ages*. New York: Norton, 1940.

————, *Music in the Renaissance*. New York: Norton, 1959.

Riedel, Johannes, *Music of the Romantic Period*. Dubuque, Iowa: Brown, 1969.

Robertson, Alec, and Denis Stevens, *The Pelican History of Music*. Baltimore: Penguin Books, 1963–68. 3 vols.

Salzman, Eric, *Twentieth-Century Music: An Introduction*. Englewood Cliffs, N.J.: Prentice-Hall, 1967.

Seay, Albert, *Music in the Medieval World*. Englewood Cliffs, N.J.: Prentice-Hall, 1965.

Slonimsky, Nicolas, *Music Since 1900*, 3rd ed. New York: Norton, 1949.

Stuckenschmidt, H. H., *Twentieth Century Music*, trans. Richard Deveson. New York: McGraw-Hill, 1969.

Szabolsci, Bence, *A History of Melody*, trans. Cynthia Jolly and Sára Karig. New York: St. Martin's, 1965.

Thomson, James C., *Music Through the Renaissance*. Dubuque, Iowa: Brown, 1968.

Yates, Peter, *Twentieth Century Music: Its Evolution From the End of the Harmonic Era Into the Present Era of Sound*. New York: Pantheon, 1967.

### J. S. Bach

Geiringer, Karl, *Johann Sebastian Bach—The Culmination of an Era*. New York: Oxford University Press, 1966.

Grew, E. M., and S. Grew, *Bach*. New York: Collier, 1962.

Schweitzer, Albert, *J. S. Bach*, trans. Ernest Newman. New York: Macmillan, 1955. 2 vols. (Boston: Humphries, 1964, paper)

Spitta, Philipp, *Johann Sebastian Bach, His Work and Influence on the Music of Germany*, trans. Clara Bell and J. A. Fuller-Maitland. New York: Dover, 1951. 3 vols. in 2.

Terry, Charles Sanford, *Bach: The Historical Approach*. New York: Oxford University Press, 1930.

### Bartók

Stevens, Halsey, *The Life and Music of Béla Bartók*, rev. ed. New York: Oxford University Press, 1964.

### Beethoven

Marek, George, *Beethoven: Biography of a Genius*. New York: Funk & Wagnalls, 1969.

Scott, Marion, *Beethoven*. New York: Farrar, Straus & Giroux, 1960.

Sullivan, J. W. N., *Beethoven: His Spiritual Development*. New York: New American Library, Mentor Books, 1954.

Thayer, Alexander Wheelock, *The Life of Beethoven*, rev. and ed. Elliott Forbes. Princeton, N.J.: Princeton University Press, 1964. 2 vols.

Tovey, Donald Francis, *Beethoven*, ed. H. J. Foss. New York: Oxford University Press, 1965.

Turner, William J., *Beethoven*. London: J. M. Dent, 1945.

### Berg

Redlich, H. F., *Alban Berg, the Man and His Music*. New York: Abelard-Shuman, 1957.

Reich, Willi, *The Life and Work of Alban Berg*, trans. Cornelius Carden. London: Thames and Hudson, 1965.

### Berlioz

Barzun, Jacques, *Berlioz and the Romantic Century*, 3rd ed. New York: Columbia University Press, 1969.

Elliot, John Harold, *Berlioz*, rev. ed. New York: Farrar, Straus & Giroux, 1967.

### Bizet

Curtiss, Mina, *Bizet and His World*. New York: Knopf, 1958.

Dean, Winton, *Bizet*. London: Dent, 1965.

### Brahms

Evans, Edwin Sr., *Handbook to the Chamber Music and Orchestral Music of Brahms*. London: W. Reeves, 1933–35. 2 vols.

Geiringer, Karl, *Brahms, His Life and Work*, trans. H. B. Weiner and Bernard Miall, 2nd ed., rev. and enl. London: Allen and Unwin, 1963.

Latham, Peter, *Brahms*. New York: Collier, 1962.

**Britten**

Mitchell, Donald, and Hans Keller, eds., *Britten: A Commentary on his Works From a Group of Specialists*. New York: Philosophical Library, 1950.

White, Eric Walter, *Benjamin Britten, A Sketch of his Life and Works*. London: Boosey and Hawkes, 1954.

**Bruckner**

Doernberg, Erwin, *The Life and Symphonies of Anton Bruckner*. New York: Dover, 1960.

Newlin, Dika, *Bruckner, Mahler, Schoenberg*. New York: Columbia University Press, King's Crown Press, 1947.

Simpson, Robert, *The Essence of Bruckner*. Philadelphia: Chilton, 1968.

**Chopin**

Abraham, Gerald, *Chopin's Musical Style*. New York: Oxford University Press, 1960.

Chissell, Joan, *Chopin*. London: Faber, 1965.

Hedley, Arthur, *Chopin*, rev. ed. New York: Farrar, Straus & Giroux, 1963.

Walker, Alan, ed., *Frederic Chopin: Profiles of the Man and the Musician*. New York: Taplinger, 1967.

**Copland**

Berger, Arthur, *Aaron Copland*. New York: Oxford University Press, 1953.

**Corelli**

Pincherle, Marc, *Corelli: His Life, His Work*, trans. Hubert Russell. New York: Norton, 1956.

**Debussy**

Lockspeiser, Edward, *Debussy*. New York: Collier, 1962.

————, *Debussy: His Life and Mind*. New York: Macmillan, 1962–65. 2 vols.

**Dvořák**

Hughes, Gervase, *Dvořák: His Life and Music*. New York: Dodd, Mead, 1967.

Robertson, Alec, *Dvořák*. New York: Collier, 1962.

**Elgar**

Reed, W. H., *Elgar*. New York: Collier, 1962.

**Fauré**

Suckling, Norman, *Fauré*. London: Dent, 1951.

**Franck**

Demuth, Norman, *César Franck*. London: Dobson, 1964.

**Gluck**

Einstein, Alfred, *Gluck*. New York: Collier, 1962.

**Handel**

Lang, Paul Henry, *George Frideric Handel*. New York: Norton, 1966.

Young, Percy M., *Handel*, rev. ed. New York: Farrar, Straus & Giroux, 1965.

**Haydn**

Geiringer, Karl, in collaboration with Irene Geiringer, *Haydn: A Creative Life In Music,* 2nd ed., rev. and enl. Berkeley: University of California Press, 1968.

Hughes, Rosemary, *Haydn.* New York: Collier, 1962.

**Ives**

Cowell, Henry, and Sydney Cowell, *Charles Ives and His Music.* New York: Oxford University Press, 1955.

**Liszt**

Beckett, Walter, *Liszt.* New York: Collier, 1962.

Searle, Humphrey, *The Music of Liszt,* rev. 2nd ed. Gloucester, Mass.: Smith, 1968.

**Mahler**

Newlin, Dika, *Bruckner, Mahler, Schoenberg.* New York: Columbia University Press, King's Crown Press, 1947.

**Mendelssohn**

Radcliffe, Philip, *Mendelssohn,* rev. ed. New York: Collier, 1967.

Werner, Eric, *Mendelssohn: A New Image of the Composer and His Age,* trans. Dika Newlin. New York: Free Press, 1963.

**Monteverdi**

Arnold, Denis, *Monteverdi.* New York: Farrar, Straus & Giroux, 1963.

Schrade, Leo, *Monteverdi: Creator of Modern Music.* New York: Norton, 1950.

**Mozart**

Blom, Eric, *Mozart.* New York: Collier, 1962.

Brophy, Brigid, *Mozart, the Dramatist.* New York: Harcourt, Brace and World, 1964.

Deutsch, Otto E., *Mozart: A Documentary Biography,* trans. Eric Blom, Peter Branscombe, and Jeremy Noble. Stanford: Stanford University Press, 1965.

Einstein, Alfred, *Mozart: His Character, His Work,* trans. Arthur Mendel and Nathan Broder. New York: Oxford University Press, 1945.

Landon, H. C. Robbins, ed., *The Mozart Companion.* London: Rockliffe, 1956.

Turner, Walter J., *Mozart: The Man and His Works,* rev. and ed. Christopher Raeburn. New York: Barnes and Noble, 1966.

**Mussorgsky**

Calvocoressi, M. D., *Mussorgsky.* New York: Collier, 1962.

**Palestrina**

Coates, Henry, *Palestrina.* London: Dent, 1948.

**Poulenc**

Hell, Henri, *Francis Poulenc,* trans. Edward Lockspeiser. New York: Grove, 1959.

**Prokofiev**

Nestyev, Israel V., *Prokofiev,* trans. Florence Jonas. Stanford: Stanford University Press, 1960.

**Puccini**

Carner, Mosco, *Puccini: A Critical Biography*. New York: Knopf, 1959.

**Purcell**

Westrup, J. A., *Purcell*. New York: Collier, 1962.

Zimmerman, Franklin B., *Henry Purcell, 1659—1695: His Life and Times*. New York: St. Martin's, 1967.

**Rachmaninoff**

Bertensson, Sergei, and Jay Leyda, *Sergei Rachmaninoff: A Lifetime in Music*. New York: New York University Press, 1956.

**Ravel**

Demuth, Norman, *Ravel*. New York: Collier, 1962.

Manuel, Roland, *Maurice Ravel*, trans. Cynthia Jolly. London: Dobson, 1947.

Stuckenschmidt, H. H., *Maurice Ravel–Variations on His Life and Work*, trans. Samuel R. Rosenbaum. Philadelphia: Chilton, 1968.

**Rossini**

Toye, Francis, *Rossini: A Study in Tragi-Comedy*. New York: Norton, 1963.

**Satie**

Myers, Rollo H., *Erik Satie*. New York: Dover, 1968.

**A. Scarlatti**

Dent, Edward J., *Alessandro Scarlatti: His Life and Work*. London: Edward Arnold, 1960.

**D. Scarlatti**

Kirkpatrick, Ralph, *Domenico Scarlatti*. Princeton, N. J.: Princeton University Press, 1953.

**Schoenberg**

Newlin, Dika, *Bruckner, Mahler, Schoenberg*. New York: Columbia University Press, King's Crown Press, 1947.

Payne, Anthony, *Schoenberg*. New York: Oxford University Press, 1968.

**Schubert**

Abraham, Gerald, ed., *The Music of Schubert*. New York: Norton, 1947.

Brown, Maurice J. E., *Schubert: A Critical Biography*. London: Macmillan, 1958.

Hutchings, Arthur, *Schubert*. New York: Farrar, Straus & Giroux, 1956.

**Schumann**

Abraham, Gerald, ed., *Schumann: A Symposium*. New York: Oxford University Press, 1952.

Brion, Marcel, *Schumann and the Romantic Age*, trans. Geoffrey Sainsbury. New York: Macmillan, 1956.

Chissell, Joan, *Schumann*, rev. ed. New York: Collier, 1967.

Plantinga, Leon B., *Schumann as Critic*. New Haven: Yale University Press, 1967.

**Schütz**

Moser, Hans Joachim, *Heinrich Schütz: His Life and Work*, trans. Carl F. Pfatteicher. St. Louis: Concordia, 1959.

**Sibelius**

Abraham, Gerald, ed., *Sibelius: A Symposium*. London: L. Drummond, 1948.

Johnson, Harold, *Jean Sibelius*. New York: Knopf, 1959.

**R. Strauss**

Del Mar, Norman, *Richard Strauss: A Critical Commentary On His Life and Works*. London: Barrie and Rockliffe, 1962.

Mann, William, *Richard Strauss: A Critical Study of the Operas*. New York: Oxford University Press, 1966.

Marek, George Richard, *Richard Strauss: The Life of a Non-Hero*. New York: Simon and Schuster, 1967.

**Stravinsky**

Vlad, Roman, *Stravinsky*, trans. Frederick and Ann Fuller, 2nd ed. New York: Oxford University Press, 1967.

White, Eric Walter, *Stravinsky: The Composer and His Works*. Berkeley: University of California Press, 1966.

**Tchaikovsky**

Abraham, Gerald, ed., *Tchaikovsky: A Symposium*. London: L. Drummond, 1946.

Evans, Edwin, *Tchaikovsky*, rev. ed. New York: Farrar, Straus & Giroux, 1966.

Hanson, Laurence, and Elisabeth Hanson, *Tchaikovsky: The Man Behind the Music*. New York: Dodd, Mead, 1966.

Tchaikovsky, Modeste, *The Life and Letters of Peter Ilich Tchaikovsky*, ed. and trans. Rosa Newmarch. New York: Dodd, Mead, 1924.

**Varèse**

Oullette, Fernand, *Edgard Varèse*, trans. Derek Coltman. New York: Orion Press, 1968.

**Vaughan Williams**

Foss, Hubert, *Ralph Vaughan Williams: A Study*. London: Harrap, 1950.

**Verdi**

Gatti, Carlo, *Verdi: The Man and His Music*, trans. Elisabeth Abbott. New York, Putnam, 1955.

Hussey, Dyneley, *Verdi*, further rev. ed. New York: Farrar, Straus & Giroux, 1963.

Martin, George, *Verdi: His Music, Life and Times*. New York: Dodd, Mead, 1963.

Osborne, Charles, *The Complete Operas of Verdi*. New York: Knopf, 1970.

Toye, Francis, *Giuseppe Verdi: His Life and Works*. New York: Random House, 1946.

**Vivaldi**

Pincherle, Marc, *Vivaldi: Genius of the Baroque*, trans. Christopher Hatch. New York: Norton, 1962.

**Wagner**

Gutman, Robert W., *Richard Wagner: The Man, His Mind and His Music*. New York: Harcourt, Brace & World, 1968.

Jacobs, Robert L., *Wagner*, rev. ed. New York: Collier, 1965.
Newman, Ernest, *The Life of Richard Wagner*. New York: Knopf, 1949. 4 vols.
————, *Wagner as Man and Artist*. New York: Random House, 1960.
Stein, Jack, *Richard Wagner and the Synthesis of the Arts*. Detroit: Wayne State University Press, 1960.
White, Chappell, *An Introduction to the Life and Works of Richard Wagner*. Englewood Cliffs, N.J.: Prentice-Hall, 1967.

### Weber

Saunders, William, *Weber*. New York: Dutton, 1940.
Stebbins, Lucy Poate, and Richard Poate Stebbins, *Enchanted Wanderer: The Life of Carl Maria von Weber*. New York: Putnam, 1940.
Warrack, John Hamilton, *Carl Maria von Weber*. New York: Macmillan, 1968.

### Webern

Kolneder, Walter, *Anton Webern: An Introduction to His Works*, trans. Humphrey Searle. Berkeley: University of California Press, 1968.
Wildgans, Friedrich, *Anton Webern*, trans. Edith Temple Roberts and Humphrey Searle. New York: October House, 1967.

### Wolf

Walker, Frank, *Hugo Wolf*, 2nd ed. New York: Knopf, 1968.

## SECTION 5: CHAMBER MUSIC

Blesh, Rudi, *Shining Trumpets: A History of Jazz*. New York: Knopf, 1958.
Cobbett, Walter Willson, *Cobbett's Cyclopedic Survey of Chamber Music*. London: Oxford University Press, 1929–30. 2 vols.
Demuth, Norman, *French Piano Music: A Survey With Notes On Its Performance*. London: Museum Press, 1959.
Gillespie, John, *Five Centuries of Keyboard Music*. Belmont, Calif.: Wadsworth, 1965.
Hodeir, André, *Jazz: Its Evolution and Essence*, trans. David Noakes. New York: Grove, 1956.
Hutcheson, Ernest, *The Literature of the Piano*. New York: Knopf, 1949.
Judd, F. C., *Electronic Music and Musique Concrète*. London: Neville Spearman, 1961.
King, Alexander Hyatt, *Chamber Music*. New York: Chanticleer Press, 1948.
Kirby, F. E., *A Short History of Keyboard Music*. New York: Free Press, 1966.
Lockwood, Albert Lewis, *Notes on the Literature of the Piano*. New York: Da Capo Press, 1968.
Loesser, Arthur, *Men, Women and Pianos*. New York: Simon and Schuster, 1954.
Robertson, Alec, ed., *Chamber Music*. Baltimore: Penguin Books, 1967.
Rowen, Ruth Halle, *Early Chamber Music*. New York: Columbia University Press, 1949.
Sargeant, Winthrop, *Jazz: A History*, new ed. New York: McGraw-Hill, 1964.
Schuller, Gunther, *Early Jazz: Its Roots and Musical Development*. New York: Oxford University Press, 1968. (Basic History of Jazz Series, Vol. 1)
Stearns, Marshall W., *The Story of Jazz*. New York: Oxford University Press, 1956.
Ulrich, Homer, *Chamber Music: The Growth and Practice of an Intimate Art*. New York: Columbia University Press, 1966.
Wilson, John Stewart, *Jazz: The Transition Years, 1940–1960*. New York: Appleton-Century-Crofts, 1966.

*Chants of the Church*, ed. and compiled by the monks of Solesmes. Toledo, Ohio: Gregorian Institute of America, 1953.

Dean, Winton, *Handel's Dramatic Oratorios and Masques*. London: Oxford University Press, 1959.

Einstein, Alfred, *The Italian Madrigal*, trans. Alexander H. Krappe, Roger H. Sessions, and Oliver Strunk. Princeton, N.J.: Princeton University Press, 1949. 3 vols.

Fellowes, Edmund H., *The English Madrigal Composers*, 2nd ed. London: Oxford University Press, 1948.

Gajard, Dom Joseph, *The Solesmes Method: Its Fundamental Principles and Practical Rules of Interpretation*, trans. R. Cecile Gabain. Collegeville, Minn.: The Liturgical Press, 1960.

Hutchings, Arthur, *Church Music in the Nineteenth Century*. New York: Oxford University Press, 1967.

Jacobs, Arthur, *Choral Music: A Symposium*. Baltimore: Penguin Books, 1963.

Larsen, Jens Peter, *Handel's Messiah: Origins, Compositions, Sources*. New York: Norton, 1957.

Liemohn, Edwin, *The Chorale*. Philadelphia: Muhlenberg Press, 1953.

Terry, Charles Sanford, *Bach: The Cantatas and Oratorios*. New York: Oxford University Press, 1925. 2 vols.

Whittaker, W. G., *The Cantatas of J. S. Bach, Sacred and Secular*. New York: Oxford University Press, 1959. 2 vols.

Wienandt, Elwyn, *Choral Music of the Church*. New York: Free Press, 1965.

Young, Percy M., *The Choral Tradition*. New York: Norton, 1962.

## *SECTION 7: DRAMATIC MUSIC*

Austin, William W., ed., *New Looks At Italian Opera*. Ithaca, N.Y.: Cornell University Press, 1968.

Briggs, Thomas H., *Opera and Its Enjoyment*. New York: Bureau of Publications, Teachers College, Columbia University, 1960.

Cooper, Martin, *French Music From the Death of Berlioz to the Death of Fauré*. New York: Oxford University Press, 1951.

————, *Opéra Comique*. New York: Oxford University Press, 1949.

————, *Russian Opera*. London: Max Parrish, 1951.

Cross, Milton, *Complete Stories of the Great Operas*. ed. Karl Kohn. Garden City, N.Y.: Doubleday, 1952.

Dent, Edward J., *Mozart's Operas*. New York: Oxford University Press, 1960.

————, *Opera*. Baltimore: Penguin Books, 1968.

Donington, Robert, *Wagner's "Ring" and its Symbols*. New York: St. Martin's, 1963.

Engel, Lehman, *The American Musical Theater*. New York: CBS-Macmillan, 1967.

Ewen, David, *Complete Book of the American Musical Theater*. New York: Holt, Rinehart & Winston, 1958.

Fellner, Rudolph, *Opera Themes and Plots*. New York: Simon and Schuster, 1968.

Green, Stanley, *The World of Musical Comedy*, rev. ed. New York: A.S. Barnes, 1968.

Grout, Donald J., *A Short History of Opera*, 2nd ed. New York: Columbia University Press, 1965.

Hamm, Charles, *Opera*. Boston: Allyn and Bacon, 1966.

Howard, John Tasker, *The World's Great Operas*. New York: Modern Library, 1959.

Howard, Patricia, *Gluck and the Birth of Modern Opera*. New York: St. Martin's, 1964.

Kerman, Joseph, *Opera as Drama*. New York: Random House, 1956.

MacKinlay, Malcolm Sterling, *The Origin and Development of Light Opera*. London: Hutchinson, 1927.

Marek, George R., *Opera as Theater*. New York: Harper and Row, 1962.

Merkling, Frank, *The Opera News Book of "Figaro."* New York: Dodd, Mead, 1967.

Moberly, R. B., *Three Mozart Operas: Figaro, Don Giovanni, The Magic Flute*. New York: Dodd, Mead, 1968.

Newman, Ernest, *More Stories of Famous Operas*. New York: Knopf, 1943.

————, *Seventeen Famous Operas*. New York: Knopf, 1955.

————, *Stories of the Great Operas and Their Composers*. Garden City, N.Y.: Garden City Press, 1930.

————, *The Wagner Operas*. New York: Knopf, 1949.

Pauly, Reinhard, *Music and the Theater*. Englewood Cliffs, N.J.: Prentice-Hall, 1970.

Peltz, Mary Ellis, ed., *Introduction to Opera*. New York: Barnes and Noble, 1961.

Robinson, Michael F., *Opera Before Mozart*. New York: Morrow, 1967.

Simon, Henry W., *100 Great Operas and Their Stories*. Garden City, N.Y.: Doubleday, 1960.

————, ed., *The Victor Book of the Opera*. 13th ed. New York: Simon and Schuster, 1968.

Smith, Cecil, *Musical Comedy in America*. New York: Theater Arts Books, 1950.

Toye, Francis, *Italian Opera*. London: Max Parrish, 1952.

Wellesz, Egon, *Essays on Opera*, trans. Patricia Kean. London: Dobson, 1950.

Westerman, Gerhart von, *Opera Guide*, trans. Anne Ross, ed. Harold Rosenthal. New York: Dutton, 1965.

## SECTION 8: ORCHESTRAL MUSIC

Bagar, Robert, and Louis Biancolli, *The Complete Guide to Orchestral Music*. New York: Grosset and Dunlap, 1947. 2 vols.

Bekker, Paul, *The Orchestra*. New York: Norton, 1936.

Carse, Adam, *Eighteenth Century Symphonies: A Short History of the Symphony in the Eighteenth Century with Special Reference to the Works in the Two Series: Early Classical Symphonies and Eighteenth Century Overtures*. London: Augener, 1951.

————, *The Orchestra from Beethoven to Berlioz*. Cambridge, Eng.: W. Heffer, 1948.

————, *The Orchestra in the XVIIIth Century*. Cambridge, Eng.: W. Heffer, 1940.

Frankenstein, Alfred, *A Modern Guide to Symphonic Music*. Des Moines, Iowa: Meredith, 1966.

Girdlestone, Cuthbert M., *Mozart and His Piano Concertos*. New York: Dover, 1964.

Goldman, Richard Franko, *The Wind Band*. Boston: Allyn and Bacon, 1961.

Grove, Sir George, *Beethoven and His Nine Symphonies*. London: Novello, 1903.

Hill, Ralph, ed., *The Concerto*. Baltimore: Penguin Books, 1952.

Hopkins, Anthony, *Talking About Concertos*. Belmont, Calif.: Wadsworth, 1960.

————, *Talking About Symphonies*. Belmont, Calif.: Wadsworth, 1962.

Hutchings, Arthur, *The Baroque Concerto*. New York: Norton, 1961.

Landon, H. C. Robbins, *The Symphonies of Joseph Haydn*. London: Universal Edition, 1955.

Nelson, Wendell, *The Concerto*. Dubuque, Iowa: Brown, 1969.

Niecks, Frederick, *Program Music in the Last Four Centuries: A Contribution to the History of Musical Expression*. London: Novello, 1907.

O'Connell, Charles, *The Victor Book of Overtures, Tone Poems and Other Orchestral Works*. New York: Simon and Schuster, 1950.

————, *The Victor Book of Symphonies*. New York: Simon and Schuster, 1948.

Saint-Foix, Georges, *The Symphonies of Mozart*, trans. Leslie Orrey. London: Dobson, 1947.

Simpson, Robert, ed., *The Symphony*. Baltimore: Penguin Books, 1967. 2 vols.

Terry, Charles Sanford, *Bach's Orchestra*. New York: Oxford University Press, 1932.

Ulrich, Homer, *Symphonic Music*. New York: Columbia University Press, 1952.

Veinus, Abraham, *The Concerto*, rev. ed. New York: Dover, 1964.

————, *The Victor Book of Concertos*. New York: Simon and Schuster, 1948.

## SECTION 9: SONG

Capell, Richard, *Schubert's Songs*. New York: Macmillan, 1957.

Hall, James Husst, *The Art Song*. Norman: Oklahoma University Press, 1953.

Miller, P. L., *The Ring of Words*. Garden City, N.Y.: Doubleday, Anchor Books, 1963.

Northcote, Sydney, *Byrd to Britten: A Survey of English Song*. London: Baker, 1966.

Noske, Fritz, *French Song from Berlioz to Duparc*, trans. Rita Benton. New York: Dover, 1970.

Prawer, Siegbert, ed. and trans., *The Penguin Book of Lieder*. Baltimore: Penguin Books, 1964.

Spaeth, Sigmund, *Tin Pan Alley: A Chronicle of American Popular Music*, with suppl. by Edward Jablonski. New York: Frederick Unger, 1961.

Stevens, Denis, ed., *A History of Song*. London: Hutchinson, 1960.

## SECTION 10: FOLK MUSIC AND MUSIC OF OTHER CULTURES

Abrahams, Roger D., and George Foss, *Anglo-American Folksong Style*. Englewood Cliffs, N.J.: Prentice-Hall, 1968.

Aptheker, Herbert, ed., *A Documentary History of the Negro People in the United States*. New York: Citadel, 1951.

Courlander, Harold, *Negro Folk Music, U.S.A.* New York: Columbia University Press, 1963.

Dundes, Alan, ed., *The Study of Folklore*. Englewood Cliffs, N.J.: Prentice-Hall, 1965.

Dunson, Josh, *Freedom in the Air: Song Movements of the Sixties*. New York: International Publishers, 1965.

Fraser, Douglas, *The Many Faces of Primitive Art: A Critical Anthology*. Englewood Cliffs, N.J.: Prentice-Hall, 1966.

Idelsohn, A. Z., *Jewish Music In Its Historical Development*. New York: Tudor, 1948.

Jackson, Clyde Owen, *The Songs of Our Years: A Study of Negro Folk Music*. Jericho, N.Y.: Exposition Press, 1968.

Jones, A. M., *Studies in African Music*. London: Oxford University Press, 1959.

Jones, Leroi, *Blues People: Negro Music in White America*. New York: Morrow, 1963.

Karpeles, Maud, ed., *Folk Songs of Europe*. London: Novello, 1956.

Kunst, Jaap, *Ethnomusicology*, 3rd ed. The Hague: Humanities Press, 1959.

Leach, MacEdward, and Tristan P. Coffin, eds., *The Critics and the Ballad*. Carbondale: Southern Illinois University Press, 1961.

Lloyd, A. C., *Folk Song in England*. New York: International Publishers, 1967.

Malm, William P., *Japanese Music and Musical Instruments*. Rutland, Vt. and Tokyo: Charles E. Tuttle, 1959.

————, *Music Cultures of the Pacific, the Near East, and Asia*. Englewood Cliffs, N.J.: Prentice-Hall, 1967.

Malone, Bill C., *Country Music, U.S.A.: A Fifty-Year History*. Austin and London: University of Texas Press, 1968.

Merriam, Alan P., "Purposes of Ethnomusicology: An Anthropological View," in *Every Man His Way: Readings in Cultural Anthropology*, ed. Alan Dundes. Englewood Cliffs, N.J.: Prentice-Hall, 1968.

————, *A Prologue to the Study of the African Arts*. Yellow Springs, Ohio: Antioch Press, 1962.

Nettl, Bruno, *Folk and Traditional Music of the Western Continents*. Englewood Cliffs, N.J.: Prentice-Hall, 1965.

————, *Introduction to Folk Music in the United States*, rev. ed. Detroit: Wayne State University Press, 1962.

————, *Music in Primitive Culture*. Cambridge, Mass.: Harvard University Press, 1956.

————, *North American Indian Musical Styles*. Philadelphia: American Folklore Society, 1954.

Odum, Howard W., and Guy B. Johnson, *The Negro and His Songs*. New York: The New American Library, 1969.

Sachs, Curt, *The Wellsprings of Music*. The Hague: Martinus Nijhoff, 1962.

Slonimsky, Nicolas, *Music of Latin America*. New York: Crowell, 1945.

## SECTION 11: RELATED ARTS

Abramson, Doris E., *Negro Playwrights in the American Theater, 1925–59*. New York: Columbia University Press, 1969.

Ambrose, Kay, *The Ballet Lover's Companion*. New York: Knopf, 1962.

Arnheim, Rudolph, *Art and Visual Perception*. Berkeley: University of California Press, 1954.

Brinton, Crane, ed., *The Portable Age of Reason Reader*. New York: Viking, 1956.

Chujoy, Anatole, and P. W. Manchester, eds., *The Dance Encyclopedia*, rev. and enl. ed. New York: Simon and Schuster, 1967.

Cohen, Selma Jeanne, ed., *The Modern Dance: Seven Statements of Belief*. Middletown, Conn.: Wesleyan University Press, 1966.

Dudley, Louise, and Austin Faricy, *The Humanities: Applied Aesthetics*, 4th ed. New York: McGraw-Hill, 1967.

Fleming, William, *Arts and Ideas*. New York: Holt, Rinehart & Winston, 1955.

Hauser, Arnold, *The Social History of Art*. New York: Knopf, 1968.

Haydn, Hiram, ed., *The Portable Elizabethan Reader*. New York: Viking, 1960.

Holt, Elizabeth B., *Literary Sources of Art History*. Princeton, N.J.: Princeton University Press, 1947.

Hughes, Langston, and Milton Meltzer, *Black Magic*. Englewood Cliffs, N.J.: Prentice-Hall, 1967.

Hugo, Howard E., ed., *The Portable Romantic Reader*. New York: Viking, 1957.

Janson, H. W., *History of Art*, 2nd ed. Englewood Cliffs, N.J.: Prentice-Hall, 1969.

————, general ed., *Time-Life Library of Art*. New York: Time-Life, 1968—. (volumes on Delacroix, Picasso, Rembrandt, Rodin, *et al.*)

Janson, H. W., and Joseph Kerman, *A History of Art and Music*. Englewood Cliffs, N.J.: Prentice-Hall, 1969.

Kernodle, George Riley, *Invitation to the Theatre*. New York: Harcourt, Brace, and World, 1967.

Kraus, Richard, *A History of the Dance: In Art and Education*. Englewood Cliffs, N.J.: Prentice-Hall, 1969.

Lawrence, Robert, *The Victor Book of Ballets and Ballet Music*. New York: Simon and Schuster, 1950.

Levey, Michael, *A Concise History of Painting*. New York: Praeger, 1967.

————, *A History of Western Art*. New York: Praeger, 1968.

Macgowan, Kenneth, and William Melnitz, *Golden Ages of the Theater*. Englewood Cliffs, N.J.: Prentice-Hall, 1959.

Mitchell, Loften, *Black Drama*. New York: Hawthorn Books, 1967.

Nettl, Paul, *The Story of Dance Music*. New York: Philosophical Library, 1947.

Praagh, Peggy Van, and Peter Brinson, *The Choreographic Art*. New York: Knopf, 1963.

Read, Herbert, *A Concise History of Modern Painting*. New York: Praeger, 1963.

Reyna, Ferdinando, *A Concise History of Ballet*. New York: Grosset & Dunlap, 1966.

Rich, Alan, *Music: Mirror of the Arts*. New York: Ridge Press, 1970.

Ross, James Bruce, and Mary Martin McLaughlin, eds., *The Portable Medieval Reader*. New York: Viking, 1949.

————, *The Portable Renaissance Reader*. New York: Viking, 1953.

Sachs, Curt, *The Commonwealth of Art*. New York: Norton, 1946.

Searle, Humphrey, *Ballet Music: An Introduction*. London: Cassell, 1958.

Sypher, Wylie, ed., *Art History: An Anthology of Modern Criticism*. New York: Random House, 1963.

Terry, Walter, *The Ballet Companion*. New York: Dodd, Mead, 1968.

Verwer, Hans, *Guide to the Ballet*. New York: Barnes and Noble, 1963.

Weismann, Donald L., *The Visual Arts as Human Experience*. Englewood Cliffs, N.J.: Prentice-Hall, 1970.

# INDEX

Page numbers in italics indicate illustrations; those followed by an asterisk refer to Short Biographies in Appendix.

# A

AB form, 94ff.
ABA form, 94ff., 172
*Academic Festival* Overture (Brahms), 225
A cappella choir, 37
Accompaniment, 69ff.
Acid rock, 124
Adam de la Halle, 275*
Aesthetics:
    art's perennial newness, 254
    communicative powers in program music, 210f.
    congregation's impact on, 253
    and the creator, 6
    definition, 4ff.
    Greco-Roman, 25
    Hellenic art, 26
    of sacred versus secular music, 252
Affection, 147
Afro-American music, 128
*Agnus Dei* (Palestrina), 182f.
*Aïda* (Verdi), 55f., 154, 230
Ailey, Alvin
    contributions to ballet, 231
    *Dancers, 231*

Air, 66
Albéniz, Isaac, 275*
    nationalism, 221
*Alceste* (Gluck), 23
*Alcina* (Handel), 54, 146
Aleatory, 13
Aleatory music, 117
*Alexander Nevsky* (Prokofiev), 176
*Also sprach Zarathustra* (R. Strauss), 108, 214f.
Alto, 35, 54, 55
Alto horn, 47
*Alto Rhapsody* (Brahms), 54, 55
Alvin Ailey Dancers, *231*
*America*, 95
American composers of symphonies, 199
*American in Paris, An* (Gershwin), 222
American music:
    art song, 139f.
    blues, 22, 75, 127–29
    electronic, 115
    jazz, 22, 63, 75, 127, 129
    nationalism in, 222
    Negro melodies, 129
    opera, 142ff.
    song, 127f.
    twentieth century, 113
*An die ferne Geliebte* (Beethoven), 138
Answer, 104
Anthem, 108, 183
*Antigone* (Orff), 164
Antiphonal chorus, 120
Antiphonal music, 54
*Appalachian Spring* (Copland), 222

## X

## Y

## Z